THE PAPERS OF
BENJAMIN FRANKLIN

SPONSORED BY

The American Philosophical Society
and Yale University

Lord North

THE PAPERS OF

Benjamin Franklin

VOLUME 17   *January 1 through December 31, 1770*

WILLIAM B. WILLCOX, *Editor*

Dorothy W. Bridgwater, Mary L. Hart, Claude A. Lopez, C. A. Myrans, Catherine M. Prelinger, and G. B. Warden, Assistant Editors

New Haven and London YALE UNIVERSITY PRESS, 1973

Library of Congress catalog card number: 59-12697
International standard book number: 0-300-01596-8

Designed by Alvin Eisenman and Walter Howe,
and printed by Cambridge University Press.

Published in Great Britain, Europe, and Africa by
Yale University Press, Ltd., London.
Distributed in Canada by McGill-Queen's University
Press, Montreal; in Latin America by Kaiman &
Polon, Inc., New York City; in Australasia and
Southeast Asia by John Wiley & Sons Australasia
Pty. Ltd., Sydney; in India by UBS Publishers'
Distributors Pvt., Ltd., Delhi; in Japan by
John Weatherhill, Inc., Tokyo.

Contents

CONTENTS

List of Illustrations

A mezzotint by Thomas Burke (1749–1815) after the portrait by
Nathaniel Dance (1735–1811). Reproduced by courtesy of Wilmarth
S. Lewis. Frederick North (1732–92) was known throughout his life
by the courtesy title of Lord North until, two years before his death, he
succeeded his father as second Earl of Guilford. The administration that
North inaugurated in 1770 was, with the exception of Walpole's and
the younger Pitt's, the longest in the century; yet he lacked the quali-
ties of leadership. Although he was skilful in debate and Parliamentary
maneuvers, he found decisions agonizing and the pressures of office so
unsettling that they frequently drove him to tears and would, if the King
had permitted, have brought him to resign. His warmheartedness and lack
of rancor made him many friends, but his sound if limited intelligence
and good intentions were no substitute for statesmanship.

A mezzotint by John Greenwood (1727–92) after the well-known portrait by Nathaniel Hone (1718–84); both were apparently executed in
1769. The mezzotint is reproduced by courtesy of the Yale University
Library. Whitefield, the great Methodist preacher and missionary, is too
familiar to readers of these volumes to need introduction; and this like-
ness of him at the close of his life is interesting in comparison with the
portrait of the young Whitefield that appears in Volume II. Franklin first
met him in Philadelphia in 1739, and their relationship continued for
more than thirty years. They were far apart in temperament and
belief, and Franklin's skepticism sometimes tried Whitefield's Christian
patience; yet each found stimulus in the other. "Ours was a mere civil
Friendship, sincere on both sides," Franklin remarked, "and lasted to his
Death." Leonard W. Labaree *et al.*, eds., *The Autobiography of Benjamin
Franklin* (New Haven, 1964), p. 270.

Contributors to Volume 17

The ownership of each manuscript, or the location of the particular copy used by the editors of each rare contemporary pamphlet or similar printed work, is indicated where the document appears in the text. The sponsors and editors are deeply grateful to the following institutions and individuals for permission to print or otherwise use in the present volume manuscripts or other materials which they own.

INSTITUTIONS

American Philosophical Society
Bibliothèque Municipale de
   Nantes
Blumhaven Library and Art
   Gallery
Boston Public Library
British Museum
Clements Library
Folger Library
Georgia Historical Society
Historical Society of
   Pennsylvania
Library of Congress
Maine Historical Society
Massachusetts Historical Society

Newport Historical Society
New York Society Library
University of Pennsylvania
   Library
Princeton University Library
Rosenbach Foundation
The Royal Society
Schaffer Library, Union College
State Historical Society of
   Wisconsin
University of Virginia Library
Henry Francis du Pont
   Winterthur Museum
Yale University Library

INDIVIDUALS

Mrs James Manderson Castle,
   Wilmington, Del.
Mr William C. Coles, Moores-
   town, N.J.

Miss Harriet V. C. Ogden,
   Bar Harbor, Me.

Method of Textual Reproduction

An extended statement of the principles of selection, arrangement, form of presentation, and method of textual reproduction observed in this edition appears in the Introduction to the first volume, pp. xxiv–xlvii. A condensation and revision of the portion relating to the method of reproducing the texts follows here.

Printed Material:

Those of Franklin's writings that were printed under his direction presumably appeared as he wanted them to, and should therefore be reproduced with no changes except what modern typography requires. In some cases, however, printers carelessly or willfully altered his text without his consent; or the journeymen who set it had different notions from his—and from each other's—of capitalization, spelling, and punctuation. Such of his letters as survive only in nineteenth-century printings, furthermore, have often been vigorously edited by William Temple Franklin, Duane, or Sparks. In all these cases the original has suffered some degree of distortion, which the modern editor may guess at, but in the absence of the manuscript can do nothing to remedy. We therefore follow the printed texts as we find them, and note only obvious misreadings.

We observe the following rules in reproducing printed materials:

1. The place and date of composition of letters are set at the top, regardless of their location in the original printing.

2. Proper nouns, including personal names, which were often printed in italics, are set in roman, except when the original was italicized for emphasis.

3. Prefaces and other long passages, though italicized in the original, are set in roman. Long italicized quotations are set in roman within quotation marks.

4. Words in full capitals are set in small capitals, with initial letters in full capitals if required by Franklin's normal usage.

5. All signatures are set in capitals and small capitals.

6. We silently correct obvious typographical errors, such as the omission of a single parenthesis or quotation mark.

7. We close a sentence by supplying, when needed, a period or question mark.

8. Longhand insertions in the blanks of printed forms are set in italics, with space before and after.

Manuscript Material:

a. *Letters* are presented in the following form:

1. The place and date of composition are set at the top, regardless of their location in the original.

2. The complimentary close is set continuously with the text.

3. Addresses, endorsements, and docketing are so labeled and printed at the end of the letter.

b. *Spelling* of the original we retain. When it is so abnormal as to obscure the meaning, we supply the correct form in brackets or a footnote, as "yf [wife]."

c. *Capitalization* we retain as written, except that every sentence is made to begin with a capital. When we cannot decide whether a letter is a capital, we follow modern usage.

d. Words underlined once in the manuscript are printed in italics; words underlined twice or written in large letters or full capitals are printed in small capitals.

e. *Punctuation* has been retained as in the original, except:

1. We close a sentence by supplying, when needed, a period or question mark. When it is unclear where the sentence ends, we retain the original punctuation or lack of it.

2. Dashes used in place of commas, semicolons, colons, or periods are replaced by the appropriate marks; when a sentence ends with both a dash and a period, the dash is omitted.

3. Commas scattered meaninglessly through a manuscript are eliminated.

4. When a mark of punctuation is not clear or can be read as one of two marks, we follow modern usage.[1]

1. The typescripts from which these papers are printed have been made from photocopies of the manuscripts, and marks of punctuation are sometimes blurred or lost in photography. It has often been impossible to consult the original in these cases.

5. Some documents, especially legal ones, have no punctuation; others have so little as to obscure the meaning. In such cases we silently supply the minimum needed for clarity.

f. *Contractions and abbreviations* in general are expanded except in proper names. The ampersand is rendered as "and," except in the names of business firms, in the form "&c.," and in a few other cases. Letters represented by the thorn or tilde are printed. The tailed "p" is spelled out as per, pre, or pro. Symbols of weights, measures, and monetary values follow modern usage, as: £34. Superscript letters are lowered. Abbreviations in current use are retained, as: Col., Dr., N.Y., i.e.

g. *Omitted or illegible words or letters* are treated as follows:

1. If not more than four letters are missing, we supply them silently when we have no doubt what they should be.

2. If more than four letters are missing, we supply them conjecturally in brackets, with or without a question mark depending on our confidence in the conjecture.

3. Other omissions are shown as follows: [*illegible*], [*torn*], [*remainder missing*], or the like.

4. Missing or illegible digits are indicated by suspension points in brackets, the number of points corresponding to the estimated number of missing figures.

5. Blank spaces are left as blanks.

h. *Author's additions and corrections.*

1. Interlineations and brief marginal notes are incorporated in the text without comment, and longer notes with the notation [*in the margin*].

2. Footnotes by the author, or by an earlier editor when significant, are printed with our notes but with a bracketed indication of the source.

3. Canceled words and phrases are in general omitted without notice; if significant, they are printed in footnotes.

4. When alternative words and phrases have been inserted in a manuscript but the original remains uncanceled, the alternatives are given in brackets, preceded by explanatory words in italics, as: "it is [*written above:* may be] true."

5. Variant readings of several versions are noted if important.

Abbreviations and Short Titles

Acts Privy Coun., Col.	W. L. Grant and James Munro, eds., *Acts of the Privy Council of England, Colonial Series, 1613–1783* (6 vols., London, 1908–12).
AD	Autograph document.[1]
ADS	Autograph document signed.
AL	Autograph letter.
ALS	Autograph letter signed.
Alvord and Carter, eds., *Trade and Politics*	Clarence W. Alvord and Clarence E. Carter, eds., *Trade and Politics 1767–1769* (Illinois State Historical Library *Collections*, XVI; Springfield, Ill., 1921).
APS	American Philosophical Society.
Autobiog.	Leonard W. Labaree, Ralph L. Ketcham, Helen C. Boatfield, and Helene H. Fineman, eds., *The Autobiography of Benjamin Franklin* (New Haven, 1964).
BF	Benjamin Franklin.
Bigelow, *Works*	John Bigelow, ed., *The Complete Works of Benjamin Franklin*...(10 vols., N.Y., 1887–88).
Board of Trade Jour.	*Journal of the Commissioners for Trade and Plantations...April 1704 to...May 1782* (14 vols., London, 1920–38).
Candler, ed., *Ga. Col. Recs.*	Allen D. Candler, ed., *The Colonial Records of the State of Georgia...* (26 vols., Atlanta, 1904–16).
Carter, ed., *Gage Correspondence*	Clarence E. Carter, ed., *The Correspondence of General Thomas Gage...* (2 vols., New Haven and London, 1931–33).
Chron.	*Chronicle.*

1. For definitions of this and other kinds of manuscripts, see above, I, xliv–xlvii.

Crane, *Letters to the Press*	Verner W. Crane, ed., *Benjamin Franklin's Letters to the Press, 1758–1775* (Chapel Hill, N.C., [1950]).
DAB	*Dictionary of American Biography.*
DF	Deborah Franklin.
Dictionnaire de biographie	*Dictionnaire de biographie française...* (11 vols. to date, Paris, 1933–67).
DNB	*Dictionary of National Biography.*
DS	Document signed.
Duane, *Works*	William Duane, ed., *The Works of Dr. Benjamin Franklin...* (6 vols., Philadelphia, 1808–18). Title varies in the several volumes.
Exper. and Obser.	*Experiments and Observations on Electricity, made at Philadelphia in America, by Mr. Benjamin Franklin...* (London, 1751). Revised and enlarged editions were published in 1754, 1760, 1769, and 1774 with slightly varying titles. In each case the edition cited will be indicated, e.g., *Exper. and Obser.* (1751).
Gaz.	*Gazette.*
Gent. Mag.	*The Gentleman's Magazine, and Historical Chronicle.*
Gipson, *British Empire*	Lawrence H. Gipson, *The British Empire before the American Revolution* (15 vols.: I–III, Caldwell, Idaho, 1936; IV–XV, N.Y., 1939–70; I–III, revised ed., N.Y., 1958–60).
Grenville Papers	William J. Smith, ed., *The Grenville Papers: Being the Correspondence of Richard Grenville, Earl Temple, K.G., and the Right Hon: George Grenville, Their Friends and Contemporaries* (4 vols., London, 1852–53).
Johnson Papers	James Sullivan, Alexander C. Flick, Almon W. Lauber, and Milton W. Hamilton, eds., *The Papers of Sir William Johnson* (14 vols., Albany, 1921–65).
Jour.	*Journal.*

Kammen, *Rope of Sand*	Michael G. Kammen, *A Rope of Sand: the Colonial Agents, British Politics, and the American Revolution* (Ithaca, N.Y., [1968]).
Lewis, *Indiana Co.*	George E. Lewis, *The Indiana Company, 1763–1798: a Study in Eighteenth Century Frontier Land Speculation and Business Venture* (Glendale, Cal., 1941).
LS	Letter signed.
Morgan, *Stamp Act Crisis*	Edmund S. and Helen M. Morgan, *The Stamp Act Crisis* (Chapel Hill, [1953]).
MS, MSS	Manuscript, manuscripts.
Namier and Brooke, *House of Commons*	Sir Lewis Namier and John Brooke, *The History of Parliament. The House of Commons 1754–1790* (3 vols., London and N.Y., 1964).
N.J. Arch.	William A. Whitehead and others, eds., *Archives of the State of New Jersey* (2 series, Newark and elsewhere, 1880–). Editors, subtitles, and places of publication vary.
N.Y. Col. Docs.	E. B. O'Callaghan, ed., *Documents relative to the Colonial History of the State of New York* (15 vols., Albany, 1853–87).
Pa. Arch.	Samuel Hazard and others, eds., *Pennsylvania Archives* (9 series, Philadelphia and Harrisburg, 1852–1935).
Pa. Col. Recs.	*Minutes of the Provincial Council of Pennsylvania...* (16 vols., Philadelphia, 1838–53). Title changes with Volume XI to *Supreme Executive Council.*
Phil. Trans.	The Royal Society, *Philosophical Transactions.*
PMHB	*Pennsylvania Magazine of History and Biography.*
Proc.	*Proceedings.*
Sibley's Harvard Graduates	John L. Sibley, *Biographical Sketches of Graduates of Harvard University* (Cambridge, Mass., 1873–). Continued from Volume IV by Clifford K. Shipton.

Smyth, *Writings* Albert H. Smyth, ed., *The Writings of Benjamin Franklin*... (10 vols., N.Y., 1905–07).

Sparks, *Works* Jared Sparks, ed., *The Works of Benjamin Franklin*... (10 vols., Boston, 1836–40).

Trans. *Transactions.*

Van Doren, *Franklin* Carl Van Doren, *Benjamin Franklin* (N.Y., 1938).

Van Doren, *Franklin–Mecom* Carl Van Doren, ed., *The Letters of Benjamin Franklin & Jane Mecom* (American Philosophical Society *Memoirs*, XXVII, Princeton, 1950).

WF William Franklin.

WTF, *Memoirs* William Temple Franklin, ed., *Memoirs of the Life and Writings of Benjamin Franklin, LL.D., F.R.S., &c.*... (3 vols., 4to, London, 1817–18).

Introduction

The year 1770 was momentous on both sides of the Atlantic. In England the fragile administration begun by Chatham and continued by Grafton came to its unlamented close in January, and was succeeded by what proved to be the longest ministry since Walpole's and the most disastrous of the century, that of Lord North. The new government was immediately confronted by the American problem, for which a number of contrasting solutions were being advanced. Franklin twice mentions, in references that are tantalizingly elusive,[1] plans for major constitutional reform in the empire; but what they were is impossible to say, and in any case they came to nothing. Another and opposite proposal was to attack the nonimportation agreements directly by a statute outlawing them; this scheme made some progress during the spring, but also proved abortive.[2] The solution that prevailed was to undermine the agreements by removing most of their cause, and to retain only one of the Townshend duties.

Would repealing them all have led in time to a resolution of the colonial problem? If Parliament had permitted its claim to tax to fall quietly into abeyance, would the colonists have fastened upon other issues to renew the quarrel, or become satisfied with a major constitutional concession? The latter possibility may well have been in Franklin's mind, although he did not say so, when he was conducting his campaign for total repeal.[3] But he was fighting against insuperable odds. Just as Rockingham had been unable to rescind the Stamp Act without simultaneously asserting the principle behind it in the Declaratory Act, so North was unable—even if he had been willing—to retreat from that principle by rescinding all the Townshend duties. One had to be retained, as symbol more than for revenue, and the one selected was that on tea. The moment passed to let the constitutional dogs go back to sleep if so inclined;

1. See the beginning of his letters below to Galloway, Jan. 11, and to Le Despencer, July 26.
2. See below, p. 169 n.
3. See in particular his eleven articles in the press, "The Colonist's Advocate," below, Jan. 4, 8, 11, 15, 25, 29, Feb. 1, 5, 12, 19, and March 2.

henceforth they were awake and growling. The government, in short, did just what Junius had blamed the Rockingham ministry for doing: it abandoned the revenue and preserved the contention.

But the immediate results in America seemed to show that this compromise would work. Long before repeal was enacted, the prospect of it had cooled colonial excitement and weakened the merchants' support of nonimportation; all Franklin's influence had been needed to keep them in line. Once partial repeal was assured, the agreements were abandoned. This was a defeat for Franklin, who had argued strongly for maintaining them, even at the risk of a rupture with Britain, until all duties were removed. His reasons were partly economic, partly political. He was as confident as ever that an embargo on British goods would promote colonial manufactures and so strengthen the whole American economy. He was now ready, as he had not been before, to say openly that any Parliamentary tax on the colonies was the exercise of a usurped and illegal power. Just when the Americans and British seemed to be moving toward reconciliation, in short, he was moving in the opposite direction. He was becoming less the irenic pragmatist, intent on calming tempers and seeking compromise, and more the theorist who was willing to follow logic to conclusions that were too extreme for many of his countrymen.

He first stated his position in a letter to Samuel Cooper (below, June 8), which he must have known would be widely circulated. He there attacked the whole concept of Parliamentary sovereignty in the empire, and urged his American friends to stop implying that they accepted it. Parliament was encroaching unconstitutionally upon their rights and those of the crown, for the empire was composed of states with coequal legislatures and a common sovereign. This idea had long been in Franklin's mind, and he had once touched upon it in a letter to the London press.[4] But he had never before interjected it so publicly into the political debate, and by broadcasting it in Boston he chose the point where that debate was at its hottest.

Although the colonists in general were showing signs of being mollified by partial repeal, Massachusetts was the exception. There the leaders in Boston who were corresponding with Franklin found one grievance to pile upon another. The Boston Massacre in the

4. See above, xv, 36–8; xvi, 277 n 1.

spring, suspicion of malicious reports to London, resentment of the Governor's secret instructions from the ministry, rumors that the colony's charter was to be altered, all combined to keep fear and antagonism at the boil. Franklin had been intermittently in touch with the situation for more than a year, but in October he was plunged into it by his election as agent for the Massachusetts House of Representatives. He had been suspect to many of its members as too conservative and too closely tied to the crown; even though his letter to Cooper and earlier letters in favor of nonimportation had allayed much of the suspicion, the election was far from unanimous. His future support in the House would depend on how well he carried out its instructions, and here he was in difficulties. His own views were not yet as radical as those of some of his constituents, and his power to speak for them was further limited by the nature of his appointment: he was agent of the lower house, at a time when the government was tightening the rules and recognizing only an agent chosen by the governor and both houses. By these rules he was agent for Georgia alone; his status in his three other agencies was shaky in the eyes of Whitehall. Yet, whatever the views of the American Department, his close connections with four of the thirteen colonies now made him more than ever before a spokesman for them all.

For this very reason he was vulnerable to attack in England as an unfaithful officer of the crown. When news of his efforts to maintain the nonimportation agreements filtered back to London, he was in danger of losing his position in the Post Office; and, in the hope of forcing him to resign it, writers vilified him in the public press. They misjudged their man. He was unrepentant and, in his words, "deficient in that Christian virtue of resignation." Again, as at the time of the Stamp Act, he said what he thought, "refused to change my political opinions every time his Majesty thought fit to change his ministers," and won enough respect in high quarters to keep his office.[5]

Franklin's other and quite different cause, that of the land speculators, seems to have made little demand upon him during the year. The reason was that negotiating with the government offered small chance of action, for every step taken was followed by interminable silence from officialdom. The Walpole Company, encouraged by

5. BF to Jane Mecom below, Dec. 30.

Hillsborough at the close of 1769, petitioned on January 4 for a grant of twenty million acres, which was almost ten times what it had previously hoped for. Thereafter it waited; its only sign of life during the rest of the year was when it absorbed a small rival.[6] What kept it waiting was not mere bureaucratic torpor; a struggle was going on within the government over what British policy should be toward the settlement of the west, but of this struggle Franklin seems to have known little. Although he doubtless wondered whether he would live long enough to see the petition acted upon, he said nothing. Perhaps he was too old a hand at the game to be surprised by what must have seemed to him like cobwebs on the wheels of government.

Several events in his private life marked 1770. One was the death in New Jersey of his old colleague James Parker, which ended both a friendship of long duration and a stream of letters that were outstanding for their dullness. Another was the marriage in August of a second close associate, John Foxcroft, who was on leave in England; Franklin gave away the bride, and his young friend Thomas Coombe, Jr., performed the ceremony.[7] A few weeks earlier Franklin had attended a wedding of far more moment to him, that of Polly Stevenson to William Hewson, the physician and anatomist. Coombe again officiated, and Mrs. Stevenson, Dorothea Blunt, and Franklin were witnesses. He and Dorothea purported to be grieved at Polly's deserting them. But his wound, whatever it may have been, quickly healed. Two months after the marriage the newlyweds, in Mrs. Stevenson's absence, came to manage the Craven Street household; and their regime inspired one of Franklin's most entertaining outbursts of nonsense.

He also found time for outbursts of a different sort, in his continuing marginalia. If the conjectural dating is correct, this was the year when they were the most profuse; in one pamphlet by Josiah Tucker, in which the Dean was singularly provocative in tone and

6. Below, May 7.

7. Thomas Coombe to his father, Aug. 4, 1770, Hist. Soc. of Pa. The bride was Judith Osgood, and BF referred to her thereafter as his daughter, presumably because he had been surrogate father at her wedding. These references led the literally-minded to believe that she was in fact his illegitimate daughter; see, for example, Sydney G. Fisher, *The True Benjamin Franklin* (Philadelphia, 1899), pp. 104–5. Van Doren has neatly disposed of this myth: *Franklin*, pp. 411–12.

the printer singularly generous with his margins, Franklin's comments are almost as long as the text. There and elsewhere he was repetitious, reiterating the same ideas—sometimes even the same words—over and over. But spontaneity compensates for redundancy, because the man at his most spontaneous is far more human and vivid than the Olympian figure of tradition.[8] The Franklin, in fact, who is talking to himself in his marginalia would have grinned at that figure.

8. This traditional view of BF, so well expressed in Carl Becker's article on him in the DAB, is still current. "Nearly always he held something of himself back, as though playing life like a game of whist. Only when digging into sciences was he wholly open and unreserved. In other matters he seemed a spectator—bland, friendly, but detached." Marshall Smelser, *The Winning of Independence* (Chicago, 1972), pp. 166–7.

Chronology of 1770

January 4: BF publishes the first in a series of eleven essays, "The Colonist's Advocate," attacking the Townshend duties; it runs for the next two months in the *Public Advertiser*. The Walpole Company petitions the Board of Trade for an enlarged grant of land.

January 9: Parliament reconvenes.

January 22: The Duke of Grafton resigns.

January 25 and February 16: debates in the Commons and Lords on the legality of Wilkes' expulsion.

January 27: London merchants meet to petition for repeal of the Townshend duties.

January 28: Lord North becomes the King's first minister.

February 6: The petition of the London merchants is presented to Parliament.

February 27: BF is belatedly reappointed agent for Georgia for the current year; on May 10 the appointment is extended for another year.

March 5: The Boston Massacre. The House of Commons debates the petition of the London merchants and votes against total repeal of the Townshend duties.

April 8–12: Legislation is passed to provide for partial repeal of the duties.

May 9: Parliament adjourns.

June 10: A Spanish force from South America captures a British settlement in the Falkland Islands, precipitating an Anglo-Spanish crisis that lasts for the rest of the year.

July 2: James Parker dies in Burlington, N.J.

July 9: New York merchants abandon their nonimportation agreement.

July 10: Mary (Polly) Stevenson marries William Hewson at St. Mary Abbots, Kensington.

August 2: John Foxcroft marries Judith Osgood in London; BF gives away the bride.

September 20: Philadelphia merchants abandon their nonimportation agreement.

September 30: John Mecom, Jane's son, dies at New Brunswick, N.J. George Whitefield dies at Newburyport, Mass.

October 11: Boston merchants abandon nonimportation.

October 17: The first trial growing out of the Massacre, that of Capt. Preston, opens in Boston.

October 24: BF is chosen agent of the Massachusetts House of Representatives to succeed Dennys DeBerdt.

November 13: Parliament reconvenes.

THE PAPERS OF
BENJAMIN FRANKLIN

VOLUME 17

January 1 through December 31, 1770

The first ascription of these fables to Franklin was by Verner Crane, and his evidence is conclusive. [1] When the second and third fables were composed, as distinct from published, is impossible to say; the genesis of the first goes back almost two years, although in the intervening period it changed considerably.

NEW FABLES, *humbly inscribed to the S——y of St——e for the* American Department.

FABLE I.

A Herd of Cows had long afforded Plenty of Milk, Butter, and Cheese to an avaricious Farmer, who grudged them the Grass they subsisted on, and at length mowed it to make Money of the Hay, leaving them to *shift for Food* as they could, and yet still expected to *milk them* as before; but the Cows, offended with his Unreasonableness, resolved for the future *to suckle one another.*[2]

FABLE II.

An Eagle, King of Birds, sailing on his Wings aloft over a Farmer's Yard, saw a Cat there basking in the Sun, *mistook it for a Rabbit,* stoop'd, seized it, and carried it up into the Air, *intending to prey on it.* The Cat turning, set her Claws into the Eagle's Breast; who, finding his Mistake, opened his Talons, and would have let her drop; but Puss, unwilling to fall so far, held faster; and the Eagle, to get rid of the Inconvenience, found it necessary to *set her down where he took her up.*

FABLE III.

A Lion's Whelp was put on board a Guinea Ship bound to America as a Present to a Friend in that Country: It was tame and harmless as a Kitten, and therefore not confined, but suffered to walk about the Ship at Pleasure. A stately, full-grown English Mastiff, belonging to the Captain, despising the Weakness of the young Lion, frequently took it's *Food* by Force, and often turned it out of it's Lodging Box, when he had a Mind to repose therein himself.

1. Verner W. Crane, "Three Fables by Benjamin Franklin," *New England Quarterly,* IX (1936), 499–503.
2. For the initial form of this fable see above, xv, 66–7. In that version the central point, both in BF's rough draft and in his printed essay, is one that he has now deleted: the cows were taxed in grass.

The young Lion nevertheless grew daily in Size and Strength, and the Voyage being long, he became at last a more equal Match for the Mastiff; who continuing his Insults, received a stunning Blow from the Lion's Paw that fetched his Skin over his Ears, and deterred him from any future Contest with such growing Strength; regretting that he had not rather secured it's Friendship than provoked it's Enmity.

Note on Post Office Accounts

AD (copy): Historical Society of Pennsylvania

April 2, 1768, to January 3, 1770

[The credit entries, running from April 2, 1768, to March 17, 1769, are of money received by Franklin and Foxcroft from American post offices. In round figures the receipts from James Parker in New York were £2,439, from Philadelphia £312, and from smaller places (Talbot Court House, presumably Talbot, Md.; Rhode Island, presumably Newport; and Annapolis) £73, a total of £2,824 sterling. The disproportion between Parker's figures and the rest was doubtless due to his collecting, as comptroller, from numerous post offices outside New York. Boston and towns to the north of it, and those south of Maryland, appear to have remitted independently. A sampling of the receipts that are given in provincial currency as well as in sterling indicates that the exchange rate was most favorable in Pennsylvania and least so in New York: in the former it ranged between £169 and £167.5 to £100 sterling, and in the latter between £180 and £177.7.

The debit entries, running from April 2, 1768, to Jan. 3, 1770, are of payments from the Post Office to Franklin and Foxcroft: two years' salary for each at £300 a year, Foxcroft's traveling expenses in America in 1769 at a guinea a day and his outlays for "Jonas Greens Suit,"[3] etc. The total of £1,861 left a balance due to the Post Office of £963.]

3. Green had been postmaster at Annapolis until dismissed for keeping improper accounts, and had died in 1767. See above, III, 153 n; VII, 277 n; XIV, 139 n. The suit was presumably brought by or against his widow in connection with those accounts.

The Colonist's Advocate: I

Reprinted from Verner W. Crane, *Benjamin Franklin's Letters to the Press, 1758–1775* (Chapel Hill, [1950]), pp. 167–70.

This essay, printed in the *Public Advertiser* on Jan. 4, 1770, was the first in a series of eleven that ran in that newspaper for the next two months. The series was designed to muster support for the total repeal of the Townshend Acts, and ended when the last hope of such repeal was dashed in March. Verner Crane, with his usual meticulous and persuasive scholarship, has demonstrated that Franklin was the principal author, but may have had some assistance from his fellow member of the Club of Honest Whigs, James Burgh.[4] The essays were the only instance during his English missions in which Franklin committed himself in advance to ongoing serial publication. Even though he did not meet the schedule as first announced, of two a week, and even if he did have Burgh's help as collaborator, the literary effort involved must have conflicted seriously with the other demands upon his time. Hence it is not surprising that the essays contain little that is original; they reiterate, and on occasion amplify, arguments that he had formulated earlier.[5]

[January 4, 1770]

The Time now approaches when the Great Council of the Nation is to meet for deliberating on the momentous Concerns of this mighty Empire; no Object of greater Importance than the present unhappy Dispute between the Mother Country, and her Colonies, is likely to come before them, I therefore beg leave to offer to the Public a few brief Considerations on this weighty Subject. The Hope that the Legislature will at length be graciously pleased to relax of the Severity heretofore exercised against our Fellow-Subjects in America, and to consult more deliberately the mutual Advantage both of them and us, has encouraged me to seize the present Opportunity. The impartial Publick will judge, from my

---

4. *Letters to the Press*, pp. 285–7, and notes on pp. 167–86, 192–7, 201–9. Burgh subsequently made free and unacknowledged use of this series and many other writings by BF, as Crane points out, in Book II of Vol. II of *Political Disquisitions . . .* (3 vols., London, 1774–75).

5. And sometimes arguments to which he returned later. Crane has traced these arguments to their sources in his excellent footnotes, to which we are deeply indebted; much of our annotation consists merely in changing his references to apply to the present edition. We have also pointed out passages that in our opinion are clearly not by BF and hence are presumably Burgh's handiwork.

Manner of treating the Subject, in the following Numbers, which will appear in this Paper on Mondays and Thursdays, what Opportunities I have had, during some Years Service in America, of knowing the Inclinations, Affections, and Concerns of the Inhabitants in the Provinces of that extensive Continent. Be it remembered by those, who may find themselves disposed to object against this Publication, that where the Matter is of such Weight, the Manner of stating it is of less Consequence, and that, while Grievances continue unredressed, the Continuance of Complaint is to be expected.

It is well known, that the late fatal Rupture between us and our Colonies, is owing to an Innovation introduced under the Administration of Mr. Grenville, by which, instead of the usual Method of Requisition, at all Times readily complied with by our Colonies to their utmost Power, we have thought fit to lay upon them sundry Taxes, with the declared Purpose of raising Money for the Benefit of the Revenue, while they have no Representation adequate, or inadequate in the Assembly, which imposes those Taxes. To this we have added an express authoritative Declaration, that the British Parliament has a Right to impose Taxes on the Colonies without their Consent given either in Person, or by Representation.

These Proceedings the Colonists consider as a direct Attack on the Vitals of their Liberty. "What is it to be enslaved?" the Colonists say, "If, being deprived of our Property, without our Consent, nay, in direct Opposition to our Inclination, by an Assembly in which not one Individual is interested, or authorized to take our Part, but, on the contrary, all think themselves interested to burthen us for their own Alleviation. What is it to be enslaved if this be not?"[6] According to Mr. Locke, the late Declaration of the Parliament's Right to tax the unrepresented Colonies, annihilates the whole Property of every British Subject in America, and at once beggars three Millions of industrious, loyal, and brave People. "I have truly no Property in that which another can, by Right, take from me, when he pleases, against my Consent," says that great Writer.[7] Now, in this very Predicament, have we, by the late Claim of a

6. See above, xv, 188.

7. His actual words were, "What property have I in that, which another may by right take, when he pleases, to himself?" *Of Civil Government*, Bk. II, chap. xi, par. 140.

6

Right to tax the Colonies, without Representation, placed a very great Proportion of the British free-born Subjects. Three Millions, out of Fifteen of which his Majesty is Sovereign, are declared no longer Masters of the Fruits of their own Industry. Their All is at the absolute Disposal of the British Parliament, to every Intent and Purpose, as effectually as the Property of every Frenchman, or every Turk is at the Mercy of their respective Governments, in which the Subjects of those unhappy Countries are wholly unrepresented, and denied all Power of refusing; in which important Respect the Case of our Colonists is equally calamitous and oppressive.

The British Subjects on the West Side of the Atlantick, see no Reason why they must not have the Power of giving away their own Money, while those on the Eastern Side claim that Privilege. They imagine, it would sound very unmelodious in the Ear of an Englishman, to tell him, that, by the Rapidity of Population in our Colonies, the Time will quickly come when the Majority of the Subjects will be in America; and that in those Days there will be no House of Commons in England, but that Britain will be taxed by an American Parliament, in which there will not be one Representative for either of the British Kingdoms.[8]

If the British Subjects, residing in this Island, claim Liberty, and the Disposal of their Property, on the Score of that unalienable Right that all Men, except those who have justly forfeited those Advantages have to them, the British People, residing in America, challenge the same on the same Principle. If the former alledge, that they have a Right to tax themselves, from Prescription, and Time immemorial, so may the latter. If the former have Charters from Princes, so have the latter. There is not one Species of Claim, natural or artificial, on which the former can found their Right to the Disposal of their own Property, to which the latter is not equally intitled. Indeed, an Empire, composed of half Freemen, half Slaves (in a very few Years the British Subjects in America will equal the Number of those in the Mother Country) would resemble the Roman Empire in it's ruinous State, as it is described in the wonderful Prediction of the Prophet Daniel, by the Representation of the Legs and Feet of an Image partly of Iron, and partly of Clay,

8. A stronger reiteration of an old point of BF's, for which see above, XIV, 131.

partly strong, and partly broken.⁹ God forbid that ever this Description should be applicable to the British Empire!

N.B. If any Fact should, in the Course of these Papers, be wrong stated, it will immediately be corrected, if candidly pointed out. But Gentlemen will please to decline urging any of the Objections already published against the Reasonings of the Colonists, because most of them will be considered in the Course of these Papers.

Petition to the Treasury from Franklin and Others for a Grant of Land   AD (copy): Library of Congress

The formation of the Grand Ohio Company in the early summer of 1769 had begun a flurry of activity among its principal promoters.[1] The original request to the Privy Council for a grant of 2,400,000 acres, to be carved out of the territory ceded to the crown by the Indians in the Treaty of Fort Stanwix, had been referred to the Board of Trade. After a five-month pause the Board held a hearing in December, 1769, at which Hillsborough made the suggestion—most surprising in the light of his previous attitude—that the grant be enlarged to a size suitable for a new colony, and himself offered to sound out the opinion of the Treasury. The promoters may have been as much startled as pleased by the American Secretary's volte-face, but they were quick to improve the shining hour. At a meeting on December 27, with sixteen in attendance and Franklin in the chair, they decided to reorganize and enlarge the Company so as to include George Croghan and his group and those in the Indiana Company, and to raise the ante by asking for a grant of twenty million acres. The petition printed below grew out of this meeting and was presented to the Lords Commissioners of the Treasury, including Grafton and North, by the signers in person on January 4, 1770. The Commissioners behaved as might be expected: they were receptive in principle but averse to reaching any quick decision, and waited on further information from the Board of Trade and opinions from other governmental departments.[2] The negotiations thereupon relapsed into their usual torpor.

9. The image in Nebuchadnezzar's dream (Dan. 2: 31–45) is now interpreted, not as a prediction of Rome, but as a reference to the past empire, that of Alexander's successors.

1. See above, XVI, 163–8, where the signers of this petition are identified.

2. Lewis, *Indiana Co.*, pp. 89–94.

8

[January 4, 1770]
The Memorial of Thos Walpole, John
Sarjant, Dr. Franklin and Saml.
Wharton for the Purchase of Lands in
America in behalf of themselves and
their Associates.

SHEWETH.

That your Memorialists propose to your Lordships to become
Purchasers of a certain tract of land within the late Cession made
to the King at Fort Stanwix by the six Nations and described in a
Paper hereto annexed paying for the same £10,460 7s. 3d. and a
Quit Rent of 2 shillings for every 100 Acres of *cultivable* Land within the said tract, which Quit Rent to commence after the expiration
of 20 years. One fifth part of the Principal Money to be paid immediately on receiving a deed of Grant under the Great Seal for the
said Tract of Land and the remaining four fifths to be paid annually
by four equal Instalments——And Your Memorialists &ca.

THOS. WALPOLE
JOHN SARJANT
B. FRANKLIN
SAML. WHARTON

To the Right Honourable the Lords Commissioners of His
Majesty's Treasury.

Copy

[*Annex:*] Beginning on the South side of the River Ohio, opposite
the Mouth of Sioto, thence Southerly through the Pass in the Ona-
sioto Mountains to the South side of the said Mountains thence
along the side of the said Mountains North Easterly to the Fork of
the Great Kenhawa made by the junction of Green Briar and New
Rivers thence along the said Green Briar River on the Easterly side
of the same into the head or termination of the North Easterly
branch thereof, thence Easterly to the Allegheny Mountain thence
along the said Allegheny Mountain to Lord Fairfax's line, thence
along the same to the Spring head of the North branch of the River
Powtomack thence along the Western Boundary line of the Province of Maryland to the Southern Boundary line of the Province
of Pennsylvania, Thence along the said Southern Boundary line of
the Province of Pennsylvania to the end thereof, Thence along the

9

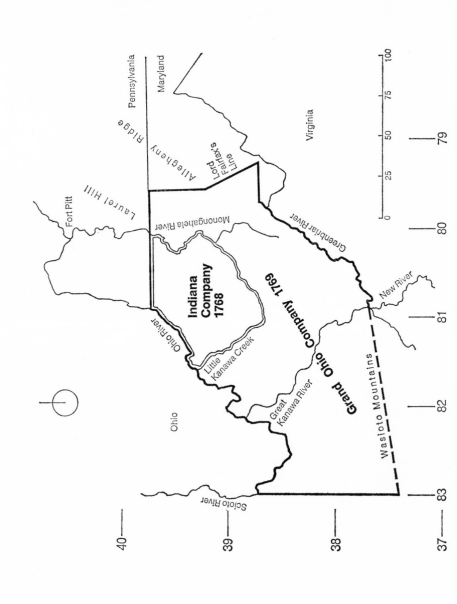

Western Boundary line of the said Province of Pennsylvania until the same shall strike the *River Ohio*, Thence down the said River Ohio to the Place of Beginning.

Copy

Endorsed: Memorial of the Honourable Thomas Walpole and his Associates to the Lords of the Treasury for Lands On the River ohio, and the Bounds of the same.

From John Ewing[3] ALS: American Philosophical Society

Sir   Philada. Janry. 4th 1769[4]
    Our Philosophical Society have at Length ordered me to draw out an Account of our Observations of the Transits of Venus and Mercury to be transmitted to you as our President thro' whose Hands we think they may most conveniently be communicated to the learned Societies of Europe to whom you may apprehend they will be agreable. The Reason of their not coming sooner to Hand was a rash Agreement of the Society not to send them abroad untill we had printed them in our own Transactions.[5] But finding that there was some Reason to suspect that some partial Accounts of them had been transmitted to England, by some of our Members privately, which possibly might be inaccurate and not much to be depended on, the Society have thought proper to reconsider that hasty Agreement, and send them without farther Loss of Time. We hope however that they will be as soon with you as those that have been made in South America and the East Indies. I have accordingly enclosed to you two Copies, one directed to the Astronomer Royal Mr. Maskelyne at Greenwich[6] and the other to be transmitted by you to any of the learned Societies of Europe you shall think

3. Pastor of the First Presbyterian Church in Philadelphia, and one of the group that had observed the transit of Venus from the Statehouse yard. See above, XI, 526 n; XVI, 241–2.
4. [BF's *note:*] should be 1770.
5. See *ibid.*, p. 241.
6. The Astronomer Royal had already received the "partial Accounts" and found them unsatisfactory; *ibid.*, pp. 257, 269–70.

proper.[7] I would have had them transcribed in a fairer Hand than my own, but only that the only Post which can reach the Packet leaves Town this morning.

You are well acquainted, Sir, with the Serenity of our Air, and the Advantages we enjoy above many other Countries in Europe for making celestial Observations could a fixed Observatory be established in Philadelphia. I have mentioned this Matter to Mr. Maskelyne and referred him to you for Advice how to bring it into Execution should it meet with your Approbation. You are well acquainted with the Views of our Assembly, and the Unreasonableness of expecting that they would lay out any of the public Money for such a Purpose, unless it was recommended by you to them, as they place an unreserved Confidence in your Judgment, concerning what Measures would Lend to the Reputation of the Province the Advancement of useful Knowledge and the Benefit of the public in general. Geography, Navigation and the Arts that depend upon them are daily reaping Advantages from the Astronomical Observations made in the different Observatories of Europe. Should you think it of any Consequence that we in this infant Country might bear any Part in these Things, your known Character and Abilities to judge in these Matters must necessarily have so much Influence with our Assembly as to induce them to bear at least a Part in the Expences of it. And possibly Mr. Maskelyne might suggest some Means of affording some Assistance from Home, from the Consideration of its being made subservient to his Observatory at Greenwich and put under his general Direction.[8]

I have not mentioned this Proposal to any Persons here but to Mr. Coomb, excepting to you, and that under a Promise that he will not speak of it, as I apprehend that there is a Propriety in its coming from you and the Astronomer Royal. So that if it does not meet with your Approbation, pray let it sleep and be so kind as to

7. BF forwarded the observations to Jean-Baptiste LeRoy, who transmitted them to the Académie royale des sciences. See BF to LeRoy below, Oct. 2, and Alexandre Pingré, "Examen critique des observations du passage de Vénus sur le disque du soleil, le 3 juin 1769; et des conséquences qu'on peut légitimement en tirer," *Histoire de l'Académie royale des sciences...*, LXXII (1770), 578–9.

8. Ewing returned to this idea in a letter to BF below, June 14; see also BF to Ewing below, Aug. 27, and Brooke Hindle, *The Pursuit of Science in Revolutionary America, 1735–1789* (Chapel Hill, [1956]), pp. 167–8.

excuse the Trouble given you by Sir Your most obedient and very humble Servant   JOHN EWING

P s. Mr. Coombe tells me that he has mentioned the above Proposal to his Son, with a Desire that he should speak to you on the Subject.[9]

Please to send me Authentic Accounts of the Observations of the Transit of Venus made in as many Places as you can conveniently procure, if your Leisure from more important Business will permit it, that we may here also endeavour to solve the curious Problem of the Suns Parallax. If it would not be trespassing too much, I should also be much obliged to you for an Account of Messrs. Mason's & Dixons Determinations of the Length of a Degree of Latitude here, as they have been employed by the R. Society to measure it in the lower Counties.[1]

Endorsed: Revd Mr Ewing Jan 4. 1770

From James Parker   ALS: American Philosophical Society

Honoured Sir   Woodbridge Jan. 4, 1769 [1770][2]

I am yet here about the Jersey Laws: I sent up to New York 8 Days ago, a Letter for you with the first of the inclosed Bill of Exchange for £200, Wats and Mc Evers on Harley and Drummond which I had of Mr. Colden: but the Weather has been so extreme severe, that I have not learnt whether it could be sent by a Merchantship, or by this Packet; but lest that should be with a Merchant Ship, I venture to send this per Packet. By that I sent a New power to you which I designed by Capt. Davis, who witnessed it, but he sailed suddenly and I knew it not.[3] The Laws will take me

9. For Thomas Coombe, Sr., BF's old friend, see above, XI, 107 n; XVI, 112. His son, Thomas Jr., had gone to England in 1768 to seek ordination, and did not return to America until 1772. The young man's letters to his father, in the Hist. Soc. of Pa., indicate that he saw a good deal of BF during his stay; see also above, xv, 286, 293.

1. The hope of determining the sun's parallax, as mentioned in Vol. xvi, was what interested the scientific world in the transit of Venus. For the involvement of the Royal Society in the Mason and Dixon survey see above, XII, 341–2.

2. Misdated by Parker, as the body of the letter makes clear.

3. For Parker's previous letter and the business matters that he is discussing see above, XVI, 264, 269.

here about two Weeks from this Time,[4] when I hope to return to New-York. I continue very Stiff and sore but seem to gather Strength a little: I have resigned the Office in the Custom-House:[5] We are otherways much as usual, and with the Utmost Regards remain Your most obliged Servant   JAMES PARKER

PS. I don't remember ever to have seen your Examination in a Quebeck Paper, it was in several of the Eastern Ones; but I write to Quebeck about it, and if I can get it I will send it.[6]

Addressed: For / Dr Benjamin Franklin / Craven Street / London / per Packet

The Colonist's Advocate: II

Printed in *The Public Advertiser*, January 8, 1770

The Absurdity of taxing the Colonies without Representation, is so glaring, that some Defenders of the late oppressive Measures have attempted to palliate it by urging, that our American Brethren are actually represented in the British House of Commons; "the most ridiculous Idea (says Lord Chatham in his Speech on the Stamp Act) that ever entered into the Head of a Man, and which does not deserve a Confutation."[7] We find a different Sort of reasoning in the Year-Book of Richard III. *Nostra statuta non ligana* [*ligant*] *Hibernos, quis non mittunt milites ad Parliamentum.* "Our Laws do not bind the People of Ireland, because they do not send Members to our Parliament."[8] But the American Colonists have ever

4. For more than a decade Parker had been public printer for the province of New Jersey.

5. See *ibid.*, pp. 137–8.

6. The *Quebec Gaz.* had printed BF's famous *Examination*, in French and English, in six issues between Dec. 1, 1766, and Jan. 5, 1767; Parker succeeded in getting copies for BF, and forwarded them with his letter of April 23 below. Two eastern newspapers that had also printed it were the *New London Gaz.* and the *Providence Gaz.*

7. Pitt's reference to virtual representation, slightly misquoted by BF, was made during the debate in January, 1766. See Cobbett, *Parliamentary History*, XVI, 100.

8. BF is apparently paraphrasing, not the Yearbook, but Sir Edward Coke's garbled version of it in discussing the judgment in the case of the Merchants of Waterford. See William Molyneux, *The Case of Ireland's Being Bound by Acts*

shewn themselves willing to obey our Laws, though they sent no Members to our Parliament, till we begun laying Taxes on them without their having one assenting or dissenting Voice in our Parliament. They then bethought themselves of the Case of the People of Ireland, and of the People of Chester and Durham, which two last mentioned Places obtained Representation in Parliament, precisely on this Account, that they paid Taxes, and because it was thought unjust to subject them to Taxes without giving them an Opportunity of assenting or dissenting. The People of Wales were not taxed till they had Representatives in Parliament, says Lord Chatham.[9] Both Ireland and Wales are conquered Countries; and yet we use greater Severity toward our Colonies, which never resisted us, while we are incomparably more obliged to our Colonies than to Ireland and Wales both put together. An incomprehensible Partiality! Nor would the taxing of Ireland or Wales without Representation, be so great a Hardship as what we have lately laid on our Colonies, because of their Proximity, which gives us an Opportunity of knowing their Abilities to bear Taxes. The same may be urged still more strongly concerning Chester and Durham, which are situated almost in the Middle of England.

To what Distress must the Defenders of the Grenvillian Measures be reduced, when they are fain to argue that the Colonists are under no greater Hardship in being taxed by an Assembly in which three Millions have not one Representative for any one of their Counties, Cities, or Boroughs, than the Mother-Country; in which, though Representation is far enough from being adequate, (an Evil which wants Redress, not Extention) yet about double or treble the Number of the British Subjects in America have 558 Representatives, and in which every Man, Woman, and Child, by living in one County or other, to say nothing of Cities or Boroughs, is represented by two Members at least, who cannot tax them without taxing themselves, their Friends, Dependents, Tenants, &c. whereas in

---

of Parliament in England, Stated ([Dublin?], 1719), pp. 54–5, 69–70. The whole complex question of English jurisdiction in Ireland had long been argued, and the "reasoning" that BF ascribes to the Yearbook was far from universally accepted legal doctrine at any time. See Robert L. Schuyler, *Parliament and the British Empire...* (New York, 1929), chap. II.

9. Cobbett, *Parliamentary History*, XVI, 100. For other references by BF, in his marginalia, to the examples of Chester and Ireland see above, XVI, 285, 312–13, and below, pp. 320, 346–7, 384.

taxing the Colonies we are under a direct Temptation to burden them, because we not only do not thereby tax ourselves, but on the contrary obtain a present Relief proportioned to the Sum we levy on them.[10] If the Cases of the Mother-Country and Colonies be, in respect to Taxation by Parliament, the same, or at all capable of Comparison, then Slavery is the same with Liberty, Tyranny with just Government, Property with Beggary. They however who attempt to gull their American Fellow Subjects into the Belief that their Hardship, in being subjected to British Taxation, is not greater than that now suffered by the People of Britain, serve the American Interest thus far, that they shew plainly they have no Shadow of Reason to urge for a Difference being made by Government between the Mother-Country and the Colonies. How they dare to enterprize so gross an Imposition on the Understandings of so great a Multitude, as alledging that there is no Difference, they themselves best know. "Woe to them who call Darkness Light, and Light Darkness," says the Scripture.[1]

We now see all England besetting the Throne with a Complaint, that one County is deprived, not of all Representation, as America is, but of one particular Person, as one of their two Representatives, and this not to Perpetuity, but only during the Space of a few Years, while the Electors were at Liberty to choose any other qualified Person in Britain.[2] We see all England alarmed, and not without Reason, on this Occasion; and we have heard, that the Inhabitants of this County have talked of refusing to pay the Land-Tax, merely on Account of their being deprived of the Man of their Choice. Can we then wonder, that three Millions of People, every Individual of which was born as free as any Freeholder of Middlesex, should complain of being taxed by an Assembly, in which their vast Multitude has not one single Representative for County, City, or Borough?

10. See BF's marginal note above, XVI, 316.

1. "Woe unto them . . . that put darkness for light, and light for darkness." Is. 5: 20.

2. The affair of John Wilkes was still boiling. In February, 1769, the House of Commons had expelled him for the second time, and in April had declared his opponent in the election, Col. Luttrell, to be the legal member for Middlesex. Petitions against this highhanded act were pouring in, and a few weeks after BF published his essay a resolution that the Commons had exceeded its authority was introduced and defeated in both houses.

The Firmness shewn by the Colonists against what to them is precisely the same Oppression as to us it would be, to have Taxes laid on us by Royal Edict, has, by some among us, been called Sedition and Rebellion. It would be curious to know those Gentlmen's Opinion of the Conduct of the brave Hampden, who thought it his Duty to resist the lawful Sovereign's illegal Demand of three Shillings and Four-pence, for the single Reason, that he had no Hand, either personally, or representatively, in consenting to the Tax of Ship money.[3] Do the Grenvillians hold this glorious Patriot to be a seditious and rebellious Person? Are all those Subjects Rebels who oppose the illegal and oppressive Proceedings of lawful Government? If this Doctrine is Orthodox, down goes the Revolution, and we are all Rebels, the Jacobites only excepted; for the Stuarts were lawful Sovereigns.

To an American Colonist our Parliament is (as far as concerns the giving and granting of his Property) the same as the Parliament of Paris. He has as much Representation in one as in the other. Nor is his Opposition to Injustice any greater Proof of his Disrespect to the Authority of the British Parliament, where it's Authority ought to take Place, than every Englishman's Resistance to an Imposition by the lawful Sovereign, on his single Authority, would be of his Aversion to monarchical Government, and of his being of a seditious and rebellious Disposition.

From Samuel Wharton   ALS: American Philosophical Society

Dear Sir   Wednesday Morning [January 10, 1770?[4]]

I was informed late last Night, That a Number of your and my Letters were lying at the New York Coffee House and Therefore I

3. Where BF found, or invented, the assessment of 3s. 4d. on John Hampden is immaterial. The total assessments for Hampden's various estates were probably many times the 20s. on which the actual trial hinged, but in any case the defendant was attempting to protect a principle rather than his pocketbook. *DNB.* Edmund Burke, in his speech on American taxation in 1774, made a similar reference to Hampden, though more accurate and eloquent. *The Works of the Right Hon. Edmund Burke* (2 vols., London, 1834), I, 158.

4. The dating is purely conjectural. Capt. Falconer, in the *Pa. Packet*, arrived at Deal on Dec. 10, 1769 (*London Chron.*, Dec. 9–12), and might well have carried mail for Wharton and BF, in which case this note could have been

went into the City early this morning and have taken up all I could find.

I send by my Boy, yours. I [am] always very respectfully your Very affectionate Friend.   S WHARTON

Addressed: To / Dr. Franklin

The Colonist's Advocate: III

Printed in *The Public Advertiser*, January 11, 1770

Suppose some long-headed Minister should invent a Tax to be imposed *only* on those Subjects, residing in Britain, who have no Vote in any Election for Members of Parliament. Suppose the British Government to publish a formal Declaration, That they have a Right to give and grant away the Property of many Millions of their Fellow-Subjects, without, or against their Consent, and for the declared Purpose of saving their own, what Idea would this Proceeding give Foreigners of the hitherto justly boasted Equity of the British Government? But does it make any Difference, as to Equity, whether the Individuals taxed without, or against their own Consent, be Subjects residing on the Eastern, or on the Western Side of the Atlantick? If it does, the Advantage is plainly on the Side of the Tax here supposed; for the Members of the British Parliament, or at least the Majority of them (and the Majority decides) cannot be supposed competent Judges of the Ability of the Colonists to bear Taxes; whereas, they are Judges of the Ability of their Fellow-Subjects resident in Britain.[5]

---

of Dec. 13; but no letters from BF's Philadelphia correspondents, written shortly before Falconer sailed, are extant. Capt. Sparks, on the other hand, who sailed in late November and arrived in London early in January, 1770 (*Pa. Chron.*, Nov. 27–Dec. 4, 1769; *London Chron.*, Jan. 4–6, 1770), carried a number of letters to BF written in late November and printed in the previous volume— from DF, Hillegas, Thomson, and Evans. We are inclined to believe that Wharton was referring to the arrival of this mail, and was writing on Jan. 10, the first Wednesday after Sparks reached Dover. His use of the first person, instead of the third as in his previous notes, tells nothing except that he was erratic in his form of address. In 1768 he had even used, for the only time as far as we know, the greeting "Dear Friend"; see above, xv, 275.

5. See below, pp. 330–1, 389.

Again, suppose the Form of Representation was the same in England, as it is in some Parts of America, viz. That every Parish should send so many Deputies to the Assembly of Lawmakers. Suppose each County to exclude one Parish from the Privilege of Representation, and yet to lay Taxes on the unrepresented Parishes, as if they were represented. Suppose the Legislature to declare, that the County of Middlesex has a Right to tax the Parish of Islington, and at the same Time a Right to refuse to admit Deputies from that Parish to the County-Meeting, in which the Contingent for each Parish was settled, could it be reasonably expected that the Inhabitants of the Parish of Islington should contentedly submit to such gross Partiality? Yet this gross Partiality would be more reasonable than the British Parliament's assuming a Right to tax the unrepresented Colonists, because the Representatives of the other Parishes of Middlesex (and so of the rest) must, at least, be supposed competent Judges of the Abilities of the Inhabitants of Islington.

There is besides the Injustice, a palpable Self-contradiction in the Idea of a Power in the British Parliament, of laying Taxes on the Colonists, without previously new-modelling their whole internal Constitution. All, who know any Thing of the Government of the Colonies, know, that their Provincial Assemblies of Representatives have always had a Power, analogous to that of our House of Commons, of laying Taxes for bearing the Expences of each respective Government. This Constitution, every Body must perceive, is founded on the prime Maxim of all free Government, viz. That no Subject is to be deprived of any Part of his Property, but by his own Consent, given either personally, or by his Representative. Now, I should be glad to learn, from the Grenvillian Theory, what is to be the Business of the provincial Assemblies of Representatives in our Colonies, if the Power of taxing be in the British House of Commons? Is it not evident, that these two Powers are incompatible? How is the Provincial Assembly of New-England,[6] for instance, to lay on a Tax of Half a Crown in the Pound for the most indispensable Exigency, at the same Time that, for aught that is known in New-England, the House of Commons may be laying on a Tax of Seventeen and Six-pence in the Pound? If we may put any Trust in the first Rule in Arithmetick, here is the whole Pound gone.

6. The pointlessness of BF's inventing this assembly suggests that it may have been born of a collaborator's ignorance.

And, that severe and disproportionate Taxes may be laid on the Colonies by a British Parliament, is naturally to be expected from the Difficulty of their coming at a competent Knowledge of the internal Circumstances of the Colonies, of which more hereafter. If it should be proposed, in order to support this double Power of Taxation, that there be an indemnifying Power vested in the American Assemblies, of retorting Taxes on Britain to the Value of the Excess above what the Colonists can fairly bear; besides, that this would, at best, be but a clumsy Kind of doing and undoing, perhaps our being subjected to Taxation by the Americans, might not be relished here. But, to be serious, as their Constitution is at present, it seems impossible to reconcile, with any clear Ideas of Business, a double Power of Taxing. And, to take away from their Assemblies the Power of Taxing, in order to place it solely in the House of Commons, would indeed effectually remove the glaring Absurdity of a Self-contradictory double Power of Taxation; but I should be glad to know, if the Grenvillians have an Idea of a State of more absolute Slavery, as to Property, than this new Constitution would, without Representation in Parliament, bring our American Fellow-Subjects into.

On this Head a most pitiful Set of Defences has been fabricated by the Enemies of Liberty: As, that the City of London is sometimes taxed by her own internal Government, to raise Funds for the particular Uses of the City, while she is subject to the general Taxes imposed by Parliament. If the Colonies sent, as London does, Members to Parliament, and their Provincial Assemblies were accidental subordinate Courts, like the Common-Council of London, and not, as at present, their whole Representation, there might be some Comparison attempted. As their Constitution is now, no two Things can well be imagined more specifically different.

Again, it has been urged, in Defence of the new Taxing-Policy, that it pleads Precedent. The Post-Office, say the Grenvillians, is, in Effect, a Tax upon America, which they never have complained of. The advancing of so frivolous an Apology for their Injustice and Oppression, shews the Difficulty they find in patching up an indefensible Cause. They might as well have drawn a Defence of their Policy from the establishing of Tolls at Turnpikes. Will any Man of common Sense attempt to force a Comparison between a Regulation evidently for the Benefit of the Colonies, and of our

Merchants trading with them, and whose Effect is a saving of Money to the Colonists, and a Scheme, whose declared Intention is, to take from them their Property, and to increase the Revenue at their Expence, and contrary to their Inclination? Our American Fellow-Subjects have never shewn the least Inclination to dispute the Power of the British Government to make Regulations either for the Mother Country, or the Colonies, so they were found to be of general Advantage. Nay, it will appear by the Sequel that they have suppressed innumerable Complaints they might have been expected to utter with a very audible Voice. They have all along acquiesced in our regulating all the Branches of the national Commerce, and among the rest, that between the Mother Country and themselves. None of the Dummers, the Otises, the Dickensons, the Dulaneys,[7] dispute, in their Writings, the Power of the British Government over the Colonies. All they oppose is the illegal and unconstitutional Application of it. The Colonists admire and celebrate the British Form of Government, and only wish to enjoy the Benefit of it. They have, in their implicit Confidence, (for, with Anguish, I write it, their confidence once was implicit) in the Wisdom of Parliament, taken for granted, that no Regulation was likely ever to be made by it, which should materially injure them; as the known Consequence of injuring or impoverishing the Colonies, must be heavy Damage to the Mother Country.

Another flimsy Apology for the Right of taxing the unrepresented Colonies, is drawn from the Tenor of some of their Charters. And here likewise the Grenvillians throw away a great deal of Toil and Sweat on an ungrateful and barren Argument. Their Manner of handling the Point is alone a sufficient Indication of the cruel Hardships with which they find themselves pinched. Sometimes they argue, that the Charters granted the original Colonists are the only Foundation on which their respective Constitutions rest; and that some of those Charters mention a Power in the Parliament to lay Taxes on the Colonists. Ergo, the late Innovations are unexceptionable. Now, the Truth is, this Mode of Expression occurs only in one or two Charters, and plainly means nothing more than a

7. Jeremiah Dummer (*c.* 1679–1739), agent for Connecticut and Massachusetts, was a staunch defender in Great Britain of New England's interests; Daniel Dulany (1722–97) wrote an influential pamphlet against the Stamp Act; James Otis and John Dickinson need no introduction.

Security against regal Taxation, too common in those despotic Times.

Nor does it exclude the Idea of Representation, so essential to the Justice of a Claim of the Power of Taxation, but leaves it unmentioned; which was to be expected from the Spirit of those Ages, when Liberty was not understood. But the Grenvillians, in arguing from the Charters when they find themselves beaten out of this Hold, immediately shift Ground, and cry out, "The Kings who granted the Colony Charters over-stretched their Power." Nothing less than the whole Legislature could reach so far. Ergo, the Colonists Immunities are what the Legislature pleases to make them. How far the Power of Kings reaches I will not enquire; nor is the Dispute, whether the Colonists are to be Free or Slaves, to be decided by a Set of hasty Charters huddled up by a Set of Kings, who did not understand Liberty, and given to a Set of People who understand it as little. Were we to be determined by what was done in those arbitrary Times, the Liberties of the Mother Country, as well as of the Colonies, would soon be shaken from their Foundation.[8]

To John Bartram

Reprinted from William Darlington, ed., *Memorials of John Bartram and Humphry Marshall* (Philadelphia, 1849), pp. 404–5.

My ever dear Friend: London, Jan. 11, 1770.

I received your kind letter of Nov. 29, with the parcel of seeds, for which I am greatly obliged to you. I cannot make you adequate returns, in kind; but I send you, however, some of the true Rhubarb seed, which you desire.[9] I had it from Mr. Inglish, who lately received a medal, of the Society of Arts, for propagating it.[1] I send,

8. These concluding sentences, with their casual attitude toward Stuart history in general and the charters in particular, suggest again the work of a collaborator. For BF's view of the charters see above, XVI, 316, 318–20, and below, pp. 335, 346, 398.

9. BF had offered the rhubarb seed in the previous July; Bartram had accepted in November and sent a packet of his own. See above, XVI, 173, 250.

1. A Dr. James Mounsey had introduced the seed into England; for raising rhubarb from it James Inglish, of Hampstead, had received the Society's gold

also, some green dry Pease, highly esteemed here as the best for making pease soup; and also some Chinese Garavances, with Father Navaretta's account of the universal use of a cheese made of them, in China, which so excited my curiosity, that I caused inquiry to be made of Mr. Flint, who lived many years there, in what manner the cheese was made; and I send you his answer. I have since learnt, that some runnings of salt (I suppose runnet[2]) is put into water when the meal is in it, to turn it to curds.

I think we have Garavances with us; but I know not whether they are the same with these, which actually came from China, and are what the *Tau-fu* is made of.[3] They are said to be of great increase.

I shall inquire of Mr. Collinson for your Journal. I see that of East Florida is printed with Stork's Account.[4] My love to good Mrs. Bartram, and your children. With sincere esteem, I am ever, my dear friend, Yours affectionately,   B. FRANKLIN

To Joseph Galloway   ALS: Clements Library

Dear Sir,   London, Jan. 11. 1770
Since mine of the 9th. past, I have received your Favour of Nov. 8. with the Bill for £500. Wharton on Whitmore; for which I am greatly oblig'd to the Assembly; and to you for your kind Care in so speedily remitting it.

---

medal in 1769: Robert Dossie, *Memoirs of Agriculture, and Other Œconomical Arts* . . . (3 vols., London, 1768–82), II, 261–4; III, 448.

2. *I.e.*, rennet, used in the generic sense of a curdling agent.

3. BF's description of garavances and their use is, to put it mildly, misleading. He was not referring to cheese but to a vegetable paste; and the paste was not made of garavances, or chick-peas, but of beans. The account he mentioned was by Domingo Fernandez Navarrete (1618–86), a Jesuit missionary to China, who published his work in Spanish in 1676. It was translated into English by Awnsham and John Churchill, published in 1704, and subsequently republished; BF probably encountered it in the third edition: *A Collection of Voyages and Travels* . . . (6 vols., London, 1744–46), I, 1–311. Tau-fu or teu-fu was there described (p. 252) as a paste of kidney beans, as it was in the original Spanish; where BF got hold of garavances we have no idea.

4. For the unpublished journal of Bartram's trip through the south see above, XVI, 110. For the published journal see William Stork, *An Account of East-Florida with a Journal, Kept by John Bartram* . . . (London, [1766]).

I am perfectly of the same Sentiments with you, that the old Harmony will never be restor'd between the two Countries, till some Constitution is agreed upon and establish'd, ascertaining the relative Rights and Duties of each. And I am pleas'd to find that the same Opinion begins to prevail here. Several have mention'd it to me in Conversation, and last Week, a Member of Parliament in high Station and in great Esteem with the present Ministry, came to visit me, and intimated that such a Constitution was now thought of, and in his Opinion a Plan might be form'd agreable to both Sides, if three or four reasonable Men were to meet for that purpose, and discuss coolly the contended Points; which he wish'd me to think of, and hop'd I would not leave England till something of the kind was done.[5]

It has been understood for some time past, that the Duties on Glass, Paper and Colours, were to be repeal'd early this Session, agreable to the Promises in Lord Hillsborough's circular Letter; and the Duty on Tea in consequence of a Petition from the East India Company.[6] This, if accomplished, will open the Trade, I suppose, between Britain and our Province; But it will still remain shut with Boston, if the other Revenue Acts are not also repealed.[7] It is talk'd, however, that a severe Law will be pass'd with the Repeal,

5. This paragraph suggests that at least in some quarters fundamental constitutional revision was being seriously considered; but we have found no other evidence to support the suggestion. BF had long believed that a federal union, however desirable in theory, was unrealizable in practice (see, for instance, above, XIV, 65; XV, 239, 241). The memorandum for British politicians that he had written less than two months before (above, XVI, 243–9) contained no ideas about constitutional reform, but may have stimulated discussion out of which such ideas emerged. The identity of the M.P. who brought them to BF cannot be established without further evidence. One possibility is Lord Le Despencer, who six months later was interested in a plan for reconciliation with the colonies; see BF's letter to him below, July 26. Thomas Pownall is unlikely, despite his concern with constitutional issues (see above, XVI, 298–303), because he was neither in high station nor in the good graces of the ministry. Other and more exciting names might be suggested, but for one reason or another each seems wholly implausible.

6. For the circular letter, of May 13, 1769, see 1 *N.J. Arch.*, X, 109–10. The petition was presumably that submitted to Parliament in 1767, in which the East India Company proposed an alteration in the duties on tea: Gipson, *British Empire*, XI, 97–8.

7. For the content of the Boston nonimportation agreement see above, XVI, 272.

to make it highly penal to enter into such Agreements not to import Goods from hence, as have lately taken Place in America. A Paragraph you will observe in the King's Speech seems intended to introduce this new Law;[8] which if brought forward we shall use our Endeavours to obstruct: tho' I do not see how such a Law could be executed; and I rather think it would tend to make such Agreements more general, and more resolutely adher'd to. In the House of Peers on the first Day of the Session, Lords Chatham, Cambden, and Shelbourne, spoke strongly for the Rights of America, insisted that we had been unjustly treated by the late Laws, and that we had a Right to use the only peaceable Means in our Power, (those Agreements) for Self-Defence: They also, as I hear, gave their Opinion, that *all* the Revenue Laws for America ought to be repealed; commended our publick Virtue and the Spirit of Liberty that existed so universally among us; and said they gloried in being considered as the Friends of such a People. Col. Barré and others in the House of Commons spoke well to the same purpose.[9] The ministerial Strength, however, is so great, that nothing will be done against their Inclination; and it is to be hoped, that by degrees they may be brought to favour us; especially as domestic Faction seem to give them Trouble enough at present.

To forward the Repeal, I have represented, that if they intend it at all, it should be done immediately; otherwise the Spring Trade will be too late and lost. I have also been in the City among the Merchants, to get them to present to the Ministry or Parliament, an Account of the Amount of their *conditional* Orders; in order to obviate an Opinion industriously propagated here, that the Trade still goes on, tho' covertly. Whether they will do it or not, I cannot yet

8. The relevant part of the speech, delivered on Jan. 9, was not a paragraph but a clause, which assailed the unwarrantable measures taken by Americans to destroy their commerce with Britain; see Cobbett, *Parliamentary History*, XVI (1765–71), 643. The law that BF feared would implement this clause was never introduced, and he believed that he played some part in its abandonment. See his letter to Galloway below, June 11.

9. None of the speakers BF mentions, insofar as they were reported, took the position with which he credits them. Even Chatham admitted that the non-importation agreements were dangerous, and argued only that they were not illegal. See Cobbett, *Parliamentary History*, XVI, 649–50; "Correspondence between William Strahan and David Hall, 1763–1777," *PMHB*, XI (1887), 226–7.

say, many of them being so averse to the Ministry as to be unwilling to have anything to do with them. We may possibly know better in a few Days what is to be expected from Parliament; and I shall send you by the first Opportunity what occurs of Importance. The internal Divisions of this Kingdom, tho' bad in themselves, may perhaps produce some Advantage to us,[1] or at least lessen the Mischiefs some threaten us with; but it is rather to be wish'd Government would relieve and treat us fairly from Principles of Wisdom and Equity.

I observe from the Committee's Letter, that the Instructions relating to the Change of Government in our Province, and other Points, are continued.[2] We shall never lose Sight of them; but use our best Endeavours, and seize every Opportunity, of fulfilling the Desires of our Constituents; attending at the same time to the prudent Cautions given us with regard to some Matters of the greatest Importance.

Be pleased to communicate this Letter to the Committee, assuring them of my Respect and most faithful Services. With great and sincere Esteem I am, Dear Sir, Your most obedient humble Servant   B FRANKLIN

Joseph Galloway Esqr Speaker.

From Thomas Viny   ALS: American Philosophical Society

This is the first extant letter from a man with whom Franklin continued to correspond intermittently for years to come. Viny was a carriage-maker in Tenterden, Kent; he and his wife were friends of the Stevensons, and their acquaintance with Franklin went back at least to the autumn of 1768.[3] The subject of this letter, obscured by the fact that a crucial part of it is missing, can be reconstructed at least conjecturally from Franklin's reply.[4] Mr. and Mrs. Viny had discussed with him their intention to emigrate to America, and he had encouraged them. They had sold part of their estate, presumably to obtain the necessary capital, and only then had belatedly revealed their plan to Thomas's brother John, whose pas-

1. A reference to the agitation over Wilkes, which was still on the boil.
2. See above, XVI, 219–20.
3. See above, XV, 238.
4. Below, Feb. 16.

sionate opposition had led them to reconsider the whole idea. The up-
shot was that they remained in England.

Sir   Tenterden Jany the 13th 1770
    I can attribute the respect you have shewn towards me to no
other Cause but the Divine and manly Benevolence and Courtesy
thats Characteristick of Dr. Franklin; It was this Captivating Disposition that encouraged my Confident address, and its this that
stimulates my reverential Esteem. Should I give [in to?] the dictates of my mind, tho' never so natural, and justly founded, they
might Savour of Flattery and must offend so dellicate a Soul. I shall
wave this gratefull Contemplation by Informing you, that I have
Sold that part of my Estate I mention'd to you and at the same price;
as this was managed with the greatest reserve none but my Wife
being privy of my Relations, the execution was Conveyd by my
Attorney to them, bef[ore we had the opportunity?] of seeing them,
this [torn] former hints I had given [torn] This Sir Brought on a most
Tender Scene and I own has so sensibly affected me, that I begin to
be very diffident of myself, and dare not say that I have Philosophy
enough to encounter so passionate a farewell, even with the most
fair probabilitys. I am inclin'd to think hardly any thing short of
Stubborne persecution can steel my fortitude. However I have not
[had yet]? extorted from me a re[straining?] promise, I shall not
then relinquish Your assistance so long as you shall think me worthy
of it, and hope I shall at least have this [merit?] of retaining and
acknowledgeing my obligations with the most ingenuous Temper
this will always engage me to be Sir Your Unfained Humble Servant
                                                    T VINY

PS I have only Room to express in General Terms my most San-
guine [hopes for?] Success In Your Important Negotiations and
Compliments [to Mrs.] Stevenson and Family in which I Include
Master T[emple].

Addressed: To / Dr. Benjn. Franklin / Craven-Street / Strand
Endorsed: Mr Viny

The Colonist's Advocate: IV

Printed in *The Public Advertiser*, January 15, 1770

To assume the Title of the *Colonist's Advocate*, is to undertake the Defence of Three Millions of the most valuable Subjects of the British Empire, against Tyranny and Oppression, brought upon them by a wrong-headed Ministry. It is to call the Attention of Government to the Injuries of the brave and free Emigrants from these Realms, who first, without the least Charge to us, obtained, and have, for many Years, at the Expence of their Sweat and their Blood, secured for themselves, and the Mother Country, an unmeasurable Territory, from whence Riches, Power, and Honour have, for many Centuries, been flowing in upon us; and (had not the evil Genius of England whispered in the Ear of a certain Gentleman, "George! be a Financier"[5]) would, for Ages to come, have continued to flow in the same happy Channel. I beg Justice for those brave People, who, in Confidence of our Protection, left their native Country, pierced into Woods, where no humanized Foot had, from the Creation, trod; who rouzed the deadly Serpent in his Hole, the Savage Beast in his Den, and the brutal Indian in his Thicket, and who have made us the Envy and the Terror of Europe.[6] The Colonists have made our Merchants Princes, while themselves are, for the most Part, Farmers and Planters. They have employed our Hands, increased our People, consumed our Manufactures, improved our Navy, maintained our Poor, and doubled, or trebled our Riches. Our Exports to Pensylvania were,

	£	s.	d.
In 1723,	15,992	19	4
In 1742,	75,295	3	4
In 1749,	238,637	2	10
In 1744, to all the Northern Colonies,	640,114	12	4
In 1748,	830,243	16	9
In 1754,	1,246,615	1	11

5. George was of course George Grenville, but BF was parodying the famous adjuration imputed to Augusta, Princess of Wales: "George, be a king!"

6. This string of clichés is like those that Lord Chesterfield mocked, "'the virtuous Spartans,' 'the polite Athenians,' and 'the brave Romans.'" Burgh reproduced the passage almost unaltered in *Political Disquisitions . . .* (3 vols., London, 1774–75), II, 282; and we suspect that he wrote it in the first place.

In 1758,	1,832,948	13	10
In 1744, to the West-India Islands,	796,112	17	9
In 1758,	877,571	19	11

Is not this a stupendous Mart for British Manufactures? But if this was not getting [rich] fast enough by our Colonies, let us proceed a little farther.

By the Easiness of settling and maintaining a Family in America, it is found, that the People do, merely by natural Population, exclusive of Additions from Europe, from whence great Numbers are continually emigrating double their Numbers every twenty Years. If, therefore, in 1758, our Exports

To the American Continent,			
were	1,832,948	13	10
And to the Islands,	877,571	19	11
Together,	2,710,520	13	9

Supposing the Exports to the Islands not to increase, but to continue the same; by the mere Increase of the People on the Continent, our Exports to both Islands and Continent, might have been expected in 1778, only seven Years hence, to amount to £4,543,469 7s. 7d. But the above Figures shew, that our Exports do much more than double themselves every twenty Years, and that the Demands of the Colonists, for our Manufactures, have grown as the Wealth and Luxury of the Colonists has increased. It is certain, that, in a short Time, the Colonies would have wanted more of our Luxuries and Manufactures, than all the working Hands in the Mother-Country could have furnished. Instead of which, in an accursed Hour comes, to use my Lord Chatham's Expression, "A wretched Financier boasting, that he can bring into the Treasury a Pepper-Corn, at the Risque of Millions to the Nation."[7] Let the Day of his Birth be a Darkness! For, what, in the Name of all that is voracious and insatiable, what would the Taxers of our Colonies have? Does not all the Wealth of these industrious People already centre in Britain? Would our Financiers have more than their All? Supposing the Colonists ever so willing to submit to Taxation without Repre-

7. Pitt's scathing reference to Grenville, which BF slightly misquotes, was in the debate in January, 1766; see Cobbett, *Parliamentary History*, XVI, 106.

sentation, and that they could command a Sufficiency of Money for the Purpose, neither of which is their Case, what should we gain by having a Pittance from them in the Shape of Taxes? We should only have their All in two Ways, instead of one; a Part in the Commercial Way, and the Remainder in Payment of Taxes: But, if by wresting from them, unjustly, a pitiful Pittance in the Form of a Tax, while we may, with a Good-will, obtain Millions on Millions by fair Commerce; if, by such dirty Doings, we are to enrage them against us; if, by a few Cutters stationed to prevent their Trade on the Spanish Main, and, by making a few Places for our needy Court-Danglers, we are to force them into Resolutions against our Manufactures, and hasten them into working for themselves, hundreds of Years before the Time, how do we shew ourselves wiser than the Savages of Louisiana, who, to come at the Fruit, cut down the Tree?[8]

To Thomas Vernon[9]   ALS: Newport Historical Society

Dear Sir   London, Jan. 16. 1770
    The Bearer Mr. Bowman, intends for New York; and as he will be intirely a Stranger in Rhodeisland, I beg leave to recommend him to your Civilities as a young Gentleman of good Character, for whom I interest myself. Your Advice may be useful to him; and every Regard you shew him, will be acknowledg'd as an Obligation confer'd on, Dear Sir, Your most obedient humble Servant
                                                    B FRANKLIN
Thos Vernon Esqr

From John Whitehurst[1]   ALS: American Philosophical Society

Dear Sir   Derby 18 Jan, 1770
    The natural tendency of philosophical minds to promote useful knowledge, seems to render an apology to you quite needless for the favour I'm going to request.

8. For the genesis of this allusion see Crane, *Letters to the Press*, p. 179, n. 8.
9. The postmaster at Newport, R.I., 1754–75, for whom see above, v, 451 n.
1. For the Derby clock- and instrument-maker and F.R.S. see above, IX, 42 n; X, 70–1.

I'm inform'd Sir, that the truely eminent Artist Mr. West is one of that Class of men who cultivates the Science he professes for the Sake of the Art only.[2] A most laudable example indeed.

A Young artist, who I humbly conceive has some merit, has expressd a strong desire of being a Student under Mr. West, but is destitute of a friend to interceed for him. His Name is Powell, a Sober worthy Youth, and Extremely Assiduous to attain a degree of Emenence. If you could with propriety name Mr. Powells inclination, to Mr. West, I verily believe, it woud give that Worthy Gentleman pleasure to see the progress he has made. But previous to your taking that Step, I presume it would be agreeable to you to see a Specimen of Mr. Powells performance. Shoud this proposal meet your approbation, Mr. Powell will wait on you when ever you are pleased to Address a line to him at Mr. Hurlstones in Cary Street, whose Son has the Honour of being a Studient at this time, and Can speak to his moral Character.[3]

Mr. Tissington[4] tells me you propose leaving England in the Spring, which gives me some Concern as well as my worthy friend. We purpose doing our Selves the pleasure to take leave of you in London, and shoud hope to be favour'd with a line a few weeks before your departure.

I hope Mrs. Stevenson is well, to whom please to present my Complements And that I hope she will spend some weeks with me when she comes down into Derbyshire who am Sir Your Most Obedient Servant JOHN WHITEHURST

PS I hope you received a Hare by the derby Stage on Wednessday morning last. Pray Sir, what will be done about the duties imposed on the North Americans? I shoud Esteem it a Singular favour to know your Sentiments on that head.

Addressed: To / Benj. Franklin Esqr / Mrs. Stevensons Craven Street / the Strand / London

2. Benjamin West, the well-known American painter, and his wife were good friends of BF and have appeared frequently in preceding volumes.

3. The "sober worthy Youth" was John Powell, who was subsequently a pupil and assistant of Sir Joshua Reynolds. He was staying with the Hurlestons near Lincoln's Inn Fields; Richard Hurleston, the "Studient," later became a portrait-painter of some note. *DNB.*

4. Whitehurst's close friend and an intermittent correspondent of BF; see above, IX, 42 n, and later volumes.

31

To Mary Stevenson ALS: American Philosophical Society

Dear Polly, Craven street Jan 22. —70
I received your Favour of Saturday early this Morning, and am as usual much obliged by the kind Readiness with which you have done what I requested.

Your good Mother has complain'd more of her Head since you left us, than ever before. If she stoops or looks or bends her Neck downwards on any Occasion, it is with great Pain and Difficulty that she gets her Head up again. She has therefore borrowed a Breast and Neck Collar of Mrs. Wilkes,[5] such as Misses wear, and now uses it to keep her Head up. Mr. Strahan has invited us all to dine there tomorrow, but she has excused herself. Will you come and go with me? If you cannot well do that, you will at least be with us on Friday, to go to Lady Strachan's.

As to my own Head, which you so kindly enquire after, its Swimming has gradually wore off, and to day for the first Time I felt nothing of it on getting out of Bed. But as this speedy Recovery is, (as I am fully persuaded,) owing to the extream Abstemiousness I have observed for some Days past at home, I am not without Apprehensions, that being to dine abroad this Day, to morrow and next Day, I may inadvertently bring it on again, if I do not think of my little Monitor and guardian Angel, and make use of the proper and very pertinent Clause she proposes, in my Grace. Here comes a Morning Visitor. Adieu. My best Respects to Mrs. Tickel.[6] I am, my dear Friend, Yours affectionately B FRANKLIN

Endorsed: Jan 22 –70
27

5. Presumably the wife of Israel Wilkes, John's brother; see above, xv, 238 n.

6. Polly's aunt, with whom she lived.

The Colonist's Advocate: V

Printed in *The Public Advertiser*, January 25, 1770

In my last Paper I shewed, from authentic and known Estimates, that, had not the Course of our Trade with the Colonies been interrupted by the Inventions of the Grenvillians, we were in the Way to have carried it, in the Space of a few Years, to such a Length, that the Mother-Country would have gained by it annually the amazing Sum of Five Millions; and that their Wants must soon have employed more manufacturing Hands than all Britain contains. Yet these People, who are of such Consequence to us, we shew ourselves indifferent how we treat. We put the whole People of America to Expence and Trouble, merely to put a little Money into the Pockets of a few Portugal Merchants. The Colonists must not import directly Wine, Oil, or Fruit from Portugal, but must have them, loaded with the Expences of a Voyage 3000 Miles round, by Way of England, which enhances every Article 30 per Cent. in War Time, empoverishes the Colonies, disables them from paying their Debts, and makes them the worse Customers to ourselves.[7] We empty on them our Gaols, and fill their Country with our Rogues. Our restraining them from the Use of Slitting Mills, and Steel Furnaces, with the Design of preventing their manufacturing of Nails, Edge-Tools, &c. is copied from the tyrannical Politicks of the Philistines with the People of Israel.[8] The Act for prohibiting the cutting of white Pines, invented on Pretence of preserving them for the Use of the Navy, has proved the Destruction of many noble Trees fit for Masts.[9] For the Custom of the Log-men, when they go into the Woods to search for Trees for the Mills, is, to cut

7. BF is here paraphrasing and expanding a point he had made in the press two years before, for which see above, XV, 9–10, 107–10. Most of the grievances discussed in this essay appeared, in roughly similar language, in the Boston Declaration of 1772, for which see Samuel E. Morison, ed., *Sources and Documents Illustrating the American Revolution, 1764–1788* . . . (Oxford, 1923), pp. 91–6.

8. BF is again repeating points made in "Causes of American Discontents before 1768," for which see above, XV, 10–11 and ns. His Biblical reference confuses, we believe, the Philistines with the Egyptians, whose "tyrannical politics" are described in the early chapters of Exodus.

9. The Naval Stores Act of 1722 (8 Geo. I, c. 12) forbade the unlicensed cutting of white pines, except those growing within townships, in all colonies from New Jersey north.

33

down as many as they can, in order to secure their Property in them. This occasions their destroying many more than they really want; and their sawing into Boards many, which, but for the injudicious Prohibition, they would have disposed of for Masts; by which they would have got more, and we should likewise have saved the ready Money we now send to Norway for Masts. It is now too late to regulate this Article in New-England, but not in Canada.

Again, how rigorous are our Regulations, which oblige them to bring us all their Products at our own Price, though they might find better Markets Abroad? How severe to prohibit their manufacturing a Variety of necessary Articles, or their purchasing them of other Nations, only that they may be obliged to have them of us at an advanced Price; for we can afford nothing at a moderate Price, loaded as we are with the yearly Interest of 135 Millions of Debt, incurred chiefly by warring in Germany; which Interest is to be paid by the Consumers of our Manufactures. Thus we make the Colonists sell as cheap, and buy as dear as we please. The Carthagenians obliged the People of Sardinia (*Væ victis!*) to buy all their Corn of them, and at the Price they set upon it.[1] But we do not hear, that those tyrannical Conquerors forced the enslaved Sardinians to sell them all their Products at a Price of their own fixing. This Law we impose, not on a conquered People, but on our own Children,[2] who have always shewn themselves dutiful, and have never complained of these Regulations, 'till we began to lay direct Taxes on them; direct Taxes, I say, because these Regulations are indirect Taxes, and severe ones, too, as we would think them, if we found our Trade hampered by a People beyond the Ocean, in the Manner we restrain that of our Colonists; which is, in many Instances, rigorous, useless, and impolitick.

Whenever we find ourselves encumbered with a needy Court-Dangler, whom, on Account of Connections, we must not kick down Stairs, we kick him up into an American Government. Many of these have proved Men of arbitrary and rapacious Dispositions. They have not, as Kings, an Interest in the Countries they govern, on Account of Children who are to succeed them. They are generally Strangers. They come only to make Money as fast as they can. Their Situation enables them to be very vexatious and injurious.

1. See above, xv, 188 and n.
2. See above, xvi, 19.

(See the Complaints of the House of Representatives of Massachusett's Bay, in their Petition to the King against Sir F.B.— Providence Gazette, No. 296.)[3] Yet, we have endeavoured to make their Governors wholly independent on them, by obtaining for them a fixed Salary, extorted from the People, without Intervention of their Assemblies. An admirable Scheme for making their Assemblies useless, and for rendering the Governors indifferent about calling them, as having nothing to hope, and perhaps something to fear, from their meeting.

The Judges we give them, being appointed from hence, and holding their Commissions, not during good Behaviour, but during Pleasure, all the Weight is thrown into one of the Scales, if the Salaries are to be paid out of Duties raised upon the People, without their Approbation, or Disapprobation of the Behaviour of the Judges.[4]

The Admiralty-Courts, whereby we allow Cognizance to be taken of all Offences against our Revenue-Acts, which deprives the People of the inestimable Advantage of being tried by Juries, are a heavy Grievance.

In reckoning up the Hardships we lay on our Colonists, the Difficulty consists not in finding Matter, but in the great Abundance of Matter, to range and dispose it in such Manner as to give some Idea of it that may be tolerably distinct. In the above-quoted Gazette I find some of them stated as follows:[5]

"Raising a perpetual Revenue, without Consent of the People, or their Representatives, in violation of the sacred Rights of Representation.

"General Warrants, under which any Officer, or Servant, in the Customs, may break open a Man's House, Closet, Chest, &c. at his Pleasure.

"Establishing the arbitrary and oppressive Powers of Excise, by

3. Or, more conveniently, see the petition against Gov. Bernard in Harry A. Cushing, ed., *The Writings of Samuel Adams* (4 vols., New York, etc., 1904–08), I, 349–54.
4. For the genesis of this and the preceding paragraph see above, xv, 7–9.
5. This statement of grievances, in the form of an unsigned letter seemingly from London, appeared in the issue of the *Providence Gaz.* in which the Massachusetts petition was printed (Sept. 2–9, 1769) but had no other connection with it.

appointing Judges during Pleasure, to try all Revenue Causes without Jury.

"Compelling his Majesty's Subjects to Trial, in all Revenue Causes, out of their respective Colonies.

"A Secretary of State sending a Requisition to the Assembly at Boston, with Threats, tending to force their Determinations, which, by the Constitution, ought to be free.

"Threatening and punishing the American Assemblies for attempting to petition the King, though the Act of Settlement expressly secures this Right, unlimited to the Subject.

"Raising a Revenue by Prerogative [Articles ordered to be furnished the Troops][6] with arbitrary Impositions; another Violation of an express Article in the Act of Settlement.[7]

"Misapplication of the permanent Revenue granted by several Assemblies in America for the Support of Government, and of the Revenue granted by Act of Parliament.

"Empowering the Crown to seize, and send over to Britain, the American Subjects without any legal Indictment, or Bill found by a Jury.

"Suspending the Legislative Power of the Assembly of New York, so as to destroy that Freedom of Debate and Determination, which is the necessary, unalienable, and constitutional Right of such Assemblies.

"Quartering Soldiers by Violence in the Town of Boston, in Defiance of an Act of Parliament."

This is our Way of treating a People, who have been the Means of our gaining Millions.

6. The phrase in brackets did not appear in the *Providence Gaz.* and was presumably BF's insertion.

7. This and the preceding reference to the Act of Settlement of 1701 should have been to the fifth and fourth provisions, respectively, of the Bill of Rights of 1689.

Request for a Reprinting

Printed in *The London Chronicle*, January 25–27, 1770

[A request to the *Chronicle*, signed "A.B.," to republish the extract of a letter from London printed in the *Boston Evening Post* of Dec. 4, 1769. The letter was Franklin's to Folger above, XVI, 207–10, where the extract is indicated.]

A Conversation on Slavery[8]

Printed in *The Public Advertiser*, January 30, 1770

To the PRINTER of the PUBLIC ADVERTISER.

Sir,   Broad-Street Buildings, Jan. 26, 1770.

Many Reflections being of late thrown out against the Americans, and particularly against our worthy Lord-Mayor,[9] on Account of their keeping Slaves in their Country, I send you the following Conversation on that Subject, which, for Substance, and much of the Expression, is, I assure you, a *real one*; having myself been present when it passed. If you think it suitable for your Paper, you will, by publishing it, oblige Your Friend,   N. N.

A Conversation *between an* ENGLISHMAN, *a* SCOTCHMAN, *and an* AMERICAN, *on the Subject of* SLAVERY.

Englishman. You Americans make a great Clamour upon every little imaginary Infringement of what you take to be your Liberties; and yet there are no People upon Earth such Enemies to Liberty, such absolute Tyrants, where you have the Opportunity, as you yourselves are.

American. How does that appear?

8. First attributed to BF by Verner W. Crane, "Certain Writings by Benjamin Franklin on the British Empire and the American Colonies," Bibliographical Soc. of America *Papers*, XXVIII, pt. 1 (1934), 19. See also the same author's "Benjamin Franklin on Slavery and American Liberties," *PMHB*, LXII (1938), 1–11, and *Letters to the Press*, pp. 186–92. The textual evidence that Crane amasses is conclusive.

9. William Beckford (1709–70), a Jamaican by birth, was serving his second term; he died in office on June 21. *DNB*.

JANUARY 26, 1770

Eng. Read Granville Sharpe's Book upon Slavery: There it appears with a Witness.[1]

Amer. I have read it.

Eng. And pray what do you think of it?

Amer. To speak my Opinion candidly, I think it in the Main a good Book. I applaud the Author's Zeal for Liberty in general. I am pleased with his Humanity. But his *general Reflections* on *all Americans*, as having no real Regard for Liberty; as having so little Dislike of Despotism and Tyranny, that they do not scruple to exercise them with unbounded Rigour over their miserable Slaves, and the like, I cannot approve of; nor of the Conclusion he draws, that therefore our Claim to the Enjoyment of Liberty for ourselves, is unjust. I think, that in all this, he is too severe upon the Americans, and passes over with too partial an Eye the Faults of his own Country. This seems to me not quite fair: and it is particularly *injurious* to us at this Time, to endeavour to render us odious, and to encourage those who would oppress us, by representing us as unworthy of the Liberty we are now contending for.

Eng. What Share has that Author's Country (England I mean) in the Enormities he complains of? And why should not his Reflections on the Americans be general?

Amer. They ought not to be general, because the Foundation for them is not general. New England, the most populous of all the English Possessions in America, has very few Slaves; and those are chiefly in the capital Towns, not employed in the hardest Labour, but as Footmen or House-maids. The same may be said of the next populous Provinces, New-York, New Jersey, and Pensylvania. Even in Virginia, Maryland, and the Carolinas, where they are employed in Field-work, what Slaves there are belong chiefly to the old rich Inhabitants, near the navigable Waters, who are few compared with the numerous Families of Back-settlers, that have scarce any Slaves among them. In Truth, there is not, take North-America through, perhaps, one Family in a Hundred that has a Slave in

1. Granville Sharp, *A Representation of the Injustice and Dangerous Tendency of Tolerating Slavery*... (London, 1769). The author (1735–1813) became involved in the question in 1767, when a former protégé of his was thrown into jail as a runaway slave. Sharp procured his release, sued his master, and began the long litigation over the status of slavery that culminated in 1772 in the judicial decision that a slave who set foot on English soil became free. *DNB.*

38

it. Many Thousands there abhor the Slave Trade as much as Mr. Sharpe can do, conscientiously avoid being concerned with it, and do every Thing in their Power to abolish it. Supposing it then with that Gentleman, a Crime to keep a Slave, can it be right to stigmatize us all with that Crime? If one Man of a Hundred in England were dishonest, would it be right from thence to characterize the Nation, and say the English are Rogues and Thieves? But farther, of those who do keep Slaves, all are not Tyrants and Oppressors. Many treat their Slaves with great Humanity, and provide full as well for them in Sickness and in Health, as your poor labouring People in England are provided for. Your working Poor are not indeed absolutely Slaves; but there seems something a little like Slavery, where the Laws oblige them to work for their Masters so many Hours at such a Rate, and leave them no Liberty to demand or bargain for more, but imprison them in a Workhouse if they refuse to work on such Terms, and even imprison a humane Master if he thinks fit to pay them better; at the same Time confining the poor ingenious Artificer to this Island, and forbidding him to go abroad, though offered better Wages in foreign Countries.[2] As to the Share England has in these Enormities of America, remember, Sir, that she began the Slave Trade; that her Merchants of London, Bristol, Liverpool and Glasgow, send their Ships to Africa for the Purpose of purchasing Slaves. If any unjust Methods are used to procure them; if Wars are fomented to obtain Prisoners; if free People are enticed on board, and then confined and brought away; if petty Princes are bribed to sell their Subjects, who indeed are already a Kind of Slaves, is America to have all the Blame of this Wickedness? You bring the Slaves to us, and tempt us to purchase them. I do not justify our falling into the Temptation. To be sure, if you have stolen Men to sell to us, and we buy them, you may urge against us the old and true saying, that *the Receiver is as bad as the Thief.*[3] This Maxim was probably made for those who needed the Information, as being perhaps ignorant that *receiving* was in it's Nature as bad as *stealing*:

2. By 5 Eliz. I, c. 4, justices of the peace were authorized to fix laborers' wages in quarter sessions, and any one who offered to pay more was subject to fine and imprisonment. By 5 Geo. I, c. 27, and 23 Geo. II, c. 13, artificers in the woollen and other trades were forbidden to emigrate.

3. The proverb goes back to the early Greek period; the wording that BF uses may be found in John Ray, *A Compleat Collection of English Proverbs . . .* (3rd ed., London, 1742), p. 150.

But the Reverse of the Position was never thought necessary to be formed into a Maxim, nobody ever doubted that *the Thief is as bad as the Receiver*. This you have not only done and continue to do, but several Laws heretofore made in our Colonies, to discourage the Importation of Slaves, by laying a heavy Duty, payable by the Importer, have been disapproved and repealed by your Government here, as being prejudicial, forsooth, to the Interest of the African Company.[4]

Eng. I never heard before of any such Laws made in America. But the severe Laws you have made, on Pretence of their being necessary for the Government of your Slaves (and even of your white Servants) as they stand quoted by Mr. Sharpe, give us no good Opinion of your general Humanity, or of your Respect for Liberty. These are not the Acts of a few private Persons; they are made by your Representatives in your Assemblies, and are therefore the Act of the whole.

Amer. They are so; and possibly some of them made in Colonies where the Slaves greatly out-number the Whites, as in Barbadoes now, and in Virginia formerly, may be more severe than is necessary; being dictated perhaps by Fear and too strong an Opinion, that nothing but extream Severity could keep the Slaves in Obedience, and secure the Lives of their Masters. In other Colonies, where their Numbers are so small as to give no Apprehensions of that Kind, the Laws are milder, and the Slaves in every Respect, except in the Article of Liberty, are under the Protection of those Laws: A white Man is as liable to suffer Death for killing a Slave, though his own, as for any other Homicide.[5] But it should be con-

4. Such prohibitions on colonial legislation began in 1731, and the most recent example was the disallowance of a New Jersey act of 1763. Elizabeth Donnan, ed., *Documents Illustrative of the History of the Slave Trade to America* (4 vols., Washington, 1930–35), III, 38; Sydney G. Fisher, "The Twenty-Eight Charges against the King in the Declaration of Independence," *PMHB*, XXXI (1907), 264–5. The African Company, which traced its beginnings to 1660 and had been reorganized in 1750 as the Company of Merchants Trading into Africa, was the chief agency for collecting slaves there. See Kenneth G. Davies, *The Royal African Company* (London, [1957]).

5. The laws varied widely. BF's generalizations are essentially correct, except that severity in the southern colonies was much more widespread than he implies. In Maryland the courts determined whether the killing of a slave was justifiable. Jeffrey R. Brackett, *The Negro in Maryland* (Baltimore, 1899), p. 76. Virginia distinguished between accidental and willful killing; only the

sidered, with regard to these severe Laws, that in Proportion to the greater Ignorance or Wickedness of the People to be governed, Laws must be more severe: Experience every where teaches this. Perhaps you may imagine the Negroes to be a mild tempered, tractable Kind of People. Some of them indeed are so. But the Majority [are] of a plotting Disposition, dark, sullen, malicious, revengeful and cruel in the highest Degree. Your Merchants and Mariners, who bring them from Guinea, often find this to their Cost in the Insurrections of the Slaves on board the Ships upon the Coast, who kill all when they get the upper Hand. Those Insurrections are not suppressed or prevented but by what your People think a very necessary Severity, the shooting or hanging Numbers sometimes on the Voyage. Indeed many of them, being mischievous Villains in their own Country, are sold off by their Princes in the Way of Punishment by Exile and Slavery, as you here ship off your Convicts: And since your Government will not suffer a Colony by any Law of it's own to keep Slaves out of the Country, can you blame the making such Laws as are thought necessary to govern them while they are in it?

Eng. But your Laws for the Government of your white Servants are almost as severe as those for the Negroes.

Amer. In some Colonies they are so, those particularly to which

---

latter was actionable, but no punishment was stipulated. William W. Henning, ed., *The Statutes at Large, Being a Collection of All the Laws of Virginia* (13 vols., Richmond, N.Y., and Philadelphia, 1809–23), IV, 133. In North Carolina even willful killing was not punishable by death until 1774, and conviction for the same offense in South Carolina brought only a fine and loss of the right to hold office. John S. Bassett, *Slavery and Servitude in the Colony of North Carolina* (Baltimore, 1896), pp. 210–11; Thomas Cooper and David J. McCord, eds., *The Statutes at Large of South Carolina* (10 vols., Columbia, S.C., 1836–41), VII, 410–11. Georgia made the murder of a slave punishable by death only if it was (a) not the result of sudden passion or "undue correction" and (b) a second offense. Candler, ed., *Ga. Col. Recs.*, XVIII, 131–2. New England and Pennsylvania, in contrast, made no distinction between the murder of a slave and of a free man, and New York forbade the master's punishing his slave to the point of death or mutilation. Lorenzo J. Greene, *The Negro in Colonial New England, 1620–1776* (Port Washington, N.Y., 1966), p. 177; Edward R. Turner, *The Negro in Pennsylvania...1639–1861* (Washington, 1911), pp. 35–6; *The Colonial Laws of New York from the Year 1664 to the Revolution* (5 vols., Albany, 1894–96), II, 680. For these details we are deeply indebted to Professor Winthrop D. Jordan and his research assistant, Mrs. Deborah Wahl.

you send your Convicts. Honest hired Servants are treated as mildly in America every where as in England: But the Villains you transport and sell to us must be ruled with a Rod of Iron. We have made Laws in several Colonies to prevent their Importation: These have been immediately repealed here, as being contrary to an Act of Parliament.[6] We do not thank you for forcing them upon us. We look upon it as an unexampled Barbarity in your Government to empty your Gaols into our Settlements; and we resent it as the highest of Insults. If mild Laws could govern such People, why don't you keep and govern them by your own mild Laws at home? If you think we treat them with unreasonable Severity, why are you so cruel as to send them to us? And pray let it be remembered, that these very Laws, the cruel Spirit of which you Englishmen are now pleased so to censure, were, when made, sent over hither, and submitted, as all Colony Laws must be, to the King in Council for Approbation, which Approbation they received, I suppose upon thorough Consideration and sage Advice. If they are nevertheless to be blamed, be so just as to take a Share of the Blame to yourselves.

Scotchman. You should not say we force the Convicts upon you. You know you may, if you please, refuse to buy them. If you were not of a tyrannical Disposition; if you did not like to have some under you, on whom you might exercise and gratify that Disposition; if you had really a true Sense of Liberty, about which you make such a Pother, you would purchase neither Slaves nor Convict Servants, you would not endure such a Thing as Slavery among you.

Amer. It is true we may refuse to buy them, and prudent People do so. But there are still a Number of imprudent People, who are tempted by the Lowness of the Price, and the Length of the Time for which your Convicts are sold, to purchase them. We would prevent this Temptation. We would keep your British Man-Merchants, with their detestable Ware, from coming among us: But this you will not allow us to do. And therefore I say you force upon us the Convicts as well as the Slaves. But, Sir, as to your Observation, that if we had a real Love of Liberty, we should not suffer such a Thing as Slavery among us, I am a little surprised to hear this from you, a North Briton, in whose own Country, Scotland, Slavery still subsists, established by Law.

6. For the Parliamentary legislation to which BF is referring see above, XIII, 240–1.

Scotchman: I suppose you mean the heretable Jurisdictions.[7] There was not properly any Slavery in them: And, besides, they are now all taken away by Act of Parliament.

Amer. No, Sir, I mean the Slavery in your Mines. All the Wretches that dig Coal for you, in those dark Caverns under Ground, unblessed by Sunshine, are absolute Slaves by your Law, and their Children after them, from the Time they first carry a Basket to the End of their Days. They are bought and sold with the Colliery, and have no more Liberty to leave it than our Negroes have to leave their Master's Plantation.[8] If having black Faces, indeed, subjected Men to the Condition of Slavery, you might have some small Pretence for keeping the poor Colliers in that Condition: But remember, that under the Smut their Skin *is white*, that they are *honest good People*, and at the same Time are *your own Countrymen!*

Eng. I am glad you cannot reproach England with this; our Colliers are as free as any other Labourers.

Amer. And do you therefore pretend that you have no such Thing as Slavery in England?

Eng. No such Thing most certainly.

Amer. I fancy I could make it appear to you that you have, if we could first agree upon the Definition of a Slave. And if your Author's Position is true, that those who keep Slaves have therefore no Right to Liberty themselves you Englishmen will be found as destitute of such Rights as we Americans I imagine.

Eng. What is then your Definition of a Slave? Pray let us hear it, that we may see whether or no we can agree in it.

Amer. A Slave, according to my Notion, is a human Creature, stolen, taken by Force, or bought of another or of himself, with Money; and who being so taken or bought, is compelled to serve the Taker, or Purchaser, during Pleasure or during Life. He may be sold again, or let for Hire, by his Master to another, and is then obliged to serve that other; he is one who is bound to obey, not only the Commands of his Master, but also the Commands of the lowest Servant of that Master, when set over him; who must come when

7. The rights, abolished by act of Parliament in 1746, of owners of certain lands to hold local courts of justice.

8. For the seventeenth-century genesis of this peculiar form of slavery see John U. Nef, *The Rise of the British Coal Industry* (2 vols., London, 1932), II, 157–64 and the references there cited.

he is called, go when he is bid, and stay where he is ordered, though to the farthest Part of the World, and in the most unwholesome Climate; who must wear such Cloaths as his Master thinks fit to give him, and no other, though different from the common Fashion, and contrived to be a distinguishing Badge of Servitude; and must be content with such Food or Subsistence as his Master thinks fit to order for him, or with such small Allowance in Money as shall be given him in Lieu of Victuals or Cloathing; who must never absent himself from his Master's Service without Leave; who is subject to severe Punishments for small Offences, to enormous Whippings, and even Death, for absconding from his Service, or for Disobedience to Orders. I imagine such a Man is a Slave to all Intents and Purposes.

Eng. I agree to your Definition. But surely, surely, you will not say there are any such Slaves in England?

Amer. Yes, many Thousands, if an English Sailor or Soldier is well described in that Definition. The Sailor is often *forced* into Service, torn from all his natural Connections. The Soldier is generally bought in the first Place for a Guinea and a Crown at the Drum-Head: His Master may sell his Service, if he pleases, to any foreign Prince, or barter it for any Consideration by Treaty, and send him to shoot or be shot at in Germany or Portugal, in Guinea or the Indies. He is engaged for Life; and every other Circumstance of my Definition agrees with his Situation. In one Particular, indeed, English Slavery goes beyond that exercised in America.

Eng. What is that?

Amer. We cannot command a Slave of ours to do an immoral or a wicked Action. We cannot oblige him, for Instance, to commit MURDER! If we should order it, he may refuse, and our Laws would justify him. But Soldiers must, on Pain of Death, obey the Orders they receive; though, like Herod's Troops, they should be commanded to slay all your Children under two Years old, cut the Throats of your Children in the Colonies, or shoot your Women and Children in St. George's Fields.[9]

9. The "massacre" in 1768, when troops fired upon a Wilksite mob; see above, XV, 127–8.

44

The Colonist's Advocate: VI

Printed in *The Public Advertiser*, January 29, 1770

I have shewn, that our Gains by our Colonies have been immensely great [and], but for the Grenvillian Taxation Scheme, would have soon come to be equal alone to the Whole of our necessary annual Expences of Government in Times of Peace. If so, how absurd are the Cavils of some among us, who argue, That we have been at great Expences for the Advantage of our Colonists; and that, consequently, it is very ungrateful in them to refuse to contribute to the general Exigencies of the State. It is an Insult on common Sense to affect an Appearance of Generosity in a Matter of obvious Interest. Is it Generosity that Prompts the Rustick to feed his Cow, which yields him Milk? Could we have been enriched by our Colonies, if we had not defended them from the common Enemy? Did we not know, that if we had left them a Prey to France, the very Accession of such a Dominion, with the additional Naval Force necessarily consequent, must have over-turned the British Empire, and unbalanced Europe? How absurd is it, then, to make a Merit of fighting our own Battles, and driving the Enemy from our Doors! Was it not the obvious Interest of both Mother-Country and Colonies to oppose the Attacks of France against whatever part of the Empire they were directed? Suppose the Inhabitants of Middlesex, and of Surrey, to raise a certain Sum of Money, and a certain Contingent of Men, respectively on Occasion of an Apprehension of a flat-bottomed Invasion, would the Middlesex Men have a Claim to the Thanks of the Inhabitants of Surrey, or the People of Surrey to those of the Middlesex Men? The Cause being common, neither one nor the other could, with Propriety, be said to have either conferred or received an Obligation. The Case with the Mother-Country, and Colonies, with Respect to the common Enemy, is the same; but with this material Difference, to the Disadvantage of the former in the present Dispute, that while we pretend to be ruined by the Defence of our Colonies, it is notorious, that the enormous Load of Debt, which sinks us almost to Perdition, is brought upon us by our romantick European Continental Connections; and, that we pretend to have borne alone the Burthen and Heat of the Day, while the Colonies have sat still, and, as if they had known their Throats to be Steel-proof, left us to defend them; whereas, the Truth is that the Colonists have never been wanting to their own Defence. New-England alone maintained, in the late War, at an Average of one Year with another, 15,000 Men, and lost, in the Course of the War, no less than 30,000. The Town of Boston paid, for several Years, Twelve Shillings in the Pound. The whole Contribution raised by New-England alone, amounted to almost Half a Million Sterling. Our Government has been so sensible of the Generosity of the Colonists on such Occasions, as to make them Remittances for reimbursing them some Part of their excessive Expences; yet they continue, to this Day, loaded with Debt. And, in the foregoing War, the taking of Louisbourg by the New-England Forces, was the only Feat that was done against the Enemy. In which Action the brave Waldo, and others, laid out, for the Good of their Country, more than they could afford; and, instead of being rewarded with Places or Pensions, as we every Day see one execrable Court-Tool or other, for doing a worthless Minister's dirty Drudgery, after spending many Years, and large Sums of Money, in endeavouring to obtain Reimbursement, were obliged to return home, disappointed and disgusted.[1] This very Conquest, gained by New-England's Blood and Treasure, was all we had to offer the Enemy, in order to obtain a Peace on any Terms; so scandalously was that War conducted. And this Conquest was accordingly sacrificed to the Duke of Newcastle's blundering Management, who would probably have conducted the late War to the same disgraceful Issue, had not Mr. Pitt taken the Reins into his abler Hand. Let us not, then, for Shame's Sake, any longer pretend, that the Colonists have been sparing of their Men, or their Money, in the common Cause. Let us, on the contrary, ingenuously allow their Merit it's due Praise, and be modestly contented with their All in the Way of Commerce, without grasping at somewhat besides, in the Form of Taxes.[2]

Or, if it should still be said, "Our Colonies have cost us so dear in

1. Samuel Waldo (1695–1759), Boston merchant and politician, was second in command of the Massachusetts forces at the capture of Louisbourg. *DAB.* He and others were subsequently involved in a long battle in London with Gov. Shirley over the expenses of the expedition. See John A. Schutz, *William Shirley, King's Governor of Massachusetts* (Chapel Hill, [1961]), pp. 149–58.

2. For other versions of many of the points covered in this paragraph see above, XIII, 24, 75–6, 133–4; XV, 239–40; and below, pp. 325–8, 340, 342–3.

defending them, that we are justified in loading them with Taxes for our Indemnification," let us carry on this Reasoning. Let it be considered, what Taxes we ought to lay on Portugal, whose Defence against Spain has cost us a large Expence, and has never yielded us an Advantage to be compared with that we have long been gaining (and, if G.G. had never been born, might have gone on gaining, no one knows how long, or to what Degree) by our Colonies; and whose Commerce we never had in exclusive Monopoly, as we have had that of our Colonies. Let us, in short, go roundly to work: Let us tax all Europe, excepting France. For it is at our Expence of Men and Money chiefly, that the Balance of Europe has been kept even, and that France has not established her favourite Scheme of universal Tyranny.

Were there nothing to be said against a ministerial Scheme for taxing the unheard and unrepresented Colonies, besides the Disgrace which the Injustice of such a Proceeding would bring on the Government, and Nation, in the Sight of all Mankind, one would imagine the generous Heart of every true Englishman would revolt against the Proposal. But when it is remembered, that it is an old Artifice of the Enslavers of Kingdoms to begin with the more distant Parts, surely every free-born Subject on this Island ought to be alarmed at the late bold Attempt on the Liberties of our brave Fellow-Subjects in America, and to think, with Horror, of the bare Possibility of it's Success. For, should an encroaching Administration prevail in enslaving the Colonies, would they not thence be emboldened to subject the Mother-Country to their Iron Rod? To tax the Colonies, without giving them, in any Shape, the Power of assenting or dissenting in the Disposal of their own Property, is not using them better than it would be to tax the Mother-Country by Royal Edict, which is declared, I. William and Mary, to be the Subversion and Extirpation of the Laws and Liberties of this Kingdom, and is expressly provided against in the Bill of Rights, &c.

I will conclude this Paper with the Words of the great Sidney's Discourse on Government, "Asiatic Slaves usually pay such Tributes as are imposed on them. We own none but what we freely give, [none is] or can be imposed on us, unless by ourselves. We measure our Grants according to our Will, or the present Occasion, for our own Safety. The Happiness of those who enjoy the like Liberty, and the shameful Misery they lie under who have suf-

47

fered themselves to be forced, or cheated out of it, may persuade, and the Justice of the Cause encourage us to think nothing too dear to be hazarded in Defence of it."[3]

From William Robertson[4]   ALS[5]: Princeton University Library

Dear Sir   College of Edinburgh Janry 30th 1770

By some unlucky accident I could find no person to take the charge of Dr. Haven's Diploma.[6] I have therefore got my Brother to put it into a box which he was sending by the waggon to his correspondents Messrs. Poole & Buckenton Jewellers in Bartholemew Closs.[7] I suppose it will be in London by the time you receive this letter, and if you take the trouble of sending for it to those Gentlemen, they will deliver it to your servant. Do me the justice to believe that I am, at all times, very happy in obeying your commands, for I am with great sincerity and respect Dear Sir your affectionate and most humble Servant   WILLIAM ROBERTSON

3. Algernon Sidney, *Discourses Concerning Government...* (London, 1763), p. 288. The words in brackets are restored from the original text; BF's other departures from it are unimportant.

4. The famous historian and principal of Edinburgh, for whom see above, IX, 220 n.

5. The MS bears a later and revealing annotation: "Note to Dr. Franklin from Dr. Robertson the author of the History of America, and Charles 5, given me by Jared Sparks Esq. in 1837. R. Gilmor."

6. Samuel Haven (1727–1806), minister of the Second or South Congregational Church in Portsmouth, N.H., received his S.T.D. from Edinburgh on Dec. 24, 1769. *Catalogue of the Graduates...of the University of Edinburgh since Its Foundation* (Edinburgh, 1868), p. 244. BF was induced to obtain the degree for him, the story goes, by Col. Samuel Sherburne of Portsmouth, to repay Haven for preaching the funeral sermon of Sherburne's father. *Sibley's Harvard Graduates*, XII, 385.

7. The brother was Patrick Robertson, a prosperous Edinburgh jeweler, and his London correspondents were Poole & Bickerton. *DNB* under William Robertson; *Kent's Directory...* (London, 1770), p. 141.

From Isaac Winn[8]

ALS: the Royal Society

Sir   [Before February 1, 1770[1]]

Tis a common and I am afraid just complaint, that Seamen are exceedingly backward in availing themselves of the discoveries which Men of Science have made, and the directions which they have given for their benefit and safety. Notwithstanding the pains several eminent Philosophers have taken, to bring Conductors into general use, as well in Ships as houses, 'tis too true that very few Vessells are furnish'd with them, tho' scarce a year passes that does not afford us Instances, (some of them terrible ones) of Ships being struck by Lightning. For my part I am never without a Conductor in my Ship. I have had them of various constructions: that which I now use is a Chain of copper wire as described in the annex'd plate: that such a Chain, so disposed may conduct the lightning, and prevent a Stroke that might destroy a Ship, has often been demonstrated: but a circumstance that occurred in my last Voyage may perhaps have greater weight with some Seamen than all the reasoning of the Electricians: If it should be a means of perswading them to make use of Conductors my Intention will be answer'd. In April last, as we approached the Coast of America we met with strong Southwesterly Gales: they had continued several days, when exceeding dark heavy clouds arose in the opposite quarter, forced against the wind that blew with us till they had cover'd all the North Eastern half of the Hemisphere; the Struggle then be-

8. A merchant captain, master of the *Dutchess of Gordon*. See *N.-Y. Gaz.* (Gaine), May 8, 15, 29, 1769.
   1. The letter cannot be accurately dated. The voyage to which it refers began in the Downs on March 7 and ended at New York on April 24, 1769. *Ibid.*, May 1, 1769; *Pa. Gaz.*, May 18, 1769. Winn returned to England, and crossed again later in the year: he left for New York in the early autumn, arrived there in November, and cleared again for London before the month was out. *PMHB*, LX (1936), 472; *N.-Y. Gaz.* (Gaine), Nov. 20, 1769; *N.-Y. Jour.*, Nov. 30, 1769. He might have written the account at sea during this second voyage, from which he would have returned to England in ample time to deliver his letter to BF on Feb. 1, 1770, for transmission to the Royal Society. It was read there on March 29 and published (with Winn's initials incorrectly given as J. L.) in *Phil. Trans.*, LX (1770), 188–91; a few words lost in the MS have been silently restored from the printed text. BF's interest in apparently similar phenomena went back for twenty years. See above, III, 473; IV, 143.

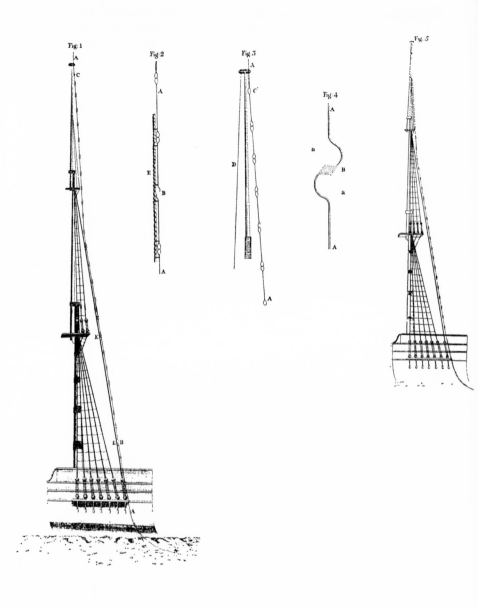

Fig. 1

Fig. 2

Fig. 3

Fig. 4

Fig. 5

50

tween the two winds was very extraordinary, sometimes one prevailing, sometimes the other. I was apprehensive we should have
much Lightning, and got my Conductor in order; when in hauling
up the Main Sail the sheet Block struck violently against the back
stays, to which the Chain was fasten'd (EE in fig: 1)[2] and, as I
found afterwards, broke the latter which occasion'd the Pheno-
menon I am going to describe. It was near midnight and very dark,
when I first observed a pale bluish light a few feet above the quarter rail; at first I thought it proceeded from the light in the Binnacle,
but finding that it frequently dissapear'd and return'd again precisely
in the same place, and that it sometimes emitted Sparks not unlike
those of a small Squib, I began to suspect that it proceeded from the
Conductor. To be certain, I order'd all the lights to be put out below,
and that no ray of Light might issue from the Binnacle I cover'd it
entirely with my Cloak. I was presently confirmed in my conjecture, that the light and Sparks which I had observed, proceeded
from the Chain; for, placing myself near it during the Space of two
hours and a half, I saw it, frequently emit continued Streams of
Rays or Sparks (See fig: 4) sometimes single drops as it were slowly
succeeding to each other, and sometimes only a pale feeble light.
On examining next morning I found the Chain broken at B, half the
eye of each Link being quite gone, and the points of the remaining
halves about three fourths of an Inch asunder: luckily the Chain was
fasten'd to a small rope (fig: 2) above and below the Eye of each
link which prevented that part of the Chain below B from falling
into the water, or of being separated from the part above B beyond
the striking or attracting distance. I am with the greatest respect
Sir Your Obliged Humble Servant   I. L. WINN

References to the Plate

AAA   The Conductor, a Chain of Copper Wire of the thickness
of the Barrel of a small quill, the uppermost and lowest
links of which terminate in fine points
B. Fig. 1. The broken Links, in passing between which the lightning became visible.

2. The drawing that accompanied the original has been lost, although
Winn's references to it at the end of the letter survived. Our illustration is
reproduced from a broadside in the Yale University Library and contains, it
will be noted, two lines of reference that Winn must have added later.

C   An Eye in the uppermost link, to which the pendant halliards are fastened.

D Fig. 3   The pendant halliards which pass over a sheave in the truck on the top gallant mast head, and are fastened to the eye at C, and hoists up the chain, till the point of the uppermost link is a foot or two above the truck

EE   The maintop mast backstay to which the chain is stopped to prevent its swinging about.

B. Fig. 4. Appearance of the lightning passing between the broken limbs.

Endorsed: Capt. Winn's Acct. of the Appearance of Lightning in his Conductor. Received Feb. 1, 1770. March 2 A Letter to Dr. Benjamin Franklin giving an account of the appearance of lightning on a conductor fixed from the summit of the mainmast of a ship Down to the water by Capn. I. L. Winn.

The Colonist's Advocate: VII

Printed in *The Public Advertiser*, February 1, 1770

Walpole, who declared in the House of Commons that he did not well understand foreign Affairs, who was as quick at smelling out where Money might be had as any Minister could well be imagined, and whose Difficulties in keeping his Place were such, that it was alledged he would have swept the Bottom of the Ocean for a Guinea, if he could: Even Walpole had Humanity enough to reject the Proposal often made to him by his hungry Hangers-on, of taxing the Colonies.[3] He had Sense enough, though far from possessing the Talents which form an able Statesman, to know that all the Colonists could raise centered in Britain, and that the Mother Country could but have their All, tho' G.G. seems to think they have two Alls.

The Manner of doing Things is of great Consequence in national Concerns. Had the good old Way of Requisition been tried, and found ineffectual, there might then have been some Pretence

3. See above, XV, 242.

52

for having Recourse to more rigorous Methods of Exaction. In better Times, and under wiser Administrations, the Colonists gave and granted, on Requisition, liberally, viz. in the Years 1756, 1757, 1758, 1759, 1760, 1761, 1762.

Government must depend for it's Efficiency either on Force or Opinion. We have been taught by our Forefathers to look upon the British Government as free. What our Sons may call it is not yet certain. Free Government depends on Opinion, not on the brutal Force of a Standing Army. What then are we to think of a British Statesman who could find in his Heart to run the desperate Hazard of shaking and overturning that on which Government depends, for the Sake of obtaining by authoritative, not to say arbitrary, Means, what might have been had more abundantly, with a good Grace, in the good old Way, and nothing moved out of it's Place.

In the Year 1710 the Colony of New York omitted levying certain Monies granted by their Assembly. The Governor, incommoded in his Proceedings in Consequence of this Deficiency, sent to the Ministry a Representation of this Affair. They threatened the Colony with a Bill for taxing them in Parliament. This put the New York People to their Trumps; and they immediately proceeded to effectual Measures for raising the Money. The Bill was dropped,[4] and the good old Way of Requisition resumed, which has been kept to ever since till the inauspicious Day that G. G. put forth his Decree, that "all the World should be stamped," not because the Colonists had refused to tax themselves, but because he would assert the ministerial Power of taxing them without their own Consent.

I have shewn in some of my former Papers, that our Laws for regulating our Colonies, and their Commerce, have not always been framed according to the purest Principles of Wisdom, Justice, and Humanity. These Errors ought to convince us, that our Parliaments (what are P——s but Assemblies of fallible Men?) are but incompetent Judges of the State and Abilities of our remote Fellow-

4. This is clearly the episode about which BF, when questioned on it before the House of Commons four years earlier, had expressed ignorance and incredulity. Above, XIII, 138–9; Crane, *Letters to the Press*, p. 193 n. 2. BF's version differs from that advanced by his questioner in 1766 and also from the actual circumstances, for which see Leonard W. Labaree, *Royal Government in America: a Study of the British Colonial System before 1783* (London and New Haven, 1930), p. 284.

Subjects, and should teach our Ministers Modesty in their Opinions concerning the Expediency of loading them with Taxes modelled in this Country. The Truth is, the Colonists are not at present in a Condition for bearing any Taxes worth the laying on; tho' their Inability is not the Principal Argument against our taxing them. At the Time when the famous Stamp Act, of blessed Memory! was invented, the Colonies were said to be indebted to Britain to the Amount of no less than Four Millions, occasioned merely by Want of Ability to make Remittances. The Colonists are almost all Farmers, depending on the Produce of their Lands, contented till lately, and happy, but in no Condition to pay us Taxes, otherwise than by their enabling us to pay our Taxes out of the great Advantage we gain by them, as I have shewn in my former Papers. How poor in Cash must those Countries be where the Sheriffs, in raising the annual Levies, are often obliged to make Returns into the Treasury of Goods taken in Execution for Want of Cash, which Goods cannot be turned into Cash for Want of monied Purchasers! where Men of the best Credit cannot raise Money to pay Debts, inconsiderable, when compared with their Estates! where Creditors, when they sue to Execution, obtain Orders for Sale of Lands and Goods, and though they offer those Lands and Goods for almost nothing, they are often nothing the nearer being reimbursed, because there are no monied Men to purchase after repeated Advertisements of the Sales; and when Sales can be made, the Debtor is stripped, and the Creditor not paid, and they break one-another all round. The more of this certainly the worse for us; and this Distress has been aggravated by those very Ministers whose Taxation Schemes particularly required all Measures to be used which were likely to promote a Circulation of Cash. Thus the Colonists, at their best, can hardly be said to be equal to the Taxes laid on by their own Assemblies; accordingly several of them are plunged into Debts, out of which they know not when they shall be able to extricate themselves. To help them the backward Way, "Come (the Grenvillians crying out) you shall pay us additional Taxes whether you can pay those laid on by your own Assemblies or not; and you shall give over your Trade to the Spanish Main. You shall make the full Tale of Bricks whether you can find Straw or Not."[5] This System

5. "There shall no straw be given you, yet shall ye deliver the tale of bricks." Ex. 5: 18.

of Politics puts me in mind of Milton's Description of Chaos, where every Thing is inconsistent with, and contrary to every Thing.[6]

From James Parker   ALS: American Philosophical Society

Honoured Sir   New-York, Feb 2. 1770

My last to you was from Woodbridge, where I have been printing the Laws of Jersey pass'd last Session, that was per Packet, with the Second of a Bill for £200 Sterling I had of Mr. Colden——the first of which I sent by a Ship bound for Bristol, along with which I sent you another Power, as should have sent by Capt. Davis, but he sail'd e're I was aware of it, as did also some other London Vessels. That Bill was drawn by Wats & McEvers on Harley & Drummond, dated Decemb. 21. 1769.[7] I now send you the First of a Bill I have received from Quebec Office, for £200 Sterling drawn by John Drummond, on Harley & Drummond also, dated 5th Decemb. 1769. I send also the First Bill of each Set of two Bills I have received from Mr. Vernon of Rho-Island, who says they are the best he can get. One of them is for £20 Sterling 60 Days sight, dated Jamaica 20 June 1769 drawn by Alexr. Findleter, on Wm. Cunningham, Esqe near Glascow. The other is for £52 Sterling 90 Days sight, dated Newport, Jan 9. 1770, drawn by Hays and Polock, on David Milligan, of London, all which I hope will come safe to your Hands, and be acceptable.[8]

According to your Permission have wrote to the Commissioners at Boston and resigned the Place in the Custom-House. My bad State of Health I had acquainted you with: I am still but poorly—— when I went to Woodbridge, I was so, and I thought myself a little restored by going; but I can't say it was a great deal; However I can walk a little. I was concerned at my Non-Ability to open and dispose of B. Mecom's Effects left in my Custody, but one Mr. Bell, who is an Auctioneer, and who had an Auction here some Time ago,

6. *Paradise Lost*, Bk. II, lines 890–906.
7. For this transaction see Parker to BF above, Jan. 4.
8. Findletter's draft was protested; see BF to Smith, Wright & Gray below, May 10. For William Cuninghame & Co., of Glasgow, a firm involved in the Virginia tobacco trade, see James H. Soltow, "Scottish Traders in Virginia, 1750–1775," 2 *Economic History Rev.*, XII (1959), 83–99. Many of the other firms and people mentioned are identified above, XVI, 130 n, 214–15 ns.

arriving here again with a Parcel of Books from Phila. and applying to me to print his Advertisement, I proposed his taking all those of B. Mecom's &c. He consented to try them at Auction, will get the best Price he can for them.[9] We accordingly open'd the Trunks, and he is now taking an Invoice of them, in order to their being printed and exposed to the Knowledge of Purchasers: He was accounted, and is a pretty good Hand, and will join them to his Sale. On Opening them, we found a pretty many of them hurt by Moths, &c. especially the lettering part, but they were other ways good clean and dry, and many of them quite good, but as Benny had had them some years, the most saleable it is thought were sold: I have not his Invoice, so I can't say. I imagine this to be the best I can do: tho' if I should thereby displease you and the others concerned, I should be very sorry. I will send you one of the Catalogues when printed, also an Account of Sales, &c——and if Exchange be not high, I will immediately purchase a Bill, and send it to you. I suppose I could make more Profit of them by retailing them in my Shop, but in the first Place, they are not now a good Assortment, and those damaged will get worse by laying, next, I imagine there will be large Assortments sent for by Noel, Rivington and Gaine, as soon as Importations are allowed: Indeed they have great Parcels here already stored, which they are not allowed to sell until the Importation takes Place; Tis said Rivington having married one of the Vanhorne's, is now in affluent Circumstances, and intends to shine away in the Book-Way; tho' such Tyrants hurt themselves and others too.[1] I told you two Scots Paper Spoilers had set up a News paper here called the New-York Chronicle——they puff'd and flourished away a While, but the Paper is now dropd.[2] They were ignorant Blockheads, but have Impudence enough. I hear they are now at work or going to work for Rivington——they must be more

9. The books came to Parker as a result of Mecom's bankruptcy; see above, XI, 240–1; XVI, 133–4. Robert Bell (c. 1732–84), a famous bookseller and auctioneer, advertised the forthcoming auction in Gaine's *N.-Y. Gaz.*, Feb. 5, 1770. For details of the auction itself see Parker to BF below, Feb. 20.

1. Garrat Noel, James Rivington, and Hugh Gaine were New York's leading stationers and booksellers; see above, XIII, 395. In March, 1769, Rivington had married Elizabeth Van Horne as his second wife. *DAB*.

2. For the journalistic debut of James and Alexander Robertson in New York see above, XV, 270 n. The brothers, like the more famous Rivington, became Loyalists during the Revolution.

skilful than I apprehend they are, or they won't hold that long. Indeed, they must be better Oeconomists than I: for tho' I drive on my Trade, as much as I can, it falls short of supporting itself——and the Moment I am turn'd out of the Post-Office, I must shut up here or leave the Country; but while I have that Office, I can make out pretty well, and hope by Degrees to work out of Debt; tho' I do not owe scarce any Thing now, but what is due to you. While it shall please God to give me Life, I will struggle hard, to do to all, as I would be done by. Holt and I nothing done yet.[3] I don't think he will hold it many years——for my own part, my Letter wears out, and I have no Appearance of being able to get new, so we shall wear out together. If his Majesty shall please to give his Assent to the Jersey Loan-Office Bills it is probable I shall have a good Job of doing the Money, if I live, but that is yet uncertain. I am satisfied you will not be wanting in your Assistance towards it.[4]

I have Nothing material to write of the Post-Office, every Thing going on generally as usual as far as I can just now tell. The Winter has been as fickle, as any I have known, extreme Cold at Times, and moderate at other Times. We all join in our respectful Complements to yourself and Mr. Foxcroft, whilst I am Your most obliged Servant JAMES PARKER.

Addressed: For / Dr. Benjamin Franklin / Craven-Street / London / per Capt Munds

Endorsed: Parker Feb. 2 ——70

From William Strahan ALS: American Philosophical Society

Dear Sir Sunday Even. 9 o'Clock [February 4, 1770?[5]]

I inclose this unfinished that I may have your Opinion whether it is, or is not, *the thing.* I can *add* or *alter* what you shall point out.

3. Parker's tangled business dealings with John Holt have appeared frequently in earlier volumes, notably XIV and XV.

4. New Jersey's currency acts of 1768 and 1769, despite BF's efforts, were disallowed. See above, XVI, 254 n; Gipson, *British Empire*, XI, 262 n.

5. The letter mentions four things: an essay, apparently by Strahan, that cannot be identified; a debate in Parliament; a contribution by BF to the *London Chron.*; a session of the House of Lords that Strahan attended. The last three, as noted below, would have been natural references in a letter written on the day we have assigned.

Please to let me have it early in the Morning. I will call in the Afternoon and bring it with me finished, with what I can recollect of Politics, and of that Days Debate.[6] Pray send also the other Paper for the Chronicle which we must have *very early*, or it will not be time enough.[7] I am sorry I missed you in the House of Lords.[8] I am Dear Sir Your most obedient Servant   W.S.

The Colonist's Advocate: VIII

Printed in The Public Advertiser, *February 5, 1770*

Lord Chatham, in his Speech on the Repeal of the Stamp-Act, said, That Debate was the most important that had come before the House since the Revolution. How differently that great Man, of whom, with all his Faults, we may well say, "We ne'er shall look upon his like again,"[9] thought of this Matter, from our Grenvillianised Ministers, it is curious to observe. Whether he or they have judged, in the soundest Manner, must be left to public Decision. Was our Ministry in Want of Money for the necessary Uses of Government (I will not say for gratifying a Set of Court-Harpies) how much better had it been to raise a few Thousands (it was but a few we expected to raise by taxing our Colonies) by taxing Luxury and Vice among ourselves, than to think of plundering our brave Colonists, the Discoverers and Settlers of a new World, from whence, as from an inexhaustible Source of Wealth and Plenty, the Means of Power, Greatness, and Glory, inconceiveable to our Ancestors, have been pouring into this Kingdom for Ages past. How much wiser to reduce exorbitant Salaries, abate, or abolish extravagant Perquisites, annihilate enormous Pensions, and useless Places, reform an odious and dangerous standing Army, lay Taxes, new, or

6. Perhaps the debate in the House of Commons, Feb. 5, on Wilkes's expulsion; see Cobbett, *Parliamentary History*, XVI, 830–1.

7. Perhaps BF's brief tribute to Pownall, printed on the first page of the *London Chron.*, Feb. 6–8; see below.

8. Perhaps the debate on the night of Feb. 2–3 on Wilkes's expulsion; see Cobbett, *op. cit.*, XVI, 814–30. Whether or not BF attended, Strahan did: "Correspondence between William Strahan and David Hall, 1763–1777," *PMHB*, XI (1887), 108–9.

9. A slight garbling of *Hamlet*, I. ii. 187.

additional, on Carriages, Dogs, Livery Servants, Cards, Assembly and Play-House Tickets? How much wiser for the Heads of the Nation to drink honest Port, instead of French Wine, to keep to their Wives, or at least to debauch at a moderate Expence, than to enrage Three Millions of People, drive the national Commerce out of it's Channel, and endanger public Credit. We have shewn our Colonists, that we think almost any Thing of more Consequence than their Friendship. We have treated them in such a contemptuous Manner, as we might reasonably suppose would irritate them to the utmost Pitch. And now we stand aghast at their shewing the Spirit of Men, of free-born British Subjects; the Spirit, which if they had not shewn, we might well have called them Bastards, not Sons. For, what their Disposition, with Respect to the Mother-Country, was, before the Year 1763, is well known to the Public, and justly described, in the following Words, by a Gentleman, who has done great Honour, and important Service to his Country by his manly Defence of her Liberties.

"The Disposition of the Americans was the best that could be. They submitted willingly to the Government of the Crown, and paid Obedience, in all their Courts, to Acts of Parliament. Numerous as the People are in the several old Provinces, they cost nothing in Forts, Garrisons, or Armies, to keep them in Subjection. They were governed by this Country at the Expence of a little Pen, Ink, and Paper. They were led by a Thread. They had not only a Respect, but an Affection, for Great Britain; for it's Laws, it's Customs, and Manners, and even a Fondness for it's Fashions, which very much increased the Trade with them. Natives of the Mother-Country were always treated with particular Regard. To be an Old-England-Man was of itself a Character of some Respect, and gave a Kind of Rank among them." [See Exam. of B. Franklin, Esq; before the House of Commons.][1]

Their sending constantly their Children home (for that was the affectionate Term they always used when speaking of England) for Education, was both a very convincing Proof of their Respect for the Principles and Manners of the Mother-Country, and was like-

1. Brackets are in the text. BF's words, like Shakespeare's, are slightly misquoted; see above, XIII, 135. Those who do not like to think that BF would have introduced himself so admiringly to his readers may conclude that the introduction was the work of his presumed collaborator, James Burgh.

wise a powerful Means of attaching them to us from Generation to Generation. For there is no stronger Attraction than to the Place where we pass our most innocent and happiest Days; nor are any Friendships stronger than those contracted at Places of Education. The Expence laid out among us by the Colonists on this Account, was likewise no inconsiderable Object. It is already lessened, and probably will be still farther reduced, and perhaps, together with our other Gains by them, may never more rise to their former Amount.

How malignant must, therefore, be the Spirit of those who labour to persuade us, that our Colonies have long been desirous of breaking off all Connection with us! Does any just Parent apprehend the Defection of his Child? A Philip, a Herod, a Solyman, may drive his Children to seek the Protection of Strangers: But it is not surely the natural Disposition of Englishmen to compel their remote Fellow-Subjects to wish themselves rather connected with other Nations, than with that Country, where their venerable Ancestors drew their first Breath. Wo to the fatal Machinations of those unnatural and churlish-hearted Men (unlike the noble Genius of this Land of Liberty) who, needlessly, wickedly and madly sowed the first Seeds of Discontent between Britain and her Colonies! But for them, Peace and Harmony would have reigned between the different Parts of this mighty Empire from Age to Age, to the unspeakable and inestimable Advantage of both. Those Men make a mighty Noise about the Importance of keeping up our Authority over the Colonies. They govern and regulate too much. Like some un-thinking Parents, who are every Moment exerting their Authority, in obliging their Children to make Bows, and interrupting the Course of their innocent Amusements, attending constantly to their own Prerogative, but forgetting the Tenderness due to their Off-spring. The true Art of governing the Colonies lies in a Nut-Shell. It is only letting them alone. So long as they find their Account in our Protection, they will desire, and deserve it. This our Experience confirms. So long as they find their Advantage, upon the Whole, in carrying on a Commerce with us, preferably to other Countries, they will continue it. Nay, unless we compel them to the contrary by our unnatural Treatment of them, they will shew a Prejudice in our Favour. Whenever they find Circumstances changed to the contrary, taxing and dragooning will only widen the Breach, and frustrate what ought to be the Intention of both Countries, viz. mutual Strength, and mutual Advantage.

On Governor Pownall's Departure from Massachusetts

Printed in *The London Chronicle*, February 6–8, 1770

To the PRINTER *of the* LONDON CHRONICLE.

SIR,

The people of the Massachusetts Bay in America, are represented here, by their enemies, as factious, quarrelsome, averse to government, &c. As a proof of the contrary, and to shew, that when they have a Governor who does not seek to raise his own character at the expence of theirs; who does not in his official letters forever *lessen* their loyalty to *magnify* his own, and describe them as *ungovernable* to excuse his own inability or mismanagement;[2] when they have a Governor who knows how to unite the service of the Crown with a just regard to the privileges and interests of the People; then they can live in harmony with him while he stays among them, treat him with respect and affection, and lament his leaving them as a public misfortune. I say, to demonstrate this, I send you the following last parting Addresses of the Council and General Assembly *of the same Province* to Sir Francis Bernard's immediate Predecessor, with his Answers, which I wish you to republish in your Chronicle.[3] The world may thence judge, whether it is likely that so great a change could so suddenly happen in the temper and disposition of the inhabitants of *a whole country*; or whether when we see the departure of one Governor attended with *benedictions*, and that of another pursued with *execrations*, the difference is not more probably in the *man* than in the *people*.

N. N.

2. The references are of course to Governor Bernard.

3. The *Chron.* did so, but under the dateline March 31, 1769, an error for 1760. In his answer to the Assembly Pownall said that he could never forget the affection and kind regard of the people of Massachusetts, to which the *Chron.* appended the following note by BF: "He has verified this declaration, being now one of their warmest friends in Parliament." The address and Pownall's reply may be found in Malcolm Freiberg, ed., *Journals of the House of Representatives of Massachusetts, 1759–1760* ([Boston], 1964), pp. 277–8.

From Joseph Smith[4]

ALS: American Philosophical Society

Respected Friend   Burlington Febry 6. 1770

I inclose thee printed Copies of the Acts pass'd last Session of Assembly[5] among which is the Act for striking £100,000 in Bills of Credit. I wish the Kings Assent may be obtaind to it before the breaking up of Parliament. I suppose a Copy of this Bill has long since been sent to the Board of Trade by our Governor.[6] This is sent for thy own information.

The Committee of Correspondence woud be glad to hear from thee in answer to their Letter. I am very Respectfully Thy Friend

Jos Smith

Doctr. Franklin

Endorsed: Mr Smith Burlington Feb 6. 1770

On Partial Repeal

Printed in *The Gazetteer and New Daily Advertiser*, February 7, 1770

For the Gazetteer.

Permit me to make a few short remarks on what is said in your paper of Feb. 5, by one who signs himself *A Merchant*. He begins by observing, "It is very *extraordinary* to hear people crying out, 'we are all ruined for want of a trade to America; and if the late acts respecting it are not totally repealed, we must all starve or leave the country.'" Thus he acknowledges this general cry to be an existing present fact; and if it be nevertheless true, that "The trade of this country was never in a more flourishing state," as he roundly asserts, I must agree with him, that there being such a cry is, indeed, "very extraordinary."

If the working hands in the manufactories have been, as he says,

4. A Quaker member of the New Jersey Assembly Committee of Correspondence, who was acting as its secretary. See above, XVI, 256 n, 264.

5. *Anno regni, Georgii III, . . . decimo. At a session of General Assembly, begun at Burlington, October 10, 1769, and continued till the 6th of December following . . .* (Woodbridge, N.J., 1769).

6. wf sent a copy to Hillsborough six days later, and defended the act. 1 *N.J. Arch.*, X, 150–2. The Board of Trade subsequently recommended that it be disallowed. See above, XVI, 254 n.

62

for some time fully employed, let me ask him, may not that be partly owing to the public declarations of the Ministry, immediately after the late sessions of parliament, that early in the ensuing sessions the anti-commercial duties should be repealed?[7] Has not this encouraged the employers to keep their hands at work, that they might have a stock of goods beforehand, to pour into America as soon as the trade should be opened? If they gave credit to those declarations, is it right not to disappoint them, by a total non-compliance, or an inefficient compliance by halves? Will such a conduct prevent a very grievous loss to all such deluded employers? Will it restore the lost business and affluent commissions of the merchants of London trading to that country? Is it certain, that the West Indian islands (at present a great market for our manufactures) will not another year accede to the North American agreements, either voluntarily with a view of recovering their rights, or of necessity, from the North Americans refusing otherwise to trade with and supply them.

Having informed us that the journeymen of all trades are now in full employ, he founds upon it this important advice: "Let not this great kingdom give up *that prerogative*, which the most *solemn determinations* have *confirmed* its right to assert." Does not this writer know, that repealing a particular tax, is by no means giving up a right to tax where we have such a right? Does he not know, that the declaration of the Ministry was, that they would propose the repeal of the duties, as being *anti-commercial*, not as being contrary to the rights of America, nor in favour of the people there, or in compliance with any demand or request of their's? Is it then to be wondered at, if they should not be quite satisfied with an incompleat repeal, which was never intended to satisfy them? But what does he mean by *solemn determinations confirming our rights?*[8] One would imagine the point had been litigated before some indifferent

7. Hillsborough's circular letter to the colonial governors of May 13, 1769. It has often been cited in previous notes, but the precise wording bears on BF's subsequent discussion. The administration did not intend to recommend further measures for raising revenue in America; "it is at present their Intention," Hillsborough continued, "to propose in the next Session of Parliament to take off the Duties upon Glass, Paper and Colours, upon consideration of such Duties having been laid Contrary to the true principles of Commerce." I *N.J. Arch.*, X, 110.

8. He meant the Declaratory Act.

impartial Tribunal, which, after due hearing of the parties, had decided against America in favour of Britain. If one of the parties, without overhearing the other, has determined for itself that it is in the right, can it be supposed that the other will ever conceive itself bound by such determination? But he apprehends "the Americans will rise in their demands, in proportion as they find our government disposed to attend to their complaints, and that nothing less than giving up all right to tax the colonies, will ultimately satisfy them." And suppose we should give them this satisfaction, together with a clear, intelligible constitution,[9] that we and they may know what we are henceforth to do and expect for and from each other; if thereby a good understanding is established between the two countries; if mutual commerce is restored; if by this commerce, and by their voluntary grants, we gain infinitely more from them with their good will, than we could have levied by force; and if the general strength of the nation is at the same time increased by our union, to the terror of our enemies; where will be the great damage of our relinquishing a right we can never exercise to advantage; and by which, in only attempting to exercise it, we have already lost more in one year, than we are likely to gain in fifty?

The Grenvillenians, who have done all this mischief, would terrify us (in case of a repeal) with the apprehensions of imaginary future demands from the Americans.[1] If I am well informed, as I think I am, they desire no more than to be put into the situation they were in before these new-fangled projects took place; I mean with regard to the exercise of their rights. I do not believe they will insist, as some suppose, on our *refunding* the money we have *extorted* from them (as they call it) *under colour of law*; they know it is all consumed in the new officers salaries, and that there is no ripping of guts; and they may well fear it would put us into too great a passion. A collector on the King's highway, who had rifled the passengers in a stage coach, desirous to shew his great civility, returned to one a family seal, to another a dear friend's mourning ring, which encouraged a third to ask a watch that had been his grandmother's? "Zounds, says he, have you no conscience? presently you will all

---

9. See the second paragraph of BF to Galloway above, Jan. 11.

1. Here, as often throughout the essay, BF is repeating points that he made elsewhere; the reader who wishes to trace these ideas should consult Crane's painstaking annotation of the text in *Letters to the Press*, pp. 197–200.

expect your money again! a pack of unreasonable dogs and b——s; I have a great mind to blow your brains out."

ANOTHER MERCHANT

To Jacques Barbeu-Dubourg

Extract: translated and printed in Jacques Barbeu-Dubourg, ed., *Œuvres de M. Franklin*... (Paris, 1773), II, 314.

Londres, 7 Février 1770.

Il est bien vrai, comme on vous l'a mandé d'Amérique, que les Trembleurs y ont donné la liberté à tous leurs esclaves, mais il est à remarquer qu'ils n'en avoient pas beaucoup. Cependant si l'effort en est moins surprenant de leur part, l'action n'en est pas moins belle en elle-même.

To Michael Collinson[2]   Copy: American Philosophical Society

Dear Sir   [February 8, 1770[3]]

Understanding that it is intended to give the Publick, some Account of our dear departed Friend Mr. Peter Collinson, I cannot omit expressing my Approbation of the Design, as the Characters of good Men are exemplary, and often stimulate the well-disposed to an Imitation beneficial to Mankind, and honourable to themselves. And as you may be unacquainted with the following Instances of his Zeal and Usefulness in promoting Knowledge, which fell within my Observation, I take the Liberty of informing you, That in the year 1730, a subscription Library being set on foot in Philadelphia, he encouraged the same, by making several very valuable Presents to it, and procuring others from his Friends; And as the Library Company had a considerable Sum arising annualy to be laid out in Books, and needed a judicious Friend in London to

2. Peter Collinson's only son.
3. So dated in the first printing of the letter in an anonymous pamphlet, *Some Account of the Late Peter Collinson*... (London, 1770), pp. 6–7, from which an error in the copy has been silently corrected. For the genesis of this pamphlet see John Elliott, ed., *A Complete Collection of the Medical and Philosophical Works of John Fothergill*... (London, 1781), p. [607].

transact the Business for them, he voluntarily and chearfully undertook that Service, and executed it for more than 30 years successively, assisting in the Choice of the Books, and taking the whole Care of Collecting and Shipping them, without ever charging or accepting any Consideration for his Trouble.[4] The Success of this Library (greatly owing to his kind Countenance and good Advice) encouraged the erecting others in different Places, on the same Plan; and it is supposed there are now upwards of 30 subsisting in the several Colonies, which have contributed greatly to the Spreding of useful Knowledge in that part of the World, the Books he recommended being all of that kind, and the Catalogue of this first Library being much respected and followed by those Libraries that succeeded. During the same time he transmitted to the Directors the earliest Accounts of every new European Improvement in Agriculture and the Arts, and every philosophical Discovery: Among which, in 1745, he sent over an Account of the new German Experiments in Electricity, together with a Glass Tube, and some Directions for using it, so as to repeat those Experiments. This was the first Notice I had of this curious Subject, which I afterwards prosecuted with some Diligence, being encouraged by the friendly Reception he gave to the Letters I wrote to him upon it.[5]

Please to accept this small Testimony of mine to his Memory for which I shall ever have the utmost Respect, and believe me, with sincere Esteem, &c Dear Sir Your most obedient humble Servant

B FRANKLIN

Endorsed: To Michael Collinson Esqr

The Colonist's Advocate: IX

Printed in *The Public Advertiser*, February 12, 1770

The Grenvillians labour to persuade us, that there is an Inconsistency in the Colonists refusing to submit to British Taxation, at the same Time that they acknowledge themselves obliged to obey the

4. For his assistance to the Library see above, I, 248–9 and subsequent volumes.

5. Collinson undoubtedly sent "An Historical Account of the Wonderful Discoveries Made in Germany &c. Concerning Electricity," *Gent. Mag.*, XV (1745), 193–7. For the effect of the glass tube that he also sent in first arousing BF's interest in electricity see above, II, 451 n; III, 118–19.

Laws of the Mother-Country. The Enemies of the Colonists must be very shallow Politicians, if they be really and sincerely at a Loss to understand, that, in a free Country, paying Taxes is, and always must be, *giving* a Part of their Property. But how can the Colonists be said to *give* what is taken from them by Force, and against their own Consent? In former Times, the Commons of England had no Legislative Power. The Kings called them together only that they might settle among themselves what they could afford to contribute for the Expences of Government. And when this was settled, they were dismissed. But does any Body, on that Account, doubt whether the People, in those Times, thought themselves obliged to obey the Laws? Our Fathers, therefore, saw a clear Difference between Legislation and Taxation, though our Grenvillians cannot, or rather will not. So lately as Queen Elizabeth's Time, that sagacious Princess used to boast, that she had seldom called Parliaments; which was saying, in other Words, that she had seldom called on her Subjects for Money. It was, in former Times, often mentioned in the Preambles of the Writs for calling of Parliaments, that it was proper that they, who were to raise the Money, should meet, and settle how much they could raise. Even in our Times, the King directs that Part of his Speech which relates to the raising of the Supplies, to the Gentlemen of the House of Commons; because the House of Commons are representatively the Persons who are to contribute the Money. A Money Bill must not originate in the House of Lords. It must not be amended, or undergo the least Alteration in the Upper House. The Lords can only pass, or reject it. And why all this Delicacy about Money-Bills, but because Property, in a free Country, is a very delicate Affair? The Peers, with all their High Honours and Privileges, and the Power of deciding all Suits about Property, finally, and without Appeal,[6] are not permitted, by the Constitution, to intermeddle in Grants of Money, because it is supposed, that the Proportion of the Taxes, contributed by them, is inconsiderable, and because giving them Power in disposing of what is not, in any considerable Proportion, their

---

6. The phrasing echoes a passage in William Blackstone: "They are . . . the last resort, from whose judgment no farther appeal is permitted; . . . upon their decision all property must finally depend." *Commentaries on the Laws of England* (4 vols., London, 1809), III, 157. BF, as far as we know, was unfamiliar with Blackstone; if so this passage was doubtless by another hand.

Property, was, by the Wisdom of our Forefathers, thought unjust and unsafe.

Thus the Grenvillian Notion of a necessary Connexion between Subjection and Taxation, appears to strike at the very Root of that important Part of our Constitution, which secures to us the Possession of our Property; and is therefore to be abhorred and opposed by every free-born Englishman, who ought to be ready to die in Defence of Lord Chatham's truly constitutional Doctrine, That Taxation, without Representation, is Slavery.[7]

If the Lords are not allowed to originate a Money-Bill, because they are to pay but a small Part of the Tax, on what Principle of Liberty or Property, do the Grenvillians argue, that the House of Commons of England may originate an American Money-Bill, of which they are to pay no Part, nay, which will serve to lessen the Burthen upon themselves? If the Lords may put a Negative upon a Money-Bill, merely because otherwise, they might alledge, they are taxed against their Will, ought not, by Parity of Reason, Three Millions of People (by whom we have been such Gainers, as I have shewn in former Papers) to have the Power of rejecting a Bill for taxing them, because otherwise they too may alledge, they are taxed against their Will?

Our Kings, in their Speeches, at the Conclusions of Sessions, are wont to thank the Commons for raising Supplies. Why? Because the Supplies granted are out of their own, and their Constituents Property. When the Commons lay a Tax on America, whom is the King to thank, the House for giving what is neither their own Property, nor that of their Constituents? Or the Americans, for being deprived of their Property, without and against their Consent? Would not either of these be a Mockery unworthy of the King, or of the House?

With what View were the Colony-Assemblies originally instituted? What has been all along the Business of those Assemblies? Why are they called Assemblies of Representatives? Why have the People all along submitted to be taxed by them? Are they to meet hereafter only to settle the Assize of Bread, and the Rates of Labour by the Day? The Grenvillians say, We are but ill-represented in

7. The actual phrase, to the best of our knowledge, was one that Pitt never used; but he had clearly set forth the doctrine in his speech of Jan. 14, 1766, for which see above, XIII, 39–44.

Parliament, where we are taxed. Is that a Reason why the Colonists must be taxed where they are not represented at all? The Colonists have all along laboured under the same Hardship as we in England. They are not represented in an adequate Manner in the Provincial Assemblies, in which they have always been taxed. Is this Grievance to be redressed by taking from them their inadequate Representation, and giving them, instead of it, no Representation?

Forty Shillings Freehold a Year in England, gives Representation in the Assembly which has the Power of Taxation. On Grenvillian Principles, Forty Thousand a Year give no Right to an American. His All may be voted away without his Knowledge. Yet the Grenvillians will tell him, he is a free British Subject, and enjoys every Privilege enjoyed by the Inhabitants of the Mother-Country. Whether this is not an Insult on Common-Sense, is submitted to the Judgment of the Reader.

To Nevil Maskelyne

ALS: the Royal Society

Dear Sir,   Craven street Feb. 12. 1770

I have just received a Letter from Mr. Winthrop, dated Dec. 7. containing the following Account, viz.

"On Thursday the 9th of November, I had an Opportunity of observing a Transit of Mercury. I had carefully adjusted my Clock, to the apparent Time, by correspondent Altitudes of the Sun, taken with the Quadrant for several Days before; and with the same Reflecting Telescope as I used for the Transit of Venus, I first perceived the little Planet making an Impression on the Sun's Limb at 2h.52′.41″; and he appeared wholly within at 53′.58″. Ap.T. The Sun set before the Planet reached the Middle of his Course; and for a considerable Time before Sunset, it was so cloudy, that the Planet could not be discerned. So that I made no Observations of consequence except that of the Beginning, at which time the Sun was perfectly clear. This Transit compleats three Periods of 46 Years, since the first Observation of Gassendi[8] at Paris in 1631." With great Esteem, I am, Sir, Your most obedient Servant

B FRANKLIN

8. Pierre Gassendi or Gassend (1592–1655) was famous in his day as an opponent of Descartes and one of the most versatile scholars of Europe—

Addressed: To / The Revd Mr Maskelyne / Astronomer Royal / at the Observatory / Greenwich

Endorsed: Winthrop's on Comet Jan. 10.[9]
　　　　Pryer

To William Mickle

ALS: Yale University Library

William Mickle, the Scottish poet (1735–88), had abandoned his Edinburgh brewery in 1763 and moved to London to be a man of letters. In 1765 he took a position with the Clarendon Press in Oxford;[1] while there he clearly met and became friendly with Ephraim Brown, the adopted son of Benjamin Franklin's brother Peter and the subject of this letter. Brown seems to have been constitutionally unable to save money, like several others of Franklin's young relatives; when he died after a long illness in the autumn of 1769, he left considerable debts.[2] Mickle's attempt to get Franklin to help discharge them elicited the courteous refusal that follows.

Sir,　　　　　　　　　　　　　　London, Feb. 15. 1770

I received yours of the 5th Instant, and in answer would acquaint you, that I have not, nor ever had, any Effects of Mr. Brown's in my Hands, out of which to pay any Debts that may be due from him.[3] Nor have I ever been in any kind of Connection with him that should make it in the least incumbent on me to discharge any such Debts. During his long Illness he from time to time acquainted me with his Distresses and Wants, which I relieved by permitting him to draw on me, to the Amount of 26½ Guineas in the whole, believing that if he recovered, he would in time repay me, as I esteemed him an honest well-disposed Man. But now that he is dead, I have not the least Expectation of ever receiving Sixpence of it,

---

linguist, theologian, philosopher, physician, astronomer. His work on Mercury was published as *Mercurius, in Sole Visus et Venus Invisa* (Paris, 1631).

9. The date in 1771 when the extract was read to the Royal Society; it was subsequently printed in *Phil. Trans.*, LXI (1771), 51–2.

1. *DNB.*

2. See above, XVI, 203–4 n.

3. Brown had left a trunk behind him in Philadelphia, which DF had eventually forwarded to him in England. But the only item in it of even potential worth seems to have been a lottery ticket, which disappeared. See above, XII, 340; XIV, 209, 282; XV, 136.

his Mother, the only Relation he has left, that I know of, being a very poor Woman.[4] As to the particular Debt you mention, that to the Apothecary, I cannot think that you will be under any Necessity of paying it. No one would recommend an Apothecary to a Patient, if by so doing he became responsible for the Bills. Mr. Stevens can hardly be so unreasonable as to think of punishing you for your Friendship to him; and as he has receiv'd a Guinea out of his Bill of £1 15s. 0d., I suppose the first Cost of his Medicines must be nearly paid, and that his Humanity will receive full Satisfaction for the rest, in the Reflection that by his kind Care and Attention, he made more comfortable some of the last Hours of a poor sick Stranger. I am, Sir, Your most obedient humble Servant

B FRANKLIN

Mr. Mickle

To Thomas Viny

Reprinted from Albert H. Smyth, ed., *The Writings of Benjamin Franklin*... (New York, 1905–07), V, 248–50.

Dear Sir.   London, Feb. 16. 1770

I received your Favour of the 13th past,[5] which I ought to have acknowledg'd sooner, but much Business and some Indisposition have occasion'd the Delay. I can easily conceive the Difficulty a Man in your Situation, with such Connections, and so well esteem'd and belov'd among them, must have in resolving to leave them with an Intention of Settling in a distant Country. And I do not wonder that your Regard for them should determine you to remain where you are. I was indeed of Opinion, from my Knowledge of that Country and of you, that if you should remove thither with your Family and Substance you would not only do extreamly well yourself, but have better Opportunities of establishing your Children in the World. Therefore I did not dissuade you when you appear'd to have such an Inclination. But at the same time, tho' I own I should have a Pleasure in adding such worthy Inhabitants to

4. Mary Franklin, his adoptive mother and Peter's wife, had died in 1766. BF must therefore be referring to his real mother, about whom nothing else is known.

5. See above, Jan. 13.

my Country as you and Mrs. Viny, and should be very happy in having you there for my Neighbours; yet as your Removal would give Pain to your good Brother here, whom I love[6] and to many others that love you, I cannot, without extreme Reluctance think of using any Arguments to persuade you. Let us then leave that Matter where we found it.

Possibly, however, as you are likely to have many Children, you may hereafter judge it not amiss, when they are grown up, to plant one of them in America, where he may prepare an Asylum for the rest, should any great Calamity, which God avert, befal this Country. A Man I knew, who had a Number of Sons, us'd to say, he chose to settle them at some Distance from each other, for he thought they throve better; remarking that Cabbages growing too near together, were not so likely to come to a Head. I shall be asleep before that time, otherwise he might expect and command my best Advice and Assistance. But as the Ancients who knew not how to write had a Method of transmitting Friendships to Posterity; the Guest who had been hospitably entertain'd in a strange Country breaking a Stick with every one who did him a kindness; and the Producing such a Tally at any Time afterwards, by a Descendant of the Host, to a Son or Grandson of the Guest, was understood as a good Claim to special Regard besides the Common Rights of Hospitality: So if this Letter should happen to be preserv'd, your Son may produce it to mine as an Evidence of the Good will that once subsisted between their Fathers, as an Acknowledgement of the Obligations you laid me under by your many Civilities when I was in your Country and a Claim to all the Returns due from me if I had been living. Pray make my best Respects acceptable to good Mrs. Viny, and give my Love to your Children. Be so good, too, as to remember me respectfully to your Sister and Brother-in-Law, to Mr. Stace and Family, and to Mr. Hancock; and believe me ever, with sincere Regard, Dear Sir, Your most obedient humble Servant,

B FRANKLIN

6. Presumably John Viny, who will appear in subsequent volumes. He was a wheelwright and, according to John Adams, a genius at his trade: Lyman H. Butterfield, ed., *Diary and Autobiography of John Adams* (4 vols., Cambridge, Mass., 1961), III, 186–7. He, as well as his brother, was a close friend of Polly Stevenson. He was also, apparently, an amateur vintner; an undated recipe in what appears to be his hand is in the Franklin Papers (APS), endorsed by BF "From Mr. Viney whose Wine was remarkably good."

The Colonist's Advocate: X

Printed in *The Public Advertiser*, February 19, 1770

The Grenvillians have endeavoured, by various Publications, in Pamphlets and News-papers, to support the Wisdom of taxing the Colonies, by sometimes alledging, that the British Trade with America is but an *inconsiderable* Object. It has never yet, they say, in any one Year, been worth to the Mother-Country quite Three Millions clear Gain. And what are Three Millions Gain to Britain? The Court has as much in her Gift; and there is not a Placeman, or a Pensioner, in the three Kingdoms, who will not tell you, he himself, and his Friends, have too little, and that the Three Millions a Year given away by the Court, are a mere Bagatelle, insufficient for producing the least Effect on the Minds, or in the Measures of the very honorable Persons who enjoy them, as appears manifestly from our [their] unbiassed and obstinate Adherence, on all Occasions, to the true Interest of their Country.

Others of that Party, taking up the Argument by a different Handle, labour to persuade us, that whatever may have been the Importance of our Commerce with our Colonies, it will not be at all *affected* by the late Revenue-Acts. It is true, those Gentlemen have not given us any Proofs of their possessing the Spirit of Prophecy. But this is no Reason why any Person, so disposed, may not be good-natured enough to give them Credit for what they pretend to. Others, indeed, of a less tractable Temper, may dispute the Matter with them, and argue, that though it were true, that *hitherto* our Commerce and Manufactures have felt no Diminution from the Grenvillian Measures, it does not, by any means follow, that the Case will not *hereafter* be found very fatally different. It is enough, they will alledge, to shew, that our offending the Colonists does *naturally tend* to alienate their Affections from us, and to force them upon striking into Tracks of Manufactures and Commerce very unfriendly to those of the Mother-Country.

But what will our Grenvillians find sufficient to invalidate the Reasonings of those, who bring Facts to prove, that the Revenue-Acts have *already* produced Effects very materially prejudicial to the British Navigation and Manufactures? Are not the Merchants judges of this Matter? Do not they *feel* a Stagnation of Trade, occasioned by the late fatal Measures? If all is going on as usual, what moves those grave and prudent Men to quit their Accounting-Houses, and Warehouses, and assemble together for the Purpose of drawing up Petitions to the Legislature for repealing the late Revenue-Acts? Do they not know, that such of them as have signed the Petition, will be examined upon the Allegations contained in it, and obliged to prove them? Do we see the Merchants of London engage themselves in such foolish Attempts as this would be, if they could not produce sufficient Reasons for the Request they make? At Bristol, when a Petition, concerning the Middlesex Election, was first proposed, some of the Merchants observed, that the Rupture with our Colonies was an Object of as great, if not greater, national Importance, than that which occasioned the numerous Petitions then preparing, and since presented; and they expressed a greater Inclination to sign a Petition for restoring Commerce, than on any other Subject.[7] Are there not now Two Hundred Ships in the River, rotting for Want of Freights to America? Are not all the Commissions from thence conditional?[8] "No Repeal; no British Goods." Are not the American Stores (Warehouses) full of British Goods, which they only keep for a short Time, with the express Design of returning them, if the late Revenue-Acts are not repealed? Have we not Ships come back loaded with the Goods they carried out?[9] Is not the Exchange between America and England, which used to be from 170, to 175, now fallen to 162?[1] What has produced this Effect, but the Decline of our Commerce with America? An Insurance of Tea, to the Value of £6000 Sterling, from Holland to New-York, alone, has been made in London within these few Weeks. A great many Six Thousand Pounds will amount to the whole Value of our late gainful Trade to America. What will the Grenvillians say, if they should quickly hear of such commercial

7. Bristol merchants in 1769 had been divided on the issue, and even the most strongly pro-American group had not given repeal the top priority that BF implies. George Rudé, *Wilkes and Liberty: a Social Study of 1763 to 1774* (Oxford, [1962]), pp. 112–13.

8. See BF to Galloway above, Jan. 11.

9. See BF to [Charles Thomson] below, March 18.

1. This remarkable statement can only be explained by assuming that BF was using the four-year-old figures for the Pennsylvania exchange that he had given the House of Commons (above, XIII, 134). He must have known from his Post Office accounts, of which a résumé appears above, Jan. 3, that in 1768–69 the colonial exchange varied between 167.7 and 180.

Projects as the following, for indemnifying America of the Sums we are to raise by our noble Taxation-Schemes, and punishing us for our ill Policy and Injustice? What will they say when they find, that Ships are actually fitted out from the Colonies (they cannot, I suppose hinder their fitting out Ships) for all Parts of the World; for China, by Cape Horn; for Instance, to sail under Prussian, or other Colours, with Cargoes of various Kinds, and to return loaded with Tea, and other East India Goods? A Master of a Vessel can go from America to France, can legally charter her from thence for Eustatia, and load her with every Species of Goods for the American Consumption. He can leave them at Eustatia 'till Winter, when it will be extremely easy to smuggle them into all Parts of North America in small Vessels. The whole Navy of England, if stationed ever so judiciously, cannot prevent smuggling on a Coast of 1500 Miles in Length. Such Steps as these will soon be taken by the Americans, if we obstinately go on with our unjust and oppressive Measures against them. And they will soon shew us, that they have it in their Power to carry Manufactures to much greater Lengths, and in a shorter Space of Time, than our Grenvillians would have us believe; of which more in my next Paper. There is no American Merchant, or Manufacturer, who does not already feel a considerable Diminution of Trade, in Consequence of the late Revenue-Acts. The fatal Innovation, which has given the Colonists such great and just Offence, is yet but recent. And it is a great while before a whole People come to act in concert on Occasion of unexpected Emergencies. It is likewise notorious, that several temporary Circumstances have partially contributed to prevent that Distress from coming upon our working Manufacturers, which otherwise they must, by this Time, have felt more severely than they do; as an unusual Trade to France, Spain, and Russia, and the Resolutions made by the Colonies to receive British Goods, and store them up, and of some Provinces to go on longer than others.

In short, it has been proved, by innumerable Writers, that taxing the Colonies, without Representation, is so unjust, that it ought not to be done, were it ever so prudent, and so impolitic, that it ought not to be done, were it ever so unexceptionably just. But if the Ministry be for the Measure, they will find Men to defend both it's Policy and it's Justice.

From James Parker   ALS: American Philosophical Society

Honoured Sir   Newyork Feb 20. 1770
    The 2d of this Month I wrote you per Capt. Munds, who was then
purposing to sail, but for some Reasons known only to the Owners,
he is not yet sail'd, tho' the Letter having been put in his Bag, I cannot get it back and he is expected to sail soon; probably this will
come to hand first. In that I sent the first of each of the three Bills,
I now send the second of viz. One from Quebec, for £200 Sterling
drawn by J. Drummond, on Harly & Drummond, dated 5 Dec.
1769——the two others from Rhode-Island, One for £20 Sterling
60 Days sight dated Jamaica 20 June 1769 drawn by Alex. Findleter
on Wm Cunningham, Esqr near Glasgow; the other for £52 Sterling 90 Days sight, dated Newport Jan 9. 1770 drawn by Hays and
Polock on Dav. Milligan of London. Mr. Vernon says they are the
best he can get, I hope them safe to Hand and all acceptable.
    Yours of the 10th December per this Packet I received. I have
resigned the Custom-House Business, and have got my pay. For
your Amusement I send you the Account of the Attorney. I have
now done with them, but I cannot help thinking it hard, as well as
absurd that the Officers must appoint such Attorney as the Commissioners please to direct and that Attorney have 5 per Cent, for
receiving the Money, and paying it away, or rather only delivering
it to Order. The Attornies of the Officers in England never had but
2½ per Cent, and this Tool of the Board has 5——whereas Mr.
Hubbart[2] would have received it for me for Nothing. This Man
must suck the Blood of about 200 Poor Officers, and make double
of what any of them can make: the King runs the Risk of the Money
going to Boston, and every Officer in America, run the risk of it
coming back to them. Such Absurdity is to me inconceivable. To
England an Officer could sell his Bills to Advantage, but to Boston,
only the Money itself must come generally. But Is done. I wonder
a good deal what is become of Robinson; he has not even wrote to
his Wife, she says.
    The Affair of Mecom's Books, I mention'd in mine per Munds,
since which have proceeded to have them all sold at Auction. Inclosed is a Catalogue of the Auction: All in this Catalogue to No 103
were Mr. Bell's own, Mecom's begins at No 104 and continues to

    2. Tuthill Hubbart, the Boston postmaster.

No 309, the last 10 Numbers are another's Parcel. The Sale is finished, but the Auctioneer has not settld the Account yet. By Act of Assembly, there is a Duty on Goods sold at Auction here, and I was the Auctioneer's Security for that Duty, which is first to be settled. As soon as we can get it done, I will take the Ballance and immediately purchase a Bill for it, and send it you, with the particular Account of Sales &c. which you will probably have by the next Packet if I am alive. I have thought I have done the best by such Auction but if it should be thought otherways by the Parties concerned, I shall be very sorry. My Reasons I give you in my Letter per Capt. Munds.[3]

My Health is much as it was, I can walk about; but so emaciated and torn by the Gout, that all the Springs of Nature fail. I think I am drawing nigh to the Grave with a good deal of Rapidity. God only knows how soon my Course will be finished: I am desirous to resign my Will to his. All our best Respects await you and Mr. Foxcroft, whilst I am your most obliged Servant   JAMES PARKER

Addressed: For / Dr Benjamin Franklin / Craven-Street / London / per Halifax Packet / Capt. Boulderson

Endorsed: Parker   Feb. 20 1770

From Noble Wimberly Jones

LS: American Philosophical Society

In the Commons House of Assembly Savannah in Georgia
Sir   21st Febry 1770
I am directed by the House of Assembly to desire you will please to purchase for the use of the House a Mace to be made of Silver and double gilt to cost a Sum not exceeding £100 Sterling also two Gowns [*in margin:* 5 foot 8 inches, 5 foot 10 inches, size of persons] such as you think would be proper for the Speaker and Clerk of an American Assembly. So soon as I can be acquainted by you what the whole expence will amount to I shall take Care to have it

3. The auction and much of the rest of what Parker is discussing he had already touched upon in his letters to BF above, Jan. 4, Feb. 2.

immediately remitted, as there is a Vote of the House to provide a Sum for that purpose, I have only at present further to inform you that the Ordinance for your Reappointment as Agent has passed both Houses of Assembly.[4] As to other matters I shall reserve myself till another Opportunity and am in the mean time with great respect Sir Your most Obedient Humble Servant

NOBLE WIMBERLY JONES Speaker

Benjamin Franklin Esqr

Endorsed: [N. W.] Jones Speaker of Georgia. *Mace and Gowns* Feb. 21. 1770.

To Joshua Babcock[5]

ALS: Yale University Library

Dear Sir, London, Feb. 26. 1770

It is a long time since I have had the Pleasure of a Line from you; indeed I have not deserv'd it; for I am a Debtor on Account of several of your Favours that remain unanswer'd. The Truth is, I have too much Writing to do. It confines me so much, that I can scarcely find time for sufficient Bodily Exercise to keep me in Health. Hence I grow more and more averse to Writing; and sometimes almost wish I had never learnt to write. The Consequence is, that when I have many Letters to answer, I take the Liberty of postponing those to Friends on whose Goodness in excusing me I can most rely. I never fail, however, of enquiring after you and yours of every one I meet with that can give me Information, and I was glad to hear by your Son,[6] that you continue well and prosperous.

I wish I could send you an Account by this Opportunity of the Redress of all our Grievances by Parliament. But tho' some here are sanguine enough to expect it this Session, I cannot say I think they have much Foundation for their Hopes. We have lately lost out of the Cabinet almost every Man that was in the least favour-

---

4. See below, Feb. 27.

5. For the physician and storekeeper of Westerly, R.I., see above, VI, 174 n.

6. Luke Babcock, who had resigned as postmaster of New Haven and gone to England, apparently to be ordained. See above, XIV, 61 n; XVI, 141 n.

ably dispos'd towards America;[7] and it will be strange if our Relief should come spontaneously from our Adversaries.

Be so good as to make my Respects acceptable to Mrs. Babcock, remember me affectionately to the Colonel,[8] and believe me ever, with great Esteem, Yours sincerely B FRANKLIN

Joshua Babcock Esqr

Ordinance of Georgia Reappointing Benjamin Franklin as Agent[9]

Copy:[1] American Philosophical Society

[February 27, 1770]

Whereas leave was Given by the late house of Assembly to bring in an Ordinance for reappointing Benjamin Franklin Esquire to be agent for Soliciting the affairs of this Province in Great Britain And Whereas the Dissolution of the said Assembly immediatly following

7. BF is presumably referring to the disappearance of Shelburne and Conway some time before, and not to the recent changes. Grafton had resigned at long last on January 22, and North had succeeded him as first minister on the 28th; but the concomitant shift in office-holders was of negligible importance. North "had not formed a ministry; he had merely inherited one." Alan Valentine, *Lord North* (2 vols., Norman, Okla., [1967]), I, 190.

8. For Joshua Babcock's wife and eldest son, Col. Henry, see above, respectively, VI, 175 n; IX, 397 n.

9. BF's initial appointment in 1768 had been for a year, until June 1, 1769. Governor Wright had dissolved the Assembly at the end of 1768, and a new one had not convened until the following October. Hence the appointment had legally lapsed, and the present ordinance renewed it for the remainder of the second year.

1. The first page of the copy is omitted. It gives the date when the ordinance became law; the dates when it passed its three readings in the Commons House, Dec. 15, 19, and 20, 1769, signed by the clerk, John Simpson; the dates when it passed the Upper House, Jan. 15 and 16, 1770, signed by the clerk, Charles Watson; and a certification that the copy is a true one, dated May 21, 1770, and signed by the deputy secretary of the province, Thomas Moodie. For Simpson, a former member of the Assembly Committee of Correspondence, see above, XV, 95. Watson, a Georgia attorney, had been clerk of the Council and Upper House since 1757; see Candler, ed., *Ga. Col. Recs.*, VII, 89, 282, 506; XV, 174. Moodie had been deputy secretary of the province since 1765; in 1776 he was restrained as a dangerous Loyalist. *Ibid.*, XV, 184, 295–6; Allen D. Candler, ed., *The Revolutionary Records of the State of Georgia...* (3 vols., Atlanta, 1908), I, 146.

prevented the said Ordinance from going through its regular forms And Whereas the said Benjamin Franklin notwithstanding the Want of Such an Appointment hath Continued to Transact the Business of this Province in Great Britain, Be it therefore Ordained And it is hereby Ordained by his Excellency James Wright Esquire Captain General and Governor in Chief of his Majestys Province of Georgia by and with the Advice and Consent of the Honourable Council and Commons house of Assembly of the said Province in General Assembly met and by the Authority of the same that the said Benjamin Franklin be and he is hereby declared Nominated and Appointed Agent to represent sollicit and Transact the affairs of this Province in Great Britain.

And be it further Ordained that the said Benjamin Franklin shall be and he is hereby fully Authorized and empowered to follow and pursue all such instructions as he shall from time to time receive from the General Assembly of this Province or from the Committee herein after appointed to Correspond with him.

And be it further Ordained That the Honourable James Habersham, Noble Jones, James Edward Powell, Lewis Johnson and Clement Martin Esquires, The Honourable Noble Wimberly Jones Esquire John Mullryne John Milledge Archibald Bullock, William Ewen, Charles Odingsall, Philip Box, William Young, and Richard Cunningham Crooke Esquires[2] untill others shall be Appointed or any Seven of them two of Which to be of the Council Provided Nevertheless that after being Summoned in Consequence of an Order from any of the Committee by the Clerk or other person appointed by them for that purpose to meet the Committee

2. The first ten names listed have already been identified above, xv, 95 n. Charles Odingsell was a South Carolinian by background, who represented Great Ogechee and St. Philip's parish; he was probably the same Odingsell who died in Rhode Island the following November. Philip Box, the Savannah postmaster, represented Acton and Christ Church parish; he was later a member of the first Provincial Congress and treasurer of Georgia. William Young, a Savannah representative, became Speaker in 1772 and was also a member of the Provincial Congress in 1775, shortly before his death. Richard Cunningham Crooke, after losing to Odingsell in 1769 as representative of Great Ogechee and St. Philip's, was returned for Augusta and St. Paul's; in 1771 he replaced Simpson as clerk of the Assembly. These biographical details have been gathered from the following sources: Candler, ed., *Ga. Col. Recs.*, x, 858, 884; xiv, 137; xv, 6, 13, 35–6, 67, 303, 338; *S.C. Hist. and Geneal. Mag.*, xvi (1915), 132; xvii (1916), 121; Ga. Hist. Soc. *Collections*, v (1901), 1, 15, 19, 44.

they shall refuse or Neglect to attend then any Seven of the persons before named shall be and they are hereby Nominated and appointed a Committee to Correspond with the said Benjamin Franklin and give him such orders and Instructions from time to time as they shall Judge to be for the service of this Province.

And be it further Ordained That there shall be Allowed and paid unto the said Benjamin Franklin for his Agency the sum of One hundred pounds Sterling money of Great Britain over and above his reasonable Charges and disbursements on his Application to the several Offices and Boards in Negociating the affairs of this Province.

And be it further Ordained That the said Benjamin Franklin shall be and Continue Agent for this Province untill the first day of June in the year of Our Lord One Thousand Seven hundred and Seventy

By Order of the Commons house of Assembly

N W Jones Speaker

By Order of the upper house of Assembly

James Habersham President

Council Chamber 27th February 1770   Assented to

Ja Wright

From Daniel Roberdeau:[3] Five Letters

These letters illustrate the complexities—perhaps increased by the writer's nature—of trying to negotiate a transatlantic sale of land. Daniel Roberdeau wanted to dispose of his plantation in the Antilles; he believed that he had one potential buyer in London, and hoped that he might find several who would vie with each other. To save himself a journey to England he sent a power of attorney to Franklin, Dr. Fothergill, and his cousin Charles Pearce,[4] and with it this bevy of letters to tell them how to act. In the first, addressed to all three, he explained the situa-

3. A former ally of BF in Pennsylvania politics, and a prominent Philadelphia merchant engaged in the West Indian trade, who in childhood had moved with his family from St. Kitts (St. Christopher). See *DAB* and above, XIII, 264 n and earlier volumes.

4. An English merchant who was Roberdeau's first cousin by marriage, and lived near Dr. Fothergill's botanical garden at Upton. See Roberdeau Buchanan, *Genealogy of the Roberdeau Family...* (Washington, 1876), p. 38.

tion in general terms. There were complicating factors, however, not all of which he wanted to confide to Pearce; the most important was the difference between his asking price and what he would settle for if need be. He explained these factors in a second letter, of the same date, intended originally for Franklin but then readdressed to him or Fothergill; a third, to Franklin alone, followed at once to explain the readdressing. As if this were not complicated enough, Roberdeau added another twist. Instead of authorizing his agents to reduce the price, if they had to, by stages to his minimum figure, he put the authorization into two separate letters, enclosed in that to Franklin or Fothergill, and dated them March 20 and April 30. The dates were of course spurious; both were written and sent in February.

To Benjamin Franklin, John Fothergill, and Charles Pearce   AL (letterbook draft): Historical Society of Pennsylvania

Dear Gentlemen   Philada. Feby. 27th. 1770

   However reluctant a man may be within his sprere of action to give trouble to another, yet the circumstance of distance of place lays him under an indispensable necessity, and when that happens his first thought leads to the object of his confidence, and he is exercised therein in proportion to the trust he is to repose. I have motives sufficient to induce me as well from your established Characters as my personal knowledge of two of you to trust all that I have unreservedly into your hands; I am only embarrassed for an Apology in so great a liberty as I have taken with you, but as every thing I could say would be insufficient to excuse my freedom, I choose rather to submit my Cause to that common humanity which distinguishes your Characters. I have a Plantation in the Island of St. Christophers called Pelhams River Plantation under lease to one Mr. Stedman Rawlins,[5] a Copy of which lease I now send you, which I incline to sell subject to the same, with all the improvements as appraised to him, before the expiration of his time. I promised Mr. Augustus Boyd in his time, the refusal, accordingly some years ago I offered it to him for £7,000 Sterling, and about 3½ years

5. The plantation contained 150 acres. *Ibid.*, p. 58. Steadman Rawlins or Rawlings (1725–88) and his brother Joseph, mentioned below, were sons of Henry and Ann Rawlins of Christ Church, Nicola Town, St. Kitts. *Caribbeana*, I (1909), 38. They are referred to briefly in Philip C. Yorke, ed., *The Diary of John Baker*... (London, [1931]), pp. 308, 333, 346, 370 n.

past I received Mr. John Boyd's answer that the Terms were too high,[6] but as he was desirous of selling his own, and it was probable from the two places joining that the person who bought the one would be glad to have the other also, for these reasons desired to know my very lowest Terms, which he would endeavour to procure for me. Although I was under great obligations to Mr. Boyd as well as his father in my earliest mercantile life, which gives me pleasure to acknowledge, and doubt not his integrity, or continued regard for me, yet as from the vicinity of our places and the greater value of mine to him than to any other Person, it is highly probable that he himself will be the purchaser; therefore besides the disadvantage a compliance with that proposal would lay me under too obvious to mention, I should thereby forego the great advantages of a rival interest that may start up, which is the spring and life of a market. In conversing with Mr. Boyd on the subject he will no doubt as he has done with me argue from the present rent which is only £280 Sterl. per Annum in Confirmation of his Opinion of my former offer being too high, but besides that I know that the present Leasee would have given £20 Sterl. per Annum more, but from an undue advantage of my absence through a false insinuation to my Attorney and the Leasee that I had offered the place for £280 Sterl. per Annum, I know not but that it is of considerable more annual worth. I have wrote to my uncle D. Cunyngham Esqr. of Ludlow,[7] who I suppose is well acquainted with the value of my Estate to favour me with his advice and assistance to you in the sale. It is also very probable that some of Mr. Pearce's other West India Connections may be of special service. Having availed yourselves of every advantage within the compass of your power, if you shall judge that

6. John Augustus Boyd was a native of St. Kitts who married the daughter of a judge on the island and then moved to London and became a merchant; his only son, also a merchant, was John Boyd (1718–1800), who was a man of means. He had held a mortgage on Roberdeau's plantation, paid off in 1769, and had a country estate at Bexley, Kent, that was landscaped by "Capability" Brown. He became a baronet in 1775. *Caribbeana*, I, 74; III (1913), 102 n; Buchanan, *op. cit.*, p. 58; Dorothy Brown, *Capability Brown* (London, [1950]), p. 78. George E. Cockayne, *Complete Baronetage* (5 vols., Exeter, 1900–06), V, 184.

7. Daniel Cunyngham, Roberdeau's uncle on his mother's side and Charles Pearce's father-in-law, had been born on St. Kitts in 1701; he moved to England, and died between 1772 and 1781. Buchanan, *op. cit.*, p. 38.

I have been too sanguine in my Expectations and that you cannot obtain £7,000 Sterl. you have my consent to take Six thousand five hundred Pounds Sterl.

Mrs. Roberdeau[8] would have freely joined me in the power sent you, which was originally intended fully to authorise you to make a conveyance, but being since better instructed by a Lawyer, we hold ourselves in readiness, God sparing our Lives, to execute deeds that may be drawn in London and transmitted here for Execution and sent from hence to St. Christophers to be registered, which as I am informed is the least expensive mode, or in any other mode to make the Conveyance effectual that Counsel shall advise and you approve. But particular care must be taken of the security and of my receiving my Annual Rent of £280 Sterl. until I can avail my self of the purchase money. In August 1752 I empowered Grosvenor Bedford Esqr. and Mr. Wm. Woodmess Mercht. in London[9] to receive of Messrs. Boyd's certain papers of which Mr. John Boyd can inform you relating to my Estate deposited in their hands agreeable to their Messrs. Boyds receipt then forwarded, there are other papers also left with them at the time I gave them a Mortgage, all which papers, you will be please first to call for receive and carefully keep for me. These papers which were sufficient for the Mortgage, will no doubt be also sufficient for the sale. I have herewith sent Instruments of writing with Certificates of their being properly recorded, which show that the late incumbrance of the Mortgage to Messrs. Boyd's long since discharged, is taken off. I beg it can be done consistent with my Interest that Mr. Boyd may have the preference of Purchase, and if it's not too much trouble to you that he may know the high sense of obligation I retain for him as a Patron and friend, which I hope I shall carry with me to my Grave. Mr. Joseph Rawlins[1] brother to Mr. Stedman Rawlins I am informed is

8. For Mary Bostwick Roberdeau (1741?–77) see *ibid.*, p. 49.

9. Grosvenor Bedford (d. 1771) had once been customs collector at Philadelphia, and was at the time a deputy usher of the Exchequer. *PMHB*, xxv (1901), 570; *Gent. Mag.*, XLI (1771), 523. William Woodmass, a merchant of Homerton, in Hackney, had gone bankrupt in 1767. *Gent. Mag.*, XXXVII (1767), 50.

1. Steadman's younger brother Joseph (1729–95) had a daughter who was married and living in London in 1783, perhaps the reason for his visit in 1771. He moved to America—when we do not know—and eventually died in Baltimore. *Caribbeana*, I, 39, 292; V (1918), 97.

in London perhaps he may incline to purchase. I depend on you in Case of sale that the security for payment on Condition of exicuting any deeds of Conveyance transmitted to me for that purpose, be abundantly sufficient. I beg leave to take my leave at present with assuring you that I am very respectfully Dear Sirs Your most obedient and very humble Servant

p. s You'll please to take particular notice to provide by *undoubted* security not only for the payment of the purchase money, but also for the Payment of an Interest, which shall commence from the time my rent shall cease equal to £280 Sterl. on the whole purchase money, and in proportion for any lesser Sum until the whole is drawn for, which you may limit to any reasonable time after that I shall have authority to draw for the purchase money.

Also when you sell I must beg you will be at the trouble to get 100 Bills of Exchange[2] numbered, with proper blanks of 4 bills to a set struck in Copper plate and sent over to me, answering to indents and numbers of each Bill transmitted, to be left in London to be compared and prevent Counterfeits.

Joseph Reed Esqr. one of the subscribing Witnesses, will prove the Power when called on.[3]

Could I have my choice, of all modes of negotiating this sale I should prefer your selling to Mr. Boyd, and the money to lay in his hands subject to my drafts from time to time without Commissions, as soon after Conveyances are made as I should think proper, but not to be obliged to draw for any or all of the purchase money under three years, as in that time I probably might make considerable advantage in the way of Exchange, he in the mean time allowing me

2. [*Roberdeau's note:*] I presume the Expence will be within the bounds of 5 or 6 Guineas.

3. Roberdeau added a note to himself that this part of the postscript was repeated in his letter to Fothergill; it was also repeated in that to Franklin below, where we have omitted it. Joseph Reed, the New Jersey lawyer, has appeared briefly in previous volumes. He embarked for England in March, 1770, and two months later married Dennys DeBerdt's daughter Esther. *DAB*; William B. Reed, *Life and Correspondence of Joseph Reed* (2 vols., Philadelphia, 1847), I, 42. Reed undoubtedly carried these five letters and Roberdeau's other documents.

interest for the whole or any part at the rate of £280 Sterl. on the whole.

Doctor Benja. Franklin
Doctor John Fothergale and } London
Charles Pearce Esqrs.

To Franklin or Fothergill   ALS: American Philosophical Society

Dear Sir   Philada. Feby. 27th. 1770

I have been for weeks past meditating a Voyage to London, which would be attended with very great inconvenience, to sell my Estate in St. Christophers, as a long lease thereon is now almost expired, when a presumptious thought occurred, that if you would condescend to look down from Affairs of the highest publick concern, to an Affair of the highest private concern of an unworthy friend, that all I could most sanguinely hope from a personal attendance, would be more than made up by your abundantly superior Capacity, with such hints as I should give on the Subject, besides the Authority vested in you in Company with two other worthy Gentlemen, and instructions to them bearing equal date herewith.

On the presumption that you will treat me as your own Child on this Occasion, which will lay me under peculiar Obligation, I proceed to mention my motives in general that you may better understand, advise and direct for me, and then descend to some particulars which may serve as a Clew. In the first place I have the pleasure to inform you that it is not necessity that urges to this matter but besides a desire of circumscribing my Affairs to Limits within my sphere of action, and of removing a temptation that at some future day might fall in the way of my Children to slave keeping, a practice I never can be reconciled to, I say besides these the Money that my place will sell for put to Interest under my own Eye, will in all probability bring me in a considerable greater yearly Income. I come next to give some hints by way of Clew.

Doctor Forthergill and Mr. Pearce being intimate, and you intimate with the worthy Doctor, thereby you will be easily lead to an acquaintance with Mr. Pearce, which will subserve the design of availing me of any assistance that my Uncle his father in Law will be pleased to give, and of his and Mr. Pearce's greater knowledge I suppose than either of you have with Gentlemen of the Island where my Estate lais, which will tend to create a rival Interest to Mr. Boyd.[4] Besides as Mr. Pearce many years ago when I think he could have no knowledge of my having any Intentions of selling, offering his assistance, if I should incline to sell, makes it no improbable Conjecture that he himself may be that Rival, which further accounts for the wary steps of this Letter. But I would have you also guarded against a very great prejudice which some years ago did and probably still subsists in my Uncle against Mr. Boyd, that no such prejudice should be a bar to my Intentions. Buyer and Seller generally have a secret that would be of mutal disadvantage to each other to be known, therefore to supply that defect on my part, which the best Representation cannot supply, I have fallen on a Stratigem, which on the possibility of Mr. Pearce's wanting to purchase forbids my including in the general Instructions; besides that it would effect a Consciencious plea of Limitation, for £6,500 Sterl. is my Limitation,[5] but should you with the other Gentlemen not succeed in getting that Sum, you would want my Authority for any Abatement in the Case, and only in that Case is my Letter of the 20th: of March to be produced, or considered as a Letter to my Attorneys, which I think can hardly fail of effecting the Bargin. But such is my desire of selling that I have provided even against the possibility of failure there, for should your best Endeavours and my highest Expectation of success on an offer of my Plantation for £6,000 Sterl. fail, in that Case and only in that Case is my Letter of the 30th: of April which exhibits my lowest Terms to be produced or considered as a Letter to my Attorneys. I have sent these two Letters without superscriptions on their out sides to guard against the possibility of a mistake before you are fully acquainted with the contents of this. If there should be occasion of producing either of the Letters, you will be pleased to consider them as inclosed to you,

4. If BF understood all the intricacies of this sentence, he had the advantage of his editors. But Roberdeau apparently hoped that Cunyngham and Pearce between them could find some one interested in competing with Boyd.

5. In other words the lowest price at which he was willing to sell at the start of negotiations. His original figure of £7,000, mentioned in the previous letter, was doubtless to impress Pearce—one of Roberdeau's "wary steps."

for the purpose of Conveyance, without any regard to the time of Reception.

You being now fully advised without any reserve or diffidence, all I could do in person can be better done by Proxy, as I anticipate the pleasure your Benevolence on all occasions prompts to the meanest Object. I shall direct this to Doctor Forthergill in your absence, as I fully include him in my confidence, nor shall I even doubt that Candour in him I flatter myself to find in a fellow Citizen in excusing the liberty this particular confidence bespeaks, when this falls into his hands and consiquently is considered as originally directed to him.

My Estate has always been Mr. Boyd's object, as from it's situation it would be of greater advantage to him than to any body else, and without it his Estate adjoining is inconsiderable. I am confident your attention being fixed on him, he will give more than any other Person, but I would not divert you from such a Tryal as will naturally engage his Attention and consiquently anxiety in proportion to the gre[ater unc]ertainty of obtaining this mode of procedure in preference to his proposal, mentioned in my general Letter, will naturally create.

I honour my Uncle and hope for his friendship and assistance, to this end beg you will take the trouble to treat with him, in such manner as will do honour to me, as your Representation cant fail to do, but at the same time remember my greater confidence is in you.

You'll please to remember that my Lease with Mr. Rawlins, including a *conditional* Covenant for 6 months longer, see the Lease, will expire in Jany. 1771, therefore all haste is to be made in the sale consistend with good speed.

I am under difficulty to provide for the small expence you will be at on my Account for postage &c. and it would be easy for me to give an order on Messrs. Wood & Trevanion[6] in whose hands I have money, but these my good friends might be offended in a transaction for such a trifle, whilst I employ others in a much greater trust, therefore choosing to be obliged to you or the worthy Doctor, I beg your reimbursement may rather be by a draft on me which shall at any time be readily honoured.

Committing myself and Affairs to your prudent and careful

6. A London mercantile firm at 33 New Broad Street, the same address as Boyd's. *Kent's Directory*... (London, 1770), p. 195.

management I beg leave to subscribe myself Dear Sir Your Affectionate and obedient humble Servant   DANIEL ROBERDEAU[7]

To Franklin   AL (letterbook copy): Historical Society of Pennsylvania

Dear Sir   Philada. Feby. 27th. 1770
    After writing the rough draft of a Letter to you this day at very considerable length, I was informed by a friend that it was highly probable that you would return by next June, which occasioned me to accomodate that Letter to that Circumstance and to direct it to you or Dr. John Fothergill refering him in a private Letter to the same. I among the Croud of your friends shall be very glad of an Opportunity most cordially to wellcome you to our shore, when you can be spared from attending on the important Businesses you are imployed in, but from motives I confess entirely selfish I cannot but hope that your Continuance in London may be a little longer for I hope to avail myself of your friendship in an Affair, the subject of the above cited Letter, to which please to be refered. I know no Gentleman on whose integrity as well as abilities I have greater reliance, I also am no stranger to your condescending disposition, therefore in an Affair of the highest Importance to my temporal Interest I hope to obtain your pardon in seeking for your friendship in a strange land. Was my business merely merchantile or was it lucrative I need not have troubled you, but although I flatter myself it will not be attended with much trouble, it requires some attention and more address and adroitness than to be committed into every hands. If this should happily meet with you and you condescend to undertake for me, my utmost wish would be satisfied and while I live I will thank you and my Children after me I am with unfeigned Regard Dear Sir Your Affectionate and obedient humble Servant

PS Joseph Reed Esqr. the bearer has orders to deliver the above mentioned letter to you if in London, and he probably may be of further service if you should require it of his profession.

Doctor Benja. Franklin

    7. The first part of the postscript to the previous letter, as mentioned above, was here repeated verbatim.

To Franklin, Fothergill, and Pearce

AL (letterbook copy): Historical Society of Pennsylvania

Dear Sirs   Philada. March 20th. [*i.e.*, February 27] 1770
  Please to be refered to what I wrote you the 27th. Ulto, on considering the possibility of your not obtaining £6,500 Sterl. for my Estate the Sum by which you were then limited, and as I would not have my purpose mared by failing of the above sum, and in Case you cannot obtain an intermediate Sum I even consent to take Six Thousand pounds Sterl. which I have no doubt you will obtain, and for which this is your Authority. I am with high Regard, but great haste, which I hope you'll excuse Dear Sir Your most obedient and obliged humble Servant

Doctor Benja. Franklin ⎫
Doctor John Fothergill and ⎬
Charles Pearce Esqr ⎭

To Franklin, Fothergill, and Pearce

ALS: American Philosophical Society

Dear Sirs   Philada. April 30th. [*i.e.*, February 27] 1770[8]
  If by this time you have not succeeded in [the sale of my Plantation,] according to what I wrote you the 27th. Feby. and 20th. March, as [I am anxious to] transfer my Property from the West-Indies to the more eligible Situa[tion of my] own residence, and as a last effort, although I have little doubt that by [the time] this gets to your hands, that you will have obtained at least £6,000 sterling my last Limitation, yet as you and I have taken such pains I would not for some hundreds that our Labour should prove fruitless, therefore you have now my Authority to make such an abatement of Price, as that I shall receive clear of all Charges in negotiating and paying, Five thousand five hundred Pounds Sterl., which is the last offer I shall make. I am with high sense of the obligation you have laid me under Dear Sirs Your much obliged and obedient humble Servant

DANIEL ROBERDEAU

Doctor Benja. Franklin Doctor John Fothergill and Charles Pearce Esqr.

  8. The place and date have been torn off the original, and are supplied from the letterbook copy in the Hist. Soc. of Pa.

The Colonist's Advocate: XI

Reprinted from Verner W. Crane, *Benjamin Franklin's Letters to the Press, 1758–1775* (Chapel Hill, [1950]), pp. 207–9.

[March 2, 1770]

The Genuineness of the following Extract from a North American Letter may be depended on. The Strain of it will shew, whether it is written by one most attached to the Ministry or to the People, and consequently whether the Information it contains is to be taken strictly, or with Allowances. One Thing I know, (though I suppose our wise Grenvillians will give little Attention to it) that the following, and many other Letters from America, agree but too well with what is now the common Talk of those native Americans occasionally resident here, who have long in vain opposed the Revenue Acts. "It is Time (they say) for us to be quiet. As Well-wishers to America, we ought to rejoice at Measures which will put our Countrymen upon what must in the End enrich and aggrandize them, though to the heavy Loss of the Mother Country, who sets the Colony Trade at Defiance. If the Colonists must pay Duties to the arbitrary Pleasure of an Assembly, in which they are not represented, it is Time they should think of what otherwise would not have come into their Minds for many Ages. It is Time they should apply to Manufactures, by which they may enable themselves to pay the Mother Country's Taxes, and lessen the Demand for her Tax-loaded Manufactures." Thus the Friends of America now talk; and this it seems our Government's noble Firmness will bring it to: Accordingly our British Manufacturers, thrown out of Employment at home, are removing to America, and carrying with them their various Arts, which have made us the Glory of all Lands, and our Goods are daily coming back unpacked, on our Merchants' Hands to the Ruin of our Country. No Matter: The Ministry have found Half a Dozen new Places for a few of their unprovided Friends. But I had almost forgot the Letter. Here it follows:

"As to Politics, I can write nothing new. The mutinous, seditious Spirit seems to have subsided, but a determined Resolution has taken Place to forbear Importation, and it seems to be supported with an Unanimity and Steadiness that exceeds their Expectations, and unless something satisfactory is soon done, I am persuaded all commercial Connection and Dependance on the Mother Country will be lost in a few Years, and political Connection, it is not likely, will long survive it. It would surprize you to see the Difference in American Manufactures. Mr. —— has lately had a Suit of Cloaths made off of his own Sheep, spun and wove in his own House; a good Piece of Cloth. It is Half the Breadth of Broad Cloth, and stands him in 4s. 6d. Sterling per Yard every Thing reckoned in; so that the Notion of the Impossibility of American Manufactures from their Expensiveness does not hold good."

Suppose this Spirit of manufacturing to spread through all America, and, in Consequence, their Want of our Commodities to lessen annually, till, in a few Years hence, our Colony Trade be annihilated, instead of being (as I have in one of my former Papers shewn it most probably would) doubled, that is amounting to Three or Four Millions clear annual Gain to the Mother Country; I say, supposing this to prove, as is reasonably to be expected, the Effect of our late wise and just Treatment of our American Brethren; I ask, whether the Annals of Government round this Globe can furnish an Instance of so prodigious a Loss voluntarily incurred by a Nation, for the sake of so small an Advantage in Prospect as Eight Thousand Pounds to come annually into the Treasury, and Bread for five Men to collect that pitiful Pittance?

From James Parker   ALS: American Philosophical Society

Honoured Sir   NYork March 8. 1770

My last to you was per Packet of the 20th Feb: and Capt. Munds being not yet sail'd, I have now to add. This covers a Bill of £250, Sterling Exchange 67½ so that it rises here, Wats & McEvers on Messrs. Harley & Drummond, dated Feb. 28. 1770. Of this Bill the Sum of £135, this Money, is on Account of B. Mecom's Books sold at Auction, and £283 15s., the same Money, on the Post-Office Account, the Bill having cost £418: 15s. As soon as the Account of the Auction can be fully made out, I shall send you a particular Account of every Article: tho' I believe there will be little more net Proceeds, when all the Charges are paid, &c. However, you will see, and if this be more than the net Proceeds, I will debit your Account for the Ballance; and if less, will debit my own Account, and credit you for it. This is all the Money I've yet got in.[9]

Mr. Hughes last Week applied to me for the Electrical Machine you sent designed for him; he says, his Brother John's eldest Son Hugh has spoke to him to get it, and will take it of you. I have let him open it, and he promises in his Nephew's stead to take it. I have not got the Invoice or Account of the Cost; having only taken down the Invoice of the Stationary that was sent designed for Hughes, and made myself Debtor for them only; so that if I had the Original Account of the Electrical Machine, I know not what is become of it. Mr. Hughes says, it will be paid according to the Charge, and your Order.[1]

The first of three Sets of Bills to you, go by Capt. Munds, by whom this is designed: The second of the same Sets were by the Packet of the 20th Feb. All which with these I wish safe to your Hands.

I having nothing else material to write, beg Leave to add, respectful Complements to Mr. Foxcroft, and self, from Your most obliged Servant   JAMES PARKER.

Addressed: For / Dr Benjamin Franklin / Craven-Street / London / per Capt. Munds

Endorsed: Parker March 8. 70

From John Perkins[2]   ALS: American Philosophical Society

Sir.   Boston March 12th. 1770
When I imagin myself possess'd of any new Thought I think it, in the first place, due to your Inspection and accordingly have in-

9. These transactions have already been dealt with in Parker's letters to BF above, Jan. 4, Feb. 2, 20.

1. This machine had been bedeviling Parker for the past four years. BF had ordered it in 1765 for Hugh Hughes, the brother of his friend John. By the time it arrived in New York Hughes was bankrupt and in hiding from his creditors; Parker had received and stored it for him. See above, XII, 259 n, 355 n, 408; XIII, 11 n, 307, 475. Even now Hughes was clearly unable to pay for the machine himself, but had managed to involve his nephew.

2. For Dr. John Perkins, BF's longtime correspondent on medical and scientific phenomena, see above, IV, 267 n.

clos'd my Conjectures on the Caudae Cometive; to gether with the small Tract on Epidemic Colds.[3]

I confess there is something unnatural in phylosophic Speculations at a Time when the Nation is involv'd in such Disorder and Confusion; and in accosting you with them in the midst of your weighty Employments, the businesses of State; in which you are so much needed; but Gratitude for very many Favours would not suffer me to be any longer Silent: They are too many for me to enumerate; the many former ones, and the latter of the Thermometer; Your Effigies; and Collection of Papers;[4] together with the honour you have done some of my Thoughts; Of all which I retain the most gratefull Sense. Sincerely wishing you all that may render Life most happy, and desireable, I am Sir Your most obliged, most obedient and Humble Servant   JOHN PERKINS

Dr: Franklin

From John Perkins

ALS: American Philosophical Society

Sir   Boston March 12 1770

Just as I was about inclosing my papers[5] it came in my head to mention to you a notion I have sometimes had that Pit-Coal is a vegitable production as of Grass or other Herbage of which the rich and fat Soil of our fresh Marshes is form'd.[6] We know that these are constantly filling up by the Annual Supplys of this kind so that perhaps many places that were formerly Boggs or Marshes are now

3. The first was perhaps the MS of his *The True Nature and Cause of the Tails of Comets. Elucidated in a Rationale Agreeing with Their Several Phanomena...* (Boston, 1772). No American work on colds as early as this has been identified. The subject was one in which BF had been and long continued to be interested.

4. For BF's gift to Perkins in 1764 of one of the Fisher prints of his portrait by Chamberlain see above, XI, 90. The "Collection of Papers" was probably one of the six copies of his *Exper. and Obser.* (1769) that BF had mentioned to Jane Mecom; see above, XVI, 52.

5. See the preceding document.

6. Pit coal and sea coal were terms for coal in the modern sense, as distinct from charcoal. This letter from Perkins may well have been what first aroused BF's interest in the subject. In 1772 he visited a mine far under the sea, and soon thereafter outlined to Barbeu-Dubourg his theory—closely akin to Perkins'—of the vegetable origin of sea coal. Jacques Barbeu-Dubourg, *Œuvres de M. Franklin...* (2 vols., Paris, 1773), II, 199.

94

uplands over which Travelers pass without imagining they were ever otherwise.

What gave occasion to these Thoughts at first was the accounts the Irish at their first coming among us many years Since, gave of their Boggs. They assure me that on drying the Substance of them they make tollerable Fewel and the better as the lower they digg it. The bottom parts dry blackest and yield a Sulphureous Smoke nearly approaching that of Pit-Coal.

I should like to visit the Coal-Mines to see the Nature and Circumstances of them Or to gain by Conversation with those who are well acquainted with them some further insight concerning these Subterraneous Stores. I am Sir, as ever, Your most humble Servant

JNO PERKINS

Endorsed: Dr Perkins. March 12, 1770

To Jane Mecom

Reprinted from Jared Sparks, ed., *A Collection of the Familiar Letters and Miscellaneous Papers of Benjamin Franklin* (Boston, 1833), pp. 123–4.

Dear Sister, London, 15 March, 1770.

I received your kind little letter of January 3d from Philadelphia. I am glad your visit thither proves agreeable to you. Since your family is so much reduced, I do not see why you might not as well continue there, if you like the place equally with Boston.[7] It would be a pleasure to me to have you near me; but your own discretion must govern you. I propose, God willing, to return this summer. With true regard, I am ever Your affectionate brother,

B. FRANKLIN.

7. For her visit to Philadelphia see above, XVI, 231–2, 262–3. Van Doren assumes that Jane, in her missing letter of Jan. 3, had suggested moving to Philadelphia (*Franklin–Mecom*, p. 16); but BF may equally well have originated the idea. Her family was indeed reduced. Of her twelve children five were still living, and of those only Jenny (Jane) gave her reason for staying in Boston. Peter was insane. Ben, on the verge of insanity, was in Philadelphia. Josiah was at sea on a whaler, and apparently hoped to be married on his return to Boston. John was in New Brunswick, already suffering from the disease that carried him off in September. *Ibid.*, p. 114.

To Cadwalader Evans

ALS: Miss Harriet V. C. Ogden, Bar Harbor, Me. (1958).

Dear Friend   London, Mar. 17. 1770

I received your Favour of Nov. 27. and thank you for the Information it contained relating to the Society.[8] Mr. Ewing has transmitted to me Copies of the Observations of the Transits of Venus and Mercury which were made in Pensilvania. Those you sent me, made by Messrs. Biddle & Bayley, will, with the others, be printed, I suppose, in the next Volume of the Transactions of the Royal Society here.

Our Friends James and Wharton, your quondam Patients, seem in pretty good Health here at present. Mr. Wharton had got a Habit of Complaining that he was not well in almost every Company; and, as is always the Case, he everywhere found somebody who would officiously prescribe to him, and he too readily made Trial of their Prescriptions; so that he was forever physicking and never better.[9] I have persuaded him to keep his Ails to himself, and he passes now for a well Man.

I am glad the Silk Books were agreable to you, and likely to be useful. With great and sincere Esteem, I am, my dear Friend, Yours very affectionately   B Franklin

Dr. Cadwalader Evans

Addressed: To / Dr Cadr. Evans / at / Philadelphia / per Capt Falconer

Endorsed: March 17th. 1770.

8. See above, xvi, 235–6, where most of the items mentioned in this letter were discussed.

9. Abel James, the prominent Philadelphia merchant, was in London on the business of his firm, James and Drinker: *PMHB*, xiv (1890), 41–5. Samuel Wharton's hypochondria must have surprised Evans, who had expected him to overindulge in the fleshpots of London. Above, xvi, 157.

To William Franklin Extract:[1] Historical Society of Pennsylvania

March 17, 1770

What you say with regard to advancing Money for Building Mills, Bloomeries, &c.[2] has a good deal in it, and I believe most of the Persons concerned will think with you when the Settlement comes under Consideration. I sent you a Part of L. Evans's Map, containing the Bounds of the intended Province: You see by that, that the Scheme is much enlarg'd since the first Proposition of purchasing only 2,400,000 Acres.[3] We had at first no Thoughts of making it a distinct Province and Government, as now it is to be. The Duke of Grafton's Resignation, and the Sickness of the two Secretaries,[4] has retarded a little the Completion of our Bargain, but we now expect it soon.

Endorsed: Extract of B. F. Letter to W. F. March 17th. 1770

1. The MS extract, like a similar one of an earlier letter from BF to WF that has also been lost (above, XII, 361–5), was probably made for circulation among American friends, in this case those interested in the Grand Ohio Company.

2. The draft articles for the Grand Ohio Company (above, XVI, 166) provided for the erection of mills and other buildings on the land to be granted. A bloomery was a furnace and forge for converting ore into wrought-iron "blooms," or large ingots.

3. Apparently a copy of Lewis Evans, *A General Map of the Middle British Colonies in America*... (London, 1755), with the boundary lines added by hand. The ambition of the Company promoters was growing fast. Their original request for 2,400,000 acres had now grown to twenty million. See above, XVI, 163, and the memorial of Jan. 4, 1770.

4. We cannot identify them, partly because the term is ambiguous. If BF was referring to secretaries of state, one likely possibility is Lord Rochford, head of the Northern Department and a patron of the Company (Lewis, *Indiana Co.*, p. 88); the other obvious possibility would be Hillsborough, except that he was well enough to attend the March meetings of the Board of Trade. If, as seems more likely, BF was referring to less exalted secretaries, one of the two he had in mind was probably John Robinson, who had been appointed secretary of the Treasury in February but did not assume his duties until autumn (Namier and Brooke, *House of Commons*, III, 364); the delay was perhaps occasioned by illness. The other may have been John Pownall, secretary of the Board of Trade and an undersecretary of the American Department. Both men were influential behind the scenes.

To Michael Hillegas[5]

Printed in *The American Museum, or, Universal Magazine*, VII (1790), 224–5.

Dear sir,   London, March 17, 1770.

I received your favour of November 25, and have made enquiries, as you desired, concerning the copper covering of houses. It has been used here in a few instances only: and the practice does not seem to gain ground. The copper is about the thickness of a common playing card: and though a dearer metal than lead, I am told that as less weight serves, on account of its being so much thinner, and as slighter wood-work in the roof is sufficient to support it, the roof is not dearer on the whole than one covered with lead. It is said, that hail and rain make a disagreeable drumming noise on copper: but this, I suppose, is rather fancy: for the plates being fastened to the rafters, must in a great measure deaden such sound. The first cost, whatever it is, will be all: as a copper covering must last for ages: and when the house decays, the plates will still have intrinsic worth.[6] In Russia, I am informed, many houses are covered with plates of iron tinned, such as our tin pots and other wares are made of, laid on over the edges of one another, like tiles; and which, it is said, last very long; the tin preserving the iron from much decay by rusting. In France and the Low Countries, I have seen many spouts or pipes for conveying the water down from the roofs of houses, made of the same kind of tin plates soldered together: and they seem to stand very well. With sincere regard, I am, your's, &c.   B. FRANKLIN

From David Hall   ALS: Historical Society of Pennsylvania

Dear Sir   Philadelphia March 17, 1770.

The last Letter I had the Pleasure of receiving from you, was dated April 14, 1767, since which I have wrote you twice, but have not been favoured with an Answer to either of those Letters.[7] In

5. See above, XVI, 8 n.
6. BF pursued the question of copper roofing; see his letter to Samuel Rhoads below, June 26.
7. For BF's letter see above, XIV, 126–8; only one of Hall's two unanswered letters has survived: above, XIV, 19.

that Letter you acknowledged the Utility of settling our Accounts, and promised to forward the Paper of Remarks you made, on looking over the Settlement by Mr. Parker, on your Behalf, with me, by the next Opportunity; but, tho' it is now very near three Years since, I have not yet received it, no Doubt owing to the continual Hurry you are in. For my own Part, I am not yet sensible of any Mistakes, or Omissions, other than what have been already taken Notice of, but still ready to rectify what is wrong in the Accounts, and to add whatever may have been omitted.

When you left Philadelphia, you thought you would return Time enough before our Contract should end, to settle the Affairs of the Partnership yourself, and tho' it has been now expired above four Years, you are not yet returned, and may still be longer necessarily detained in England on the Business of the Province. And as we are now both growing old fast, and one, or both, may be taken off before the Settlement is accomplished, which may prove most inconvenient to our Families; I think nothing further need be said to urge you to comply with my Request, in sending your Remarks, with Orders for Mr. Parker to finish the Affair in the Manner you may imagine is right.

In my Letter to you, of January 27, 1767, I sent you a State of our Accounts from February 1, 1766, to that Date;[8] which State you will be pleased to take no Notice of, farther than the Balance of £993 11s. 6d., thought to be due to me from you, by Mr. Parker's Settlement; as, in the Room of that, I have now sent you an exact Account of all the Money received for our Partnership, from February 1, 1766, to February 16, 1770. Likewise an Account of all the Monies received by Mrs. Franklin from me, from February 1, 1766, to March 16, 1770, for which I have her Receipts. All which have been most carefully taken [as] by the Books will appear, viz.

For the Gazette, from February 1, 1766, to
February 16, 1770 - - - - - - - - - - - - - - £1457 8s.
For Public Work, received June 18, 1767, of
Samuel Preston Moore Esqr. - - - - - - - - - 318 5s.
By Cash received for Work done, as credited
in the Leidger, in the above mentioned Time 389 14s. 1d.

£2165 7s. 1d.

8. Above, XIV, 19.

Account of Money received by Mrs. Franklin.

March 8, 1766,	Cash	- - - - - - - -	£200
July 12, - -	Ditto	- - - - - - - -	91
November 25,	Ditto	- - - - - - - -	50
December 27,	Ditto	- - - - - - - -	160
January 18, 1768,	Ditto	- - - - - - - -	100
September 1,	Ditto	- - - - - - - -	30
March 16, 1770,	Ditto	- - - - - - - -	45
To Sundries out of the Shop		- - - - - - -	11 3s. 6½d.

£687 3s. 6½d.

As you mentioned in one of your Letters, some Time ago, no Doubt you have a large Sum of Money owing you from our Customers,[9] which I should be very glad to be instrumental in recovering, both on your Account and my own, because wherever you lose, I must also be a Sufferer, and yet I cannot devise how to get it, or the greatest Part of it, in, the People lie so scattered, the Sums, most of them so small, many of the People dead, others left the Country, and a great Number of them pretend to have paid Posts, &c. on our Account. And as to impowering People to receive for us, we have succeeded so poorly in that Way, that I don't know but it will be better to trust it with the Multitude, than to let it get into the Hands of a few Individuals, we might appoint to collect for us, as Fifty or One Hundred Pounds might be a Temptation to be roguish, when Thirty, Forty or Fifty Shillings will not. It is true, there are certainly a Number of very honest Men in the different Quarters of the Country, but then such Men have generally Business enough of their own to mind, and would hardly care to be troubled with ours.

John Jones, one of our Posts, who, you may remember, was impowered to collect for us in the Lower Counties, has never yet finished his Collection, as he pretends, and puts off coming to a Settlement from Time to Time. Chapman, the Post for the Eastern Shore, Maryland, I believe paid all the Money he received for us, which amounted to but little more than One Hundred Pounds. And about Twelve Months before our Partnership ended, Mr. William Goodwin, of Baltimore County, Maryland, was recommended to me as a very honest Man, and would gather in our Gazette Money

9. *Ibid.*, p. 127.

on the Western Shore; upon which I got the Accounts made out, to the Amount of about Eight Hundred Pounds, and sent them to him, and tho' I believe he was most faithful, and, at the same Time, very industrious, yet all he was able to collect for us in two Years, neated only £53 2s. 8d., which he paid, and delivered up the Accounts, after having gone through a good Deal of Fatigue. Thus, Sir, you see what a bad Prospect we have of getting in our News Money, or any tolerable Proportion of it.

I should be glad to hear from you immediately on the Receipt of this, and that you would let me know when you think I may have the Pleasure of seeing you here.

My Wife, who has now been in a poor State of Health for these fourteen Years, is still but poorly, tho' rather better than she has been for some Years past, owing, we imagine, to the great Benefit she received from the Bristol Bath, last Summer. My eldest Son, Billy, is now turned of Eighteen, is learning the Printing Business with me, promises pretty well, and, in all Probability, will be a very stout Man, being now very little short of six Feet high. My Daughter Debby, tho' but just turned of Fifteen, is well grown too, being something taller than her Mother; she was seized with the Palsy in one Side last Summer, which frightened us a good Deal; but we sent her to the Bristol Bath, where, by the Blessing of God, she recovered, and is now very hearty. And David, the youngest, past Fourteen, is still at the Academy, is but small as to Heighth, but well set.[1] They all, with their Mother, desire to be remembered in the most affectionate Manner to Mr. Franklin. I hope you will excuse my taking up any of your Time about them.

Your own Family are all well. I saw Mrs. Franklin this Day. Mrs. Bache, and her Child (a fine Boy) are at Burlington, both well, as is Mr. Bache. If you have any Thing in the News Way, should be much obliged to you for it; and to hear from you frequently, will be most agreeable to me. In the mean Time, you may believe me to be, Dear Sir, Yours most affectionately,   DAVID HALL.

1. Mary Leacock Hall, DF's second cousin, seems to have thriven on ill health: she outlived her husband by nine years and died in 1781. The two Hall boys, young as they were, took over their father's business when he died in 1772. *PMHB*, X (1886), 87. For the baths at Bristol, in Bucks County, see F. H. Shelton, "Springs and Spas of Old-time Philadelphians," *ibid.*, XLVII (1923), 217–21.

Addressed: To / Benjamin Franklin Esqr. / At Mrs. Stevenson's in Craven-Street / London / Via Liverpool / By the Speedwell / Capt Le Cocq / Q.D.C.

Endorsed: Letter from D Hall to B.F. dated March 17th 1770

From Rudolph Erich Raspe[2] ALS: American Philosophical Society

Sir   Cassell. March. 17. 1770.

I sympatize still so much with Your publick Spirit and Your Genius, You have happily devoted to Your countries service and the improvement of natural Philosophy, that the keeping me in Your good remembrance is the least liberty I can indulge me with. I cannot therefore neglect to trouble You with these lines and to recommend You Mr. Lichtenberg Professor of Mathematics and natural Philosophy in the University of Giessen. He is very desirous to be nearer acquainted with a Man he values so high and in so many respects; and besides he himself will plead the liberty I take and easily gain a part in the friendship You have bestow'd on me.[3]

The compliments for me, which last Summer You order'd to Mr. Merk, who had the honour to see You in Switzerland, have been deliver'd to me.[4] They were very welcome to me, as shall be too

2. For the adventures and misadventures of this odd character, whom BF had met in 1766 and who later presented the world with the tales of Baron Munchausen, see above, XIII, 345 n.

3. Georg Christoph Lichtenberg (1742–99) later became an eminent writer and physician. In 1767 the government of the Landgraf of Hesse had named him professor of mathematics and reader in English at the University of Giessen, but he continued to study at Göttingen until his brief visit to England in 1770. While in London he was presented to the King, who as Elector of Hanover authorized his appointment to a professorship at Göttingen; Hessian efforts to get him back were unsuccessful. Carl Brinitzer, *A Reasonable Rebel, George Christoph Lichtenberg* (New York, 1960), pp. 34, 47–8. The presence of Raspe's letter among BF's papers would suggest that Lichtenberg delivered it in person; but the indications are that he did not, and that Raspe's effort to introduce the two came to nothing. Robert L. Kahn, "Meeting between Lichtenberg and Franklin?", *German Life and Letters*, new ser. (Oct., 1955), 64–7.

4. Johann Heinrich Merck (1741–91) was an author and critic, who later became a friend of Goethe and exercised considerable influence on the writers of the *Sturm und Drang*. When, where, or even whether BF had met him we cannot say, but a meeting in Switzerland in the summer of 1769 seems virtually

the dearer proof of Your continuing my worthy friend the new Edition of Your Electrical Letters, which I hope will now be finish'd.

I recommend me to Your and to Mr. Pringle's further favour and have the honour to be with the highest and warmest regard Dear Sir Your most obedient humble Servant   R E RASPE.

For Dr. Franklin.

To Deborah Franklin   ALS: American Philosophical Society

My dear Child,   London, March 18. 1770
My Letters are all in Capt. Falconer, but as Capt. Sparks has just been so kind as to call and acquaint me that he sails to day, and I understand that Falconer will not sail till the 20th. I just write this Line to acquaint you that I am well. Mrs. Stevenson and Polly, join me in best Affections, &c. My Love to our Children, &c. I am, my dear Debby, Your ever loving Husband   B FRANKLIN

Addressed: To / Mrs Franklin / Philadelphia / per favour of / Capt. Sparks.

To Thomas Gilpin   ALS: University of Virginia Library

Sir   London March 18. 1770
I receiv'd your Favour by the Hand of Mr. Abel James. An Accident happen'd to it in his Chest by the Breaking of a Bottle of some Liquid that obliterated part of it.[5] I see however that it contains some good Remarks on the Advantages of Canals for internal Navigation in our Country, to which I heartily wish Success. What you tell me of the Practicability of navigating down Sasquehanah pl[eases] me extremely, as hitherto I had understood that to be impossible.

---

out of the question. BF left London on July 14 of that year and was back again on Aug. 24, and would not have had time for such a journey; and we have encountered no reference to his ever being in Switzerland.

5. For Abel James, the bearer of the letter, and his business trip to London see BF to Evans above, March 17; for Gilpin's letter see XVI, 216–18, where the extracts reprinted are presumably from a copy that Gilpin made for himself.

I wrote to you last Summer that I purpose to show your Machine to the Society of Arts.[6] Since their Meeting I have till now been otherwise too busy to attend to such Things: but I lately pack'd it in its Box and sent it to their Store and am next Week to meet a Commitee of theirs to explain it to them. Many ingenious Men [have] seen it at my House and were much pleas'd with it. What they chiefly admire is not the Construction of the Sails but the Application of a single Crank to three separate Pumps.

I suppose you may not have had an Opportunity of knowing that the Manner of fixing your Sails, tho truly invented by you, has before been thought of by others. I did myself about 25 years ago make a little Model for W. Masters who had thoughts of executing it in large for Use.[7] It was in all respects the same, except the Cord and Spring to each Sail which are in yours, and which I think may be a great Improvement; and except that I plac'd my Sails upright on their Ends; which I mention now for your Consideration whether the Force or Purchase is not thereby greater, no Part of it being so near the Center of Motion as when they lie on their Sides, and fall inwards; but of this I would not be positive. In a second Model I plac'd six Sails instead of four, for which there is good room when so plac'd upright, and I thought the Motion might thereby be more equable. A Friend of mine in Maryland, Mr. H Jones, to whom I had communicated this horizontal Windmill wrote a Paper about it which he printed, and with some Alterations erected a large one on his Land intending to apply it to the grinding of Corn; he nam'd it *the Elephant* from its suppos'd Strength: and when used in a Current of Water, which he also propos'd, would then have it call'd *the Whale*; but before his Elephant was finish'd a great Storm shatter'd it to Pieces, and he never repair'd it.[8] My Son has now a Dr[aft?] of

6. See above, XVI, 175, where BF acknowledged receipt of a model of Gilpin's pump. The only extant description of this model, and an inadequate one, is in APS *Trans.*, I (1771), 339.

7. Presumably the small windmill that BF designed to assist his electrical experiments, for which see above, III, 130. Masters was almost certainly William Masters, an experimental farmer and BF's associate in civic enterprises in Philadelphia; see above, IV, 193 n, 214; VI, 312 n.

8. BF's friend was in all likelihood the Rev. Hugh Jones, an erstwhile professor of natural philosophy at William and Mary, who at the time of his death in 1760 had a parish and a farm in Maryland. See above, III, 324 n; Richard L. Morton, ed., *The Present State of Virginia...by Hugh Jones...* (Chapel Hill, [1956]), pp. 42–3. We have found no pamphlet by Jones on windmills.

those Sails of mine done by Lewis Evans, in an 8vo manuscript Volume of Inventions collected by him.[9] There is both a Plan of the Arms and Sails in their several Positions, and an upright View of them as applied to a travelling Carriage, which he fancied might be moved by them. My Son will readily shew it to you if you desire to see it.

Horizontal Windmills are not any where in general Use, except, as I have heard, in Poland. The Form there, is this. The Sails are all fix'd (in such a Position with regard to the Axis as the Radii of a Circle are to its Center) and upright Boards are fix'd all round them so as to throw the Wind to most Advantage against the Sails, let it come which way it will.

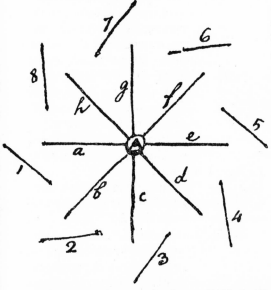

A the Axis. a, b, c, d, e, f, g, h, the Sails fix'd to the Arms. 1, 2, 3, 4, 5, 6, 7, 8, the standing Boards to throw the Wind against the Sails.

I have seen but two horizontal Windmills in all my Travels. The first was at Rhodeisland, where the Sails were in the Form of the Foresail and Mainsail of a Sloop, four little Masts with such Sails were fix'd upright on the four Ends of a horizontal Cross; the Sails fill'd and jib'd successively as the Cross went round: It was over a

9. For Lewis Evans, surveyor, draftsman, and cartographer, see above, III, 48 n. He drew "all sorts of maps, plans, seacharts, prospects, and machines": *Pa. Gaz.*, Jan. 2, 1749/50.

Turner's Work Shop and the Application was to drive a large Lathe for turning heavy Mortars of Lignum Vitae. The other is now here at Knightsbridge near London, on the Top of a House for manu-

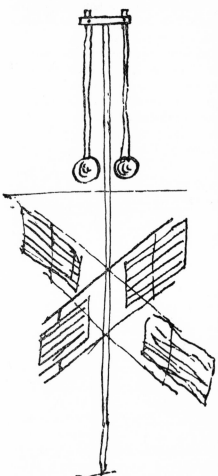

facturing painted Oil Cloths, and is used for grinding the Colours. The horizontal Wheel is in an octagon Tower with a Roof, but open all round the Sides; the Vanes are fix'd as in the Polish Mill; but to make it go, there are moveable Shutters, sufficient when properly plac'd to prevent the Wind acting on the coming Side of the Sails, and by leaving half the Tower open suffer it to act on the going side. This needs Attention and Care to shift the Shutters as the Wind changes and therefore seems not so good as the Polish Mill; nor is either of them so good as yours.

The Advantages of a Horizontal Windmill seem to me to be that the Building need not be so high as for the vertical one, therefore not so strong, therefore not so expensive; and it is always ready to receive the Wind from any Quarter, without the Trouble and Machinery necessary to bring the others about to face the Wind. But probably the others have the Advantage in some other respects which has continued them in general Use: their Force perhaps is greater.

I shall be glad to see your Contrivances for stopping or regulating its Motion. I dare say they are very ingenious. I once saw a very simple and as I thought it a very clever Method of regulating a Motion where the Power was applied unequally. It was this. From the Top of the upright Axis is hung two moveable Arms, with a Weight at the End of each. When the Axis began to turn, the Weights naturally receded farther from the Center rising higher at the same time; the greater the Force applied, the larger Circle they describ'd; and as the Force abated they sunk and describ'd smaller Circles in Proportion. By this Means the Excess of the Force applied was spent in raising the Balls and occasioning them to describe a greater Circle, whereby they pass'd thro' more Space in the same Time, instead of its occasioning more Revolutions of the Axis in the same Time: thus those Revolutions continued to be equable. And this applied to your Windmill, by lengthening the Axis upwards to give room for hanging the Weights might I imagine occasion an equality of Motion always regulating itself, tho' the Wind should be squally and unequal.

It must give you Pleasure to see the Contrivance of horizontal Wind mills become generally useful, and therefore you will excuse my mentioning a Manner of constructing them that almost every Farmer may execute without the help of any Workman, and which, or something like it, I have had an imperfect Account of as used in China.

Pumps in your ingenious Manner, tho' very proper for Mines, &c. when skilful Persons could readily be had to repair them, might neither suit the Purse nor be so easily kept in order by the common Countryman, and so the Use of them would not generally obtain for the Purpose of Watering Lands. Suppose then that in an open Field by the Side of a Brook or Pond, one of those Windmills is to be fix'd in the cheapest and easiest Manner to raise Water: A short Stake drove into the Ground might receive the lower Point of the Axis, its upper End might be supported by Cords made of Leatherwood Bark carried out on all Sides and fasten'd to Pins drove into the Earth: If the Arms are to be six it might be cut three square above and below where the Arms are applied to it, which might be of Saplins, the Buts a little flatted next to the Axis, and bound on; their small Ends being out every way to make the Circumference of the Circle. The Sails might be of Reed or Rush Mats extended on slight Frames and hung above and below by bits of Rope or Cord. An open Trough of plain Boards laid slanting up from the

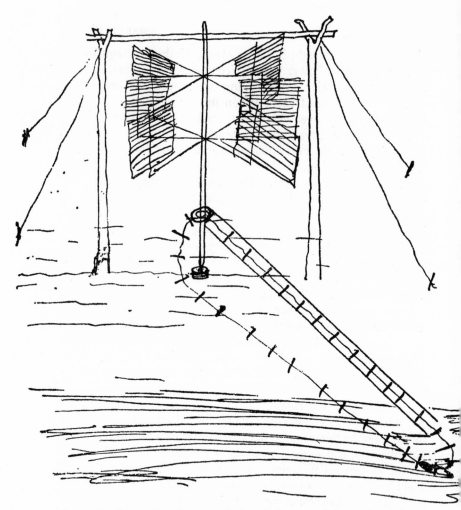

A very bad Drawing, but may help a little to explain my Meaning.[1]

1. More than a drawing is needed to explain what BF means, for his skill as an artist did not match his mechanical skill. The vanes appear to be hung on cords that act as pivots, but three of the cords are in the center of the vanes and three are eccentric. In fact they would all have to be eccentric, so that as the arm moved into the windward side of its revolution the vane would rotate to point into the wind. BF also omitted the "spring" that he spoke of in Gilpin's model; this was presumably a second cord, or some similar stop, that held the vane rigid on the arm when before the wind. Without these details, which may be implied but are certainly not mentioned, the salient characteristic of the windmill would be that it did not work.

Water, and a Number of little square Boards nearly fitting that Trough, fix'd at proper Distances to a small Rope in the Manner of a Chain Pump, and kept going by the Motion of the Axis, might bring the Water continually from the lower End of the Trough to the upper, and there discharge it into the Channel made to carry it away. If one Set of these Vanes does not raise it high enough, as they are cheap and easily made a second or third, or any Number might be used in different Parts of the Field one taking the Water from the Level where the other leaves it. Any Man with Hands might mend such a Machine when out of order. And in the Season of the Year when they would not be wanted to Work, they might easily be taken to pieces, and the Parts carried in under Shelter to preserve them from the Weather. This Idea I submit to your Consideration, and am with much Esteem, Your most humble Servant

B Franklin

[*The drawing on the opposite page follows here in* MS.]

To Humphry Marshall   ALS: Yale University Library

Sir,   London, March 18. 1770
   I was duly favoured with yours of Oct. 30, and glad to hear that some of the Colours on Experience were found useful. I show'd the Specimens you sent me to an ingenious skilful French Chemist, who has the Direction of the Royal Porcellane Manufacture at Seve near Paris, and he assured me that one of those white Earths would make a good Ingredient in that kind of Ware.[2]
   Our People in Philadelphia have done well in keeping, as you say they do, steady to their Agreements for Non Importation. The Duties on Paper, Glass and Colours, are now repealed; and if our Merchants continue their Resolutions another Year, there is good reason to believe all the rest will follow. Should any of the Merchants give way, and import, which I trust they will not, I hope the Country People will have the Good Sense and Spirit not to buy,

2. In his first surviving letter to Marshall BF had acknowledged specimens of colors that Marshall had sent him. See above, XVI, 173. The chemist to whom BF showed them—presumably during his visit to France the preceding summer —was Pierre Joseph Macquer (1718–84), a member of the Académie des sciences, who in 1760 had become director of the Royal Porcelain Factory at Sèvres. See Leslie J. M. Coleby, *The Chemical Studies of P. J. Macquer* (London, [1938]), pp. 96–110.

and then the others will soon be weary of Importing. Certainly we are under small Obligation to the Merchants here, who grow rich by our Folly,[3] and yet mov'd in this Affair but slowly; and under none to the Manufacturers, who refus'd to move at all. The Nation are all besotted with the Fancy that we cannot possibly do without them, and must of course comply at last. But if we encourage necessary Manufactures among ourselves, and refrain buying the Superfluities of other Countries, a few Years will make a surprizing Change in our favour, in the Plenty of real Money that must flow in among us, and the rising Value of our Estates. Immediately on the Receipt of your Letter, I ordered a Reflecting Telescope for you which was made accordingly. Dr. Fothergill had since desired me to add a Microscope and Thermometer, and will pay for the whole.[4] They will go with Captain Falconer.

I thank you for the Seeds, with which I have oblig'd some curious Friends. I am, Sir, Your most obedient Servant,   B Franklin

Mr Humphry Marshall.

Addressed: To / Mr Humphry Marshall / Chester County / per Capt. Falconer / with a Box

To [Charles Thomson]

ALS (copy):[5] Schaffer Library, Union College

This well-publicized letter arrived in America in May, at the height of the controversy over whether to relax or maintain the nonimportation agreements now that Parliament had repealed most, but not all, of the Townshend duties. An extract containing virtually the entire letter was

3. The past folly of buying British luxuries? the possible future folly of abandoning nonimportation prematurely?

4. Fothergill, writing to Marshall three days earlier, had given him the same assurance. William Darlington, *Memorials of John Bartram and Humphry Marshall* (Philadelphia, 1849), p. 501.

5. The copyist is unidentifiable, but the end of the letter, from "the least prospect" through the signature, has been added in a hand that is almost unquestionably Jared Sparks's; in that case an amanuensis must have copied the rest for him. He included the letter, without naming the recipient, in *A Collection of the Familiar Letters and Miscellaneous Papers of Benjamin Franklin* (Boston, 1833), pp. 224–7, and from this text we have silently corrected errors in the MS copy.

sent to Boston and promptly printed and reprinted there, while Thomson was using the original to good purpose in Philadelphia. On May 15 Galloway laid before the Assembly his letter from Franklin of March 21, printed below, and it too had great effect on rallying the waverers to stand fast. Although the rally was short-lived, Franklin was credited with it on one side of the Atlantic and blamed for it on the other; in Britain his intervention brought on him, as might be expected, the accusation of betraying his position as an officer of the crown.[6]

Dear Sir   London March 18th. 1770

Your very judicious Letter of Novemr. 26th. being communicated by me to some Member of Parliament, was handed about among them, so that it was sometime before I got it again into my Hands. It had due Weight with several, and was of considerable Use. You will see that I printed it at length in the London Chronicle with the Merchants' Letter.[7] When the American Affairs came to be debated in the House of Commons, the Majority, notwithstanding all the Weight of ministerial Influence, was only 62 for continuing the whole last Act; and would not have been so large, nay, I think the Repeal would have been carried, but that the Ministry were persuaded by Governor Bernard and some lying Letters said to be from Boston, that the Associations not to import were all breaking to Pieces, that America was in the greatest Distress for Want of the Goods, that we could not possibly subsist any longer without them, and must of course submit to any Terms Parliament should think fit to impose upon us. This with the idle Notion of the Dignity and Sovereignty of Parliament, which they are so fond of, and imagine will be endanger'd by any farther Concessions, prevailed I know with many to vote with the Ministry, who otherwise, on Account of the Commerce, wish to see the Difference accommodated.[8] But though both the Duke of Grafton and Lord

6. See Crane, *Letters to the Press*, pp. 209–12, and the extensive references there cited.

7. For Thomson's letter see above, xvi, 237–40; the letter printed with it in the *London Chron.* of March 1–3, 1770, was from Philadelphia merchants.

8. North opened the debate in the Commons on March 5 on whether to repeal the Townshend Acts in their entirety or to retain the duty on tea. He expressed his own preference for total repeal, but then gave the ministerial argument, much as BF sketches it, for maintaining the single duty as an assertion of the right to tax. Cobbett, *Parliamentary History*, xvi, 853–5. The "lying letters" to which BF refers were presumably those discussed in the *London*

North were and are in my Opinion rather inclined to satisfy us, yet the Bedford Party are so violent against us, and so prevalent in the Council, that more moderate Measures could not take Place. This Party never speak of us but with evident Malice; Rebels and Traitors are the best Names they can afford us, and I believe they only wish for a colourable Pretence and Occasion of ordering the Souldiers to make a Massacre among us.

On the other Hand the Rockingham and Shelburne People, with Lord Chatham's Friends, are disposed to favour us if they were again in Power, which at present they are not like to be; tho' they, too, would be for keeping up the Claim of parliamentary Sovereignty, but without exercising it in any Mode of Taxation. Besides these, we have for sincere Friends and Wellwishers the Body of Dissenters, generally, throughout England, with many others, not to mention Ireland and all the rest of Europe, who from various Motives join in applauding the Spirit of Liberty, with which we have claimed and insisted on our Privileges, and wish us Success, but whose Suffrage cannot have much Weight in our Affairs.

The Merchants here were at length prevailed on to present a Petition, but they moved slowly, and some of them I thought reluctantly; perhaps from a Despair of Success, the City not being much in favour with the Court at present.[9] The manufacturing Towns absolutely refused to move at all; some pretending to be offended with our attempting to manufacture for ourselves; others saying that they had Employment enough, and that our Trade was of little Importance to them, whether we continued or refused it. Those who began a little to feel the Effects of our forbearing to purchase, were persuaded to be quiet by the ministerial People; who gave out that certain Advices were

---

Chron. of Feb. 24–27, 1770; they insisted that the rise of between 25% and 90% in the price of British imports in Boston would soon dissolve the Massachusetts nonimportation agreements. Partial repeal, according to reports from America received in early February, would end all the agreements: Albert Matthews, ed., "Letters of Dennys DeBerdt," Colonial Soc. of Mass. *Publications*, XIII (1912), 396, 398.

9. The petition for repeal of the Townshend Acts, which had been formulated at a meeting of merchants reported in the *London Chron.*, Jan. 30–Feb. 1, 1770, occasioned the debate in the Commons on March 5. The substance of the petition may be found in *The Va. Mag. of History and Biography*, XII (1905), 164–6.

receiv'd of our beginning to break our Agreements; of our Attempts to manufacture proving all abortive and ruining the Undertakers; of our Distress for Want of Goods, and Dissentions among ourselves, which promised the total Defeat of all such Kind of Combinations, and the Prevention of them for the future, if the Government were not urged imprudently to repeal the Duties. But now that it appears from late and authentic Accounts, that Agreements continue in full Force, that a Ship is actually return'd from Boston to Bristol with Nails and Glass, (Articles that were thought of the utmost Necessity,) and that the Ships that were waiting here for the Determination of Parliament, are actually returning to North America in thier Ballast;[1] the Tone of the Manufacturers begins to change, and there is no doubt, that if we are steady and persevere in our Resolutions, these People will soon begin a Clamor that much Pains has hitherto been used to stifle.

In short, it appears to me, that if we do not now persist in this Measure till it has had its full Effect, it can never again be used on any future Occasion with the least prospect of Success, and that if we do persist another year, we shall never afterwards have occasion to use it. With sincere regards I am, Dear Sir, Your obedient Servant,

B. FRANKLIN

From Edward Nairne[2]   ALS: Historical Society of Pennsylvania

Sir: Cornhill March 19. 1770

When You did me the pleasure of calling on me last week, I mention'd to You that I had been trying to freeze water in which dif-

1. The *London Chron.* reported on March 10–13, 1770, that a ship had returned to Bristol with a considerable part of its cargo, which had been consigned to Boston and refused there. In its previous issue the paper reported that ten merchant captains from New York, who had been waiting all winter for repeal of the duty on tea in order to take on British goods to the value of some £300,000, had now refused all such goods in accordance with their orders, were returning to New York in ballast, and were advertising for artisans who might be attracted to settle in America.

2. The electrician and instrument-maker, an old acquaintance of BF; see above, x, 171 n. His letter is the first indication in these volumes that his experimental interests extended beyond electricity. But he had already acquired a transatlantic reputation, for at about this time he was elected, presumably at BF's initiative, to membership in the APS. Thomas Coombe to his father, Sept. 11, 1770, Hist. Soc. of Pa.

ferent quantities of Sea Salt had been dissolv'd, You then said You wish'd I had tasted the Ice, for it was thought to be fresh; At that time I had not tasted it, but since have tried the following Experiment; I took two ounces (averdupoise) of common Sea Salt and dissolv'd it in three pints and a half wine measure of Thames water, which I think is the proportion of Salt in Sea water according to Mr. Canton.[3] I then put some of this salted water in a wide Stone dish about the depth of an inch and set it out on the leads, in hopes it woud be froze by morning, the next morning it was froze about the thickness of $\frac{1}{2}$ an inch. I then took out the Ice and put it in a seive and wash'd it in a large Cistern of Thames Water, and afterwards let the water drain from it. Then I put the Ice in a Bason and kept it in a warm Room till it was dissolvd, and on tasting the dissolvd Ice I found it was so fresh, that if I had not put the Salt to the water my Self I Shoud not have suspected there had ever been a grain of Salt mixd with the water. I have sent You three Vials, in that markd A, is the dissolv'd Ice. In the Vial B is some of the same salted water that was *not* set out to freeze. In the Vial C is some of the water that was left in the dish that I took the Ice out of, (which appears to the taste to be considerably salter than that in the Vial B). I have tried the experiment twice and find the result exactly the same, the Thermometer out of doors between 7 and 8 o Clock Yesterday and this morning which were the times I washd the Ice was at 25 degrees of Farenheits. If You think this Experiment not conclusive Your objections would greatly oblidge Your most Obedient Humble Servant   EDWD. NAIRNE

P. S. The Salted water has been filtrated but the dissolvd Ice has not been filtrated.

To Dr. Franklin

Addressed: To / Dr: Franklin

To Joseph Galloway   AL (incomplete): the Rosenbach Foundation

The movement to secure total repeal of the Townshend duties failed in the House of Commons on March 5, when the government succeeded in having the duty on tea retained as proof that Parliament still had the right

3. For John Canton's experiments on the compressibility of rain and sea water see above, XI, 245–6; XII, 220 n.

to tax. This failure was more than a routine setback for Franklin. It forced him to face the question of whether the whole policy of nonimportation should be abandoned, now that it had achieved a substantial success, or continued in the hope of complete success and at the risk of a complete rupture. The answer that he reached, as this letter indicates, was to continue at all risk. He was now less concerned with restoring harmony within the empire than with encouraging colonial economic, and by inference political, autonomy. He had no doubt of America's manufacturing potential, and he saw British society as distracted to the point where civil war was a real possibility. In these circumstances he wanted the colonies to take a strong line with the mother country. Whether or not he expected Galloway to agree is a matter of conjecture, if only because the letter is incomplete; but the way in which he couched his arguments suggests that he may already have been unsure of the younger man's support. In the short run, however, he obtained it; Galloway lost no time in laying the letter before the Assembly.

Dear Sir,   London, March 21. 1770
    In my last[4] I acknowledg'd the Receipt of your Favour of Nov. 8. since which I had no Line from you.
    American Affairs which we were made to expect would be brought on early in the Session, have been postpon'd from time to time, chiefly, I imagine, from Irresolution in the Ministry, who were perplext with different and opposite Accounts of the State of Things in our Country, and knew not which to rely on, or what Steps to take in consequence. For some time there was nearly an equal Ballance in the Cabinet between those who were for repealing only the Duties mentioned in Lord H's circular Letter,[5] and those who were for giving America compleat Satisfaction, and getting rid of the Dispute forever. But when the Duke of Grafton, General Conway and Lord Cambden retired or were turned out, the Bedford Party prevailed who are violently against us; and on some false Advices from Boston, communicated as is said by Govr. Bernard, that all our Agreements were dissolved or dissolving, and the Trade opened again, the Business was brought on, and the Re-

4. Of Jan. 11, above.
5. Hillsborough's letter of May 15, 1769 (*N.Y. Col. Docs.*, VIII, 164–5), in which he assured the colonial governors that the ministry did not intend to levy taxes on America for revenue, and would move in the next session for repeal of some specified duties.

peal, of those Duties only, voted in the House of Commons.[6] Gov. Pownall moved for the Repeal of the whole, and supported his Motion by a very able Speech;[7] but on a Division it was carried against his Motion, in a pretty full House, by a Majority of 62 only, which, the great Weight of ministerial Influence being considered, shows that the independent Body of the Nation is rather favourably dispos'd towards us, and desirous of being on good Terms with us. Three Days after the Vote, a Ship arriv'd at Bristol, from Boston, with a return'd Cargo of those very Goods that Country was suppos'd most to want, and least able to subsist without; bringing also authentic Advices, that the Resolutions of Non-Importation continu'd in full Force, rather increasing than diminishing in strength, both in that and all the other Provinces. This, with the sudden Preparation of all the Ships to depart without Goods, and the actual Departure of several, has a little stagger'd the Ministry again, and Hints have been thrown out that possibly the whole Act may yet be repealed:[8] But finally it seems to be concluded to let the Matter rest where it is for the present, and make Trial whether the Americans will not, as some pretend they will, be contented with what is done, submit to pay the other Duties, and go on with the Trade as usual.

Supposing the Session should end without repealing the Duty on Tea with the hateful Preamble of the Act that gives it,[9] I imagine it will come under Consideration on your Side the Water, what Conduct to hold on the Occasion. Probably some will be for giving way a little, taking what is done as a Concession on the part of Government, and willing to show an equal Disposition to be Friends on our part. Others perhaps, esteeming this partial Repeal as no Favour to us (and indeed it appears by Lord H's Letter, that those 3 Duties were to be taken off merely as being anti-commercial and prejudicial to the Trade of Britain, not as inconsistent with our

6. Here and elsewhere in the letter BF is repeating the substance of what he had written to Thomson above, March 18. For the background of these comments see the annotation of that letter.

7. See Cobbett, *Parliamentary History*, XVI, 855–70.

8. "It is reported that all American matters will shortly be settled in a manner satisfactory to all parties." *London Chron.*, March 17–21, 1770.

9. 7 Geo. III, c. 46, the act imposing the Townshend duties. The preamble was "hateful" because it clearly stated that the purpose of the act was to raise a revenue in America, in order to support a colonial civil list.

Rights) will be for persisting; and some may be for going farther. If my Opinion were asked, it should be to adhere firmly to our Agreements till the End for which they were entred into was *fully* obtained. But as yet I would not advise *extending* the Conditions (as the Boston People lately attempted) on which the Trade should be renewed;[1] tho' I am still for keeping up our full Claim, which on some future Occasion may be peremptorily insisted on, and I think will finally be obtained. Lord H. and the Bedford Faction have confidently always predicted that our Agreements would not hold, that the known Self-interestedness of Merchants would soon overcome their pretended Patriotism, that the Distresses of the People for want of British Goods, without which they could not subsist, would compell an Importation; that the different Colonies were a Rope of Sand, and could not long hold together for any one purpose; and that a little Firmness shewn by Government here, would infallibly break us all to pieces. On this Principle they have acted. If we give way, they and their Friends will exult; their Judgment and Foresight will be admired; they will be extolled as able Statesmen, worthy to hold the Reins in governing America, and be established in their Administration; which, as they are far from being our Friends, may be attended with very disagreable Consequences. And we, if we break thro' the Agreement, can never promise ourselves any Effect from like Agreements hereafter: For it will always be said here, Be firm and their Associations will come to nothing. Therefore I should be for adhering at all Events; and the rather, as I am assured, that the Manufacturers cannot another Year be kept quiet by all the Artifices of our Adversaries, as they begin now seriously to feel the Effects of their late Credulity. The British Merchants too, will be stimulated by the *continued* Stop of Business, to act with a little more Vigour than they have shown on this Occasion; tho' to do them Justice, I believe their Backwardness was partly owing to their Unwillingness to be obliged to the present Ministry; and their little Weight when they did move, to the unfavourable

1. At a meeting in October, 1769, the Bostonians voted to maintain their embargo until not only the Townshend duties but all others for raising a revenue in America were repealed. When the New York and Philadelphia merchants failed to support them, however, they retreated from this position. Charles M. Andrews, *The Boston Merchants and the Non-importation Movement* (New York, [1968]), p. 73.

Light in which the whole City now stands at Court.[2] This Steadiness on our part is in my Opinion the more adviseable, as there are few here who are not reasonable enough to allow, that even were there no Dispute, it is very justifiable in us to refuse buying if we find we cannot well afford it, and to manufacture what we can for ourselves, so that no general National Resentment is to be apprehended from it. And this Stoppage in the Trade, if it should continue longer, will have this good Effect among us, to assist several new Manufactures in striking Root so as afterwards to support themselves in a flourishing Condition. Great Sums of Money too, for our Produce, will come into the Country and remain there to the Improvement of our Estates, and Increase of their Value; so that tho' a few Traders may be hurt at present, not having English Goods in such Quantities as heretofore to sell; yet in a little Time, those who cannot turn to other Businesses, will have their Shops and Stores replenished with our own Commodities; while their Customers, grown richer by Industry and Frugality, tho' they do not buy so much, will be enabled to make better Pay for what they do buy. (And what is more to be considered and valued than everything else, our Rights will finally be established, and no future Attempts will be hazarded here to deprive us of them.) If the Value of our annual Produce were computed, and how much of it is parted with for the Superfluities of Britain and the East and West Indies, the Sum would appear astonishing, and convince everybody that nothing can contribute to increase more rapidly the Wealth and Prosperity of our Country, than a total Forbearing of those Luxuries, or Providing them within ourselves: For as our Produce consists of the Necessaries of Life, which other Countries must have, and pay us for in Money if we refuse their Superfluities, our Stock of Currency would soon be increas'd to a greater Sum than is even wish'd of Paper Money, and from the Plenty of the former we should have little Occasion to sue here, or to the Proprietor, for Permission to make the latter.

The Publick Affairs of this Nation are at present in great Disorder, Parties run very high, and have abus'd each other so thoroughly that there is not now left an unbespatter'd Character in the Kingdom of any Note or Importance; and they have so expos'd one another's Roguery and Rapacity, that the Respect for Superiors, Trust in Parliament, and Regard to Government, is among the

2. Because of the Londoners' support of Wilkes.

generality of the People totally lost; for even the King himself is treated in Publick Papers with a rude Freedom hitherto unexampled. How far the Opposition intend to proceed (many of whom I know to be strong Republicans) or to what Lengths they will go, it is impossible to say, or what the Event may be. To such as reflect, that when a Quarrel is once on foot, even those who are at first *least in the wrong*, are often provok'd to do something that makes them *most so*; and that mutual Injuries are apt to increase Animosity till the worst of Remedies becomes the only one, the Sword: I say, to such the present Prospect is very gloomy; for in the early Part of Charles the first's Reign, there was perhaps for several Years less reason to apprehend a Civil War than there seems to be at present. I send you Samples [*remainder missing.*]

Jos. Galloway Esqr

From the New Jersey Assembly Committee
of Correspondence   LS: American Philosophical Society

Sir   Burlington March 27th. 1770.

In our last[3] we inform'd you of a Bill, that pass'd the House and Council for amending the practice of the Law which the Governor did not then think proper to assent to, and directed you not to solicit the Royal Assent to a Bill pass'd and sent over in 1765; In this Session a Bill has been agreed upon by the whole Legislature, Intitled "An Act to provide a more effectual remedy against excessive Costs in the recovery of Debts &c".[4] As this Bill will, we expect be opposed, perhaps by some holding offices, not so much that it will abridge the Fees of the office, altho' it will be made the pretence, but will affect them as practising Attorneys, We request you will use your utmost Interest in preventing such opposition proving effectual, for which purpose we have by the direction of the House, given you the earliest intelligence. We are very anxious to hear the

3. Above, XVI, 253–6.
4. See *ibid.*, p. 254 n; *Votes, N.J.*, March, 1770 (Burlington, 1770), pp. 5, 6, 23; 1 *N.J. Arch.*, XVIII, 170; Edgar J. Fisher, *New Jersey as a Royal Province, 1738 to 1776* (New York, 1911), pp. 256–62.

119

resolutions of Parliament upon the Acts laying Duties &ca.[5] And the determinations of his Majesty's Ministers upon the Laws, we recommended to you in our last, and are, Sir, Your very Humble Servants[6]

> HENDK. FISHER   CORTD: SKINNER
> EBENEZ MILLER
> AARON LEAMING
> ABRM. HEWLINGS
> JOS. SMITH

Dr. Franklin.

Addressed: To / Benjamin Franklin Esqr. / Agent for the Colony of New Jersey, / London.

Endorsed: Committee of N Jersey Ass[embly] March 27. 1770

To [Joseph Smith?[7]]

ALS (postscript only): William C. Coles, Moorestown, N.J. (1954)

P.S.   April 12, [1770]

Yesterday I attended the Board of Trade and the Objections to the Bergen Act were repeated by my Lord Hillsborough, viz. that it related to private Property; in a Course of Trial at Law, which was stopt by the Act. I alledg'd that it was only a supplementary Act for compleating a Business directed by a former Act and partly executed, which former Act had received the Royal Approbation. His Lordship answered, that in the former there was the Consent of all Parties; but to this Act, one Side not only did not consent, but had opposed and entred a Caveat against it, notwithstanding which it had been passed. I mentioned that the Opposer had approv'd and solicited the former Act, and this was only to finish, &c. To which it was answered, that in this the Commissioners were totally

---

5. John Pownall at the request of Lord Hillsborough sent a circular letter to the governors of the American colonies, April 14, 1770, enclosing a printed copy of 10 Geo. III, c. 17, which partially repealed the Townshend duties. See 1 *N.J. Arch.*, X, 191.

6. The members of the Committee are identified above, XVI, 256 n.

7. The letter was certainly intended for the New Jersey Committee of Correspondence, of which Smith was acting as secretary; BF's tone implies to us that he was writing to an individual.

changed, it was a new Sett. On the whole I endeavoured to clear the Legislature from any Suspicion of Injustice or Partiality, they having had only the Publick Peace in View, &c &c. But it seem'd determin'd to report the Act as unfit for his Majesty's Approbation.

The Paper-money Act then came on, when I was told that an Act of the same kind pass'd by Governor Colden in New York had been considered by His Majesty's Law Servants who had reported it repugnant to the Act of Parliament inasmuch as it made the Bills a legal Tender to the Treasurer in Discharge of Publick Debts, whereas the Statute says they shall be a legal Tender in no Case whatever. I urg'd that it was impossible to suppose that the Parliament intended to leave the Governments at Liberty to refuse their own Bills; that this Act of New Jersey only oblig'd the Loan-Offices that issued the Bills to receive them again when tender in Discharge of the Mortgages on which they had been issued, &c. On which I was cut short with this, That the Board could not judge of the Intention of an Act of Parliament but by its Words, and if a Colony Act was against the Words of an Act of Parliament, that was sufficient to obstruct its being allowed. However, I was told, that it was their Lordship's Purpose to report the Matter specially, viz. That this Act of New Jersey contain'd a Clause similar to that in the Act of New York, on Account of which the latter had been repealed; and so submit it to his Majesty. Thus ended that Matter.[8]

Mr. Charles, I understand, is urged by Lord Dunmore, to petition the Parliament to explain that Act.[9] He has been unwilling to do it without express Orders from his Province, as our Business in the Confirmation of Laws is constitutionally with the Crown only; and applying to Parliament to obtain Leave of the King to pass Colony Acts, would be a Novelty, and possibly be hereafter attended with disagreable Consequences: And the Ministry, who procured the Act, were the properest to procure its Explanation. I think he was right. He has however, as I understand, lately received such Orders, and will now petition, in order if he succeeds,

8. For the two acts in question see above, XVI, 254, 265–8, and *Board of Trade Jour.*, 1768–75, p. 184.

9. Robert Charles (1706?–70) was agent for New York. John Murray, fourth Earl of Dunmore (1732–1809), had been appointed governor of New York the previous December to succeed Sir Henry Moore, and took up his position in the following October. Only a few weeks after that he was promoted to succeed Lord Botetourt as governor of Virginia.

to obtain an Allowance of the Act passed by Sir Henry Moore, previous to that by Governor Colden. Should this be done, the Removing of the Objection with regard to that Act will operate in our favour likewise; and if done before ours is actually repealed, we may still obtain the Royal Assent. But I have little Expectation of it, as I know that Paper Currency in general are much against the Grain here.

I [mov'd] for their Lordship's favourable Reporting two former Laws, that for Septennial Assemblies and that for giving Representatives to the Counties of Morris Cumberland and Sussex, which they were pleased to say should be taken into speedy Consideration. I mention'd too the Desire of Assembly, that the Act for amending the Practice of the Law might not as yet be pass'd upon, as they had in Contemplation the forming one that might be better adapted to the purpose of which Notice was taken.[1] And I shall continue my best Attention to these Affairs of your Province on all Occasion.

Mr. Jackson is now appointed Counsellor to the Board of Trade.[2] All Colony Acts are submitted to the Examination of that Officer; and as he well understands our Affairs, and is a Friend to America, I hope we shall not hereafter be pestered with ignorant frivolous Objections to our Laws, as heretofore has sometimes been the Case.   BF.

I send you inclosed Govr Pownall's Speech in Parliament, when he mov'd for the total Repeal of the last Duty Act; only 20 were printed. Also his State of the Case of America as to the Military Power there.[3]

Endorsed: Letter from Dr. Franklin April 12.

1. BF is here responding to the Committee's letter of Dec. 7 above, XVI, 254.
2. Richard Jackson's appointment was not formally announced to the Board until April 30: *Board of Trade Jour.*, 1768–75, p. 185.
3. The first was Pownall's speech of March 5, reported in Cobbett, *Parliamentary History*, XVI, 855–70. The second was presumably his privately printed *State of the Constitution of the Colonies*, although only a part of that pamphlet dealt with the military power; see above, XVI, 302–3.

To Samuel Cooper[4]   ALS: British Museum

Dear Sir,   London, April 14. 1770

I suppose Govr. Pownall acquaints you with what has pass'd this Session relating to our American Affairs:[5] All Europe is attentive to the Dispute between Britain and the Colonies; and I own I have a Satisfaction in seeing that our Part is taken every where; because I am persuaded that that Circumstance will not be without its Effect here in our Favour. At the same time the malignant Pleasure other Powers take in British Divisions, may convince us on both sides of the Necessity of our Uniting. In France they have translated and printed the principal Pieces that have been written on the American Side of the Question; and as French is the political Language of Europe, it has communicated an Acquaintance with our Affairs very extensively.[6] Mr. Beaumont, a famous Advocate of Paris, the Defender of the Family of Calas, wrote the *Reflexions d'un Etranger desinteressé*, which I send you.[7] The Manuscript is an original Letter from a Gentleman (of Note I am told) as far off as the Austrian Silesia, who, being concern'd for us, wrote it to the Parliament, directing it to the late Speaker. The Speaker read only the first Side, was offended at the Freedom and Impertinence (as he call'd it) and return'd the Letter to the Office refusing to pay the

4. The minister of Brattle Street Church, Boston. See above, IV, 69 n, and his correspondence with BF in 1769.

5. Pownall's extant letters to Cooper are printed in Frederick Griffin, *Junius Discovered...* (Boston and London, 1854). These letters, like many of BF's to Cooper and other Boston correspondents, fell into British hands in 1775 and are now in the British Museum.

6. John Dickinson's *Farmer's Letters* and BF's *Examination* and "Positions to be Examined" were published in France; see Alfred O. Aldridge, "Jacques Barbeu-Dubourg, a French Disciple of Franklin," APS *Proc.*, XCV (1951), 362–3.

7. For Beaumont see above, XVI, 205. His *Reflexions* were printed for BF by William Strahan, and extracts in English were published in the *Pa. Gaz.*, May 31, 1770, and the London *Public Advertiser*, July 23, 1770; they appear to have been, according to Verner Crane, "publicity hand-outs from Craven street." *Letters to the Press*, p. xlix. Crane conjectures that the two extracts may have been translated by BF (*ibid.*, p. 294), and we have examined them with care. They are similar but far from identical. Each shows some touches that are reminiscent of BF and some that are not, and it is impossible to say that one extract is closer to his style than the other. He could have translated either or both, but we have no evidence whatever that he did.

123

Postage.[8] Accept it as a Curiosity. I send you also a late Edition of Molineux's Case of Ireland, with a new Preface shrewdly written.[9] Our Part is warmly taken by the Irish in general, there being in many Points a Similarity in our Cases. My Respects to Mr. Bowdoin, and believe me ever, Dear Sir, Yours affectionately

B FRANKLIN

Revd. Dr. Cooper

To Timothy Folger
ALS: American Philosophical Society

Dear Kinsman   London, April 14. 1770

Enclos'd with this, I send you a Map of the Island of St. John's made from actual Survey, with a particular Map of one of the Shares, which the Owner desires to have settled, and will give you any Terms you please.[1] In haste, I am, Yours affectionately

B FRANKLIN

Capt. Folger

Endorsed: Dr. Benjn. Franklin's letter to Timothy Folger

8. Sir John Cust, the irate Speaker, had died the previous January, presumably soon after returning the letter unpaid for. Hence, instead of going to Parliament, as the writer intended, it went via the Post Office and BF to Cooper. It was in French, dated Nov. 22, 1769, at Orlau in Austrian Silesia (now Orlova, Czechoslovakia), and signed de Bludowski. We are unable to identify the author, or explain why he felt moved to address Parliament on the colonial question. The Stamp Act, he argued, had destroyed the old bond between Britain and her colonies, and the only long-term hope of keeping them in the empire was to give them greater autonomy and representation in the Westminster Parliament. BF must have forwarded the letter less for its argument, which though cogent was scarcely original, than as an example of concern in a distant corner of Europe.

9. William Molyneux, *The Case of Ireland's Being Bound by Acts of Parliament in England Stated...* (London, 1770). This work, first published in 1698, was one which BF had been reading earlier in 1770; see above, p. 14 n. Molyneux's purpose had been to demonstrate Ireland's legislative independence of England, but his argument when he published it had been rejected by the House of Commons. *DNB.* It had been specifically denied in the Declaratory Act of 1719 (6 Geo. I, c. 5), and had gained no acceptance in the intervening years; BF must have known that, whatever its usefulness in America, it was an old and broken reed in Britain.

1. Folger had been interested in acquiring land on St. John's (now Prince Edward Island) since 1763, when he had addressed to Sir Jeffrey Amherst a

To Deborah Franklin ALS: Munson-William-Proctor Institute

My dear Child   London, April 20. 1770
   This will be delivered to you by Miss Farquarson and Miss
Smith, the one bred a Miliner, the other a Mantuamaker, who, by
the Advice and Consent of their Friends, go to Philadelphia, with
an Intention of following their respective Businesses there. They
are Persons of good Character, and very well recommended to me;
therefore I recommend them warmly to you and my dear Daughter,
desiring you would show them all Civility as Strangers, and afford
them your best Advice and Countenance in the Prosecution of
their Design, which will greatly oblige Your affectionate Husband
                                                                     B FRANKLIN
Mrs. Franklin

From [Jean-Baptiste] LeRoy[2]

ALS: American Philosophical Society

                                        De Paris ce 22 Avril [1770]
Il y a des Siecles que je n'ai eu de vos nouvelles Monsieur cependant
vous savez combien elles m'intéressent. J'attends avec impatience
le moment de nos fêtes pour le mariage de M. Le Dauphin[3] parce-
que jespere bien qu'elles nous ameneront des Anglois et qu'il y en
aura quelques uns qui m'apporteront quelques lettres de vous.
Vous ne doutez pas du plaisir que j'aurai à les recevoir. Je comptois
vous aller rendre une petite visite ce printemps mais comme jamais
presqu'on ne fait ses volontés dans ce monde des affaires de famille
que la perte que j'ai faite ont entrainées m'en ont empêché. Cependant si mes voeux sont remplis l'année ne se passera pas sans que je
fasse un tour en Angleterre, et j'espere bien que les affaires d'amer-

---

petition drafted by BF for a grant to himself and other inhabitants of Nantucket.
See above, X, 429–31; XI, 187. The map must have been that published in 1765
by Rocque, Jefferys & Faden of London, based on Capt. Samuel Holland's
survey. What is probably the same map, reduced, is printed in *Acts Privy
Coun., Col.*, V, facing p. 602.
   2. See above, X, 61 n, and later volumes.
   3. The Dauphin, who four years later became Louis XVI, married Marie
Antoinette on May 16, 1770.

ique vous empêcheront d'y retourner et qu'aussi j'aurai le plaisir de vous y retrouver. J'ai prié dernierement M. Francis de vous faire parvenir un Exemplaire de L'Ouvrage de mon frère qui contient les détails des principes et de la construction de la montre marine. Vous avez pu la voir annoncé dans les nouvelles publiques. Je ne puis vous dire combien j'ai été fâché de ne vous l'avoir pas envoyé plutôt. Je comptois sur des gens qui devoient aller en Angleterre et qui m'ont fait faux bond mais je l'ai bien recommande à M. Francis et j'espere qu'il vous le fera tenir bientôt. Je crois que vous serez content de cet ouvrage qui n'est autre chose que le memoire de mon frère, qui a remporté le prix de L'Académie, vous le trouverez un peu plus clair que l'Ouvrage de M. Harrison.[4] Je voulois vous envoyer cet hyver celui de l'Abbé Galliani sur le commerce des bleds qui a éxcité ici une grande rumeur parmi les œconomistes[5] mais je n'ai pu trouver dans le moment où c'étoit une nouveauté une occa-

4. Jacques Batailhe de Francès (*c.* 1724–88) was secretary to the French Ambassador, the Duc du Chatelet-Lomont, and later became chargé d'affaires; he appears frequently in Wilmarth S. Lewis and Warren H. Smith, eds., *Horace Walpole's Correspondence with Madame du Deffand*... (6 vols., New Haven, 1939), III, *passim.* The book that LeRoy entrusted to him had recently been crowned by the Académie des sciences; it was Pierre LeRoy's *Mémoire sur la meilleure manière de mesurer le tems en mer*.., printed with Jean Dominique Cassini's *Voyage fait par ordre du roi en 1768, pour éprouver les montres marines inventées par M. LeRoy*... (2 vols., Paris, 1770). Francès eventually got the book to BF through an intermediary; see [Michael] Francklin to BF below, June 22, 1770.

Pierre LeRoy (1717–85) claimed to have invented a chronometer accurate enough to determine a ship's longitude at sea. John Harrison (1693–1776) was his more famous British counterpart, whose instrument eventually received a prize from the government of £20,000; see above, VII, 208–10. LeRoy is probably alluding to *The Principles of Mr. Harrison's Time-Keeper, with Plates of the Same*... (London, 1767), which Harrison wrote with the help of Nevil Maskelyne. Among BF's papers in the APS is a short printed pamphlet dated 1770, *The Case of Mr. John Harrison*; it describes the inventor's long struggle to obtain the prize first offered by Parliament in 1714.

5. Ferdinando Galiani (1728–88), an Italian writer and economist, was secretary to the Neapolitan Ambassador to France, 1759–69, and popular with the Encyclopedists. His *Dialogues sur le commerce des bleds* was published in 1770 under a spurious London imprint, as was often done with controversial works, and has recently been reprinted: *Dialogues entre M. Marquis de Roquemaure, et Ms. le Chevalier Zanobi: the Autograph Manuscript of the DIALOGUES SUR LE COMMERCE DES BLEDS Diplomatically Edited...by Philip Koch* (Frankfurt-am-Main, [1968]).

sion de vous le faire passer. Depuis j'ai imaginé qu'il vous étoit tombé entre les mains cependant si vous ne le connoissiez pas un mot et vous l'aurez. Monsieur Franklin ne pourra jamais me fournir autant d occasions que je le désirerais de pouvoir faire ici quelque chose qui lui soit agréable.

Ne m'en voulez pas si je n'ai pas encore revu la Traduction de votre ouvrage que M. Du Bourg a fait faire par un religieux. Je n'en ai pas encore entendu parler.[6]

Je ne sache ici rien de nouveau dans les sciences qui puissent intéresser votre curiosité, mais dans les lettres vous saurez que marchant de loin sur les traces des anglois les gens de lettres ont fait une souscription pour ériger une Statue à Voltaire *de son vivant*, c'est Pigal chez qui nous avons été voir le mausolée du m[aréch]al de Saxe qui est chargé de le faire, il doit partir incessamment pour Fernet pour faire le portrait de ce grand homme. Ce sera le premier Exemple de pareille chose parmi nous on dit, qu'il y a commencement à tout je le souhaite, mais enfin cette marque publique de la reconnoissance des gens éclairés de la nation et qui doivent tant à Voltaire a été arretée Mardy dernier dans une grande assemblée.[7] Ce qu'il y a de singulier c'est que rien n'est encore plus incertain que le lieu où on la placera. Nous tenons toujours par un coin à la barbarie. Je vous ai mandé Monsieur tout ce qui peut vous intéresser. Dans peu de Jours il ne sera question que de Feux d'artifices et de Fêtes. Je voudrois bien que vous fussiez un peu moins Philosophe j'espererois qu'elles vous rameneroient parmi nous. Voici je crois le temps de l'election des membres étrangers de la Societé Royale. Je

6. This is scarcely surprising, because *Œuvres de M. Franklin...* did not appear until 1773. Although Barbeu-Dubourg's name appears on the title page, the actual translator was Abbé Jean Baptiste l'Écuy (1740–1834). See Antoine A. Barbier, *Dictionnaire des ouvrages anonymes...* (3rd ed.; 4 vols., Paris, 1872–79), III, 673–4; Berthe Ravary, *Jean-Baptiste l'Écuy, dernier abbé général des Prémontrés en France...* (Paris, [1955]).

7. At the end of a bibulous dinner party at the Neckers on Tuesday, April 17, the plan had been unveiled and wildly approved of commissioning a nude statue of Voltaire from Jean-Baptiste Pigalle (1714–85), the leading sculptor of his day. The idea of nudity bothered the aged philosopher and delighted his many enemies. But Pigalle persisted (his only concession was a scroll that does duty for a fig leaf), and the statue now stands in the Bibliothèque de l'Institut in Paris—"oeuvre unique dans l'oeuvre de Pigalle, unique aussi dans toute la statuaire du XVIIIe siècle." Samuel Rocheblave, *Jean-Baptiste Pigalle* (Paris, [1919]), p. 277; for further details see pp. 277–88.

n'ai pas besoin de vous recommander mon frère le Medecin. J'espere bien et je me flatte que vous et M. le Ch[evalie]r Pringle voudrez bien engager vos amis à lui être favorable. Je compte écrire au premier Jour au Dr. Matty et à quelques autres amis que j'ai dans la Société Royale pour leur faire la même priere.[8] Il est bien temps de finir une si longue lettre en vous assurrant de tous les sentimens de l'estime et de l'amitié les plus sinceres avec lesquelles je suis et je serai toute ma vie Votre très humble et très obéissant serviteur

LE ROY

J'espere que vous voudrez bien ne pas m'oublier auprès de notre digne ami M. Le Ch[evalie]r Pringle.

P.S. Je suis votre débiteur Monsieur pour cette lunette que vous avez eu la bonté de m'envoyer de grace daignez donc me mander à quoi se monte ma dette pour que je l'acquitte. J'ai deja prié M. Ourry il y [a] trois mois de vous faire la même prière de ma part.[9]

Addressed: To / Benjamin Franklin Esq. / Deputy Postmaster of / The English Colonies / York buildings / London

C.O. at / Ld Visct. Gallway / Hill Street Berkley Square

From Francis Hopkinson[1]   ALS: American Philosophical Society

My dear Sir   Phila. April 23d. 1770
    My Lord North being at the Head of Affairs and having show'd an Inclination in my Favour upon an Application made in my Behalf by Mrs. Johnson makes me flatter myself that, something or other may possibly be obtain'd for my Benefit. To this purpose I have wrote to the Bishop of Worcester, and as he is in the Country during the Summer Season have told him that you will be so kind as

8. In the previous November BF, Pringle, and others had recommended Charles LeRoy (1726–79), a professor of medicine at Montpellier, and he was elected to membership on May 21, 1770. See above, VIII, 359; Thomas Thomson, *History of the Royal Society* (London, 1812), p. lviii.
    9. The "lunette" was probably an achromatic telescope: see BF's letter above, XVI, 206. Lewis Ourry, DF's and BF's old friend, had become tutor to Lord Galway's son; see BF to DF below, June 10. This fact may explain the otherwise mysterious second address below, if LeRoy decided to send his letter in care of C[apt.] O[urry].
    1. See above, XII, 125 n.

to let him know by a Line if any proper Opening should offer.[2] When a Person is asking a Favour they may as well put in for a great Matter as a small One. I have therefore thought that if Beckford should compleat what he has been so long about and really and truly die, an immediate and close Application by my Friends for the Collectorship of this Port might possibly meet with Success.[3] If you are not pre-engaged in this Matter may I presume so far upon your Friendship as to Request that you would keep a watchful Eye upon that Post, and if it lies in your Way give me your Interest. I am more than half inclin'd to take a Trip Over to England so as to return in the Fall either to push my Fortune in this Way or to settle a more enlarg'd Plan of Trade. With Compliments to my good Friends Mrs. Stevenson and Daughter I am obliged for want of Time to conclude more hastily than I intended with Assuring you that I am at all Events Your sincere and affectionate Friend

F. HOPKINSON

Addressed: To / Dr Franklin / Craven Street / London / per Packet

Endorsed: F. Hopkinson April 23. 1770

From James Parker

ALS: American Philosophical Society

Honoured Sir   New York, April 23[–24]. 1770

Yours of Feb 10. by the Harriot Packet, I just received. She and the Lord Hide Packet came both in at Once. My last to you was the 8th March, by Capt. Munds, who had lain here a long While: Since that having received some Money from Boston and Bills being low here, only 6½, I laid it out in a Bill for £150 Sterling drawn by Wats

2. Miss Sarah Johnson (1715–95) was the Bishop of Worcester's sister; she lived with him and inherited his fortune when he died in 1774. Walter Money, "The Family of James Johnson...," Bristol & Glos. Archaelogical Soc. *Trans.*, VIII (1883–84), 332. Hopkinson was related to the Johnsons and, much more indirectly, to Lady North; he had tried once before, without success, to use this route to favor. Above, XII, 124 n; George E. Hastings, *The Life and Works of Francis Hopkinson* (Chicago, [1926]), pp. 140, 147.

3. We find the reference to Beckford incomprehensible. William Beckford, M.P. and Lord Mayor of London, died in June, 1770, and as far as we know had no connection with the customs service. The collector at Philadelphia at the time was John Swift (1720–1802), and we have had no more success than Hopkinson's biographer in unearthing a Philadelphia Beckford: *ibid.*, p. 166.

and McEvers, on Harley and Drummond, the first of which I now send you; Also another Bill I just received from Quebec for £100 Sterling J Drummond, on Nesbit, Drummond and Franks, Esqrs in London, the first of which I send you. The 2d of each I shall send per the Harriot. I also send the 2d of a Bill for £250 Sterling the first of which was sent by Capt. Munds. I hope them all safe to your Hands. Of this last Bill for £250, Sterling which cost 67½ (£135 this Money) is on Account of B. Mecom's Books sold at Auction the Remainder Post-Office Money. The Auctioneer was obliged to repair to Philadelphia before we had finally settled, and he promised to be here again shortly, otherways that Account should have been sent you, tho' there will be little more coming any Way. Holt and I were beginning to make some Settlement, but we are in Trouble other ways, and I so poorly that little Progress has yet been made. I have Hopes we shall proceed, tho' I fear I shall get but little. I think he does not get a-head any Thing; and I less.

Agreeable to your Request, I wrote to Quebec, for the Papers that have your Examination in, and this is the first Opportunity I have had to send them since I received them. I hope them safe to your Hand, and that they will be agreeable.[4] Is it consistent to have some Post-Horns sent us——the Posts are out of them? None to be got here.[5]

I have now a melancholly Tale to tell: Lewis Jones, the young Man who was assigned to you from London, and by you assigned to me, having served out his Time with me, left me directly after. He first got to work with the Robinson's.[6] After that he got to Mr. Gaine's, where he work'd something more than one Year, got a Wife among the poorer sort, but never came near me after he first left me——perhaps from a Fraca I had with him a little before his

4. The letter to this point largely repeats what Parker had already dealt with in his letters to BF above, Jan. 4, Feb. 2, 20, and March 8.

5. He had asked the same question more than a year before; see above, XVI, 44. In June, 1770, BF charged the Post Office with a guinea paid for horns. Jour., p. 24. The Post Office subsequently disclaimed responsibility, and insisted that the riders must pay for their own: Samuel Potts to BF, Feb. 15, [1773], APS.

6. In 1763 Griffith Jones had sent his son Lewis to Philadelphia as an apprentice assigned to BF, who had promptly reassigned him to Parker. Above, X, 343–8. On completing his apprenticeship the young man had been hired by James and Alexander Robertson: XVI, 75 n.

Time was out on this Occasion. At the Time my Son went for England,[7] there was a Company of Players here. Gaine did all their Work, and printed their Tickets: soon after my Son was gone, one of the Actors found a Number of Counterfeit Play Tickets, as they were done with the same Flowers as the true ones, he applied to Gaine about them. Lewis Jones had been that Night at the Play with one of those Tickets given him by one of Gaine's Hands: they impeach'd Lewis, and Lewis said he had got them of my Son, who had been then 10 Days absent. The injured Player then came to me, but after canvassing the Matter with him, I demenstrated, to him that the Counterfeits were done with the same Flowers and Types that the true Ones were done; and that they could not be possibly done in my House, as I had not the same Flowers——tho' Gaine was so base, as to suppose they might be done at my House. Altho' my Son was bad enough, yet I thought it unmanly Usage, and afterwards putting it close to Lewis, he cleared Sammy, and own'd he had them of Gaine's Lad. Lewis was soon after free, and he came no more near me. About 3 Weeks ago, he was apprehended and taken up, for Uttering Counterfeit Jersey Bills. What the Evidence is I know not, but tis said several Bills he has pass'd away is return'd on him, and I was told, that Saturday last, three Bills of Indictment were found against him on which he has been arraign'd, and this Afternoon I hear he is to have his Trial, when its generally thought he will be convicted, and I know of no Instance of that Sort in this Colony ever being pardoned.

So far Monday P M.

Tuesday April 24.

Last Night Lewis Jones was tried on two of the Indictments: about 9 o'Clock at Night, his Friends came to me, pleading for me to assist him with a Character, &c. I had not been out of my Room for 8 Days, and I could scarce crawl. I went, and the Court indulged him by Waiting till I came. I related how he came to this Country, and spoke all I could in his Favour, and the Judge gave as favourable a Charge as a Man could do, on which the Jury acquitted him, on those two Indictments; but there is still another to come on this Day, which I hear has a more unfavourable Aspect. If, he should be found guilty, I think he will certainly be hang'd. I have done all I

7. For Samuel Parker's trip to England in 1768 see the numerous references in Vol. xv.

can, out of Regard for his Parents, who I know must pungently feel the Grief it must occasion to them. If his Trial is over before this Letter is sealed I will acquaint you of his Fortune:[8] as it is probable none else will yet write his Friends about it. Printers ought to be doubly on their Guard with respect to counterfeit Bills, as the Probability of Truth is much against them. As to Lewis, he never was any Advantage to me, but as my Son informed me, his Father was peculiarly kind to him in London. I should be ungrateful if I did not do my Possibles in Favour of his unhappy Son; and wish my Ability was such as would enable me to do more. With this I must close at present, and am with Respects Your most obliged Servant

JAMES PARKER.

PS. Lewis is acquitted.

Addressed: For / Dr Benjamin Franklin / Craven-Street / London / per Lord Hide Packet / Capt. Goddard.

Endorsed: J. Parker April 23. 1770 about Lewis Jones.

From James Parker

ALS: American Philosophical Society

Honoured Sir   Newyork Wednesday Night April 25, 1770

Some Hours after I had sent my Letter to the Office to go with this Packet, Mr. Colden's young Man brought me the inclosed Bill of Exchange for £50 Sterling which he offered me as he had just bought it @ 62½——and it being 2½ per Cent. cheaper than any to be got, I took it drawn this Day, Henry Thompson on Messrs. Pearson & Baillie of Liverpool——on which I instantly wrote this, as the Mail closes in an Hour.

Lewis was just now here, he came to thank me for the Assistance I had given him, to help him escape &c.[9] He intreated I would not write the News to his Father——he promises Amendment of Life,

8. In a letter to DF on the same day, April 24 (APS), Parker added that suspicion of Jones was strong; but the person from whom the young man said he had received the bills had run away, and the evidence might prove insufficient. "Tho' I have laboured to clear him and would do what I could for the Sake of his Connections at home, yet from many Circumstances, I cannot help thinking him faulty." For Parker's final involvement in this episode see the next document and his last letter to BF, below, May 10–14.

9. See the preceding document.

so I submit to you not to acquaint his Friends with it. He may thank your Name for the Judge's favourable Opinion of him, from Your most obliged Servant   JAMES PARKER.

Addressed: To / Dr Benjamin Franklin / Craven Street / London / per Lord Hide Packet

Circular to American Postmasters

Printed notice: American Philosophical Society

[General Post Office, North America, April 26, 1770. An unsigned circular letter, by order of the Deputy Postmaster General, enclosing the table of postal rates established by act of Parliament and instructions for handling foreign mail, and enjoining the recipients to observe them.[1]]

To Smith, Wright & Gray   ALS: Boston Public Library

[April 1770]

[No place or date, but April, 1770.[2] Encloses four bills: on Harley & Drummond for £200, on W. Cunningham for £20, on D. Milligan for £52, and on Alex. Grant for £30, and asks for a receipt by bearer for £302.[3]]

To Noble Wimberly Jones

ALS: State Historical Society of Wisconsin

Sir,   London, May 2. 1770
    Your Favour of Feb. 21. was duly delivered to me by Mr. Preston.[4] I immediately bespoke the Mace agreable to your Orders, and

1. The table and instructions, which are missing, implemented the Postal Act of 1765, 5 Geo. III, c. 25.
    2. BF entered these bills in his Jour., p. 23, under April 2, 1770.
    3. The first three, remittances by Parker on his postal accounts, were mentioned in his letters to BF above of Jan. 4 and Feb. 2. The fourth is identified in the Jour. as drawn by DF on Grant—Sir Alexander Grant, a leading West Indian merchant in London, for whom see Namier and Brooke, *House of Commons*, II, 628.
    4. For Jones' letter, with its request for a mace and gowns, see above,

133

was assured it should be work'd upon with Diligence, so that I hope to have it ready to send with the Gowns by a Ship that I understand goes directly to Georgia sometime next Month. By the Estimation of the Jeweller who undertook it, the Cost will not exceed £80. What the Gowns will amount to, I have not yet learnt; but suppose £100 will be more than sufficient for the whole.[5]

I esteem myself highly honour'd by your Government, in being appointed, as you inform me, a second time their Agent. I shall rejoice in any Opportunity of rendring effectual Service to the Province. I beg you will present my thankful Acknowledgements to the several Branches of your Legislature, and assure them of my faithful Endeavours in the Execution of any Commands I may receive from them. With great Respect, I am, Sir, Your most obedient and most humble Servant   B FRANKLIN

N. W. Jones Esquire, Speaker of the honble. Commons House of Assembly.

From Robert Rogers   ALS: American Philosophical Society

During the French and Indian War Robert Rogers and his Rangers had become a byword on both sides of the Atlantic. They had raised more havoc and killed more of the enemy, Franklin wrote in 1759, than all the British regulars had.[6] After the war Rogers fell on bad times. In the autumn of 1764 Franklin, it is said, offered to recommend him to the government; Rogers accepted the offer and came to London to seek advancement. In 1765 he secured the command of Michilimackinac, and returned to take up his new post. While there he wrote a long report, dated May 27, 1767, in which he surveyed the resources of the region for lucrative trade with the Indians and concluded that Michilimackinac should be made into a separate government. In 1768 he was arrested at

---

Feb. 21. Henry Preston was a curious emissary to choose: in the previous November he had been called before the Commons House for having made a public statement impugning its honor. Candler, ed., *Ga. Col. Recs.*, XV, 37–9, 45. He had sailed for London on Feb. 23: *Savannah Gaz.*, Feb. 28, 1770. Six years later he was imprisoned in Georgia as a dangerous Loyalist, but released on giving security for good behavior. Allen D. Candler, *The Revolutionary Records of the State of Georgia...* (3 vols., Atlanta, 1908), I, 146.

5. See BF to Jones below, June 7, July 6.

6. Above, VIII, 344–5.

the fort, court-martialed in Montreal for treasonable dealings with the French, and acquitted. He returned to London in the following year, harried by his creditors, and bombarded the government with petitions and memorials for a variety of projects, among them the old plan for a province of Michilimackinac. Franklin was only one of the many friends and acquaintances whom he tried to enlist in his campaign. There is no indication that he succeeded; two years later he was committed to the Fleet Prison for debt.[7]

Sir   4th of May 1770
The following is an Estimate and account of the Peltry and Firr Trade in the District of Michilimakinac made from many Years carefull Observation whilst I commanded in that Country.

As I have another Copy desire you will make any Use of this that you think proper. I am Sir with the Greatest Respect Your most Obedient Humble Servant   ROBERT ROGERS

To Doctr. Frankland

Agreement to Admit the Ohio Company as Co-Purchasers with the Grand Ohio Company

Reprinted from *The Historical Magazine and Notes and Queries, Concerning the Antiquities, History and Biography of America*, second series, III (1868), 18.[8]

As soon as word got about that the Grand Ohio Company had asked in January for a grant of twenty million acres,[9] rival claimants to western lands became intensely active in London. The Mississippi Company, represented by Arthur Lee, had a claim that overlapped that of the new company; the agent for Virginia urged that nothing be done until that province could be heard from; the Pennsylvania proprietors asked for full information because their interests might be affected. None of these

7. See John R. Cuneo, *Robert Rogers of the Rangers* (New York, 1959), pp. 177–8, 183–4, 246, 249, and for a brief résumé of the Michilimackinac plan pp. 205–6. BF's copy of that plan, now incomplete, is filed with Rogers' letter in the APS. Cuneo does not mention one key detail in the proposal, to garrison the new province with Rangers, which is a clear indication that Rogers envisaged himself as commander and governor.

8. The original was at that time, according to a footnote, in the possession of M. M. Jones, Utica, N.Y.; we have been unable to trace it.

9. See above, Jan. 4.

moves turned out to be dangerous to Franklin and his fellow promoters, but another threat acquired at least some nuisance value. The Ohio Company of Virginia had been allotted a half-million acres in the area in question by the provincial council, and was attempting to get the grant confirmed; its London agent, George Mercer,[1] had protested to the Board of Trade as early as December 18, 1769, against permitting the new company to encroach. The Board seems to have turned a deaf ear, as it had to Mercer's earlier importunings. In the spring, discouraged about his prospects, he decided to merge his company with the Grand Ohio on the best terms he could, and those he obtained are set forth in the agreement below. They apparently satisfied him, for on the following day he withdrew his protest to the Board of Trade.[2]

May 7, 1770

We the Committee of the Purchasers of a Tract of Country for a New Province on the Ohio in America do hereby admit the Ohio Company as a Co-Purchaser with us for Two Shares* of the said Purchase in consideration of the Engagement of their Agent Col. Mercer to withdraw the application of the said Company for a Separate Grant within the limits of the said Purchase. Witness our hands this 7th day May 1770

THOMAS WALPOLE
T. POWNALL
B. FRANKLIN
SAML WHARTON

* The whole being divided into seventy-two equall Shares—by the words "two shares" above is understood two Seventy Second parts of the Tract so as above Purchased.

THOMAS WALPOLE
T. POWNALL
B. FRANKLIN
SAML WHARTON

1. See above, XII, 99 n.
2. For the information in this headnote see Lewis, *Indiana Co.*, pp. 94–5, 98–100.

To Smith, Wright & Gray

AL: New York Society Library

[Craven Street, May 10, 1770. Asks for the protest of the bill on W. Cunningham in order to send it to America.³ Wants to know what happened to the two lottery tickets bought last year for Mr. Williams of Boston.⁴]

From the Georgia Commons House of Assembly: Instructions to Its Agent

ADS (copy): American Philosophical Society

Georgia Commons House of Assembly Thursday May 10th: 1770

Mr. Graeme⁵ from the Committee appointed to draw up such Instructions as may be thought proper to be transmitted to the Agent reported that the Committee had come to several Resolutions which they had directed him to report to the House and he read the Report in his place and afterwards delivered the same in at the Table where the Resolutions were severally again read and agreed to by the House and are as follow Vizt.

Resolved

That it is the Opinion of this Committee that the Agent be instructed by the Committee of Correspondence to use his utmost endeavours to obtain his Majestys Royal Assent as soon as possible to the Act passed this Sessions for ordering and governing Slaves &ca. [*In margin in Franklin's hand:* Have attended Mr. J. on it.]⁶

3. The bill for £20 sterling drawn on William Cunninghame, near Glasgow, by Alexander Findletter of Jamaica, with which Thomas Vernon of Newport had attempted to settle his postal account. See James Parker to BF above, Feb. 2.

4. See above, XVI, 211, and BF to Jonathan Williams below, June 6.

5. William Graeme, or Groeme, was a lawyer who had been elected to the Assembly in 1768 but had been denied his seat because he had not been a resident for a year. He was re-elected in 1769, to represent Darien and St. Andrew's Parish; he may also have been the William Graeme who was attorney general that year. He died in 1770, soon after presenting the Committee's report. *Savannah Gaz.*, Nov. 1, 1769; Candler, ed., *Ga. Col. Recs.*, XIV, 599; XV, *passim*, XIX, pt. 1, 131, 191, 470; *S.C. Hist. and Geneal. Mag.*, XVI (July, 1915), 131.

6. For five years the Assembly had been trying to frame a code acceptable to Whitehall for governing Georgia slaves; the most recent effort was the act referred to here. See William W. Abbot, *The Royal Governors of Georgia*,

137

Resolved

That it is the Opinion of this Committee that the Agent be instructed to use his utmost endeavours to obtain an Instruction from his Majesty permitting his Excellency the Governor to issue Writs for electing Members to represent the Parishes of St. David, St. Patrick, St. Thomas and St. Mary.[7] [*In margin in Franklin's hand: Done.*]

Resolved.

That it is the Opinion of this Committee that the Agent be instructed to use his Utmost endeavours to obtain an Instruction from his Majesty permitting his Excellency the Governor to give his Assent to a Law of the same Tenor and purport as a Bill passed both Houses of Assembly this Session Intitled an Act to amend an Act to ascertain the manner and form of electing Members to represent the Inhabitants of this Province in the Commons House of Assembly.[8]

Resolved

That it is the Opinion of this Committee that the Agent be instructed to use his utmost endeavours to obtain from William Knox Esqr. (lately Agent for this Province) the plan of the Land claimed by the late Sir William Baker deceased and the Petition accompanying it which was transmitted to him to be presented to his Majesty and that the Agent be further instructed to present the

---

1754–1775 (Chapel Hill, [1959]), p. 153; Candler, *op. cit.*, XIX, pt. 1, 209–49. BF took the matter to Richard Jackson as counsel to the Board of Trade. On March 6, 1771, the Board considered the act and, in the light of a favorable report from Jackson, recommended to the King that it should be confirmed. *Board of Trade Jour.*, 1768–75, p. 237.

7. The four parishes had been created out of territory annexed to Georgia in 1763. As the number of settlers grew, Governor Wright urged the home government to allow them representation. Nothing happened. The Assembly refused to tax unrepresented parishes, and exempted them in its tax bill of March, 1770. See Kenneth Coleman, *The American Revolution in Georgia, 1763–1789* (Athens, Ga., [1958]), pp. 32–3; Abbot, *op. cit.*, pp. 153–4; Candler, *op. cit.*, XIX, pt. 1, 163.

8. The Governor had refused his consent on the ground of his instructions, and the Assembly had requested him to attempt to have the instructions changed; he had forwarded to London the request and the act in question. *Ibid.*, XVII, 593–6. For the changes in representation that the Assembly was attempting to make, and its reasons for them, see the Georgia Committee of Correspondence to BF below, May 23.

said Petition to his Majesty with all Convenient speed.[9] [*In margin in Franklin's hand:* done.]

Ordered

That the above Resolutions be referred to the Committee of Correspondence as an Act of this House.

A true Copy from the Original Journals of the Commons House of Assembly examined   JNO SIMPSON Clk[1]

Endorsed: Copy Resolutions of the Commons House of Assembly— to be transmitted to the Agent May 10th. 1770 A.

Ordinance of Georgia Reappointing Benjamin Franklin as Agent

AD (copy): American Philosophical Society

[May 10, 1770. The ordinance appoints Franklin for a year from June 1, 1770. Except for the difference of dates the wording is virtually identical with that of the ordinance printed above, February 27, which renewed the appointment until June 1, 1770. The same clerks attested the passage of the act through the Commons House and the Upper House, on May 1–3, 1770, and on May 21 Thomas Moodie again certified that this was a true copy. The same group of fourteen men was named as the Assembly's Committee of Correspondence, except that John Graham and James Read[2] replaced

9. For William Knox see above, xv, 94. Sir William Baker (1705–70) had been a London alderman and M.P., one of the foremost merchants trading with America, and a member of Rockingham's inner circle; he had died the previous January. He had extensive landholdings throughout the southern colonies, part of them in territory transferred from Carolina to Georgia, and his claims conflicted with those of settlers who had moved into the lands in question; the problem is discussed at length in the letter from the Committee of Correspondence to BF below, May 28. See also Namier and Brooke, *House of Commons*, II, 40–1; Ga. Hist. Soc. *Collections*, VI (1904), 33–5; Henry A. M. Smith, "The Baronies of South Carolina," *S.C. Hist. and Geneal. Mag.*, XI (April, 1910), 75–6, XIV (April, 1913), 61–3; William S. Powell, *The Proprietors of Carolina* (Raleigh, 1963), pp. 56–7; Robert L. Gold, *Borderland Empires in Transition . . .* (Carbondale and Edwardsville, Ill. [1969]), p. 127.

1. Identified above, xv, 95 n.

2. John Graham was a Scot who emigrated in 1753; after some years as a Savannah merchant he became one of the largest landholders in Georgia. During the Revolution he was a Loyalist, and he eventually returned to

Lewis Johnson and Clement Martin. The ordinance was signed as before by Jones, Habersham, and Wright.]

From James Parker

ALS: American Philosophical Society

Honoured Sir   NYork, May 10. 1770

This only covers the 2d of each of three Setts of Bills of Exchange, the first of which I sent per Lord Hide Packet, Capt. Goddard, the 23d and 25th of last Month, not having any new Acquisitions or Receipts since: One is for £150 Sterling Wats & McEvers on Harley and Drummond——Another for £100 Sterling from Quebec, Colin Drummond on Nesbit, Drummond & Franks; and the other for £50 Sterling H. Thompson on Pearson & Bailie of Liverpool. This last was sent me by Mr. Colden just as the last Packet was going, and cost but 62½——All upon the Post-Office Account. I believe Bills might be had of private Drawers in general for 62½——but good and publick ones are 65 yet.[3] Money indeed grows very scarce here. The Duke Packet, Capt. Goodridge arrived here the 3d Instant I had not a Word from you; I hope you are well, Suppose she is to sail the Beginning of June. Its now eight Months since I have been able to walk well, and I dont know if I ever shall again be able, so that it was Time I quitted the Land-Waiter's Place, when I could scarce crawl. I wish I could get into some warmer Climate in my Old Age; but as 'tis not likely I can hold long, it is little Matter where I be——a few Days more, it will be all over with

---

Britain. *DAB*. James Read was a South Carolinian by birth, but was in Georgia by 1755; he was a member of the provincial Council, 1756–75. During the Revolution he was imprisoned for a time and then confined to his plantation. Candler, ed., *Ga. Col. Recs.*, VII, *passim*; XII, 421; *S.C. Hist. and Geneal. Mag.*, XVII (Oct., 1916), 148; Robert W. Gibbes, *Documentary History of the American Revolution . . .* (3 vols., New York, 1853–57), I, 251–3.

3. Parker had covered most of these business details, as usual, in his letters to BF earlier in the year. The exchange rate, as he pointed out, had fallen drastically: four months earlier it had been £177–£180 in New York currency to £100 sterling. See the Post Office account above, Jan. 3, 1770, and Parker's postscript to this letter. The reason was presumably that the shortage of goods and the concomitant rise in prices had accentuated the scarcity of provincial paper money and raised, for New York merchants, its value in relation to sterling.

me.[4] I shall try to do my Duty while here, and leave the rest to Providence.

In my last I acquainted you with Lewis Jones' Affair. He being happily got clear, came to thank me, and intreated me not to acquaint his Father. Indeed, I never wrote at all to his Father; and in a Day or two after, finding it would not either be safe or beneficial to him to stay here; he solicited Help to go off: I contributed as much as I could, towards getting him a Passage to So. Carolina, where he will get Employ, and if he behaves well think he may retrieve some of his bad Fortune.[5] My Son told me Mr. Jones had been kind to him in London. I think I have paid that Debt in part at least.

May 14. PS. Having represented to Mr. Colden, that as Bills were low now, I should be glad to take Advantage of it, to send all I could; for that if Importation took place again, it was thought they would infallibly rise; he this Day sent me £300 this Mony, with which and some Money I had already, I immediately purchased a Bill of £200, Sterling which cost but 62½, being the lowest they have been known for many years, drawn by Wats & McEvers, on Harley & Drummond, dated this Day, the first of which I inclose you, and the 2d shall send the first Opportunity.

Mr. Bell the Auctioneer not returned yet from Philadelphia. The Amount of the Whole of the Sales of B. Mecom's Books came to £175 this Money, but the Commissions, Duty, Rent of a Room, &c. not yet settled, so cannot tell what more will be coming, if any.[6] All our best Respects await you, and Mr. Foxcroft, wishing you Health and Happiness, I am Your most obliged Servant

JAMES PARKER

Addressed: For / Dr Benjamin Franklin / Craven-Street / London per the Harriot Packet / Capt Lee

Endorsed: J. Pa[rker] May 10. 1770

4. For once he was right that his time was running out. This was his last extant letter to BF, and he died on July 2.

5. For Jones's trial see Parker to BF above, April 23–24, 25.

6. For the auction see Parker to BF above, Feb. 2, 20.

From the Georgia Assembly Committee of Correspondence

AD (letterbook copy): Georgia Historical Society

Sir   Savann[ah in Georgia, 11 May 1770]

As we expect a Ship is now at Cockspur Road at the entrance of this River bound for England[7] and as we hope to get this on board we embrace the Opportunity of acquainting you that two Ordinances have been passed by the General Assembly, one reappointing you Agent for this Province passed the 27th. Febry last ending the first June next and another passed yesterday for another year ending the 1st. June 1771.[8] We have not a moments time (the Boat waiting to Carry this on board) to say any thing on Publick Business of which we have several Matters in Charge and will be prepared to go by a Ship now here that will sail in all [likelihood?] this Month with Copies of the Ordinances properly authenticated. There is £100 provided for you [this] present year and inclosed you have our Governor's Certificate for one hundred Pounds Sterling (for payment of which you will apply to John Campbell Esqr. his Majestys Agent for this Province[9]) for your Service from June 1768 to 1st. June 1769.

We are Sir &ca.[1] J HABERSHAM
NOBLE JONES
J: E POWELL
N W JONES
WM EWEN
PHILIP BOX
RD CUNYM. CROOKE

To Benjamin Franklin Esqr. Agent for the Province of Georgia in London.

7. A marginal note, slightly mutilated, makes clear that this was the snow *Britannia*, Stephen Deane master. She cleared for Cowes on May 11 but was still windbound five days later. *Savannah Gaz.*, May 16, 1770.

8. See the ordinances above, Feb. 27 and May 10.

9. Campbell (1708–75) was a writer of some repute at the time, and crown agent for Georgia during the last decade of his life. *DNB*.

1. For the first five signers see above, xv, 95 n; for the other two see the Georgia ordinance above, Feb. 27.

Account with James Parker

[The accounts of Parker's remittances as comptroller of the Post Office run from May 1, 1769, to May 14, 1770; the sixteen bills of exchange listed total £1,899 19s. 1d.[2] The endorsement, in Franklin's hand, refers to Parker as the "late Comptroller."]

From Thomas Gilpin

Reprinted from "Memoir of Thomas Gilpin," *Pennsylvania Magazine of History and Biography*, XLIX (1925), 311–12.

Esteemed Friend   May 17th 1770

By letters received here yesterday by Falconer, Sparks and Friend the inclination of altering the non importation agreement is discouraged tho I still think some regulations will be made on the 5th of June[3] and if wisely done I believe it will be for the best for then it may be confidently expected that the colonies will abide by the measures they have adopted and do without one half the manufactures of Great Britain the consequence of which will be that considerable capital employed in trade will be converted to manufactures of our own as indeed has been the case already in many instances and when once these are established they will not be easily destroyed but will daily decrease the demand for foreign articles, invite the artists of England to settle among us and confirm the self-dependance and prosperity of the colonies.

Certain it is that by the adoption of a wise and paternal conduct towards us Great Britain may eminently accelerate her own prosperity and unite it with those of her colonies so that both may pro-

2. The details of these transactions appear above, XVI, 130, 159, 162, 180, 185, 186, 215–16, 269, and in Parker's letters to BF earlier in the present volume.

3. Extracts of the letters from London brought by Capts. Falconer, Sparks, and Friend were published in the *Pa. Chron.*, May 14–21, and the *Pa. Gaz.*, May 17, 1770; they contained the news that all the duties levied under the Townshend Acts had been repealed except that on tea. It likewise might be rescinded, one of the extracts suggested, if the colonists stood firm. The same issue of the *Pa. Chron.* carried a letter announcing that the Philadelphia merchants had recently decided to hold a meeting on June 5 to decide their future policy.

ceed in a happy union she as the affectionate parent and we as dutiful children: that there are many intemperate persons on both sides there is no question and it is undeniable that there are some here who would prefer offensive measures; altho' it seems to me that every law imposed upon us by Great Britain may be rendered nugatory and the repeal of it compelled by firm defensive conduct without distressing ourselves or losing our valuable trade and in this too we should not weaken the cause by giving grounds to believe that we are actuated by ambition or revenge or afford our enemies an opportunity to triumph in our adopting measures so high that we might be compelled to rescind or be beaten from them and especially from our non importation agreement. I remain respectfully Thy sincere friend   T. GILPIN

From the Georgia Assembly Committee of Correspondence   AD (letterbook copy): Georgia Historical Society

Sir   Savannah in Georgia 23d May 1770
   The 11th. Instant we wrote you a Short Line by the Britannia Captain Deane of which you have now a Copy inclosed principally to acquaint you of your being reappointed by the General Assembly Agent to sollicit the Affairs of this Province in Great Britain for the Present year ending the first day of next month and also of your being reappointed for the ensuing year ending the first day of June 1771 and with this you will receive authenticated Copies of the two ordinances empowering you to Act in that Capacity and at the same time We enclosed you our Governors Certificate payable by the Kings Agent for this Province (John Campbell Esqr.) for one Hundred pounds Sterling for your allowance as Agent ending the first of June last and you have now a second Certificate and as soon as the Publick Treasurer can invest the like Sum provided for you in the last Tax Act in a Bill payable in England it will be transmitted.
   Perhaps it may be necessary to make an Apology for an Intermission in our Correspondence with you as a Committee which however you will be pleased to believe did not arise from the least doubt of your Intention or Abilities to serve us but from Circumstances

arising from the Dissolution of the late Assembly which are now subsided.[4]

You will see by a Copy of the Resolutions of the Commons House of Assembly enclosed to which the Upper House agreed the Matters we have in Charge to recommend to your Sollicitation and to that end We have sent you a Copy of an Act for the better ordering and Governing Negroes and other Slaves &ca to which the Governor has Assented but with a suspending Clause till his Majestys pleasure is known thereupon agreable to an Instruction to him for that purpose.[5] You will please to refer to the Committees Letter of the 19th. May 1768 in which they informed you that an Act similar to this had been disallowed by his Majesty but that the Reasons for such disallowance was not communicated to the Governor, and therefore we were at a loss to know how to frame another that might be unexceptionable and at the same time answer our local Circumstances;[6] since which we have understood that the Council to the Board of Trade reported that slaves should be made real Estate, and go with the Lands they were employed upon. In a young and extensive Country like this, Where Property must necessarily be frequently Aliened and new Settlements daily made, many cogent Reasons might be urged against such a Measure but as we are informed our Governor has fully given his Reasons to remove this Objection which have been approved of, We need not add thereupon and have only to remark that in our unavoidable Situation this Law is of the utmost Importance and without it we cannot well subsist and as the greatest Care has been taken to frame it on the most humane Principles that the Nature of such a Law can admit we can make no doubt but it will meet with his Majestys Royal and speedy Approbation which you will please to lose no time in solliciting.

The next matter under Consideration is the Address of the Com-

4. At the end of 1768 Governor Wright dissolved the Assembly because it was attempting to address to the King a protest against the Townshend Acts similar to those from Massachusetts and Virginia. A new Assembly convened in October, 1769, and sat until the following May; tensions by then had relaxed, and the session was reasonably harmonious. William W. Abbot, *The Royal Governors of Georgia, 1754–1775* (Chapel Hill, [1959]), pp. 148–53; Candler, ed., *Ga. Col. Recs.*, XIV, 656–9.

5. See the Assembly's instructions to BF above, May 10.

6. See above, XV, 133–4.

mons House to the Governor requesting him to issue Writs for the electing a Representative for each of the Four new Southern Parishes of St. David St. Patrick St. Thomas and St. Mary lying between the Rivers Alatamaha and St. Mary. These were part of the Lands ceded by Spain to his Majesty by the last Treaty of Peace and were annexed by his Royal Proclamation to this Province but as the Governor did not think himself authorized to add to the number of Representatives without an Instruction from the Crown for that purpose in which Opinion his Majestys Council concurred tho' you will see by his Answer to the said Address of which you have now a Copy that he thought it right and just that every Parish should be represented as also did the Council, and therefore We are perswaded he has stated or will state the Matter to Government and We have no doubt but he will receive orders to issue Writs accordingly and it may be proper to acquaint you that in the last Tax Act these four Parishes are expressly exempted from paying any because not Represented, and as all Taxation should be equal and not partial we cannot conceive that there can be any Objection to obtain the Redress requested.[7]

We are now to acquaint you that the Commons and Upper Houses of Assembly have passed a Bill intitled an Act to amend an Act intitled an Act to ascertain the manner and Form of electing Members to represent the Inhabitants of this Province in the Commons House of Assembly of which the Governor said he would Consider being framed as we understand contrary to a Royal Instruction and afterwards both Houses presented an Address to him rquesting him to use his utmost Endeavours to obtain an Instruction from his Majesty permitting him to assent to a Law of the same Tenor and purport, a Copy of which with his Answer a Copy of the Bill not assented to and of the Law it was intended to amend passed the 9th. of June 1761 are herewith transmitted that by comparing them you may be the better furnished with the Reasons that induced the Assembly to pass the Amendment Bill, which among others was to make the Qualifications of the Electors and Elected more equal and better adapted to our local Circumstances. In the subsisting Law you will observe that a person possessed of fifty Acres of Land tho' in some Instances not worth five Pounds is qualified to Vote when another Person not having 50 Acres of Land tho' possessed

7. See the Assembly's instructions to BF above, May 10.

of Town Lots and Buildings to the Value of a thousand fold more cannot an Impropriety which we think will appear at first View to require an Amendment and the same reasoning must hold good as to the Qualification of the Elected, as it is no difficult matter for a Person wanting to be a Representative to get five hundred Acres of Barren or Lands of little Value to qualify him for that purpose tho' perhaps in every other respect he is very improper to Act in that Capacity. The method of balloting for Representatives has been found very Salutary in other Provinces on this Continent particularly in South Carolina and has prevented undue and improper Influence of designing Men who have got themselves Elected too often, not to serve, but to distress Government and carry on their own private and selfish Views. We are apprehensive that the Clause for limiting the Duration of the Assembly for three Years in the proposed Bill may meet with Objections tho' the same Clause is in the Election Law in South Carolina and has never that we know of been attended with the least Inconvenience to the Public Good and you know that in Pensylvania some of the Northern Provinces and some of the West India Islands the Assemblys are chosen annualy. In this Climate where the Inhabitants are so often subject to change their Situation three Years is a long time to attend, and even this Term has been found extremely inconvenient to many who tho' well disposed and qualifyed to serve their Country have declined Acting and if the Duration should remain undetermined by Law we may and shall be deprived of the Service of some of the most usefull Members of the Community. We do not urge this Matter from the Conduct of our present Governor whom we have no reason to believe would keep the Assembly sitting longer than three Years and perhaps the same Reasons operate with him as We have offered and would his Instructions admit of his Assenting to the proposed Bill We are of Opinion he would not object to it.

The Committee have another matter in Charge of which they write to you in a seperate Letter.[8] We need not say that any expence you may find necessary in the execution of the Business recommended to you by the Committee will be reimbursed you with thanks. We are Sir Your most Obedient Servants[9]

8. See the following document.

9. The copy is unsigned, but the accompanying minutes list the Committee members as Habersham, the two Joneses, Ewen, Box, Crooke, Read, and

From the Georgia Assembly Committee of Correspondence

AD (letterbook copy): Georgia Historical Society

Sir   Savannah in Georgia the 28th. May 1770

We are now to take under Consideration the Instructions of the Assembly respecting a Claim of Lands made by the late Sir William Baker of London deceased, in this Province, which We are directed to instruct you to Represent to his Majesty.[1] These Resolutions were drawn up tho' the Substance of them was long before agreed to, in too great a hurry, perhaps not half an Hour before the Prorogation of the Assembly, and this in particular which we are now to remark upon, was for that Reason in part mistaken. It directs that we should instruct you [to] apply to "William Knox Esqr. (lately an Agent for this Province) for the Plan of the Lands claimed by the late Sir William Baker and the Memorial accompanying it, which was transmitted to him to be presented to his Majesty." The mistake is that no Memorial was sent to Mr. Knox as you will see by a Copy of the Committees letter to him on that Occasion herewith enclosed but only a Copy of a Petition to both Houses of Assembly of the Inhabitants settled on the Lands supposed to be within the said Claim[2] of which you have now another Copy and therefore we have only to desire you to apply to Mr. Knox for the Plan referred to.

In November 1759 the General Assembly passed an Act Intitled an "Act for establishing and Confirming the Titles of several Inhabitants of this Province to their respective Lands and Tenements"[3] as the Legislature then understood that this and some other obsolete Claims of Lands not till about that time heard of and never to our knowledge made here (which ought to have been done) were intended at a future day to be produced perhaps at a time when the Lands became more Valuable from the Industry and labour of the present Occupants; which Opinion is now strengthned by the Assigns of Sir William Baker having lately lodged a Power of Attorney here to treat with the Persons supposed to be settled

---

Young. All of these have been identified above; see the ordinances of Feb. 27 and May 10 and the Committee's letter to BF of May 11.

    1. See the Assembly's instructions to BF above, May 10.

    2. For the petition see Candler, ed., *Ga. Col. Recs.*, XVII, 184–5.

    3. *Ibid.*, XVIII, 357–9.

within the Lands by them claimed for a certain Sum of money to relinquish their Pretensions.

On part of those Lands many of the early Adventurers had been quietly seated since the first Settlement of the province and the before recited Law, tho' on further Consideration it appears to be framed to operate too extensively. (We mean that the Provisions and exceptions necessary in such a Law were not sufficiently adverted to) was then thought to be founded on the most equitable Principles and doubtless was intended to prevent People who had left their native Country and Friends to seek a Retreat in a Climate and Situation subject to numberless Inconveniencies and Hardships from being harrassed and dispossessed of their Lands and Labour and in some Instances of their All.

Upon the Board of Trade taking this Law under Consideration Sir William Baker was heard by his Sollicitor and in Consequence their Lordships reported against it to his Majesty and it accordingly met with his Royal Disallowance.[4] Enclosed you have a Copy of their Lordships Report by which you will be furnished with the Arguments then urged on both sides.

Upon this Report being known here the Petition before mentioned was presented to both Houses of Assembly who in consequence instructed their Committee to write to Mr. Knox then Provincial Agent thereupon which they did and a Copy of the said Letter dated the 14th. May 1765[5] you have as before mentioned enclosed and as we think the matter was then fully set forth which we now confirm we have only to add that we desire you will pursue the Instructions therein given which is that a dutifull Petition or Address be presented to his Majesty humbly praying for the Relief requested in such manner as you may be advised or may yourself think proper. Mr. Knox we apprehend mistook the Committees meaning in this Point as he did not make such Application; however as it did then and does now also appear to be the most effectual means to obtain Relief for the Petitioners who must be otherwise on their parts innocently oppressed, many of whom being utterly

---

4. The Board's only recorded action, as far as we can discover, was in January, 1761, when it postponed the whole matter until Governor Ellis's return to England. *Board of Trade Jour.*, 1759–63, pp. 156, 158.

5. "The Letters of Hon. James Habersham, 1756–1775," Ga. Hist. Soc. *Collections*, VI (1904), 33–5.

incapable of making the Compensation required notwithstanding they or their Fathers have defended their particular Property as well as the Province in general not only when invaded by the Spaniards but on many other perilous Occasions.

It may be necessary to acquaint you that a Law Intitled an "Act for limitation of Actions and for avoiding of Suits in Law" was passed the 26th. March 1767[6] which was intended to answer as far as might be the Purposes of the former repealed Act and to remove every exception and we have not heard of any having been made to it. The following Clause was inserted "Provided also and Be it further Enacted that nothing in this Act Contained shall extend or be construed to extend to take away or prejudice the Claim of Sir William Baker of the City of London Knight or his Heirs or Assigns in and to a Certain Barony or Tract of Land within the Parish of Christ Church in the Province aforesaid." However it was not intended by this Clause to establish Sir William Bakers Claim (and we are clear it does not) but only to leave it open and not to debar him from making such Claim at any future time.

As this is a Matter We on behalf of the distressed Petitioners very much wish to have settled we hope you will lose no time in using your utmost endeavours to have it brought to an agreable Issue and any Expence that may be Necessary in effecting it will be thankfully reimbursed you. We are &ca.[7]

NB The Plan in Mr. Knox's hands is only supposed to be the Barony claimed being never executed by any Actual Survey that we know of and was solely meant for his private Information. It will therefore answer the same purpose with you.

From Humphry Marshall ALS: American Philosophical Society

Chester County Pensilvania the 28th
Esteemed Friend of the 5th mo 1770
I Recieved thy favour of the 18th. of the 3d mo. Last In Which thou informs me that "The Nation Seems Besotted With the Fancy

6. Candler, *op. cit.*, XVIII, 802–10.
7. The copy is unsigned, but the accompanying minutes list the same Committee members, except for the absence of William Young, as those who signed the letter to BF above, May 23.

that We Cannot Possily Do Without them, and must of Course Comply at Last."[8] I am almost ready to Doubt that our merchants Will not hold out Long Enough tho' there Seems Spirit and Resolution Enough in Some of them to Do it. But there is Somany Weaklings and Such that have had no other Way to Get a livelyhood and So loath to turn their hands to any other Employments that its Hard to Judge What Will Be the Event.[9] But I may Inform thee that there appears a Spirrit of Industry among the People Both in our Province maryland, and Virginia I having Lately Been through Part of Both of them Provinces, and had an oppertunity of Conversing With the People, on that Subject. Our people Seems to make a great Noise about raising Silk how it will turn out I Know not.[1] But I think not very Well this Season because We have had a severe frost So late this Spring as to kill the first Shooting of the Budds of our Mulberry. I am Greatly obliged to thee for thy Complying With my request to thee Concerning the Getting and Sending me a Small reflecting Telescope Which I have Received in Good order With the other Instruments, for [which] I Look on my Self much Indebted to thee and highly Favoured and Gratefully acknowledge the Kindness,[2] and if it Should Ever be in my Power to oblidge thee as much I hope I Shall Do it With Pleasure. Thou Will its Possible Reccieve Later accounts than mine by the Same Vessells by my Living Distant from the City hath not an opportunity to Write So late [as] the people Who Live in the City. The inhabitants in the City at this time Seems to Be resolute to not import till the Whole affairs of Duties is taken off. I hope they Will Continue in their Resolutions. I Like wise hope that although the Duties Should be all taken of that there Will Be Such a Spirit of resentment Raised in the people of America against Being Brought under Slavery to a British Ministry, that Would impose Burdens on them; that they Won't Easily forget it But remember to be Industrious to Manifacture Every article that they Conveniently Can that is Necessary for their own Consumption; By the Latest accounts We have yet

8. Marshall slightly misquotes; see above.
9. Philadelphia reduced British imports in 1770 more than any other port, and without violence. Arthur M. Schlesinger, *The Colonial Merchants and the American Revolution, 1763–1776* (New York, 1918), pp. 193–4.
1. See above, XVI, 179, 200–2.
2. See BF to Marshall above, March 18.

from your Side there Seems to be Great Confusion amongst the Great ones in England it's well if matters Settles [down?] Without Some Blood being Shed on the one Side or the other. Thy Real Well Wisher in Haste HUMP. MARSHALL

Addressed: To / Benjamin Franklin / in London / per Favour of / Capn. Sparkes

Endorsed: May 28. 1770 Humphry Marshal

To Mary Stevenson
ALS (draft): Library of Congress

Dear Polly   Thursday May 31. 70

I receiv'd your Letter early this Morning, and as I am so engag'd that I cannot see you when you come to-day, I write this Line just to say, That I am sure you are a much better Judge in this Affair of your own than I can possibly be; in that Confidence it was that I forbore giving my Advice when you mention'd it to me, and not from any Disapprobation. My Concern (equal to any Father's) for your Happiness, makes me write this, lest having more Regard for my Opinion than you ought, and imagining it against the Proposal because I did not immediately advise accepting it, you should let that weigh any thing in your Deliberations.[3] I assure you that no Objection has occur'd to me; his Person you see, his Temper and his Understanding you can judge of, his Character for any thing I have ever heard is unblemished; his Profession, with that Skill in it he is suppos'd to have, will be sufficient to support a Family; and therefore considering the Fortune you have in your Hands, (tho' any future Expectation from your Aunt should be disappointed)[4] I do not see but that the Agreement may be a rational one on both sides. I see your Delicacy; and your Humility too; for you fancy that if you do not prove a great Fortune you will not be belov'd; but I am sure that were I in his Situation in every respect, knowing you so well as I do, and esteeming you so highly, I should think you a

3. Polly had met William Hewson (above, XVI, 191 n) in 1768: George Gulliver, *The Works of William Hewson . . .* (London, 1846), p. xiv. She soon accepted him, and they were married on July 10.

4. This presumably refers to Mrs. Stevenson's sister, Mrs. Tickell, with whom Polly had lived and whose estate she eventually inherited. Above, VIII, 339 n.

Fortune sufficient for me without a Shilling. Having thus more explicitly than before, given my Opinion, I leave the rest to your sound Judgment, of which no one has a greater Share; and shall not be too inquisitive after your particular Reasons, your Doubts, your Fears, &c. For I shall be confident whether you accept or refuse, that you do right. I only wish you may do what will most contribute to your Happiness, and of course to mine; being ever, my dear Friend, Yours most affectionately   BF.

Don't be angry with me for supposing your Determination not quite so fix'd as you fancy it.

Endorsed: May 31–70

From Sarah Franklin Bache   AL: American Philosophical Society

Honored Sir   Philadelphia. May [1770]
   I am much obliged to you for asking Sir John Pringles opinion about Franklin, it has made me easier, but if it please God to spare him to us, intend having him Inoculated again when he has done cutting Teeth.[5] I take the earliest opportunity of telling my dear Papa I have altered my intention of going to Jamaica, it never was Mr. Baches design to setle there. All the Uneasiness I sufered during his absence made me get a promise of him that we should never more seperate; and that he would take me to Jamaica with him, when his Business called him, and if we had gone it would have been with a full hope of having it in our power to return to Phila. to live in a few years. Mr. Bache never urged me in the least to go, but as he had made the promise, would not go back from it, and left it entirely in my own choice whether to go or stay; your last letter has ditermined me; no Sir, Your Child will not give you pain. She will stay, and prove to you through life what She realy is Your Dutiful and Afectionate Daughter

Addressed: To / Benjamin Franklin Esqr.

Endorsed: Daughter Bache May 1770

5. BF had answered Sally's inquiry about inoculation by Capt. Falconer (BF to DF below, June 10); Falconer's ship, the *Pa. Packet*, reached Philadelphia on May 24: *Pa. Gaz.*, May 24. Hence Sally must have written in the last days of May, immediately after receiving her father's letter.

From Thomas Gilpin

Extract: reprinted from "Memoir of Thomas Gilpin," *Pennsylvania Magazine of History and Biography*, XLIX (1925), 312–13.

This extract and three others that follow, from letters by Gilpin of June 8, July 19, and November 15, may or may not have been to Franklin. The extracts hitherto printed in this and the preceding volume are described in the memoir from which they come, written by Thomas Gilpin, Jr. and found among his papers, as addressed to Franklin. These four are not. A fifth included among them, of September 28, was clearly addressed to someone else, because it covered the same ground as Gilpin's letter to Franklin of that date printed below; hence Gilpin had at least two correspondents in England. Because the author of the memoir did not bother to distinguish them, no editor can distinguish now. We therefore print the four extracts on the chance that they belong within the rubric of the Franklin Papers.

June 1st 1770

Since the repeal was announced and the public sentiment respecting it had time to mature itself the partiality in repealing the several other duties and leaving that on Tea seems to be considered as the effect of weakness in the ministry and an act of ill grace which can answer no end except to confirm the jealousy of their principles and the opinion of their weakness and ill intentions:[6] the measure will drive the Americans into manufactures and frugality, a repugnance to foreign articles and to independence. If the minister was hired to hasten these measures he could do it by no means so effectually as by these he has adopted and in contending for a battle of form he will lose every thing of substance: in despite of the pretended right and laws they have founded on it, we save more by it in one year than the ministry could collect in three: we save in luxury and the gratification of our desires for which we paid a large tax to England without complaint——at present the exchange with England is extremely reduced, produce at a very reasonable price, and the country free from luxury; in this situation it must grow rich and tho' a few individuals will suffer there is not the least disposition

6. An extract from a letter from London of March 27, printed in the *Pa. Gaz.* on May 31, 1770, asserted that North favored total repeal but, because of the weakness of the ministry and the divisions in Westminster, might not have enough support to carry it.

to give up the non-importation agreement. Some would have been glad if a few more articles of general necessity had been permitted as has been done in Maryland,[7] but they seem bent not to relax in the system which has been agreed on.

From Joseph Priestley   ALS: Massachusetts Historical Society

Dear Sir   Leeds. 2 June 1770.

I inclose a few copies of my *Proposals*, with the catalogues much inlarged.[8] I therefore beg you would destroy the former, and dispose of these as you shall think most conducive to the design. I shall send a greater number soon to Mr. Johnson,[9] from whom you may have whatever you want. In the mean time, I am obliged to take the liberty to inclose a small parcel for him in a cover to you. I hope you received Beccaria[1] safe. I am Dear Sir Yours sincerely

J PRIESTLEY

Addressed: To / Doctor Franklin / at Mrs Stevenson's / in Craven Street in the Strand / London.

Endorsed: Dr Priestly May 1770

7. Gilpin is misleading: many Philadelphia merchants insisted that only goods still subject to duties should be boycotted. The original agreement, however, was kept until September. See Gilpin to BF below, June 8, 19, Sept. 21, 28; Theodore Thayer, *Pennsylvania Politics and the Growth of Democracy* . . . (Harrisburg, 1953), pp. 145–8.

8. Priestley was intending to expand his *History and Present State of Electricity* into a comprehensive study of the development of experimental philosophy. He had just drafted his proposals for this work, and made lists ("catalogues") of the books that he had and was going to need for the purpose. Frederick W. Gibbs, *Joseph Priestley, Adventurer in Science and Champion of Truth* ([London], 1965), pp. 50–3; Robert E. Schofield, ed., *A Scientific Autobiography of Joseph Priestley* (Cambridge, Mass., and London, [1966]), pp. 75–9. BF had presumably received earlier drafts, which these were to replace.

9. Joseph Johnson, the London bookseller and publisher, for whom see above, XI, 258 n.

1. Presumably the copy of Beccaria's *Dell' elettricismo artificiale e naturale* (Turin, 1753) which BF had sent to Priestley when the latter was working on his *History and Present State of Electricity.* See above, XIII, 246, 421.

To Smith, Wright & Gray ALS: Yale University Library

[Craven Street, June 5, 1770. Encloses three bills: Watts & McEvers on Harley & Drummond for £150, Colin Drummond on Nesbit, Drummond & Franks for £100, and Henry Thompson on Pearson & Baillie for £50, and asks for a receipt by bearer for £300.² Again requests the protest of the bill on Cunningham.³]

To Jonathan Williams, Sr. ALS: American Philosophical Society

Dear Cousin,   London, June 6. 1770

Your Favour of Jan. 8 came duly to hand, but I have been so much engag'd during the Sitting of Parliament, that I could not correspond regularly with all my Friends, and have of course trespass'd most with those on whose Good Nature and Indulgence I could most rely. I am however asham'd of being so long silent. It is but the other Day that I enquired after the Fate of your Tickets, when I receiv'd the enclos'd Answer, whereby you will see that the whole Cost has not been lost.⁴ I only wish'd to see three O's more following the Sum. I have not any farther Orders from you, but think to take at a Venture two Tickets more on your Account. If you disapprove, and chuse to rest where you are, signify it by a Line before the Drawing, directed to Messrs. Smith, Wright & Gray; who may then dispose of the Tickets.

I am glad to hear the old Gentleman, your Father-in-Law is still alive and happy.⁵ Please to remember me to him respectfully. Probably he can recollect but little of me, as it is a good deal more than half a Century since he has seen me: but I remember him well, a lively, active, handsome young Man, with a fine full flowing Head of Hair. I suppose he must now be near Fourscore.

If I could have given you any Intimation of the Intentions of Government with regard to America that might be depended on,

2. These were Parker's remittances from New York on his postal accounts, sent in his letters to BF above, April 23–24, 25.

3. See BF to Smith, Wright & Gray above, May 10.

4. For the affair of Williams' lottery tickets see above, XVI, 211, and BF to Smith, Wright & Gray, May 10.

5. William Harris, of Ipswich, had married BF's half-sister Anne in 1712. Above, I, lvii.

you should have had them in good time for Use in the Views of Trade you hint at. But there have been this last Winter such Changes of Men and of Minds, and such continual Expectations of more and other Changes, that nothing was certain; and I believe that to this Day the Ministry are not all of a Mind, nor determin'd what are the next Steps proper to be taken with us. Some are said to be for severe, others for lenient Measures; others for leaving Things as they now are, in confidence that we shall soon be tired of our Non-Importation Agreements, Manufacturing Schemes, and Self-denying Frugalities, submit to the Duties, and return by degrees to our dear Luxuries and Idleness, with our old Course of Commercial Extravagance, Folly and Good Humour. Which of these Opinions will prevail and be acted on, 'tis impossible yet to say. I only know that generally the Dispute is thought a dangerous one; and that many wish to see it well compromis'd in time, lest by a Continuance of mutual Provocation the Breach should become past healing.

I am much oblig'd to you and Cousin Hubbard for your Kindness to my Friend Hughes, of which he acquainted me, with many Expressions of Gratitude for your Civilities. He would have been very happy in that Station, and in your Acquaintance so nigh him: but he is now remov'd to Carolina.[6] My Love to your good Wife and Children, and believe me ever Your affectionate Uncle

B FRANKLIN

Mr. Jona. Williams

Addressed: To / Mr Jonathan Williams / Mercht / Boston / B Free FRANKLIN

Endorsed: June 6, 1770

6. John Hughes, BF's old political ally in Philadelphia, had been appointed a customs collector in New Hampshire to compensate him for his losses in the Stamp Act crisis; and Williams and the Boston postmaster, Tuthill Hubbart, had befriended him. Meanwhile BF in London had worked for Hughes's transfer to a collectorship in South Carolina, presumably because it was more lucrative; the transfer had gone through, according to Thomas Coombe, not so much because of BF's influence as because of Hughes's sacrifices as a stamp-collector. Coombe to his father, Dec. 6, 1769, Hist. Soc. of Pa.

To John Winthrop

ALS: Massachusetts Historical Society

Dear Sir, London, June 6. 1770

I find among my Papers a Letter of yours, dated Dec. 7. 1769, which I must have had some Months in my Hands; and tho' I think I have answered it, I am not certain; a Multiplicity of Business during the late Sessions of Parliament having occasioned a Forgetting of some Circumstances. It will only be a little unnecessary Labour if I answer it again.[7]

I did give a particular Answer to Mr. Maskelyne's Queries relating to Lightning Rods. I have likewise given Sets of Directions for erecting them to several Persons who desired it; and I think that all I know of the matter may be collected from different Parts of my printed Papers. But, as many have not an Opportunity of seeing that Book, to make the thing more publick, I purpose to follow your Advice, and draw up a more compleat Instruction to Workmen than I have yet given, to be inserted in the Magazines. St. Paul's Church is now guarded agreable to the Directions of a Committee of our Society; and many Gentlemen's Houses in the Villages round London are now furnished with Conductors.[8]

You will see in the last and the next Volume of Transactions whatever the Society think fit to publish of the Observations received relating to the Transit. Those made in the South Sea are not yet come to hand, but are now daily expected.

Capt. Hall paid me the 52s. you sent per him. I have sent you the Transactions, and I think the Print you mention also, but am not certain.[9] Please to say if you have receiv'd it.

7. An extract of Winthrop's letter had gone to the Royal Society months before; see BF to Maskelyne above, Feb. 12.

8. The Astronomer Royal's queries and BF's answer have been lost. For BF's role in protecting St. Paul's see above, XVI, 145–51. See also I. Bernard Cohen, "Prejudice against the Introduction of Lightning-Rods," Franklin Institute *Jour.*, CCLIII (1952), pp. 393–440. BF, as far as we know, never did compile his instructions to workmen.

9. The worldwide observations of the transit of Venus appeared mainly in *Phil. Trans.*, LIX (1769) and LX (1770); those communicated by Captain James Cook from Tahiti did not appear until LXI (1771), 433–6. Capt. James Hall, master of the ship *Dartmouth*, later lost his cargo in the Boston Tea Party. The print, whatever it was, had not been sent; see Winthrop's reply below, Oct. 26.

I wonder much that you had not received the Galilean Glasses; and shall write again to Philadelphia about them this Day.

I bespoke your Achromatic Telescope, and I now understand that it is finished. It shall be sent by the first Ship.[1]

Towards the Beginning of last Winter Spots were seen in the Sun here by the naked Eyes of Multitudes of People, the Streets being full of Gazers for several Hours. The Smoke of the Town serv'd the purpose of colour'd Glasses.[2]

Your Observation of the Transit of Mercury I gave to Mr. Maskelyne and to the Society. I suppose it will be printed with one you sent formerly to Mr. Short, which it seems was never published.

I inclose an Extract of Mr. Maskelyne's Letter to me relating to your last Observation.[3] With the greatest Esteem and Respect, I am ever, Dear Sir, Your most obedient humble Servant

B FRANKLIN

John Winthrop Esqr
Endorsed: Recd Septr. 20.

To Noble Wimberly Jones

ALS: Bibliothèque Municipale de Nantes

Sir   London, June 7. 1770

I wrote to you sometime since that I had receiv'd your Orders to procure a Mace and Gowns suitable for your Assembly, and that I hoped to have them ready to go by this Ship.[4] The Gowns are accordingly ready; but the Silversmith has not kept his Time. So I think it best to send the Whole together, which I shall do by the first Opportunity after the Mace is finished. Inclos'd I send the Silversmith's Note of the Cost of one he lately made. I suppose his

1. For the glasses see above, XVI, 66, and for the telescope XV, 166.
2. For the sunspots see *Gent. Mag.*, XXXIX (1769), 630. The chance to observe them with the naked eye must have been the one benefit that Londoners derived from their smog, for which see above, XVI, 159.
3. See *ibid.*, pp. 257, 269–70.
4. See BF to Jones above, May 2.

Bill for this will not differ very widely. The Gowns cost £19 4s. 9d.[5]
With great Respect, I am, Sir, Your most obedient humble Servant
B FRANKLIN

P.S. With this I send you Copies of two Speeches made by a Member of Parliament who is a Friend of America, in the last Session. On the last, some Expectations were given by the Ministry that the Troops should be withdrawn.[6] The Duty on Tea still remains.

N. W. Jones, Esqr

Endorsed: Dr. Franklin 7th. June 1770

To Samuel Cooper[7]   ALS: British Museum

This letter contains Franklin's first extant response to the Boston Massacre.[8] He mentions it in closing, almost in passing, but news of it certainly underlay his discussion of the larger issue of a standing army in America. That discussion led him on to the argument, more carefully worked out than ever before, that for a century past Parliament had usurped an authority over the empire which it did not rightfully possess,

5. BF bought the gowns from Stone & Schudell and the mace from William Pickett, a goldsmith and silversmith of 32 Ludgate Hill; the bill for this was £88 8s. See the entry of June 21, 1770, in BF's Jour., p. 24; *Kent's Directory*... (London, 1770), p. 138; and BF to Jones below, July 6.

6. The speeches were undoubtedly those of Thomas Pownall in the Commons on March 5, during the debate on repealing the tax on tea, and on May 8, when he moved to clarify the legal position of the military in Massachusetts. The ministry replied to Pownall's motion through Lord Barrington, Secretary at War, who assured the House that the troops would be withdrawn because no civil authority in Boston would use them. Cobbett, *Parliamentary History*, XVI, 855–70, 979–95, 998. In fact the two regiments remaining in the town had withdrawn to Castle William in Boston harbor on March 10, five days after the Massacre. On June 12 Hillsborough approved Gage's request to send the 29th, the regiment involved in the shooting, to New Jersey: Carter, ed., *Gage Correspondence*, I, 255; II, 103.

7. See above, IV, 69 n, and the exchange of letters in Vol. XVI.

8. A town meeting on March 13 ordered a committee to compile an account of the Massacre, which was quickly written and printed: *A Short Narrative of the Horrid Massacre in Boston*... (printed by order of the Town of Boston, 1770). Copies were sent to BF and other friends in England on March 22. Cooper doubtless gave his own views in the missing letter of March 28.

because the mother country and the colonies were in fact separate states with coequal legislatures, and were held together only by their loyalty to a common sovereign. Each colony was in a contractual relationship with the crown, expressed in the solemn compact of its charter, and Parliament had no right to alter that compact or impinge on the autonomy that it guaranteed.

This idea of a compact was thoroughly familiar to the colonists and, even though it was largely a fiction, had long played an implicit or explicit role in the development of their thinking about government.[9] They held themselves to be Englishmen who, because they lived outside the realm, were exempt from many of the obligations of those within the realm (such as obedience to the game laws, to church courts, and above all to Parliament) and yet possessed all the rights of Englishmen at home. To the latter, understandably enough, this concept was incomprehensible and intolerable: a people whom they often referred to as their subjects was claiming all their rights and repudiating many of their obligations. The compact theory therefore held no hope of resolving the quarrel, but merely increased misunderstanding on both sides. Yet the theory had great future importance for both. It contained the seeds, for the United States, of divisible sovereignty and balanced government, and for Britain of the Commonwealth of Nations.

Did Franklin believe that this constitutional concept could be applied in practice to the empire of 1770? He did not commit himself,[1] but two points about his argument are worth noting. The first related to Britain: he clearly recognized that his view of the constitution would be anathema to Lords and Commons. The second related to Massachusetts: although he emphasized that loyalty to the King was the colonists' best protection against a corrupt and hostile Parliament, he failed to point out (though he may have implied) that such loyalty was scarcely consonant with the Bostonians' attitude toward the King's agents. These points do not suggest that his logic of empire was a mere polemical exercise; they do, perhaps, suggest that he was too much of a realist to expect his logic to prevail on either side of the Atlantic.

Dear Sir, London, June 8. 1770

I received duly your Favour of March 28. With this I send you two Speeches in Parliament on our Affairs by a Member that you

9. See Charles H. McIlwain, *The American Revolution: a Constitutional Interpretation* (New York, 1932), *passim*; Bernard Bailyn, *The Ideological Origins of the American Revolution* (Cambridge, Mass., [1967]), pp. 175–229.

1. A few months later, however, he wrote of a future when the colonists would "come to be considered in the light of *distinct states*." To Cushing below, Feb. 5, 1771.

know.[2] The Repeal of the whole late Act would undoubtedly have been a prudent Measure, and I have reason to believe that Lord North was for it, but some of the other Ministers could not be brought to agree to it. So the Duty on Tea, with that obnoxious Preamble, remains to continue the Dispute.[3] But I think the next Session will hardly pass over without repealing them; for the Parliament must finally comply with the Sense of the Nation. As to the Standing Army kept up among us in time of Peace, without the Consent of our Assemblies, I am clearly of Opinion that it is not agreable to the Constitution. Should the King by the Aid of his Parliaments in Ireland and the Colonies, raise an Army and bring it into England, quartering it here in time of Peace without the Consent of the Parliament of Great Britain, I am persuaded he would soon be told that he had no Right so to do, and the Nation would ring with Clamours against it.[4] I own that I see no Difference in the Cases. And while we continue so many distinct and separate States, our having the same Head or Sovereign, the King, will not justify such an Invasion of the separate Right of each State to be consulted on the Establishment of whatever Force is proposed to be kept up within its Limits, and to give or refuse its Consent as shall appear most for the Public Good of that State. That the Colonies originally were constituted distinct States, and intended to be continued such, is clear to me from a thorough Consideration of their original Charters, and the whole Conduct of the Crown and Nation towards them until the Restoration. Since that Period, the Parliament here has usurp'd an Authority of making Laws for them, which before it had not. We have for some time submitted to that Usurpation, partly thro' Ignorance and Inattention, and partly from our Weakness and Inability to contend. I hope when our

2. Presumably the same speeches enclosed in his letter to Jones; see the preceding document.

3. See BF to Galloway above, Jan. 11, March 21, and to Thomson, March 18. On April 9 Alderman Trecothick moved unsuccessfully for the repeal of the last remaining duty, that on tea. *Journals of the House of Commons*, XXXII, 750–1; Jack M. Sosin, *Agents and Merchants: British Colonial Policy and the Origins of the American Revolution, 1763–1775* (Lincoln, Neb., 1965), p. 127.

4. For slightly different versions of BF's argument see above, XVI, 302–4, and BF to Galloway below, June 11. The fear of a standing army in peacetime was an old Whig bogy; see Caroline Robbins, *The Eighteenth-Century Commonwealthman . . .* (Cambridge, Mass., 1959), pp. 103–5.

Rights are better understood here, we shall, by a prudent and proper Conduct be able to obtain from the Equity of this Nation a Restoration of them. And in the mean time I could wish that such Expressions as, *The supreme Authority of Parliament*; *The Subordinacy of our Assemblies to the Parliament* and the like (which in Reality mean nothing if our Assemblies with the King have a true Legislative Authority) I say, I could wish that such Expressions were no more seen in our publick Pieces. They are too strong for Compliment, and tend to confirm a Claim [of] Subjects in one Part of the King's Dominions to be Sovereigns over their Fellow-Subjects in another Part of his Dominions; when [in] truth they have no such Right, and their Claim is founded only on Usurpation, the several States having equal Rights and Liberties, and being only connected, as England and Scotland were before the Union, by having one common Sovereign, the King. This kind of Doctrine the Lords and Commons here would deem little less than Treason against what they think their Share of the Sovereignty over the Colonies.[5] To me those Bodies seem to have been long encroaching on the Rights of their and our Sovereign, assuming too much of his Authority, and betraying his Interests. By our Constitutions he is, with [his] Plantation Parliaments, the sole Legislator of his American Subjects, and in that Capacity is and ought to be free to exercise his own Judgment unrestrain'd and unlimited by his Parliament here. And our Parliaments have Right to grant him Aids without the Consent of this Parliament, a Circumstance which, by the [way] begins to give it some Jealousy. Let us therefore hold fast [our] Loyalty to our King (who has the best Disposition towards us, and has a Family-Interest in our Prosperity) as that steady Loyalty is the most probable Means of securing us from the arbitrary Power of a corrupt Parliament, that does not like us, and conceives itself to

5. BF here touches on a point that completely precluded British acceptance of his doctrine. Ever since the Glorious Revolution and the Act of Union the course of constitutional development had increasingly emphasized the sovereignty of the crown in Parliament. Any sphere of royal influence outside the purview of Parliament was suspect, as appeared soon afterward in the controversies over reforming the government of India. BF's doctrine, however, entailed far more than a sphere of influence; it meant dividing sovereignty itself into parts, the crown in each colonial legislature as well as in the British. The Lords and Commons, and for that matter the King, would have considered such a division unconstitutional.

have an Interest in keeping us down and fleecing us. If they should urge the *Inconvenience* of an Empire's being divided into so many separate States, and from thence conclude that we are not so divided; I would answer, that an Inconvenience proves nothing but itself. England and Scotland were once separate States, under the same King. The Inconvenience found in their being separate States, did not prove that the Parliament of England had a Right to govern Scotland. A formal Union was thought necessary, and England was an hundred Years soliciting it, before she could bring it about. If Great Britain now thinks such an Union necessary with us, let her propose her Terms, and we may consider of them.[6] Were the general Sentiments of this Nation to be consulted in the Case, I should hope the Terms, whether practicable or not, would at least be equitable: for I think that except among those with whom the Spirit of Toryism prevails, the popular Inclination here is, to wish us well, and that we may preserve our Liberties.

I unbosom my self thus to you in Confidence of your Prudence, and wishing to have your Sentiments on the Subject in Return.

Mr. Pownall, I suppose, will acquaint you with the Event of his Motions, and therefore I say nothing more of them, than that he appears very sincere in his Endeavours to serve us; on which Account I some time since republish'd with Pleasure the parting Addresses to him of your Assembly, with some previous Remarks, to his Honour as well as in Justification of our People.[7]

I hope that before this time those detestable Murderers have quitted your Province, and that the Spirit of Industry and Frugality continues and increases. With sincerest Esteem and Affection, I am, Dear Sir, Your most obedient and most humble Servant

B FRANKLIN

P.S. Just before the last Session of Parliament commenced a Friend of mine, who had Connections with some of the Ministry, wrote me a Letter purposely to draw from me my Sentiments in Writing

6. The picture of England soliciting for a century is false. When James I and VI attempted to achieve more than a dynastic union, he was defeated by English resistance; the England of Cromwell did not solicit a union but briefly imposed one; no real solicitation occurred until shortly before the Act of Union, and then because of a particular emergency. BF had little interest in a similar union of the empire; see above, XV, 239.

7. See above, Feb. 6.

on the then State of Affairs. I wrote a pretty free Answer, which I know was immediately communicated and a good deal handed about among them. For your *private Amusement* I send you Copies.[8] I wish you may be able to read them, as they are very badly written by a very blundering Clerk.   BF

Revd. Dr Cooper.

To Samuel Franklin[9]

Reprinted from [Jared Sparks, ed.,] *A Collection of the Familiar Letters and Miscellaneous Papers of Benjamin Franklin* (Boston, 1833), pp. 132–3.

Loving Cousin,   London, 8 June, 1770.
    I received your kind letter of the 23d of March. I was happy to find that neither you, nor any of your family, were in the way of those murderers.[1] I hope that before this time the town is quite freed from such dangerous and mischievous inmates.
    I rejoice to hear that you and your good wife and children continue in health. My love to them. I still enjoy a considerable share of that blessing, thanks to God, and hope once more to see Boston and my friends there before I die. I left it first in 1723. I made a visit there in 1733; another in 1743; another in 1753; another in 1763. Perhaps if I live to 1773, I may then call again and take my leave.
    Our relation, Sally Franklin, is still with me here, is a very good girl, and grown up almost a woman.[2] She sends her love to you and yours. I am, with sincere regard, Your affectionate cousin,
                                                          B. FRANKLIN.

8. William Strahan's queries and BF's answers are printed above, XVI, 233–5, 243–9. Cooper, as he mentions in his letter below of Nov. 6, showed the answers to members of the Massachusetts House when BF was being considered as agent.
    9. BF's first cousin once removed; see above, XIV, 215 n.
    1. A reference to the Boston Massacre.
    2. Sarah Franklin (A.5.2.3.1.1.1) was the daughter of Thomas Franklin, who like Samuel was BF's first cousin once removed. She had been living in Craven Street off and on since 1766.

From Thomas Gilpin[3]

Extract: reprinted from "Memoir of Thomas Gilpin," *Pennsylvania Magazine of History and Biography*, XLIX (1925), 313.

June 8th. [1770]

As the late repeal of the acts in England more fully developes itself the singularity of its not taking effect till December next makes it appear the more as if the ministry had adopted a system of traps and decoys. But they have alarmed the game and it will require considerable time if it ever is accomplished to forget the snares; the disposition now seems to be to adhere to the non-importation agreement untill all the acts are repealed and such repeal actually commences.[4] The people will never be reunited while England shall attempt to impose any laws in the making of which they have no voice.

To Deborah Franklin

ALS: American Philosophical Society

My dear Child,   London, June 10. 1770

I received your kind Letters of March 12 and April 24. I think you are the most punctual of all my Correspondents; and it is often a particular Satisfaction to me to hear from you, when I have no Letter from any one else.

I did per Capt. Falconer answer Sally's Letter about her Son's being inoculated; and told her Sir John Pringle's Opinion as to the Probability of his not having the Small Pox hereafter. I think he advised, as no Eruption appeared, to make sure of the thing by inoculating him again.[5] I rejoice much in the Pleasure you appear to take in him. It must be of Use to your Health, the having such an Amusement. My Love to him, and to his Father and Mother.

3. But perhaps not to BF; see the headnote to Gilpin's letter above, June 1.
4. A meeting of Philadelphia merchants on June 5 decided, almost unanimously, to keep in force their original agreement of March, 1769. See *Pa. Gaz.*, June 7, 1770, where similar action by the New York merchants was reported.
5. Sally's inquiry and BF's answer have been lost, but her acknowledgment of the latter is printed above at the end of May, and makes clear that Sir John did advise a second inoculation.

Capt. Ourry is gone abroad as a travelling Tutor to Lord Galway's Son;[6] Mrs. Strahan is at Bath; Mr. Strahan and Children, Mr. and Mrs. West and their Son,[7] are all well at present, tho' Mr. West himself has had a long Illness. They always enquire after you and I present your Compliments. Poor Nanny was drawn in to marry a worthless Fellow, who got all her Money and then ran away and left her. So she is return'd to her old Service with Mrs. Stevenson, poorer than ever, but seems pretty patient, only looks dejected, sighs sometimes, and wishes she had never left Philadelphia.[8] Mr. Montgomery died at Sea, as we have lately heard, and Mrs. Montgomery, who has lain in at Lisbon, will return from thence with her Boy to Philadelphia.[9]

As to myself, I had from Christmas till Easter, a disagreable Giddiness hanging about me, which however did not hinder me from being about and doing Business. In the Easter Holidays being at a Friend's House in the Country, I was taken with a Sore Throat, and came home half strangled. From Monday till Friday I could swallow nothing but Barley Water and the like. I was bled largely and purged two or three times. On Friday came on a Fit of the

6. For Lewis Ourry see above, VII, 62 n. William Monckton (after 1769 Monckton Arundell), second Viscount Galway, had two sons; the younger, Robert (1752–1810), who succeeded his brother in 1774 as fourth viscount, seems the more likely one to have been making the Grand Tour.

7. The senior Strahans and Wests need no introduction. The Strahan children were William, his father's former partner, who had by now left home and apparently set up his own printing business; George, then a fellow at Oxford and, in his mother's phrase, "breeding for a clergyman"; Andrew, overseer of his father's printing business; and Peggy (Margaret Penelope), BF's "little Wife," who had finished school and was living at home. See Mrs. Strahan to David Hall, Jan. 16, 1770, APS; above, X, 169 n. The Wests' young son Raphael was about six at the time: Charles H. Hart, "Benjamin West's Family...," *PMHB*, XXXII (1908), 9–10.

8. Ann Hardy, Mrs. Stevenson's servant, had spent several years in America, some of them with the Franklins in Philadelphia; see above, XIV, 279. The runaway husband was named Elliot.

9. The Montgomerys were a Delaware family. Robert (1743–70) died on April 28 on his brig in the Bay of Gibraltar, returning from a voyage in the Mediterranean that he had made in hopes of recovering his health. His wife was the former Dorcas Armitage of Newcastle, Del.; she gave birth to his son Robert (1770–1809) at Valformosa, near Lisbon. Thomas H. Montgomery, *A Genealogical History of the Family of Montgomery...* (Philadelphia, 1863), p. 152.

Gout, from which I had been free Five Years. Immediately the Inflammation and Swelling in my Throat disappeared; my Foot swelled greatly, and I was confined about three Weeks;[1] since which I am perfectly well, the Giddiness and every other disagreeable Symptom having quite left me. I hope your Health is likewise by this time quite re-establish'd; being as ever, my dear Child, Your affectionate Husband   B FRANKLIN

To Joseph Galloway   ALS: Clements Library

Dear Sir,   London, June 11. 1770
I wrote to you per Capt. Falconer, and since by the April Packet.[2] None went from hence in May, there being no Boat on this side. It is now long since I have received any of your Favours. I think the last was dated Nov. 8. 1769. I suppose your Indisposition, with too much Business, has prevented your Writing. I am glad to hear from our Friend Dr. Evans, that you think of affording your self more Leisure.[3]
The Parliament is up without repealing the Tea Duty: but it is generally given out and understood that it will be done next Winter. Lord North, I have reason to believe, was for doing it now; but was over-rul'd.[4] A general Act is talk'd of, revising all the Acts for regulating Trade in America, wherein every thing that gives just Cause of Offence to the Colonists may be omitted, and the Tea with its odious Preamble may be dropt, without hurting the Honour of Parliament, which it seems was apprehended if it had been repeal'd this Year. But it is by no means certain yet that such an Act will take place. The Act intended at the Beginning of the Session, and alluded to in the King's Speech, for punishing the Combinations of Merchants not to import, &c. was never brought forward. I flatter my-

1. The attack began on April 20. Thomas Coombe, writing to his father on May 5 (Hist. Soc. of Pa.), mentioned that he was dining that evening with BF, who had been confined for a fortnight with gout but appeared to be tolerably well recovered.
2. Probably the letters printed above, Jan. 11 and March 21.
3. Galloway's illness was presumably that mentioned by Cadwalader Evans a year before: above, XVI, 157.
4. See BF to Cooper above, June 8.

self I may have had some Share in discouraging it, by representing the Difficulties and even Impracticabilities of carrying such an Act into Execution in the Colonies, showing that Government here would by such a Measure only expose its own Weakness and Imprudence in a fresh Instance, and produce an Effect contrary to that intended, rendering the Agreements more general and more firmly adhered to, by souring still farther the Minds of the People.[5] Towards the Conclusion of the Session Govr. Pownal made another Speech and Motion relating to the military Power kept up in America, a Copy of which I send you inclos'd. It is a curious Question, how far it is agreable to the British Constitution, for the King who is Sovereign over different States, to march the Troops he has rais'd by Authority of Parliament in one of the States, into another State, and quarter them there in time of Peace, without the Consent of the Parliament of that other State. Should it be concluded that he may do this, what Security has Great Britain, that a future King, when the Colonies shall become more powerful, may not raise Armies there, transport them hither, and quarter them here without Consent of Parliament, perhaps to the Prejudice of their Liberties, and even with a View of subverting them?[6] The House got

5. For BF's hope, earlier in the year, that colonial trade regulation would be sweepingly reformed, and his balancing fear of an act to curb nonimportation in America, see his letter to Galloway above, Jan. 11. Neither the hope nor the fear was realized. Whatever impetus the reform movement may have had was apparently spent during the spring in the partial repeal of the Townshend Acts. The act against nonimportation also died aborning. The House of Commons requested and received documents on the subject, and a bill was drafted but not brought before the House. Historical Manuscripts Commission, *Fourteenth Report, Appendix, Part X . . .* (Dartmouth MSS., Vol. II, American Papers; London, 1895), pp. 50, 75–6; *Journals of the House of Commons*, XXXII, 717, 745. What influence BF had in quashing the bill is impossible to say, or even whether his lobbying was directed toward merchants, private M.P.s, or ministers. But other factors were probably the decisive ones. First, the merchants were more interested in repealing the duties than in attacking directly the American boycott on their goods (see BF to Thomson above, March 18), and their pressure tended to focus Parliament's attention on repeal rather than on nonimportation. Second, a ban on associations of American merchants was of doubtful legality. Third, rumors were rife in Britain that those associations were breaking up, in which case no ban was needed. These factors in conjunction suggest that BF was exaggerating the danger as well as his own role in obviating it.

6. BF is here conjuring up precisely the future peril that he himself had

over Mr. Pownal's Motion, by a Declaration of the Ministry that the several Matters contain'd in it were already under Consideration of his Majesty's Law Servants, and that every thing would be done conformable to the Law and the Constitution; that the Troops would not be return'd to Boston, unless call'd for by the Civil Power, &c. I inclose also a Paper he gave me sometime before, proposing a Case to be tried in America; but perhaps that will become unnecessary.[7] On the whole, there seems a general Disposition in the Nation (a particular Faction excepted) to be upon good Terms with the Colonies, and to leave us in the Enjoyment of all our Rights. It is universally thought that no future Impositions on America will ever be attempted here; only it is not to be expected that Parliament should formally renounce its Claim; that, they say, would be inconsistent with its Dignity, &c. And yet I think all this is not quite to be relied on. There is a Malice against us in some powerful People, that discovers itself in all their Expressions when they speak of us; And Incidents may yet arise on either Side of the Water that may give them Advantage, and prevent those healing Measures that all good Men wish to take place.

I hear that a Paper-money Bill was in hand during your last Session, but fail'd. Had it pass'd, it would have been repeal'd here, if the Bills were made a Tender even to the Loan-Office in Discharge of the Mortgages. Poor R. Charles, our former Agent, was put upon an Application to Parliament for an Act permitting the As-

---

ridiculed two and a half years before; see above, xv, 19. He did substantially the same conjuring in his letter to Cooper above, June 8, but his argument to Galloway is fragmentary by comparison. Except for this one aside about the prerogative and the military, he did not raise with him any of the large issues that he raised with Cooper. The difference between the two letters is striking, even if it does not warrant any conclusions. It may be accidental, and again it may not be.

7. For Pownall's speech and motion on the military see BF to Jones above, June 7. An incomplete copy of the motion, in Pownall's hand and dated March 8, 1770, is in the Franklin Papers in the APS; this is presumably part of what BF copied for Galloway. The other enclosure, Pownall's paper, was doubtless a by-product of his earlier consultation with BF, for which see above, xvi, 298. After the House of Commons voted down Pownall's motion on May 8, Edmund Burke introduced resolutions censuring the administration's entire recent policy. These too were voted down, and the Lords rejected identical resolutions on May 18, ending for that session any possibility of reform. Cobbett, *Parliamentary History*, xvi, 1002–28.

sembly of New York to make their Bills such a Tender. In the Progress of his Bill it was so alter'd, as to make him apprehend it would be of no Use to the Province, at the same time it was to be consider'd as a kind of private Bill, of which he was to pay the Expence and Fees, amounting (as he told me) to near £200, and he fear'd that would not be approv'd of: In a word he was so bewilder'd and distress'd with the Affair, that he finally put an End to his Perplexities—by a Razor![8] The Objection to such a Tender was frivolous; for it was certainly never the Intention of the Act of Parliament to forbid the Government's being oblig'd to take its own Notes. If the Words were so ambiguous or so general as to create a Doubt, such Doubt should have been remov'd by an Explanatory Clause in a Publick Act. But this, tho' urged by me and others to several Members, could not be attended to; it must be a particular Favour to each Province that should apply for it, acknowledging by such Application the Authority of Parliament over our Legislatures: But perhaps a principal Motive was (at least with some) to make more special Acts for the sake of more Fees.

Mr. Jackson being now appointed Council to the Board of Trade,* thinks his continuing in the Agency of any Province will be judg'd incompatible with that Office, and therefore declines serving us any longer in that Station, but professes a Continuance of his Good-Will to us, and Readiness to assist your Agent with his best Advice on all Occasions. He presses me very much to continue here another Winter, alledging that it may be of great Use, and giving Reasons, that I cannot repeat.

I send you herewith the Remainder of the Votes; and am, with best Wishes for your Health and Prosperity, my dear Friend, Yours most affectionately   B FRANKLIN

* This Office having been vacant near two Years, is the Reason that many Colony Acts have lain so long here, not pass'd upon; it being that

---

8. For the progress of Robert Charles' bill see *Journals of the House of Commons*, XXXII, 895–6, 899, 908, 919, 962, 982; *Journals of the House of Lords*, XXXII, 585–6. One historian has questioned BF's statement that Charles committed suicide: what ground had the agent to "fear the bill would not be approved when it had passed the House of Commons—the decisive chamber—the week before?" Jack M. Sosin, *Agents and Merchants...* (Lincoln, Neb., 1965), p. 137 n. 45. The question is groundless if BF meant what we believe he did, that Charles feared disapproval in New York, not Westminster.

Officer's Business to peruse them all and Report his Opinion of them in Law Points.[9] Be pleased to communicate this Letter, with my sincere Respects, to the Committee. Your Votes and Laws are rarely sent me.

Joseph Galloway Esqr

To David Hall
ALS: American Philosophical Society

Dear Mr. Hall,   London, June 11. 1770

I received your kind Letter of March 17. The continual Employment of my Time here in other Affairs, together with the Expectation I have had every Year of Returning, have prevented my considering the Accounts between us so as to compleat the Settlement, which indeed can be much better done when we are together with Mr. Parker, who may be able in a Word to explain things that would require much Writing.[1] I hope it will not now be long before we meet, as I am determin'd to see Philadelphia, God willing, next Spring at farthest, if not sooner. I rejoice to hear of the Welfare of your Family, to which I wish all Prosperity. With the greatest Esteem and Regard, I am ever, my dear Friend, Yours most affectionately   B FRANKLIN

Addressed: To / Mr David Hall / Printer / Philadelphia / via New York / Per Packet / B Free FRANKLIN / June 11, 1770.

To the New Jersey Assembly Committee of Correspondence
ALS: William C. Coles, Moorestown, N.J. (1954)

Gentlemen,   London, June 11. 1770

I received your Letter of March 27. acquainting me that a Bill

9. The previous counsel, Sir Matthew Lamb, had died on Nov. 5, 1768 (*DNB*); Jackson's appointment was not formally announced to the Board until April 30, 1770. *Board of Trade Jour.*, 1768–75, p. 185.

1. Hall had been arguing for years that the accounts should be settled, lest he or BF die with the matter still unresolved. BF had little reason to suppose that James Parker would be on hand for explanations the following spring: Parker had written him often enough that he was not long for this world, and in fact he died three weeks after BF sent this note. Hall survived only until the end of 1772. BF's casualness about the whole affair is hard to understand; he might well have foreseen the complications that it caused in later years, for which see above, XIII, 100–1.

had been agreed upon by the whole Legislature, to provide a more effectual Remedy against excessive Costs in the Recovery of Debts, &c. Mr. Morgann, Secretary of your Province had called upon me just before that Letter came to hand, mentioned his being informed that an Act was likely to pass intended to lessen the Profits of his Office, in which case his Deputy could not afford to remit him so much as heretofore and that he should be oblig'd to enter a Caveat against its receiving the King's Approbation; to which I could then say nothing, as I knew not the Nature of the Act but from his Information. But assoon as I receiv'd your Letter, apprehending that the Application of a Patent Officer[2] here against an Act of any Assembly, might have too much Weight, I thought it best, if possible, to take off his Opposition in time; and to that End got a Friend of his to represent to him; that the Act would really be of little or no Prejudice to him; that as the Province increased, the Business and Profits of his Office would be continually augmenting; that the Fees of Practising Attorneys, against which the Act was chiefly levelled, had long been complain'd of as a grievous Oppression on the People; that those Gentlemen were the Persons who would principally be affected by it, and that probably the Insinuations to him against it had come from that Quarter; that any Opposition to it from him would appear in an exceeding ungracious Light in the Province, give great Offence to the General Assembly there, who might have it in their Power sometime or other to hurt or help his Office more than any thing in this Act could amount to; and therefore I wish'd, in Friendship to him, that he would take no Step against it. On which he sent me a very obliging Answer, that he would not oppose it. So I hope we shall find no great Difficulty in getting it approved.

I am sorry to acquaint you that the Paper-money Act is disapprov'd by the King.[3] The Objection to it was, its making the Bills a legal Tender in Payment of the Mortgages and Interest to the Loan-Officers, which is said to be contrary to the Act of Parliament, that forbids their being made a legal Tender in any Case whatever. As

2. Presumably an officer appointed by letters patent. Maurice Morgann (1726–1802), secretary of New Jersey since 1767, remained in England and discharged his duties through deputies. See above, XIII, 430 n.

3. One of the acts that the Committee had asked BF to work for; he had done so with no success. See above, XVI, 254.

your Loan-Officers can have no Interest in refusing the Bills, and there is not the least Likelyhood that they will ever refuse them, and it would be a Breach of their Bonds for the due Execution of their Office; I would submit it to your Consideration whether such a Clause might not in a future Act be omitted, whereby the Objection would be taken away, and then perhaps the Act might be allowed. Mr. Charles, Agent for New York, was put upon Applying to Parliament for an Act giving Leave to his Province to make their Bills a Tender to their own Treasurer, the Act of Parliament notwithstanding. Those who had the Direction would not agree to put into some Publick Act an Explanatory Clause to set that Matter right; which I thought the best way, as all acknowledged that it was a mere Mistake; but it must be done by a kind of private Act, and a particular one for each Province that should petition, for which I could see no reason but to increase Fees, which for each Act would be near £200. So Mr. Charles went in alone in his Application, his Bill was altered in the House not much to his Liking; and apprehending his Conduct might be blamed, the poor Gentleman grew delirious thro' want of Sleep, and unhappily put an End to his own Life.[4] The Secaucus Law is also repealed;[5] but the others have received his Majesty's Royal Assent. The original Repeals, &c. as I am assured by the Secretary, will be sent to the Governor by to-morrow's Mail, and I shall send you Copies from the Council Office by the next.

Before this reaches you, you will see by the Public Papers that all the Duties in the last Revenue Act are repealed, except that on Tea. It is generally thought, that will follow next Session, but it is not certain. There seems however a Disposition to be on good Terms with us, saving the Dignity of Parliament. With great Esteem and Respect, I have the Honour of being, Gentlemen Your most obedient and most humble Servant   B FRANKLIN

Cortland Skinner, Hendrick Fisher, Ebenezer Miller, Aaron Leaming, Abraham Hewlings, and Joseph Smith Esqrs. Commee. of Correspondence

Endorsed: Benjamin Franklin 1770
          11th. June 1770

4. See BF to Galloway above, June 11.
5. See above, XVI, 266–8.

174

From Deborah Franklin

ALS: Mrs. James Manderson Castle, Wilmington, Del. (1955)

My Dear Child   June the 13[-15] 1770
this afternoon I heard Capt. Friend is to Saile to morrow and I Cold
not let him go with oute a line or two to let you know that I am
much as I have bin for sume time. I have not heard that Sister is a
rived as yit but it gives me much trubel.[6] My King bird is verey
well att this time all thow he has bin verey ill with a Sever Cold
proseded from a verey Cold spell of Cold wather and a long Spell
of Esterly raine but the wather is much better and we air all well.
Billey has bin and is att this time he is verey fond of the Child and
thinkes he is like Frankey Folger. I thoute so two and had the
pickter broute down to look and everey bodey thinkes as much as
thow it had bin drawn for him.[7] When we Show it to the Child and
tell him he is his littel unkill he will pat it and kiss it and Clape his
hand to it and everey morning he Gowes and Clapes to his Granda-
dey but I wonte say aney more now. Mr. Parker has bin heare and
is gon to mareyland he is verey un well in dead So ill I wold not let
him go a lone So Gorge is gon with him[8] he is gon 5 Days. I Shold
tell you that he billey is gon over Schuelkill after Some buisnes for
Sum Gentel man in Ingland but that is all I know of it. I expeckte
him to night. My love to all friends. I donte write a boute aney
bodey but my Self I conclud youre a feckshonet wife
                                                           D FRANKLIN
But if to morrow will pordues aney Thing I will write a line or two
more.

June the 15 Billey Came back and Stayed one night and Dined with
us yesterday and Mr. Parker came back yesterday is verey ill. I
Sente for Dr. Bond and desires to due what he Can and I will Due
all I Can for him. The Aprill packit I had a letter dated 10 I Shall

---

6. DF is worried, in other words, because she has not yet heard of Jane
Mecom's safe return to Boston from her visit to Philadelphia. Jane subse-
quently apologized for not writing her more promptly. Van Doren, *Franklin–
Mecom*, pp. 113–14.

7. For the portrait of Francis Folger Franklin, BF's and DF's son, who had
died at the age of four, see above, VIII, 92 n.

8. James Parker was indeed at death's door; he had only a few more weeks to
live. George was the Franklins' Negro servant; see above, XIV, 282 n.

write by that. The in closed is what B Franklin wrote to me from Burlinton Mr. Odel was his Secketarey.[9] Not any new of Sister I am yours   D F.

Addressed: To / Benjamin Franklin Esqr / Craven Street / London

From John Ewing   ALS: American Philosophical Society

Sir   Philada. June 14th 1770

I received your very agreeable Letter, in which you acknowledge the Receipt of our Observations of the Transit of Venus. I herewith send you a few Copies of them as they are printed in our Transactions; and I suppose in a more perfect Form than that in which they were sent before, as that was done in an Hurry and I have not a Copy of what I sent. If what you received before is not printed in the Philosophical Transactions, please to request Mr. Maskelyne to insert them as they are here, unless he should think it better to abridge or alter them, as to their Dress or Form, which he has full Liberty to do, as he is much better acquainted with Publications of this Kind than I can be supposed to be.[1]

I mentioned to our Society your Proposal to purchase the Transactions of the learned Societies in Europe, and they have taken the Matter under their Consideration. They approved of your Reasoning on the Subject, when I read it to them, and Nothing will prevent their coming into the Resolution if their Poverty does not.[2]

I hope before this Time that Mr. Maskelyne has given you an

9. This is whimsy. Sally Bache and her baby, Benjamin Franklin, had been visiting the WFS in Burlington for the past three months; see David Hall to BF above, March 17. Jonathan Odell, the WFS' Anglican minister, has appeared frequently in recent volumes.

1. For the various observations of the transit sent from Philadelphia and printed (or not printed) in *Phil. Trans.* see above, XVI, 257 n. Ewing's reference to those printed in the APS *Trans.* is baffling, because the first volume did not appear until 1771, and it seems unlikely that even proof sheets of the papers for 1769 existed at the time he wrote. If they did not, the only printed paper he could have sent was his "Proposal for Observing the Transit of Venus, June 3, 1769," which was among the transactions that were printed in the *Amer. Mag.* (1769), pp. 40–4.

2. BF had presumably made, in a missing letter to Ewing, the same suggestions to the APS that he had already made to the Library Company of Philadelphia, for which see above, XVI, 171.

Estimate of the Expence and Apparatus necessary for erecting an Observatory here, where we are blessed with so happy a Serenity of Air for astronomical Observations. I have not yet mentioned this Matter to our Society, but wait untill I hear farther from you, and would still chuse, that when it is proposed it should come from you and the Astronomer Royal, to whose Judgments our Society pay the greatest Respect in these Matters.[3]

Please to accept of my hearty thanks for the Perusal of your last Volume of the Phil. Transactions. I shall deliver it safely to Mrs. Franklin. When the Observations of the Transit of Venus come to Hand from the East Indies the North of Europe or from South America, I shall be much obliged to you for a Copy of them, as I am anxious to know how they correspond with ours.[4] I am Sir your most obedient and very humble Servant   JOHN EWING

Please to deliver one of the Copies with my Compliments to the Astronomer Royal the Revd. Mr. Maskelyne

To Benjamin Franklin Esqr. L.LD.

Endorsed: Mr Ewing June 14. 1770

From Joseph Galloway   ALS: American Philosophical Society

Dear Friend   Philada. June 21. 1770

A number of new Engagements occasioned by the Death of Mr. Growdon,[5] which detained me in the Country for the most part of several Months, prevented my acknowledging the Receipt of your Favors of Jany. 11. Mar. 21. and April 10th. I am much obliged to you for the State of American Affairs on your Side the Water, containd in yours of Mar. 21. The M[inistr]y are much Mistaken in imagining that there ever will be an Union either of Affections or Interest between G. Britain and America untill Justice is done to

3. Ewing is here repeating the suggestion made in his letter to BF above, Jan. 4.

4. If any observations were made in South America, they were not published; the others appeared in *Phil. Trans.*, LIX (1770), 262–72, 327–32.

5. For Lawrence Growdon, the father of Joseph Galloway's wife, see above, XI, 527 n. He had died on March 29: *Pa. Gaz.*, April 12, 1770.

the latter and there is a full Restoration of its Liberties. The People here are resolved to adhere to their former Non Importation Agreement. The People of Boston and Maryland are of the same Opinion untill the Duty on Tea is taken off. The Yorkers and Rhode Islanders seem to be divided among them selves, but I think they will soon concur to support the Cause of Liberty.[6]

I am greatly Surprized at the Conduct of Administration in Relation to the New York and New Jersey Paper Money Bills.[7] The Reason assigned for their Rejections are really rediculous——And can be accounted for on no other Ground, than that they are determined, the Americans shall not have any Paper Medium at all. Is not every Promisor in a Promisary Note obliged to receive his Note, every Banker to take his Bill and every Drawer of a Bill of Exchange to take it back if not paid, and yet I never understood that such Notes or Bills were ever deem'd Legal Tender? When I Lend to or deposit with another £100 he gives me Paper, or a Promisory Note for Repayment. Is he not Obliged to receive his Paper and deliver me my deposit? Such is the Case of a Bank Bill, and Inland Bill of Exchange as well as foreign, and the same is the Case with Respect to American Paper Money. A Farmer Pledges his Land with the Government and takes Paper——when he comes to redeem his Pledge ought he not to return the Paper, and ought not the Government to be obliged to receive [it] in Discharge of the Land? To say that the Statute [is] intended to prevent this is to say it is Prohibitory of all Paper Money in America. But How is their Conduct on this Occasion to be reconciled with what has passed heretofore? Several of our late Laws for the support of Government and the Act for Payment of the Debts of the House of

6. Word reached Philadelphia in early June that the Boston merchants had agreed to adhere to their nonimportation agreement until the duties were totally repealed, whereupon a meeting in Philadelphia came to the same decision. The Annapolis merchants quickly followed suit, and similar action was reported at Newport, Providence, and New York. *Pa. Gaz.*, June 7, 14, 1770. In fact the New Yorkers were beginning to abandon their agreement by June 16; a few weeks later their defection was complete, and it undermined the whole movement. See Gilpin to BF below, July 19; Arthur M. Schlesinger, *The Colonial Merchants and the American Revolution, 1763–1776* (New York, 1918), pp. 223, 226–7.

7. The Board of Trade had recently recommended disallowing the New York and New Jersey acts; see *Board of Trade Jour.*, 1768–75, pp. 173, 184.

Employment[8] were liable to the same Objection, and yet they have been laid before the King in Council and passed unrepealed.

I am much pleased with your Information that Mr. Jackson is appointed Council to the Board of Trade.[9] From his good Disposition towards America, his Knowledge of our Affairs and his great Candor and Integrity we have good Reason to hope our Laws will not be rejected on frivolous Pretences and Partial Policy.

Nothing occured in our Winter or Spring Sittings worth communicating, or engaged as I have been, I shoud have wrote to you on what Passed. Several Matters of Consequence was agitated, but faild, some in the House Some with the Governor——particularly a Loan Office Bill which he rejected, (tho the Disposition of the Money was to have been by Act of Assembly) because we would not give him, in a Manner the sole Nomination of the Trustees.[1] But this I do not now regret, since I have been informed of the Temper the Ministry are in with respect to American Currency. I am, Dear Friend, with great sincerity Yours most Affectionately

J. GALLOWAY

Addressed: To / Benjamin Franklin Esquire / Deputy Post Master General / of North America in / Craven Street / London

Endorsed: Mr Galloway June 21. 1770

From [Michael] Francklin[2]   AL: American Philosophical Society

Duke Street York Buildings 22 June 1770.

Lieut. Governor Francklin presents his best Compliments to Doctor Franklin and has sent him a Book Mr. Frances the Minister of

8. See *The Statutes at Large of Pennsylvania from 1682 to 1801* (15 vols., Harrisburg, 1896–1911), VII, 197–204. The House of Employment was the Bettering House mentioned above, XIII, 262 n, 267, 284, 495–6.

9. The information was presumably in BF's missing letter of April 10. On Sept. 18, 1770, Galloway laid before the Assembly Jackson's resignation of his agency because he had been appointed counsel to the Board. *Votes, Pa.,* 1769–70, p. 172.

1. For the points at issue between the Governor and the Assembly see *Pa. Col. Recs.,* IX, 648–9, 652–3.

2. For the Lieutenant Governor of Nova Scotia see above, XIV, 292 n. He had been in London for more than a year, and in the period 1769–72 he appeared intermittently before the Board of Trade on matters connected with Nova Scotia. *Board of Trade Jour.,* 1768–75, pp. 83, 94, 196, 281.

France sent to his Lodgings, which he apprehends was designed by Mr. Le Roy for the Doctor.[3]

Mr. Francklin hopes he shall be excused for not sending it sooner as he has been out of town and otherwise extremely employed lately.

Addressed: To / Doctor Franklin / Craven Street

To Joseph Galloway

ALS: Yale University Library

Dear Sir, London, June 26. 1770.

Since mine of the 11th. Instant per Packet, I am favoured with yours of May 16. viâ Bristol, acquainting me with what was like to be the Determination of our Merchants relating to Importation, for which I am much oblig'd to you. I hope if in any thing they vary their Agreement, it will be only to make it more uniform with the other Colonies, and in itself more tenable with less Inconvenience, and of course more durable. A Report had been industriously propagated here immediately on the Arrival of the May Packet, that the Agreement was dissolved or broken through at Philadelphia, and that immense Orders were sent hither from thence; on which certain People exulted greatly; and ventured to say with Assurance that New York and Boston would soon follow. But this Intelligence from you and others by the Chalkley, together with the actual Return of the Goods by Scot from Boston, begins to change their Countenance.[4]

I am greatly obliged by your Endeavours to prevent the Publishing of those indiscrete Letters. I must be more prudent, and for the future shall write with reserve on publick Matters, except to yourself.[5]

3. Frances was not the Minister but the secretary to the French Ambassador; the book was by Pierre LeRoy, and had been sent by his brother, Jean-Baptiste. See the latter to BF above, April 22.

4. The *Chalkley*, Capt. Peter Young, sailed from Philadelphia in mid-May for Bristol. The *Lydia*, Capt. Scott, sailed from Boston at the beginning of May and arrived in the Thames on June 13. *Pa. Chron.*, May 7–14, and *London Chron.*, June 13, 1770.

5. One of these letters was to Thomson above, March 18; see also Galloway to BF below, Sept. 27. What the other letters were we have no idea. That to

Nothing material has occurr'd here since my last, except the Death of Mr. Beckford, who is a Loss to the general Interest of America, as he had really a considerable Weight, particularly with Lord Chatham.[6] Party Heats are at present a little abated: But many think the Fire is only smothered, and will break out again before the Meeting of Parliament.

I wish you would write a Line or two to Mr. Strahan, who often enquires of me concerning your Welfare, and wonders he does not hear from you in Answer to some Letter of his. With the greatest Esteem, I am, my dear Friend, Yours most affectionately

B FRANKLIN

Jos. Galloway Esqr

Endorsed:[7] Saile and Wallace Monday
  Story and Meredith Tuesday
  Cox and Garrigues Wednesday
  Lowden[?] and Wharton Freyday
  Middeltown and Moreland

To Samuel Rhoads[8]

ALS: Historical Society of Pennsylvania

Dear Friend, London, June 26. 1770

It is a long time since I had the Pleasure of hearing from you directly. Mrs. Franklin has indeed now and then acquainted me of your Welfare, which I am always glad to hear of. It is, I fear, partly, if not altogether, my Fault that our Correspondence has not been regularly continued. One thing only I am sure of; that it has been from no want of Regard on either side, but rather from too much Business and Avocations of various kinds, and my having little of Importance to communicate.

Galloway of March 21 could scarcely have been one of them because, although it might be called indiscreet, it had been promptly publicized by Galloway himself.

6. William Beckford, M.P. and Lord Mayor of London, died in office on June 21.

7. Not in Galloway's hand. The names were familiar in Philadelphia at the time, but we have no reason to suppose that they were a list of those to whom the letter was to be shown.

8. The carpenter who built BF's Philadelphia house. See above, II, 406 n.

One of our good Citizens, Mr. Hillegas, anxious for the future Safety of our Town, wrote to me some time since, desiring I would enquire concerning the Covering of Houses here with Copper. I sent him the best Information I could then obtain;[9] but have since receiv'd the enclos'd from an ingenious Friend, Mr. Wooller, who is what they call here a Civil Engineer.[1] I should be glad you would peruse it, think of the matter a little, and give me your Sentiments of it. When you have done with the Paper, please to give it to Mr. Hillegas. I am told by Lord Despencer, who has covered a long Piazza or Gallery with Copper, that the Expence is charged in this Account too high; for his cost but $\frac{1}{10}$ per foot, all Charges included. I suppose his Copper must have been thinner.[2] And indeed it is so strong a Metal, that I think it may well be used very thin.

It appears to me of great Importance to build our Dwelling-Houses, if we can, in a Manner more secure from Danger by Fire. We scarce ever hear of a Fire in Paris. When I was there, I took particular Notice of the Construction of their Houses; and I did not see how one of them could well be burnt. The Roofs are Slate or Tile; the Walls are Stone; the Rooms generally lin'd with Stucco or Plaister instead of Wainscot; the Floors of Stucco, or of sixsquare Tiles painted brown; or of Flag Stones or Marble; if any Floor were of Wood, it was Oak Wood, which is not so inflammable as Pine. Carpets prevent the Coldness of Stone or Brick Floors offending the

9. See above, XVI, 236, and BF to Hillegas, March 17.

1. John Wooler, despite his interest in fireproof roofing (for which see also BF to Rhoads below, Feb. 10, 1771), seems to have been primarily a bridge-builder. He was subsequently employed by the corporation of Newcastle to rebuild a portion of the bridge over the Tyne that was destroyed by flood in 1771. See P. W. Hosley, *Eighteenth-Century Newcastle* ([Newcastle upon Tyne, 1971]), pp. 15, 20, 22; Albert E. Richardson, *Robert Mylne, Architect and Engineer, 1733 to 1811* (London, [1955]), p. 26.

2. Le Despencer told BF, in other words, that Wooler's estimated cost was ten times higher than what he himself had paid, for what BF conjectures was much thinner and hence cheaper roofing. For Francis Dashwood, Lord Le Despencer, see above, XIII, 44 n, which refrains from mentioning that he had been one of the outstanding rakes of his day. He was now taking out his energies in building: Robert Adam had added a library to his town house, and Nicholas Revett had recently completed a portico (doubtless the gallery in question) on the front of his country house at West Wycombe. H. M. Colvin, *A Biographical Dictionary of English Architects, 1660–1840* (London, [1954]), pp. 32, 494.

Feet in Winter. And the Noise of Treading on such Floors overhead is less inconvenient than that on Boards. The Stairs too, at Paris, are either Stone, or Brick with only a Wooden Edge or Corner for the Step; so that on the Whole, tho' the Parisians commonly burn Wood in their Chimneys, a more dangerous kind of Fuel than that used here, yet their Houses escape extreamly well, as there is little in a Room that can be consumed by Fire, ex[cept] the Furniture. Whereas [in] London, perhaps scarce a Year passes in which half a Million of Property and many Lives are not lost by this destructive Element. Of late indeed they begin here to leave off Wainscotting their Rooms, and instead of it cover the Walls with Stucco, often form'd into Pannels like Wainscot, which, being painted, is very strong and warm. Stone Staircases too, with Iron Rails, grow more and more into Fashion here. But Stone Steps cannot in some Circumstances be fixed; and there methinks Oak is safer than Pine; and I assure you that in many genteel Houses here, both old and new, the Stairs and Floors are Oak, and look extreamly well. Perhaps solid Oak for the Steps would be still safer than Boards; and two Steps might be cut diagonally out of one Piece. Excuse my talking to you on a Subject with which you must be so much better acquainted than I am. It is partly to make out a Letter for renewing our Correspondence, and partly in hope that by turning your Attention to the Point, some Methods of greater Security in our future Building may be thought of and promoted by you, whose Judgment I know has deservedly great Weight with our Fellow-Citizens. For tho' our Town has not hitherto suffered very greatly by Fire, yet I am apprehensive, that some time or other, by a Concurrence of unlucky Circumstances, such as dry Weather, hard Frost, and high Winds, a Fire then happening may suddenly spread far and wide over our Cedar Roofs, and do us immense Mischief.

If you favour me with a Line, let me know how good Mrs. Rhoads does, and every one of your Children; and how it fares with my dear old Friend Mrs. Paschal.[3] With sincere Esteem, I am, Yours most affectionately,   B FRANKLIN

Mr. Rhoads.

3. For Mrs. Rhoads and the children see above, XII, 205 n. Mrs. Thomas Paschall was Rhoads's widowed sister-in-law; see William W. Hinshaw, *Encyclopedia of Amer. Quaker Genealogy* (6 vols., Ann Arbor, 1936–50), II, 403, 615, 632.

Addressed: To / Samuel Rhoads, Esqr / Philadelphia / viâ N York / per Packet / B Free FRANKLIN

To Noble Wimberly Jones

ALS (copy in Franklin's hand): American Philosophical Society

Sir,   London, July 6. 1770

I have now sent you the Mace and Gowns you ordered.[4] They are in two Boxes marked NWJ. No. 1, 2. and directed for you. I have put them into the Care of Mr. Crouch of your Province, who promises to ship them with his own Things. The Gowns are exactly such as are commonly used by the Speaker and Clerks here: It is only when the House goes up to wait on the King in the House of Lords, that the Speaker wears a Gown with Gold Loops. The Mace is allow'd to be an admirable Piece of Workmanship. I supposed the Impression of your great Seal to be the Arms of your Province, and therefore ordered that to be put on one of the Sides; [but] if there be any other, or if you would have any Inscription engrav'd on the Mace, there is a vacant Place to receive it. I wish them safe to hand, and hope they will please. Inclos'd I send the Bills. Be pleased to present my best Respects to the Assembly, and assure them of my most faithful Services. With great Esteem I have the Honour to be Sir, Your most obedient humble Servant

B FRANKLIN

Honble. N. W. Jones, Esqr

Copy

Verte

Endorsed: Dr. B. Franklin 6th. July 1770

From Samuel Parker

ALS: American Philosophical Society

James Parker has occupied so many pages of these volumes that his departure from the scene deserves an obituary. His friendship with Franklin extended over almost three decades, during which their careers were in some respects strikingly parallel. Both were runaways in their youth;

4. See Jones to BF above, Feb. 21, and BF's replies of May 2 and June 7.

both helped to establish a number of newspapers on the eastern seaboard; both were postmasters and comptrollers of the Post Office; both were instrumental in the development of public libraries. But it was printing that brought them together in partnership in 1742, and it was as a printer that Parker made his principal reputation. He is said to have been better at his trade than Franklin and certainly did more for it, because he trained a number of young men who later established themselves throughout the colonies.[5]

His letters in his last years, when he was in wretched health, are often tedious to a degree. They give the impression of a long-winded, fussy, and self-pitying mediocrity. But Parker had his troubles (the worst of them with the son who wrote the letter that follows) and bore up under them with considerable stoicism. He saw death coming long before it came, yet continued until the last moment to discharge his obligations with diligence and punctuality; for he was above all conscientious—a faithful servant, as his widow rightly called him.[6] If he was not an endearing man, let alone a great one, he did exemplify most of the small virtues that Poor Richard had extolled.

Honoured Sir,   New York, July 7, 1770.
I have just Time to let you know that my poor Father departed this Life on Monday the 2d. Instant; his Disorder was the nervous Fever, he died in Burlington. I suppose Mr. Foxcroft has the immediate Care of the Affairs he left concerning the Post Office. My Mother joins in best Respects, I am Your obedient humble Servant
SAML F. PARKER

Addressed: For / Benjamin Franklin, Esqr / Craven Street / London / Via Packet
Endorsed: S. Parker   July 7. 1770.   His Father's Death

To Mary Stevenson   ALS: American Philosophical Society

Dear Polly   Wednesday P M. [before July 10, 1770[7]]
I send you a few of your Translations.[8] I did not put your Name

5. *DAB.*
6. See her letter to BF below, Aug. 12.
7. The date of Polly's marriage to William Hewson.
8. Jared Sparks, in one of his editorial vagaries, attached the first sentence of this letter to another from Polly in 1782, and printed the whole as a single letter under the later date. *Works,* IX, 224. The translations were of Barbeu-Dubourg's *Petit code de la raison humaine,* for which see above, XVI, 204 n, and Barbeu-Dubourg to BF below, Nov. 25.

as the Translator, (which I at first intended) because I apprehended it might *look like* Vanity, in you, and as I shall otherwise make it known, I think the omitting it, will *look like* Modesty. Mr. H. is here, requesting me to speak to Mrs. Tickell, which I have promis'd to do on Friday morning.[9] Adieu, Your affectionate Friend

B FRANKLIN

100 are printed, to give to our Friends. Send for as many of them as you please.[1]

Addressed: To / Miss Stevenson / at Mrs Tickell's / Kensington

From a Committee of the Town of Boston

DS: Massachusetts Historical Society

The Bostonians had long suspected that they were being traduced in England by false reports of what was happening in the town.[2] After the Massacre the suspicion grew. On March 16 a Captain Robson sailed for London with dispatches from Lieutenant Colonel William Dalrymple, commander of the troops, and with Captain Preston's account of his part in the shooting; on the same ship went John Robinson, the member of the Board of Customs Commissioners who six months before had assaulted James Otis. The Bostonians responded to the threat of Robson's documents and Robinson's tongue by drawing up their own narrative of events, backed by depositions, and hiring a sloop to carry this material at once to friends in England, Franklin among them.[3] On April 28 the London *Public Advertiser* printed some of the material that Dalrymple had sent, including a doctored version of Preston's account. This version

9. William Hewson was presumably trying to persuade Mrs. Tickell to accept his suit for her niece's hand. BF was successful enough as a go-between, it may be conjectured, so that Hewson wrote Mrs. Tickell the letter referred to in BF to Polly below, July 24.

1. Alfred O. Aldridge mentions the mystery of a "ghost" edition, which has not survived, of Polly's translation of the *Code*. "Jacques Barbeu-Dubourg, a French Disciple of Benjamin Franklin," APS *Proc.* xcv (1951), 383 n. BF is clearly referring, not to a published edition, but to a small private printing, the disappearance of which would be no mystery.

2. See above, XVI, 44.

3. See BF to Cooper above, June 8; W. H. Whitmore *et al.*, eds., *Reports of the Record Commissioners of the City of Boston* (39 vols., Boston, 1881–1909), XVIII, 15–16, 18, 34; Frederic Kidder, *History of the Boston Massacre...* (Albany, 1870), pp. 110–13; Randolph G. Adams, "New Light on the Boston Massacre," Amer. Antiquarian Soc. *Proc.*, new ser., XLVII (1938), 314, 319.

created a furor in London; it was promptly sent back across the Atlantic, and appeared on June 25 as a supplement of the *Boston-Gazette.* Apprehension was further increased in Boston on July 3, when John Hancock's brigantine *Lydia* sailed for England with dispatches from the Board of Customs Commissioners, immured in Castle William. The response to these developments was quick. Samuel Adams drafted the letter below, to Franklin and others in England; it was presented to and approved by a town meeting on July 13, and dispatched the following day.[4]

Sir   Boston July 13th: 1770
  It affords very great Satisfaction to the Town of Boston to find that the Narrative of the horrid Massacre perpetrated here on the 5th: of March last which was transmitted to London, has had the desired effect; by establishing truth in the Minds of honest Men, and in some Measure preventing the Odium being cast on the Inhabitants, as the Aggressors in it. We were very apprehensive that all attempts would be made to gain this Advantage against us: and as there is [no re]ason to think that the Malice of our Enemies is in the least degree abated, it has been thought necessary that our friends on your side the Water, should have a true State of the Circumstances of the Town, and of every thing which has Materially occured, since the removal of the Troops to the Castle. For this purpose we are appointed a Committee: But the time will not admit of our writing so fully by this Conveyance, as we intend by the next, in the mean time we intreat your further friendship for the Town, in your Endeavours to get the Judgment of the Public Suspended, upon any representation that may have been made by the Commissioners of the Customs and others, until the Town can have the Opportunity of knowing what is alleged against it, and of answering for itself. We must confess that we are astonished to hear that the Parliament had come to a determination, to admit Garbled extracts from such Letters as may be received from America by Administration and to Conceal the Names of the Persons who may be the Writers of them.[5] This will certainly give great Encouragement

  4. *Boston Gaz.,* July 16, 1770. The letter is printed in Harry A. Cushing, ed., *The Writings of Samuel Adams* (4 vols., New York, 1904–08), II, 10–18, from which minor errors in the MS have been silently corrected.
  5. On May 7 the House of Commons received copies of the Bostonians' *Narrative* and other material, including unidentified depositions: *Journals of the House of Commons,* XXXII, 961–2. The House did nothing except debate the

to Persons of wicked Intentions to Abuse the Nations and injure the Colonies in the grossest manner with Impunity, or even without detection. For a Confirmation hereof we need to recur no further back than a few Months, when undoubtedly the Accounts and Letters carried by Mr. Robson would have been attended with very Unhappy if not fatal effects, had not this Town been so attentive as to have Contradicted those false Accounts by the depositions of many credible persons under Oath. But it cannot be supposed that a Community will be so Attentive but upon the most Alarming Events: In general Individuals are following their private concerns; while it is to be feared, the restless Adversaries are forming the most dangerous Plans for the Ruin of the Reputation of the People, in order to build their own Greatness on the Distruction of their liberties. This Game they have been long playing; and tho' in some few instances they have had a loosing hand yet they have commonly Managed with such Art, that they have so far succeeded in their Malicious designs as to involve the Nation and the Colonies in Confusion and distress. This it is presumed they never could have accomplished had not those very letters been kept from the View of the Public, with a design perhaps to conceal the falshood of them the discovery of which would have prevented their having any mischievous Effects. This is the Game which we have reason to believe they are now playing: With so much Secrecy as may render it impossible for us fully to detect them on this Side the Water; How deplorable then must be our Condition, if Ample Credit is to be given to their Testimonies against us, by the Government at home, and if the Names of our Accusers are to be kept a profound Secret, and the World is to See only such parts or parcells of their Representations as Persons, who perhaps may be interested in their favor, shall think proper to hold up. Such a Conduct, if allowed, seems to put it into the Power of a Combination of a few designing Men to deceive a Nation to it's Ruin. The Measures which have been taken in Consequence of Intelligence Managed with such Secrecy, have already to a very great degree lessened that Mutual Confidence which had ever Subsisted between the Mother Country and the Colonies, and must in the Natural Course of things totally alienate their Affections towards each other and

general disorders in America, but in late June the Privy Council held a full inquiry: *Acts Privy Coun., Col.,* v, 246–62.

consequently weaken, and in the End destroy the power of the Empire. It is in this extended View of things that our Minds are affected. It is from those Apprehensions that we earnestly wish that all Communication between the two Countries of a public Nature may be unvailed before the public: with the Names of the persons who are concerned therein, then and not till then will American affairs be under the direction of honest Men, who are never affraid or Ashamed of the light. And as we have abundent Reason to be jealous that the most mischievous and virulent Accounts have been very lately sent to Administration from Castle William, where the Commissioners have again retreated for no reason that we can conceive but after their former manner to misrepresent and injure this Town and Province, we earnestly intreat that you would use your utmost influence to have an Order passed that *the whole* of the packetts sent by the Commissioners of the Customs and others under the Care of one Mr. Bacon late an Officer of the Customs in Virginia, who took his passage the last Week in the Brigantine Lydia Joseph Wood Commander may be laid before his Majesty in Council.[6] If the Writers of those Letters shall appear to be innocent, no harm can possibly arise from such a Measure; if otherwise, it may be the Means of exploring the true Cause of the National and Collonial Malady, and of affording an easy remedy, and therefore the Measure must be justified and applauded by all the World.[7]

We have observed in the English Papers, the most notorious falsehoods published with an apparent design to give the World a prejudice against this Town, as the Aggressors in the unhappy Transaction of the 5th: of March, but no account has been more repugnant to the truth, than a paper printed in the public Advertiser

6. The commander's last name was Hood. For his sailing see *Mass. Gaz.;* and the *Boston Weekly News-Letter,* July 5, and for his arrival *Lloyd's Evening Post,* Aug. 10–13, 1770. His ship is not to be confused with another of the same name and also out of Boston, mentioned in BF to Galloway above, June 26.

7. This attempt to bring anonymous writers into the open, although it did not succeed as the Committee had hoped, may have had some effect in inducing Stephen Sayre, an American-born merchant in London, to warn Samuel Adams a few months later of damaging letters from Lieut. Gov. Thomas Hutchinson: Cushing, *op. cit.,* II, 67–8. The Committee's reasons, as given here, for wanting to expose such correspondence are similar to those BF advanced in 1772, when he sent the original letters of Hutchinson and others to Thomas Cushing; see Smyth, *Writings,* VI, 166.

of the 28th: of April which is called *The Case of Capt. Preston*. As a Committee of this Town We thought ourselves bound in faithfulness to wait on Capt. Preston to enquire of him whether he was the Author. He frankly told us that he had drawn a state of his Case, but that it had passed thro different hands and was altered at different times, and finally the Publication in the Advertiser was varient from that which he sent home as his own. We then desired him to let us know whether several parts which we might point to him and to which we took exception were his own, but he declined Satisfying us herein, saying that the Alterations were made by Persons who he supposed might Aim at Serving him, though he feared they might have a Contrary effect, and that his discrimenating to us the parts of it which were his own from those which had been altered by others might displease his friends at a time when he might stand in need of their essential Service, this was the Substance of the Conversation between us, whereupon we retired and wrote to Capt. Preston a Letter the Copy of which is now inclosed.[8]

The next day not receiving an Answer from Capt. Preston at the time we proposed, we sent him a Message desiring to be informed whether we might expect his Answer to which he replyed by a Verbal Message as Ours was that he had nothing further to add to what he had said to us the day before, as you'l please to observe by the inclosed Certificate.

As therefore Capt: Preston has utterly declined to make good the Charges against the Town in the Paper called his case or to let us know to whom we may apply as the Author or Authors of those parts which he might have disclaimed, and especially as the whole of his Case thus Stated directly Militates not only with his own Letter published under his hand in the Boston Gazette, but with the depositions of others annexed to our Narrative which were taken, not behind the Curtain as some may have been, but openly and fairly, after notifying the Parties interested, and before Magistrates to whose Credit the Governor of the Province has given his full Attestation under the Province Seal, we cannot think that the Papers called the case of *Capt. Thomas Preston*, or any other Paper of the like import can be deemed in the opinion of the sensible and impartial part of Mankind as sufficient, in the least degree to prejudice the Character of the Town. It is therefore altogether need-

8. Printed in Adams, *op. cit.* n. 3, pp. 314–17.

less for us to point out the many falsehoods contained in this Paper; nor indeed would there be time for it at present for the reason above mentioned. We cannot however omit taking Notice of the Artifice made use of by those who drew up the Statement in insinuating that it was the design of the People to plunder the Kings Chest; and for the more easily effecting that to Murder the Centinel posted at the Custom House where the money was lodged. This intelligence is said to have been brought to Capt. Preston by a Townsman, who assured him *that he heard the Mob declare* they would Murder the Centinel. The Townsman probably was one Greenwood a Servant to the Commissioners whose deposition Number 96 is inserted among others in the Narrative of the Town and of whom it is observed in a Marginal Note that "Through the whole of his examination he was so inconsistent, and so frequently Contradicted himself, that all present were Convinced that no Credit ought to be given to his deposition, for which reason it would not have been inserted had it not been known that a deposition was taken relating to this affair, from this Greenwood by Justice Murray and carried home by Mr. Robinson," and further "this deponent is the only person, out of a great Number of Witnesses examined, who heard any thing mentioned of the Custom house".[9] Whether this part of the Case of Capt: Preston was inserted by himself or some other person we are not told: It is very much to be questioned whether the information was given by any other than Greenwood himself, and the *Sort of Character* which he bears is so well known to the Commissioners and their Connections some of whom probably assisted Capt: Preston in Stating his Case, as to have made them ashamed if they regarded the truth, to have given the least credit to what he said. Whoever may have helped them to this intelligence, we will venture to say, that it never has been and never can be supported by the Testimony of any Man of a tolerable reputation. We shall only observe upon this occasion, how inveterate our Enemies here are, who, rather than omit what they might think a lucky opportunity of Slandering the Town, have wrought up a Narrative not only un-

9. Thomas Greenwood's deposition is in Kidder, *op. cit.*, n. 3, pp. 106–9. Bostonians were quick to distrust any deposition taken by Justice James Murray, a fervent Loyalist who insisted that justice be done to Preston. See Adams, *op. cit.*, p. 324; Nina M. Tiffany, ed., *Letters of James Murray, Loyalist* (Boston, 1901), pp. 158–61, 173–4,

supported by, but contrary to the clearest evidence of facts and have even prevailed upon an unhappy Man under pretence of friendship to him, to adopt it as his own: Though they must have known with a common share of understanding, that it's being published to the world *as his own*, must have injured him, under his present circumstances, in the most tender point, and so shocked was Capt: Preston himself, at its appearing in the light on this side the Water, that he was immediately apprehensive so glaring a falsehood would raise the indignation of a people to such a pitch as to prompt them to some Attempts that would be dangerous to him, and he accordingly applyed to Mr. Sheriff Greenleaf for special protection on that Account. But the Sheriff assuring him there was no such disposition appearing among the People (which is an undoubted truth) Capt. Prestons fears at length Subsided: And he still remains in safe Custody, to be tried by the Superior Court of Judicature at the next term in August; unless the Judges shall think proper further to postpone the Trial, as they have done for one whole term, since he was indicted by the Grand Jury.[1]

Before we conclude it may not be improper to observe that the removal of the troops was in the Slowest order, insomuch that eleven days were spent in Carrying the two Regiments to Castle Island, which had before landed in the Town in less than forty eight hours; Yet in all this time, while the Number of the Troops was daily lessening, not the least disorder was made by the inhabitants, tho' filled with a just indignation and horror at the blood of their fellow Citizens so inhumanely Spilt! And since their removal the Common Soldiers, have frequently and even daily come up to the Town for necessary provisions, and some of the officers, as well as several of the families of the Soldiers have resided in the Town and done business therein without the least Molestation. Yet so hardy have our Enemies been as to report in London that the enraged populace had hanged up Capt: Preston.

The strange and irreconcileable conduct of the Commissioners of the Customs since the 5th: of March, their applying for leave to retire to the Castle so early as the tenth, and spending their time in

1. Sheriff Stephen Greenleaf was the brother of the Greenleaf who signed this letter; see *Sibley's Harvard Graduates*, VII, 188. For the long delay before Preston was tried see Hiller B. Zobel, *The Boston Massacre* (New York, [1970]), pp. 206–40.

making excursions into the Country 'till the 20th: of June following, together with other material Circumstances, are the Subject of our present enquiry; the result of which you will be made acquainted with by the next Conveyance. In the mean time we remain with strict truth, Sir Your much Obliged and most Obedient Servants

THOMAS CUSHING	WM: PHILLIPS
R DANA	W MOLINEUX[2]
SAML ADAMS	EBENEZER STORER
JOHN HANCOCK	WM GREENLEAF

Benjamin Franklin Esqr

Endorsed: Comtee of Boston about abuse of the Town in England 1770

From John Pownall   ALS: Library of Congress

[Whitehall, July 14, 1770. Requests Franklin's attendance at the Board of Trade on Wednesday next, the 18th, in regard to several laws passed in Pennsylvania in 1769.[3]]

From W. Masters   ALS: American Philosophical Society

Sir   Philadelphia July 17th: 1770
    Your kind reply to what I formerly wrote you in favour of Thos: Truck a Soldier in the trane,[4] together with his and Father in law's perpetual entreaties that I would once more befriend them by writing to you; emboldens me to remind you off your Promise of Endeavouring to procure his discharge; which would be a completion of Earthly Happiness to a poor yet Honest Family, and a favour conferr'd on your humble Servant   W MASTERS

Addressed: To / Doct: / Benjamine Franklin / London / per Capt: / Scott

2. The only signer not identified above (XVI, 45, 223, 273). He was a leader of the Sons of Liberty, but his conduct had already roused suspicion; see G. B. Warden, *Boston, 1689–1776* (Boston, 1970), pp. 251, 253. A ninth member of the Committee was Dr. Joseph Warren.
    3. Pownall was writing as secretary to the Board. For the meeting in question see *Board of Trade Jour.*, 1768–75, pp. 200–1.
    4. For Masters' letter see above, XVI, 276; BF's reply has not been found.

To Mary Stevenson Hewson

ALS: American Philosophical Society

Dear Polly,   London, July 18. 1770

Yours of the 15th. informing me of your agreable Journey and
safe Arrival at Hexham gave me great Pleasure, and would make
your good Mother happy if I knew how to convey it to her; but 'tis
such an out-of-the-way Place she is gone to, and the Name so out
of my Head, that the Good News must wait her Return. Enclos'd I
send you a Letter which came before she went, and, supposing it
from my Daughter Bache, she would have me open and read it to
her, so you see if there had been any Intrigue between the Gentleman and you, how all would have been discovered.[5] Your Mother
went away on Friday last, taking with her Sally and Temple, trust-
ing me alone with Nanny, who indeed has hitherto made no Attempt upon my Virtue. Neither Dolly nor Barwell, nor any any
other good Female Soul of your Friends or mine have been nigh me,
nor offered me the least Consolation by Letter in my present lone-
some State.[6] I hear the Post-man's Bell, so can only add my affec-

5. We are at a loss to explain this teasing. The letter could have been either
to Mrs. Stevenson or to BF, but there is no indication who wrote it or who the
gentleman was.

6. Sally was Sarah Franklin, BF's remote cousin (A.5.2.3.1.1.1), who was
staying at Craven Street; Temple was of course WF's son. For Nanny, Mrs.
Stevenson's servant, see BF to DF above, June 10. Polly's friend Dolly Blunt
has frequently appeared before. Barwell has not, but reappears in later correspondence, where the references to her make clear only that she was a friend of
BF and Dolly and the Stevenson clan, and give no hint of the notable woman
she was. Mary Barwell (b. 1733) belonged to a rich Anglo-Indian family. Her
father had been Governor of Bengal, and her half-brother Richard (1741–
1804), a member of the Council in Calcutta, was by this time amassing the
fortune that enabled him to return home a decade later as one of the outstanding
"nabobs" of the period. *DNB* under Richard Barwell; *Bengal Past & Present*
(Calcutta Hist. Soc. *Jour.*), VI (1910), 160–1. His sister Mary managed his
business affairs at home. She was wealthy in her own right but also handled
large sums of his money, and he instructed her on how to further his interests
with the public and the ministry. She was close to India House, and a power in
the political and financial world. See "The Letters of Mr. Richard Barwell,"
ibid., VIII–XVIII (1914–19), especially XI, 49; XII, 212, 228; XIII, 74, 88, 255;
XVI, 79.

The identification of BF's Barwell with this redoubtable woman rests on
numerous scraps of evidence. To him and Dolly Blunt their friend was a by-

194

tionate Respects to Mr. Hewson, and best Wishes of perpetual
Happiness for you both. I am, as ever, my dear good Girl, Your
affectionate Friend   B FRANKLIN

To Deborah Franklin   ALS: American Philosophical Society

My dear Child,   London, July 19. 1770
    This will be delivered to you by our ingenious Countryman Mr.
Benbridge, who has so greatly improv'd himself in Italy as a Portrait Painter, that the Connoisseurs in that Art here think few or
none excel him. I hope he will meet with due Encouragement in
his own Country, and that we shall not lose him as we have lost Mr.
West: For if Mr. Benbridge did not from Affection chuse to return
and settle in Pensilvania, he certainly might live extreamly well in
England by his Profession.[7]
    I have just received Letters from you and Mr. Bache and Sally,[8]

word for the busy female, and her first name began with an M. (Smyth,
Writings, VII, 15; Dolly to BF, March 18, 1779, APS.) A young man who was
a member of BF's circle in 1768, T. Henckell, seems to have been the same
Henckell whom Mary recommended to Richard in India. (Above, XV, 237–8;
Bengal Past & Present, X, 254; XIII, 88.) John Hawkesworth, BF's old acquaintance, was a close friend of both Barwells. (*Ibid.*, XI, 50–1; XIII, 74, 119.) When
Jonathan Williams, Jr., wanted to get a consignment of East India Co. tea sent
to him in Boston after his return there, he wrote to invoke Miss Barwell's assistance. (BF to Williams, July 7, 1773, APS.) All these signs, taken together,
indicate that BF's friend was the nabob's sister.
    7. Mr. West was of course the expatriate American painter and old friend of
BF, Benjamin West. Henry Benbridge (1744–1812) was a Philadelphian who
had been studying for several years in Italy; in 1769 he had painted a portrait
of Pasquale Paoli, commissioned by James Boswell, which was exhibited in
London. Benbridge arrived there at the end of 1769 with a letter of introduction from his step-father to BF (above, XVI, 38), through whom he met the
latter's young friend Thomas Coombe. As his introduction to the art world of
London, Benbridge did portraits of BF and Coombe for the spring exhibition
at the Royal Academy, where both were shown; afterward one was to go to DF
and the other to Coombe's father. They have disappeared. Charles C. Sellers,
Benjamin Franklin in Portraiture (New Haven and London, 1962), pp. 190–1.
BF's failure to mention a portrait in this letter is clear indication that something
had already happened to it and Benbridge was not taking it with him. He did
take the Coombe portrait: Thomas Coombe to his sister Sally, Aug. 17, 1770,
Hist. Soc. of Pa.
    8. DF's letter of June 13 appears above; the other two have been lost.

which I shall answer fully per next Opportunity, having now only time to add my Love to you and them, and to your dear little Boy. I am, as ever, Your affectionate Husband   B FRANKLIN

Addressed: To / Mrs Franklin / at / Philadelphia / per favour of / Mr Benbridge

From Thomas Gilpin[9]

Extract: reprinted from "Memoir of Thomas Gilpin," *Pennsylvania Magazine of History and Biography*, XLIX (1925), 313.

July 19th [1770]

Since my last New York has relaxed from the non-importation agreement but this and the other provinces stand fixed[1] although we have an account here from a vessel spoken in going to Boston that the Tea duty has been taken off.[2]

From Abel James[3]   LS: American Philosophical Society

Dear Friend   London 19 July 1770

I take the Liberty to repeat my Request to thee that Thou wilt lay before James West Esqr. the Inclos'd Paper, hoping that, that worthy Gentleman will give Orders to the Executor of Peter Razor deceased to let me dispose of the Trunk of Cloaths as he desir'd me to do by the within mention'd Paper, which I got proved before I left Philada. The other Trunk referr'd to was never deliver'd to me, but this is in my Custody, and I can [*torn*] our Friend West that Peter

9. But perhaps not to BF; see the headnote to Gilpin's letter above, June 1.

1. On July 10 the New York merchants decided to renew the importation of everything except articles that were "subject to Duty for the Purpose of raising a Revenue in America." On the 14th a meeting of Philadelphia merchants condemned this action and resolved, until it was rescinded, to import nothing from New York except in a few enumerated categories. *Pa. Chron.*, July 9–16, 1770.

2. A ship arriving at Salem in mid-July reported speaking a packet bound for New York, and getting the news that the Townshend Acts had been totally repealed. *Pa. Gaz.*, July 26, 1770. The news was of course false.

3. BF's old Philadelphia acquaintance, who was in London on business. See BF to Evans above, March 17.

Razor repeatedly requested [*torn*] his mind fulfill'd therein.[4] Thy Attention hereto will [*torn*] Addition to the many Benevolent Actions of thy Life, [*torn*] him that is with perfect Esteem Thy Affectionate Friend   ABEL JAMES

From James Gambier[5]   AL: American Philosophical Society

[Before July 20, 1770?[6]]
Capt. Gambiers Compliments to Dr. Franklyn, and calld on him to have askd the favor of his Sentiments relative to a Man that Comm[issione?]r Robinson[7] mentiond to Mr. Gambier as a proper person to recomend to take lease of a light House.

4. "Our friend West" was presumably the James West (1703–72) who was president of the Royal Society and M.P. for Boroughbridge, and who had spent many years at the Treasury. Namier and Brooke, *House of Commons*, III, 624–5; *DNB*. Peter Razor's financial affairs in 1759 appear briefly above in Vol. VIII, where he is not identified. He was presumably the Peter Razer who was at that time a customs collector at Lewes, Del., and who was corresponding with West in 1755. 1 *Pa. Arch.*, III, 546; IV, 76; *PMHB*, LXXXIII (1959), 130 n. In that case his customs accounts may well have been still unsettled, so that no part of his estate—even clothes—could be disposed of without consent of the Treasury.

5. For the naval career of James Gambier (1723–89) see *DNB*.

6. The note is said to be *c*. 1784 and in French in I. Minis Hays, ed., *The Calendar of the Papers of Benjamin Franklin*... (5 vols., Philadelphia, 1908), III, 236. Our dating, although conjectural, is at least a better conjecture than that. Gambier was appointed commander in chief on the North American station in 1770; he left London on July 20, and sailed from Spithead on the 27th. *London Chron.*, July 19–21, 28–31. It is a reasonable assumption that he would have inquired of BF about a lighthouse-keeper in the area of Boston, for which he was bound. BF knew a number of his relatives, was a particular friend of his uncle, Samuel Mead, and by this time was at least acquainted with Gambier himself. See above, VII, 325 n; X, 60 n; Cooper to BF below, Aug. 23, 1771; and BF to Cooper, Jan. 13, 1772.

7. Probably John Robinson, a member of the American Board of Customs Commissioners, who had sailed home from Boston on March 16, 1770.

To Mary Stevenson Hewson ALS: Library of Congress

Dear Polly,   London, July 24[-25]. 1770

I wrote a few Lines to you last Week in answer to yours of the 15th.[8] Since which I have been in the Country; and returning yesterday found your good Mother was come home and had got a Letter from you of the 20th. She has just put it into my hands, and desires me to write to you, as she is going into the City with Miss Barwell to buy things. Whether she will have time to write herself I cannot say, or whether if she had, she would get over her natural Aversion to writing. I rather think she will content herself with your knowing what she should say and would say if she wrote; and with my letting you know that she is well and very happy in hearing that you are so. Your Friends are all much pleas'd with your Account of the agreable Family, their kind Reception and Entertainment of you, and the Respect shown you. Only Dolly and I, (tho' we rejoice and shall do so in every thing that contributes to your Happiness) are now and then in low Spirits, supposing we have lost each a Friend. Barwell says she conceives nothing of this; and that we must be two Simpletons to entertain such Imaginations. I show'd her your Letter to your Mother, wherein you say, "Dolly is a naughty Girl, and if she does not mend I shall turn her off, for I have got another Dolly now, and a very good Dolly too." She begg'd me not to communicate this to Dolly, for tho' said in jest, yet in her present State of mind it would hurt her. I suppose it was for the same good-natur'd Reason that she refus'd to show me a Paragraph of your Letter to Dolly that had been communicated by Dolly to her.

July 25. The above was written yesterday, but being interrupted I could not finish my Letter in time for the Post, tho' I find I had little to add. Your Mother desires me to express abundance of Affection to you and to Mr. Hewson, and to say all the proper Things for her with respect to the rest of your Friends there: but you can imagine better than I can write. Sally and little Temple join in best Wishes of Prosperity to you both. Make my sincere Respects acceptable to Mr. Hewson, whom, exclusive of his other Merits, I shall always esteem in proportion to the Regard he manifests for

8. See above, July 18, where most of the people mentioned in the rest of this letter are identified.

198

you. Barwell tells me, that your Aunt had receiv'd his Letter, and was highly pleas'd with it and him; so I hope all will go well there; and I shall take every Opportunity of Cultivating her good Dispositions, in which I think you us'd to be sometimes a little backward; but you always had your Reasons.[9] I am apt to love every body that loves you, and therefore I suppose I shall in time love your new Mother and new Sister, and your new Dolly. I find I begin to like them already, and if you think proper you may tell them so. But your old Dolly and I have agreed to love one another better than ever we did, to make up as much as we can our suppos'd Loss of you. We like your Assurances of continued Friendship unimpair'd by your Change of Condition, and we believe you think as you write; but we fancy we know better than you: You know I once knew your Heart better than you did your self. As a Proof that I am right, take notice, that *you now think this the silliest Letter I ever wrote to you, and that Mr. Hewson confirms you in that Opinion.* However, I am *still*, what I have been so many Years, my dear good Girl, Your sincerely affectionate Friend, and Servant

B FRANKLIN

Endorsed: July 24–70 29

To Lord Le Despencer   ALS: American Philosophical Society

My Lord,   Cravenstreet, July 26. 1770
I heartily wish your Lordship would urge the Plan of Reconciliation between the two Countries, which you did me the Honour to mention to me this Morning. I am persuaded that so far as the Consent of America is requisite, it must succeed. I am sure I should do everything in my Power there to promote it.[1]

9. Polly was spending at least part of her honeymoon with her husband's family, who lived in Hexham, Northumberland. William Hewson's father had died in 1767, and the surviving family then consisted of the widow, son, and three daughters. George Gulliver, ed., *The Works of William Hewson, F.R.S. . . .* (London, 1846), p. xv. One of these daughters was Polly's new sister; the new Dolly might have been a young niece of William Hewson, or even a pet. The recipient of Hewson's letter was Mrs. Tickell; for Polly's earlier difficulties with her, and the reasons behind them, see above, xv, 244–5.

1. This reference is as tantalizing as the similar one in BF to Galloway above, Jan. 11. We have found no other evidence that Le Despencer was concerned with plans for reform, and he was anything but a noted constitutional theorist.

I beg leave to lay before your Lordship, and to request you would be so good as to peruse the enclos'd original Letters to me from Gen. Bouquet, who commanded the British Troops in Pensilvania in 1764, when I was one of the Commissioners of the Board of Treasury there.[2] He was then on an Expedition against the Indians in the Ohio Country. Your Lordship will in these Letters see the effectual Use I made from time to time of my Influence in America, for his Majesty's Service. Gen. Bouquet in that Expedition fought and defeated the Indians, and compell'd them to sue for Peace. He afterwards own'd great Obligations to me for the Assistance I procur'd him from our Province.

I have Enemies, as every public Man always has. They would be glad to see me depriv'd of my Office; and there are others who would like to have it. I do not pretend to slight it. Three Hundred Pounds less would make a very serious Difference in my annual Income. But as I rose to that Office gradually thro' a long Service of now almost Forty Years, have by my Industry and Management greatly improv'd it, and have ever acted in it with Fidelity to the Satisfaction of all my Superiors, I hope my political Opinions, or my Dislike of the late Measures with America (which I own I think very injudicious) exprest in my Letters to that Country; or the Advice I gave to adhere to their Resolutions till the whole Act was repealed, without extending their Demands any farther, will not be thought a good Reason for turning me out.[3] I shall, however,

---

The plan was doubtless not his own, but whose and what it was we cannot say. It is an interesting sign, nevertheless, that in the aftermath of the struggle for total repeal of the Townshend Acts ideas were astir in some quarters for restructuring imperial relations.

2. For Bouquet see above, VII, 63 n and, for his letters to BF, XI, 266–7, 321–6.

3. Several of BF's letters to America during the spring, urging continuance of the nonimportation agreements, had got back to England and caused enough of a furor to endanger his position in the Post Office; hence this appeal to one of the Postmasters General. We have been unable to identify more than one of the letters in question; see above, p. 180 n. Neither can we explain why BF feared, as early as July, being ousted from the Post Office; the main attack on him came later. In early August he spoke of a letter that we have not located, supposedly in Goddard's *Pa. Chron.*, which asserted that BF had been appointed to the Post Office because he was agent for Pennsylvania. Thomas Coombe to his father, Aug. 4, 1770, Hist. Soc. of Pa. This was scarcely a serious attack, and we have found none in the London press before late August, when a writer

always retain a grateful Sense of your Lordship's Good-will and many Civilities towards me, and remain as ever, with the greatest Respect, Your Lordship's most obedient and most humble Servant

B FRANKLIN

P.S. There are Letters also in the Secretary of State's Office, from Gen. Braddock to the then Sir Thos. Robinson, expressing his great Obligations to me for the Services I rendered him.[4]

Lord Le Despencer

Endorsed: Doctor Franklin

From Dorothea Blunt   ALS: American Philosophical Society

Dear Sir   Bromley July 26 [1770]

Be assur'd that I feel very kindly to you for the favour I receiv'd this Morning. It was not more than I wanted, tho much more than I expected——not because more than you would have given sooner if the state of my Mind had been known to you, but because you gave me unask'd the strongest proof of a tender and disinterested friendship, which tho I had no foundation for such fear, yet I did fear wou'd gradualy decay whenever it shou'd cease to be supported by our Polly. She taught you to esteem me which for her sake and mine you soon learnt to do. She has now another employment, or the same thing to do for others. Most joyfully therefore shall I assume one so pleasing as that will be to me of paying more attention to you than I have hitherto paid tho not more than I have always been prompted from affection to pay. Yes indeed My Dear Sir I do feel and think exactly as you think and feel——that what Mrs. Hewson will gain, you and I must lose. My friendship was strong enough to enable me to suppress my feelings at a time I felt most, and therefore tho my spirits sink when I reflect upon our friends absence, no more to return the same to you, and me, she

calling himself Veritas assailed BF in the *Gazetteer* as Dr. Doubleface and, later, as a modern Judas; see the issues of Aug. 23 and Oct. 17. Veritas had been excoriating the Americans since late June; we suspect that he was John Robinson, the customs officer who had sailed from Boston on March 16.

4. For this and other expressions of Braddock's sense of obligation in 1755 see above, VI, 14–15.

once was, yet when I likewise reflect that it may be for her good, I submit, nay I do more——I am thankful. I have also heard from her that she is happy in her new Relations. I am sure I wish her all possible happiness, and therefore, that part of it she already possesses, from these new Connections. Yet I will own to you that when I first read it something rose within too much like Jealousy, but which till I could examine was by self love call'd injury and therefore poor Dol at first thought herself so. It is probable I may see you before you see this as I have a half promise from Mr. Brown of a place in his Chaise tomorrow,[5] but as next to a Woman, Man is the most variable creature that never changes its appearance, nor wou'd be suppos'd capable of changing, I write this least so common a thing shou'd come to pass. With the love that I at this time, and which I shall at all times feel for you you must be content, as I have none of those amiable persons with me that you remember'd in your letter being perhaps the only inhabitant in this Mansion, at this Moment as I know the family to be far from hence, and I hear the servants out of doors. The Dr. is in London, Mrs. H: at Hackney, My Sister at Sir Charles's and the rest dispers'd various ways.[6] Thus circumstanc'd, I shou'd have been gloomy if by Conferring a favour you had not given me the most agreable employment I cou'd have desir'd, of returning it in part, by assuring you that I am your much pleased and oblig'd Friend &c   D. BLUNT

I desire to be remember'd to S: Franklin——and Mrs. S: tho I take for granted she is not at home.

Upon a recollection of *what* I have written and *how* I have written, I feel asham'd, as I have neither tried to amuse, nor to amend those faults, you lov'd me well enough to wish me to amend; and which I do hope to repeat no more.

Addressed: Doctor Franklin / Craven Street / Charing Cross

5. Probably Benjamin Brown of Bromley, who was later buried beside John Hawkesworth and seems to have been his brother-in-law. See *Gent. Mag.*, LI (1781), 370.

6. The Dr. and Mrs. H. were the Hawkesworths. For Dolly's sister and brother, Catherine and Sir Charles, see above, respectively, IX, 327 n; XIV, 93 n.

To the Georgia Assembly Committee of
Correspondence
Letterbook copy: Georgia Historical Society

Gentlemen London August 10th. 1770

Your several Favours of May 11, 23, and 28 came duly to hand.[7] The first contained a Certificate for One Hundred Pounds, which will be paid, and carried to the Credit of your Province, Please to accept my Thanks for your Care in transmitting it. With the second I recieved, The two Ordinances appointing me your Agent till June 1771, The Act for ordering and governing Slaves, &c. A Copy of the Commons Address to the Governor of Nov. 16, 1769 relating [to] the four Southern Parishes, A Copy of the Act to amend an Act intitled An Act to ascertain the manner and Form of Electing Members, &c. presented May 10, The Address of both Houses to the Governor on that Act; and a Copy of the Act it was intended to amend, which pass'd June 9, 1761. And with the third I received, A Copy of the Assembly's Instructions to the Agent: A Copy of the Petition of the Inhabitants of Lands said to [be] claimed by Sir William Baker: Copy of the Committees Le[tter] to Mr. Knox: And a Copy of the Report of the Board of Trade on the Act for confirming Titles, &c, On all which I can now only say, that I have carefully perused the several Papers, to acquaint myself well with the Matters contain'd in them; and that as soon as the great Officers of State return to Town; and the respective Public Boards enter again on Business, I shall not fail to proceed with Dillgence in prosecuting every Point recommended to my Care, agreable to the Instructions of the Assembly and the Directions contained in your Letters. I beg you would be so good as to present my dutiful Respects and Thanks to His Excellency the Governor and to both Houses, for the Honour done me by those repeated Appointments; and assure them of my Intention in all things faithfully to endeavour the Service of the Province. With great Esteem and Regard, I have the Honour to be Gentlemen Your most Obedient and most humble Servant BENJAMIN FRANKLIN

7. The annotation of those letters explains the matters referred to in this one.

From Mary Parker ALS: American Philosophical Society

New York August 12th 1770

It is with inexpressable Grief that I am Obliged to give you an Account of my Dear Mr. Parkers Death. He kept his house the Greatest part of the Winter with the gout and an inflamation in his Legg. The 4 June as soon as he could git Abroad, his Anxiety to doe his duty as Comptroller Carried him Down to New Town; On his return he fell ill at Bristol; was Carried over to Burlington, and Died there 2d. July of a nervous fevor. Presently after his Death Mr. Thomas Foxcroft came here, and took with him all the Comptrollers Books of the post office, and I at the same time paid him £19 3s. 8½d. I received, on the post office Acct in Mr. Parkers absence. How his Acct. Stands with the Post Master's General as I have not the Books nor a Copy of his General Account I am at present an utter Stranger to. It gives me great uneasiness that Mr. Parkers friends blames me much for parting with the Books out of my hands (to Mr. Foxcroft or any other person) which is now the reason that I cannot Answer that part of your Letter relating the £135 5s., £1 2s. 7d., and £48 10½d. The Bill in yours with protest a Copy of which have sent Mr. Vernon; his answer as soon as git shall Acquaint you. Mr. Parkers friends think I have done injustice to myself and family and that the Profits of the Office ought to be for the benefit of his heirs, untill a Comptroller was appointed as he was a faithful Servant, but this must be left to you who I am assured will do what is right; be it as it will I shall be Satisfied if you think I have done what will please you. I have this day wrote Mr. Foxcroft to send me the books by my Daughter.[8] I am afraid Mr. Parker has not left me and his family in so good a Situation as we Expected.[9] However I must be Content. Inclosed the Copy

8. Thomas Foxcroft and Thomas Vernon were postmasters respectively of Philadelphia and Newport; the Parkers' daughter Jane (Jenny) later married Gunning Bedford.

9. In that case their expectations must have been high, for he left a considerable estate. It went to his wife for her lifetime, and she was sole executrix; at her death it was to be divided between their two children and other relatives. In addition to unstipulated private property it consisted of four printing presses (one in New Haven, one in Woodbridge, and two in New York), four houses, more than three thousand acres of land in the Hardenbergh Patent in the northern Catskills, another tract in the Wyoming Valley, and a sawmill and

204

of a Recet, for a bill Gov. Franklin took out of Mr. Parkers pocket after his Death. I am after my Prayers for your Prosperity, with Great Gratitude for your friendship to Mr. Parker your assured and faithfull Humble Servant   MARY PARKER

Benjamin Franklin Esqr:

Addressed: Benjamin Franklin

From Deborah Franklin   ALS: American Philosophical Society

My Dear Child   August the 16 1770
      yisterday I reseved yours of June the 10. I am verey Sorrey to thinke I shold not have it in my power to atend on you. When will it be in your power to Cume home? How I long to see you but I wold not say one word that wold give you one momentes trubel. I will then tell you that as to my helthe I am as well as I ever ex-peckte to be and I thinke better then I ever did [expect] I Shold be. I have recoverd flesh and look more then I did for a yeair but my memerey but I muste expeckte when I am a verey old women. If your haveing the Goute is of Servis to you I wonte say one word only I wish I was near aneuef to rube it with a lite hand. As to Naney I am Sorrey shee has Such hard lucke what buisnes and name had her husband. Tell her I am glad shee is with good mrs. Stephen son I supouse shee was verey happey when shee lived with her.[1] I hope shee will be verey obligeing to her. Now I am to tell you a boute my King bird he has bin verey ill indead we thought we shold lues him so bad he was that he was so much altred in a boute 30 ouers was surprised that we thoute he was so altred that we never flattered he Cold recoverd. His father and mother was Sadley distresed but it plesed god to bles what was dun to him and mended as faste. Mr. Bache was a going to Jamaco. Billey Come to town and in vited them up to his house so I was verey glad as thay Cold ride everey day. But I shold tell you mr. Banton sente him a Carraig to take him oute and as soon as mrs. Masters knew he was

---

some nine hundred acres of pine barren in New Jersey. The last was left to his nephew, but Mrs. Parker wanted it set aside for BF's use. Francis Panton to WF, [Aug., 1770?], APS.

    1. For the gout and Nanny see BF's letter above, June 10, to which DF is replying.

un well shee sente twise a day to take him oute.[2] His dadey stayed
tell he was pronounesd oute of dainger. In a boute two weeks after
mr. Bache was gon his unkill Come down and took him and his
mother and maid up[3] and he is perfecktely recovered. I wold give
much for you to see him if he was not our one [own] I wold say that
I never saw a finer Child. When his maid is a takein him oute he is
stoped by everey bodey to aske who he is and is much admired by
everey bodey. Maney ses he is like you and sume his father. He is a
manly child a fine temper one thing I forget wather I told you he is a
graite admierer of Singing and musick. His father wold play on
your instruyment I wold hold him and when he wold plaid a softe
or tender tune he wold be in anentexey and bow doune and the
tears wold flow doune his cheeks as wold his dadey and Joyne his
with his kis and blsse him and Cole him his angel. When his father
and mother wold [sing] a Song in the Padlocke[4] he woud Joyne
with them and sing with them. Tell mrs. Stephenson I did thinke to
write to her and tell her what a fine child he is a fine skin a charming
pair of fine eyes it was a dispute wather he wold have blew or Black
but I think thay air Black. When he was borne his hair was verey
darke but it is fair. His unkill has shaifed his head and dipes him in
the river everey day and [he] behaves like a Jentelman. His maid
is a strong woman for a gorle cold not a tend him. His dadey had a
Negrow Boy for a house servent but when his master was a going
desired him to leve him with his master as he love him so he was lefte
so he was invited to go up as it was thoute it is easy [?] to a tend him
when he walkes. I never knew a finer Nurse then Salley makes and
a verey good mother. He was [*torn*] to have aney you mers [hu-
mors] tell he was sick and one day he freted and showed Sum you

2. John Baynton was an old friend of the family; see above, XII, 274. Mrs.
Masters was, we believe, Mary Lawrence Masters, the widow of William Masters, Sr., and the stepmother of his son by the same name; see above, XVI, 275 n.
She lived on Market Street, only a few blocks from the Franklins; see the cita-
tion from Keith in that note.

3. The Kingbird's uncle, WF. The baby's illness was undoubtedly after DF's
missing letter of April 24; BF's response (above, June 10) and the tone of the
present letter make clear that she is here giving him the first news of the crisis.
It may have been induced by the child's second inoculation, which was im-
minent in May; see Sally to BF above, end of May.

4. A play by Isaac Bickerstaff, which had run in Philadelphia the previous
autumn. Thomas C. Pollock, *The Philadelphia Theatre in the Eighteenth
Century* (Philadelphia, 1933), p. 108.

m[ers. His] mother set him on her lape and told him he had as much
good senes as aney of his [*torn*] but he semed displesed she laid him
over her knee and whiped him and then told him [what] for and
looked at him. In an instant he smiled on her and held oute his
mouthe and kised her[5] and be haved himsealf charminly his dayey
[daddy] by and I was all. Sume time after shee asked if shee did doe
well yis sed Mr. Bache and mother for we sed not one word nor did
we say one word to him. I donte remember he ever showed aney
tember or aney pashon he semes to give pleshuer to all a round.
While he was ill what is inseydent to Children he was his Gumes so
Sweld the Dr. lansed one tuthe out senes he has cute 4 more and is
so pleased with them that he is a showing of them. While I write I
long to see him I donte know what to due a boute it.

You see I never say aney thing a boute aney bodey but my self
and our one [own] children but I will tell you that a boute two weeks
a go our friend mr. Rhodes Come and took me down to his plase and
I spente the day. We talked much of you. I told him that you had
sente me one of your Books he sed he wished he Cold get one but he
never saw one asked me if I knew if thay air to be sold. I sed I did
not know. The nexte day I sente it to him. He and his kind good wife
and his Dafter desired to be rememberd to you in a porticker manner. I sume times [see] our good old friend mr. Wharton Sener and
he desier me to menshon me to you his son Franklin is a fine Lad
indead. Nansey Clifton came in shee desired me to give her love to
you but thinkes you donte remember her.[6] I promised so I wrote
and my poor mrs. Sumain come in and did desier me to desier you
if you Cold let her Dafter know shee had reseved her letter. Thay
air in a miserabel Staite he has loste all Senes and wants every
nesesarey seven years loste to him self shee is not a bove half so
big as shee was when you yoused to Cole her a threed paper.[7] I am

5. DF meant, we believe, that his daddy and she were the only bystanders.
BF's reply (below, Oct. 3) praised her for not intervening.

6. For the Rhoads family see BF to Samuel Rhoads above, June 26; the book
that the latter wanted was *Exper. and Obser.* (4th ed., 1769). Franklin Wharton,
a three-year-old at the time, was the youngest of Joseph Wharton's eighteen
children; see *PMHB*, I (1877), 327; II (1878), 55–6. For Anna Maria Clifton
see above, XVI, 262.

7. Thread paper, folded to hold skeins of thread; hence something long and
narrow. The parlous state of the Soumaines was much as DF had described it
the previous autumn; see above, XVI, 213.

verey busey att this time a geting our wood for the whinter and am ofen hinderd by the men. I have yousd to due it my self of Laite but it is a mersey I Can get it I am thankfull for it now. I have looked over this letter and I wold write it over a gen but the poste will go befor I Cold due it. My beste Compley mentes to Mr. and Mrs. Strahan to Mr. and Mrs. Weeste tell his pickter has bin att our house.[8] Kiss him for me due my bete regardes to all that remember. I was glad to hear of Mr. Orrey dus Sir John make you a visit sume times? I did reseve a letter from him but I did not write to him a gen. I supose Sister has wrote to you shee wished me not to write tell I shold hear from her so I have not had leve as yit. I nead not tell you as you muste see in the papers we have loste our friend mr. Parker. Mrs. Parker and her children and we correyspend senes his death. My beste Love to our good Miss Polley Stephenson. We ofen talke of her. I will write by a shipe I hear is to saile from N yorke. God bles you is the desier of your afeckshonet wife   D FRANKLIN

From John Bard[9]   ALS: American Philosophical Society

Dear Sir   Augst: 18 1770
    Altho the reluctance I have to ask favours of my Friends, Especially when there is too great a probability of its not being convenient, or in their power, to grant them; greatly discourages me in the request I am about to make. Yet while there is the most distant prospect of Success, I can not but hope your Friendship will Excuse me, as a Parent, in Ventureing to recommend to you, my Son Sam-

8. This sentence gives particular reason to wish that DF had had time to rewrite the letter. She presumably meant "tell Benjamin West," which suggests that she had received a portrait by him of BF. No such portrait from this period is known, although there is some slight evidence that West did paint one. See Charles C. Sellers, *Benjamin Franklin in Portraiture* (New Haven and London, 1962), pp. 402–3. Another explanation, attractive except for the timing involved, is that DF meant to write "tell Mr. Coombe," whose portrait by Henry Benbridge that painter was bringing to Philadelphia. BF to DF above, July 19. But Benbridge clearly did not sail before July 20 at earliest, and could scarcely have reached Philadelphia by Aug. 19.

9. A New York physician and surgeon, and an old friend of BF; see above, III, 49 n.

uel, as a Successor to the late Mr. Parker, in the office he held in the post office.[1] I hope Dr. Franklin will not attribute it to my Partial affection, when I tell him his Acknowledg'd Character in this place —his Integrity and merit render him worthy of such a Trust— and if it should not be Inconvenient, or Interfere with any other Views you may have; it will be adding an obligation, to the many Instances I have received of your Friendship and good will; which we shall ever remember with the warmest Gratitude and Affection. I am Dear Sir your most obliged and most Humble Servant

JOHN BARD

Addressed: To / Doctr. Benjn. Franklin L.L.D. / Craven Street / London

To Timothy Folger

ALS: Folger Library

Loving Kinsman,   London, Aug. 21. 1770

I received yours of June 28. and immediately sent the same to the Proprietor Capt. Campbell, who was in the Country, desiring he would enable me to give you an explicit Answer. Yesterday being in Town he call'd upon me, and said, that he look'd upon his Lot to be full as good as Mr. Pownal's which was sold for £500 but after some Discourse he agreed that to save Time, as you were at such a Distance from each other, it would be best to name his lowest Price at once, which he accordingly did, and it is £350 to be paid down on his making the Conveyance. You will be so good as to let me know your Mind by the first Opportunity, as he stands engag'd to me not to treat with any other Person till such time as an Answer might reasonably be expected from you.

On perusing again your Letter, I do not find which of the two Lotts that I sent you Drafts of, you now desire me to enquire the Price of. The first Draft was enclos'd with my Letter of Feb. 25. and went with your Son; and is that refer'd to above. The second was sent some time after, being of another Lot belonging to another

1. Samuel Bard was following in his father's footsteps, and also became a successful New York physician; see above, XII, 158 n. James Parker's position in the Post Office had been that of comptroller and secretary general of the northern district.

Person, Mr. Adair.[2] I forget by whom I sent it. It was about 20,000 Acres also, if I forget not. I hope it came duly to hand, and that I shall soon hear from you upon it. I should be glad you would give me your private Opinion freely, as I may have other Offers of the same kind, and could rely on your Judgment whether it might be worth while for me to be concern'd in that Island.

I hope your Son got safe to you, and is well, though you do not mention him. I have since received a Box of Spermaceti Candles from you that are excellent, and I thank you for them very heartily. Those made in Boston sent me by Mr. Tuthill Hubbard,[3] were not near so good. I have always found Palmer's the best.

Mrs. Stevenson presents her best Respects. Her Daughter is married to a very worthy young Gentleman, Mr. Hewson. Nancy Johnson is also married to Capt. Clark of the Navy, Son of Gidney Clark of Barbadoes, said to be very rich.[4] I think you must remember her at my House learning Musick. With sincere Regard, I am, Your affectionate Kinsman   B Franklin

Mr Folger

To Cadwalader Evans

Reprinted from Samuel Hazard, ed., *Hazard's Register of Pennsylvania*, XVI, No. 5 (Aug. 1, 1835), 92.

Dear Doctor   London, Aug. 27, 1770.
I am favoured with yours of June 10. With this I send you our last

2. The three lots that BF mentions were all on what is now Prince Edward Island, and had been allocated in 1767. The first two were adjacent, the third in another parish. *Acts Privy Coun., Col.*, V, 63; *Board of Trade Jour.*, 1764–67, pp. 413–14. For Capt. (later Vice-Adm.) John Campbell (1720?–90) see *DNB*, and for Robert Adair (1711?–90), a prominent surgeon, *Gent. Mag.*, LX (1790), 282. John Pownall, secretary to the Board of Trade, has often appeared in these pages. BF's letter to Folger of Feb. 25 has not survived; for the bearer, Silvanus Folger, see above, XVI, 208.

3. BF's step-nephew and the Boston postmaster.

4. Anne Johnson Clarke (C.5.7.2) was BF's grandniece, who had married Peter Clarke, R.N. Her father-in-law, Gedney Clarke (1711–64), had been a native of Salem, Mass. who had emigrated to Barbados and become a merchant and customs collector at Bridgetown. Henry F. Waters, "The Gedney and Clarke Families of Salem, Mass.," Essex Institute *Hist. Collections*, XVI (1879), 271; *The Diary of William Bentley...* (4 vols., Salem, Mass., 1905–14), IV, 494–5; *Gent. Mag.*, XXXIV (1764), 498.

Volume of Philosophical Transactions, wherein you will see printed the Observations of Messrs. Biddle and Bayley on the Transit, as well as those of Messrs. Mason and Dixon relating to the Longitude of Places.[5] When you and your Friends have perus'd it, please to deliver it to Mrs. Franklin to be put among my Books.

Thanks for the Books on the Silk Affair.[6] It will give me great pleasure to see that Business brought to Perfection among us. The Subscription is a noble One, and does great Honour to our Public Spirit.[7] If you should not procure from Georgia, as you expected, one that understands the Reeling, I believe I can procure you such a Hand from Italy, a great Silk Merchant here having offered me his Assistance for that purpose if wanted.[8]

I am happy beyond Expression to see the Virtue and Firmness of our Country with regard to the Non-importation. It does us great Honour. And New York is in great Disgrace with all the Friends of Liberty in the Kingdom,[9] who are, I assure you, no contemptible Number, who applaud the stand we have made, wish us Success. I am, my dear friend, Yours most affectionately,   B. FRANKLIN.

Dr. Cad. Evans.

To John Ewing

ALS: Yale University Library

Reverend Sir,   London, Augt. 27. 1770.

I received your Favour of June 14. with several Copies of your Observations of the Transit of Venus, for which I thank you. I have sent one of them to Mr. Maskelyne as you desired, with an Extract from your Letter, and another to Paris. I have not yet obtain'd

5. "Observations of the Transit of Venus over the Sun, June 3, 1769; made by Mr. Owen Biddle and Mr. Joel Bayley," *Phil. Trans.*, LIX (1769), 414–21; the article includes some remarks by Nevil Maskelyne about the observations of Mason and Dixon published in the previous volume of *Phil. Trans.*

6. Odell's translation of a French work that BF had sent to Evans; see above, XVI, 200.

7. The prospectus for an organization of subscribers to encourage the culture of silk in Pennsylvania was published in *Pa. Gaz.*, March 8, 1770, and the same paper carried an article on the subject a week later.

8. The merchant was probably BF's partner in land speculation, the Hon. Thomas Walpole. See BF to Evans below, Feb. 10, 1771.

9. For the action of the Philadelphia merchants and the vacillation in New York see Thomas Gilpin to BF above, July 19.

from him the Estimate he promis'd me, but hope to have it soon; tho' by what I hear from others I begin to fear the Expence will be thought too heavy for us.[1] I shall send the new Volume of the Transactions to Mrs. Franklin, where you will find what Observations have been received and published here.[2] I am, very respectfully, Reverend Sir, Your most obedient humble Servant

B FRANKLIN

Mr Ewing

Addressed: To / The Revd. Mr Ewing / at / Philadelphia / per Capt. Osborne

From Jonathan Williams, Sr.

ALS: American Philosophical Society

Honoured Sir   Boston Augt 27th. 1770

My Son Josiah is determined to go to London and I Belive Will Sail in about a month. I wish he might be accomidated at Good Mrs. Stevensons if agreeable if this Cant be please to direct the unfortinate Stranger to Some Other Good place. I Shall Send his Brother to take Care off him, it may apper to you Very extrodnary for us to Consent to Such a Step[3] but the Happiness of his whol Life Seemes to Depend on his Going to England and Some of the best Gentlemen in town adviz'd to it. He has for a long time been Very anxious to Se the Famus Mr. Stanley Who he thinks Can Serve him in the Siance of Musick in which he has made Some Proficance and is Very fond of Excelling, but Dispares allmost of all Instruction

1. Ewing had asked for an estimate of the expense of erecting an observatory in Philadelphia; see his letters to BF above, Jan. 4, June 14.

2. See the preceding document.

3. Because Josiah (C.5.3.1), his eldest son, was blind; see above, X, 156. In spite of his handicap he had become proficient on the spinet and BF's harmonica; see above, XI, 179. The young man feared for some reason that BF would disapprove of his coming and send him packing home by the first ship. Jane Mecom to BF below, Sept. 25. The fear was groundless. Mrs. Stevenson took in Josiah and Jonathan (with whom BF was later closely associated), and BF promised to do all he could for them; see the postscript of his letter to Jane Mecom below, Nov. 9. The two young men were accompanied by their uncle, John Williams the customs inspector: Van Doren, *Franklin–Mecom*, pp. 118–19. If he also lodged with them, the Craven Street house must have been capacious.

but this Great Blind man Who he Says can give him more Light in this matter then any man living that Can See.[4]

We have no Business nor likley to have owing to the unhappy differance between Great Britain and her Collines Which will consequenthaly prove the total Ruin of thousands.

Aunt Mecom is well Settled in the Old place tho almost a N House;[5] we flatter ourselves that you Will on your Return Call at Boston if So I Shall take it kind if you make my [House] your Home, I am Sinesible you are much engag'd in Public Concerns and I dont mean by Writing to you to give you too much Concern or troble with my Sons tho I Shall esteem it a great favour if you take notice of them if Only as Strangers in London. Your advice may not only Save my money but them from Ruin in [*in the margin:* Plas to turn over] Such a place as London is tho thay are Good Lads and I belive have Some Merit Otherwise I Should not have trustd them.

We Want a Governor and all most every Body Wishes Doctor Franklin might Come[6] as well as your Dutifull Nephew and Humble Servant   JONA WILLIAMS

Endorsed: Jona Williams Aug. 27. 1770

From Robert Alexander[7]   ALS: American Philosophical Society

Dear Sir,   3 Sepr. 1770
Since my return to Scotland, I have been some days in the Country by which means I did not receive your Letter before yesterday. I return you a Thousand Thanks for the Trouble you have taken about the Harpsichord, the one you describe at 33 Guineas is precisely what is wanted and therefore you will please give orders to have it immediately packt up and Sent down, after putting it in the best order and I desire you will give Mr. Bar-

4. For John Stanley, the organist and composer, see above, IX, 320 n. He had not taught for years, but took on Josiah at BF's request and was pleased with him. BF to Jane Mecom below, Dec. 30.

5. Henhouse? Jane was settled after her long visit to Philadelphia and Burlington.

6. For an earlier version of the wish, see above, XVI, 129–30.

7. An Edinburgh merchant and banker, for whom see above, VIII, 444 n; XIV, 75 n.

ron who has assisted you whatever you think he deserves.[8] Both my Brothers[9] desire to be remembr'd to you in the kindest manner and with my best Compliments to Mrs. Stevenson and your other Friends I remain Dear Sir, Your most humble and most obedient Servant ROBERT ALEXANDER

[*In the margin:*] There are every Week Ships going from London to Leith.

Addressed: To / Dr Ben. Franklin / Craven Street / London

Extract of a Letter[10]

Printed from *The Pennsylvania Gazette*, September 6, 1770

[Before September 6, 1770]

Mr. Wilkes seems to be enjoying the solid Advantages of his Popularity with little Noise. The Boston Affair is a general Subject of Conversation, but, like every other American Concern, is so enveloped with Prejudices and Misrepresentations, that the still Voice of Truth and Candour is not heard. They are Rebels——Aggressors, with a long &c. of ministerial Epithets. I am sorry to find an Observation made concerning Corsica, verified in England. Every Englishman considers himself as King of America,[1] and peculiarly interested in our Subjection; it gratifies his Pride, and he is at the same Time free from any Apprehensions of suffering himself. As to Relief from the Wisdom and Tenderness of Administration, Hope itself is gone, even with our most sanguine Friends. We have no other

8. Possibly one of the Barron Brothers, Hugh and William Augustus, both of whom were mediocre painters and excellent violinists. *DNB.* Either one might have met BF through the Wests or otherwise, although we have no evidence that he did. The harpsichord was cheap; for prices at the time see Frank Hubbard, *Three Centuries of Harpsichord Making* (Cambridge, Mass., 1965), p. 160.

9. One was William, whose daughter later married Jonathan Williams, Jr. (above, XIV, 75 n), and the other was Alexander John. Both were bankers, like Robert; in later years they were in France during BF's mission there, and corresponded with him at length.

10. We follow Crane's reason for assigning this extract to BF: *Letters to the Press*, p. 212 n. As pointed out below, however, we believe that much of the final paragraph is by another hand.

1. See below, p. 311 n.

Resource but in our own Virtue and Resolution, which our Enemies allow will prevail, if we can but persevere.

You desired me to write you, whether your Non-importation was really felt, and if not, to what it is owing? I have made the best Enquiry, and find it has had little Effect on the Manufacturers, who, like stupid Animals, must smart before they will move.[2] The Russian War has had some Effect——Germany, and even France, it is said, take off very considerable. That the Ministry play into each others Hands, to serve their own arbitrary Purposes in each Kingdom, so as to relax the former Systems of Politics and Commerce, seems too forced a Conjecture——but that Merchants are encouraged by the Promises of Ministry, even to Indemnification, is universally believed; and the Owner of the Malt-ship, sent back from Philadelphia, now makes no Secret of the Intention of his Voyage. Unjust and tyrannical Notions of Colony Government, seem too much to prevail, even among the Sons of Liberty.[3]

From Mary Hopkinson   ALS: Historical Society of Pennsylvania

Dear Sir   philada Septr 6 1770

My Son Thomas will have the Honor to deliver this to you; shall I beg you will condescend to advise and instruct a young Man; although honest and open hearted, yet intirely unacquainted with the world and the Dispositions of those whome it is his Interest to please.[4] Any other Man in your place and Station I could not ask

2. We suggest that the extract from BF ends here.

3. The three final sentences are, for various reasons, completely unlike BF. The first is awkward in wording, and does not explain why the Russo-Turkish war, which had broken out in 1768, should have affected French and German imports of British manufactures. The second, at least after the semicolon, is incomprehensible: the malt ship, the *Charming Polly*, had made her fruitless voyage to Philadelphia in the summer of 1769 (*PMHB*, LIV [1930], 366–7), when no owner in his right mind would have expected indemnification. The concluding sentence is merely paranoid. The three taken together form a passage that we are convinced BF could not have written. Crane suggests (*op. cit.*, p. 212) that it may have been garbled in printing; we suggest that the printer either invented it or extracted it from a letter by some supremely inept writer.

4. Thomas Hopkinson (1747–84), a younger brother of Francis, graduated from the College of Pennsylvania in 1766, studied divinity, and was now going

such a Favor of engaged, as you are, in such a multiplicity of Business and that for your country. But I know I write to a Gentleman who is capable of carrying on the greatest affairs and yet can attend to the most minute, whenever called upon by friendship or charity. You will answer both by this Condescension, and will add one more obligation to the many my family have receivd from you. Mr. Warrin has been so good as to invite him to lodge at his House,[5] his Goodness to my other Son, and this new favor I Shall never forget, it calls for my utmost Gratitude and my sincere prayer is, that it may be returned to him by the Father of the fatherless in Blessings Seventy fold. And do you think, Sir I can seperate in my heart the obligations I am under to you as the Instrument in the Hand of God in making me acquainted with such kind Relations. I canot——but shall with great Gratitude ever think my Self your obliged humble Servant   MARY HOPKINSON

Dr Franklin

From John Borthwick[6]   ALS: American Philosophical Society

Dear Sir,   New York, 8 Septemr. 1770.
    I used the Freedom to write you a few Lines at two times from Philadelphia.
    I have been here for sometime in the high part of the Town and continue to grow better.
    I had the pleasure of seeing the Governor his Lady, Mrs. Beache

to England to prepare for holy orders. He also carried a note of introduction to BF from WF, which, like this one, mentions the young man's innocence of the world; see below, Sept. 23. After his ordination in 1773 Hopkinson returned to Philadelphia, and subsequently had parishes in Maryland and Virginia. See Charles P. Keith, *The Provincial Councillors of Pennsylvania*... (Philadelphia, 1883), pp. 266–7.

5. Perhaps the Rev. John Warren (above, xv, 87 n); probably his brother James, mentioned below, BF to Jonathan Williams, Sr., Jan, 13, 1772.

6. The identity of the author baffles us. He was a Scot, to judge not only by his name but also by the many other Scots who appear in his letter. He writes as one who was a good acquaintance, perhaps even a good friend, of BF and his family and circle in America; and it is puzzling that such a man should not have appeared before in these volumes or, as far as we yet know, in BF's later correspondence.

and the young Dr. at Burlington, as I passed, in good health, stayed a few days with Mr. Laurence the Mayor with whom I went and saw Judge Reids Iron Works by which he is no danger of growing too rich. Mr. Beache is at Jamaica.[7]

I say nothing of the Transactions here, O homines ad servitudem paratos.[8]

As I hope to be well soon, and am determined to remain on this Continent, I must not remain idle, and I now presume on your Goodness to make this Application to you as I apprehend it may be in your power to procure something for me, if Mr. Alexander is in London I hope he will assist. I had wrote for recommendations to Lord D—re but there's no news of him,[9] and I am told nothing can be done with him without m——y, not in my Power to give. I desire not your immediate Answer, that you may think of it at your Leisure. I shall return to Philadelphia in a few days——the other day a Gentleman here made me a present of a Manuscript entitled "An Examination into the Value of Canada and Guadaloupe with an impartial Account of the latter in answer to a late Pamphlet entitled 'The Interest of Great Britain's considerd with regard to her Colonies' in a Letter to a Gentleman in England." He says he believes it was not publishd as it contains some curious particulars. I will in a Subsequent Letter send you what he says about Cayenne by which you'll recollect if you have ever seen it. It is dated "New York 5 January 1761" and contains 86 pages besides an Appendix,

7. Sally and her infant son, "the young Dr.," were staying with the WFS while Richard Bache was in Jamaica on business; see DF to BF above, Aug. 16. John Brown Lawrence (d. 1796), the father of the captain who later commanded the *Chesapeake*, was a prominent lawyer and the mayor of Burlington; he subsequently became a Loyalist. 1 *N.J. Arch.*, x, 302 n; Sabine, *Loyalists*, II, 3. Charles Read, justice of the New Jersey Supreme Court, has appeared before: x, 313 n; XI, 97 n. In 1765 he had announced his intention of establishing iron works at different sites in the province, and had invited other investors to join him. For his career as an ironmaster see Carl R. Woodward, *Ploughs and Politicks, Charles Read of New Jersey and His Notes on Agriculture*... (New Brunswick, 1941), pp. 86–96.

8. "O men ready for servitude" was the comment of Tiberius upon the Roman Senators.

9. Alexander was in all likelihood BF's old acquaintance, the Edinburgh merchant and banker, who had recently written BF: above, Sept. 3. Dunmore, also a Scot, had been appointed governor of New York in January, but did not arrive there until October. *DAB*.

and was said to be wrote by one Mr. Kennedy alias Scott.[1] For the meaning of the word alias see P—y Johnson's Dictionary 1st Edition.[2] I was at Mr. Levisey's some day's and had the pleasure of reading your Lucubrations.[3] I forgot to tell you in a former Letter that the Old Duke of Wharton has a Duplicate of the Plan of Philadelphia the same with the one I gave you.[4] I remain with Esteem [*torn*] Your most Obedient   JOHN BORTHWICK

Direct for me to the care of Mr. Joseph Wharton ju Philadelphia.

Addressed: To / Doctor Benjn. / Franklyn / to the care of / Mr. Strahan Printer / in / London. per Paquet.

Endorsed: Mr Borthwick

From Thomas Fitzmaurice[5]   ALS: American Philosophical Society

Dear Sir,   Knighton House. Isle Wight. Septr. 10. 1770.

I promised Dr. Hawkesworth that I w'd by this post acquaint you how eagerly we expect your arrival here, we were in hopes that possibly you might have arrived yesterday with Sir Chas. Knowles who means to make a stay of some days here.[6] I flatter myself that you and he will meet yet; he purposes to make a very curious Experiment upon the force and direction of the Winds

1. For BF's pamphlet, to which the author was replying, see above, IX, 59–100. The reply is unlisted in standard bibliographies, and doubtless remained unpublished. Its author, we assume, was Archibald Kennedy, still another Scot, for whom see above, IV, 117 n.

2. The joke in this reference eludes us. Samuel Johnson's famous dictionary contains an unexceptionable definition of alias.

3. Perhaps an allusion to the most recent letter that has survived from BF to Thomas Livezey (above, XV, 54), although that brief note scarcely qualifies as lucubration.

4. Joseph Wharton, the head of the large Wharton clan and the old friend of BF and DF, was known as the Duke: above, XIV, 158 n. What the plan or map was we have no idea.

5. For the younger brother of the Earl of Shelburne see above, X, 348 n.

6. For BF's and Polly Hewson's old friend, John Hawkesworth, see above, IX, 265 n and later volumes. Sir Charles Knowles (d. 1777) was a distinguished and highly controversial admiral. He resigned his command in the following month to take service in the Russian navy for the duration of the Russo-Turkish war. *DNB.*

upon one of our highest neighbouring Downs. Dr. H. and myself have declared that if you dont come soon we will Libel you in the public Advertiser, you don't know what inferences may be drawn from many of your Experiments which appear so inoffensive at the same time that they are so usefull. In short we shall pour down a sort of Thunder and lightening upon you that you are little conversant with, that is we will abuse you plentifully, tho' in the mean time he joins his best respects to you with those of, Dear Sir, Your very faithfull and Obedient Humble Servant

THOMS. FITZMAURICE

From Thomas Gilpin

Extract: reprinted from "Memoir of Thomas Gilpin," *Pennsylvania Magazine of History and Biography*, XLIX (1925), 308–9.

Philadelphia Sepr. [21,⁷] 1770.

The silk business is in a fair way and I am convinced will be of consequence if attended to——there are also numbers of minor manufactures which would succeed if parliament would but lay on a few more duties, or as I may say bounties here, for such is the effect of their duties; it is nothing but the easy terms upon which we obtain all sorts of manufactures from abroad and the more free and relaxed life it affords that hinders our manufacturers from starting up and making a rapid progress. I should be glad to see the unanimity of the two countries restored and Great Britain succeed in her manufactures as we in ours and in our agriculture but no restrictions; at a meeting of the merchants here last night it was agreed to give notice to the other provinces of an intention to make some alterations in our own non-importation agreement so as to admit the importation of some articles which we cannot at present do without, and increase the restrictions upon others in order that it may not be said we cannot hold out until a change of ministry or policy takes place.

7. The meeting of merchants "last night," to which Gilpin refers, must have been that held at Davenport's Tavern on Thursday, Sept. 20: *Pa. Gaz.*, Sept. 27; Gilpin to BF below, Sept. 28. The action taken at the meeting conforms to Gilpin's description.

This famous blend of parody and nonsense reveals, under its genial persiflage, more about the details of Franklin's daily life in London than anything else in his papers. The setting of the Gazette can only be deduced from its contents. Mrs. Stevenson and Sally Franklin had left to visit relatives or friends in Rochester about whom nothing is known, except that their hostess—a widow, because she is referred to as the Duchess Dowager—invited the Craven Street household to join them there.[8] Before Franklin's landlady left, she had apparently arranged for Polly and her new husband, William Hewson, to move into the house and take care of him in her absence. For his own entertainment and that of his circle, he wrote this account of the results. His audience could doubtless identify the members of the household more confidently than his editors can, but we are inclined to think that there were only four: Franklin, the maid Nanny, and the two Hewsons. Polly in that case was Cook, Lady Chamberlain of the Household, Lady of the Bedchamber, and first Ministress, while her husband was Groom Porter and first Minister.

[September 22–26, 1770]

THE CRAVENSTREET GAZETTE. No 113

Saturday, Sept. 22. 1770

This Morning Queen Margaret, accompanied by her first Maid of Honour, Miss Franklin, set out for Rochester. Immediately on their Departure, the whole Street was in Tears——from a heavy Shower of Rain.

It is whispered that the new Family Administration which took place on her Majesty's Departure, promises, like all other new Administrations, to govern much better than the old one.

We hear that the *great* Person (so called from his enormous Size) of a certain Family in a certain Street, is grievously affected at the late Changes, and could hardly be comforted this Morning, tho' the new Ministry promised him a roasted Shoulder of Mutton, and Potatoes, for his Dinner.

It is said, that the same *great* Person intended to pay his Respects to another great Personage this Day, at St. James's, it being Coronation-Day;[9] hoping thereby a little to amuse his Grief; but was

---

8. The hostess, whoever she was, may well have been the same one whom Polly had visited five years before: above, XII, 222–3.

9. The ninth anniversary of the King's and Queen's coronation.

prevented by an Accident, Queen Margaret, or her Maid of Honour having carried off the Key of the Drawers, so that the Lady of the Bedchamber could not come at a laced Shirt for his Highness. Great Clamours were made on this Occasion against her Majesty.

Other Accounts say, that the Shirts were afterwards found, tho' too late, in another Place. And some suspect, that the Wanting a Shirt from those Drawers was only a ministerial Pretence to excuse Picking the Locks, that the new Administration might have every thing at Command.

We hear that the Lady Chamberlain of the Household went to Market this Morning by her own self, gave the Butcher whatever he ask'd for the Mutton, and had no Dispute with the Potatoe Woman——to their great Amazement——at the Change of Times!

It is confidently asserted, that this Afternoon, the Weather being wet, the great *Person* a little chilly, and no body at home to find fault with the Expence of Fuel, he was indulg'd with a Fire in his Chamber. It seems the Design is, to make him contented, by Degrees, with the Absence of the Queen.

A Project has been under Consideration of Government, to take the Opportunity of her Majesty's Absence, for doing a Thing she was always averse to, viz. Fixing a new Lock on the Street Door, or getting a Key made to the old one; it being found extreamly inconvenient, that one or other of the Great Officers of State, should, whenever the Maid goes out for a Ha'pworth of Sand[10] or a Pint of Porter, be obliged to attend the Door to let her in again. But Opinion, being divided, which of the two Expedients to adopt, the Project is for the present laid aside.

We have good Authority to assure our Readers, that a Cabinet Council was held this Afternoon at Tea; the Subject of which was a Proposal for the Reformation of Manners, and a more strict Observation of the Lord's Day. The Result was, an unanimous Resolution that no Meat should be dress'd to-morrow; whereby the Cook and the first Minister will both be at Liberty to go to Church, the one having nothing to do, and the other no Roast to rule. It seems the cold Shoulder of Mutton, and the Applepye, were thought sufficient for Sunday's Dinner. All pious People applaud this Measure, and 'tis thought the new Ministry will soon become popular.

We hear that Mr. Wilkes was at a certain House in Craven Street

10. The blotting paper of the day.

this Day, and enquired after the absent Queen. His good Lady and the Children were well.

The Report that Mr. Wilkes the Patriot made the above Visit, is without Foundation, it being his Brother the Courtier.[1]

Sunday, Sept. 23.

It is now found by sad Experience, that good Resolutions are easier made than executed. Notwithstanding yesterday's solemn Order of Council, no body went to Church to day. It seems the *great* Person's broad-built-bulk lay so long abed, that Breakfast was not over 'till it was too late to dress. At least this is the Excuse. In fine, it seems a vain thing to hope Reformation from the Example of our great Folks. The Cook and the Minister, however, both took Advantage of the Order so far, as to save themselves all Trouble, and the Clause of *cold Dinner* was enforc'd, tho' the *going to Church* was dispens'd with; just as the common working People observe the Commandment; *the seventh Day thou shalt rest*, they think a sacred Injunction; but the other *Six Days shalt thou labour* is deem'd a mere Piece of Advice which they may practice when they want Bread and are out of Credit at the Alehouse, and may neglect whenever they have Money in their Pockets.[2] It must nevertheless be said in justice to our Court, that whatever Inclination they had to Gaming, no Cards were brought out to Day. Lord and Lady Hewson walk'd after Dinner to Kensington to pay their Duty to the Dowager, and Dr. Fatsides made 469 Turns in his Dining Room as the exact Distance of a Visit to the lovely Lady Barwell, whom he did not find at home, so there was no Struggle for and against a Kiss, and he sat down to dream in the Easy Chair that he had it without any Trouble.[3]

1. Israel Wilkes was a courtier because a frequent visitor. Thomas Coombe came to know him well, presumably through those visits, and less than five months before had reported him grief-stricken at the death of a fifteen-year-old daughter; Israel, Coombe added sententiously, was as remarkable for his virtues as John for his vices. To Thomas Coombe, Sr., May 5, 1770, Hist. Soc. of Pa.

2. BF is repeating himself: see above, xv, 107.

3. The Dowager was undoubtedly Polly's aunt, Mrs. Tickell, who lived in Kensington; Lady Barwell is discussed above, p. 197 n.

Monday, Sept. 24.

We are credibly informed, that the *great* Person dined this Day with the Club at the Cat-and-Bagpipes in the City,[4] on cold Round of boil'd Beef. This, it seems, he was under some Necessity of Doing (tho' he rather dislikes Beef) because truly the Ministers were to be all abroad somewhere to dine on hot roast Venison. It is thought that if the Queen had been at home, he would not have been so slighted. And tho' he shows outwardly no Marks of Dissatisfaction, it is suspected that he begins to wish for her Majesty's Return.

It is currently reported, that poor Nanny[5] had nothing for Dinner in the Kitchen, for herself and Puss, but the Scrapings of the Bones of Saturday's Mutton.

This Evening there was high Play at the Groom Porter's in Cravenstreet House. The Great Person lost Money. It is supposed the Ministers, as is usually supposed of all Ministers, shared the Emoluments among them.

Tuesday, Sept. 25.

This Morning the good Lord Hutton call'd at Cravenstreet House, and enquired very respectfully and affectionately concerning the Welfare of the absent Queen. He then imparted to the big Man a Piece of Intelligence important to them both, which he had just received from Lady Hawkesworth, viz. That [the] amiable and excellent Companion Miss Dorothea Blount had made a Vow to marry absolutely him of the two, whose Wife should first depart this Life.[6] It is impossible to express with Words the various Agitations of Mind appearing in both their Faces on this Occasion. *Vanity* at the Preference given them to the rest of Mankind; *Affec-*

4. If BF did not invent the dinner (as he did the name of the coffee house), he doubtless attended John Ellicot's Monday club at the George & Vulture, for which see above, x, 250 n.

5. See BF to DF above, June 10.

6. Mrs. John Hawkesworth has appeared frequently before, and so has Dorothea Blunt, who had written BF of her devotion: above, July 26. Lord Hutton was unquestionably James Hutton (1715–95), the virtual founder of the Moravian church in England, for whom see *DNB*. This is his first appearance, but a later letter from him to BF (Oct. 23, 1772; APS) makes clear that he was then, and presumably had been for some time, an habitué of Craven Street.

tion to their present Wives; *Fear* of losing them; *Hope*, (if they must lose them) to obtain the propos'd Comfort; *Jealousy* of each other, in case both Wives should die together; &c. &c. &c. all working at the same time, jumbled their Features into inexplicable Confusion. They parted at length with Professions and outward Appearances indeed of ever-during Friendship; but it was shrewdly suspected that each of them sincerely wished Health and long Life to the other's Wife; and that however long either of those Friends might like to live himself, the other would be very well pleas'd to survive him.

It is remark'd that the Skies have wept every Day in Craven-street the Absence of the Queen.

The Publick may be assured, that this Morning a certain *great Person* was ask'd very complaisantly by the Mistress of the Houshold, if he would chuse to have the Blade Bone of Saturday's Mutton that had been kept for his Dinner to Day, *broil'd* or *cold?* He answer'd gravely, *If there is any Flesh on it, it may be broil'd; if not, it may as well be cold.* Orders were accordingly given for broiling it. But when it came to Table, there was indeed so very little Flesh, or rather none at all (Puss having din'd on it yesterday after Nanny) that if our new Administration had been as good Oeconomists as they would be thought, the Expence of Broiling might well have been sav'd to the Publick, and carried to the Sinking Fund. It is assured the great Person bears all with infinite Patience. But the Nation is astonish'd at the insolent Presumption that dares treat so much Mildness in so cruel a manner.

A terrible Accident had *like to have happened* this Afternoon at Tea. The Boiler was set too near the End of the little square Table. The first Ministress was sitting at one End of the Table to administer the Tea; the great Person was about to sit down at the other End where the Boiler stood. By a sudden Motion, the Lady gave the Table a Tilt. Had it gone over, the great *Person* must have been scalded; perhaps to Death. Various are the Surmises and Observations on this Occasion. The Godly say, it would have been a just Judgment on him, for preventing by his Laziness, the Family's going to Church last Sunday. The Opposition do not stick to insinuate that there was a Design to scald him, prevented only by his quick Catching the Table. The Friends of the Ministry give out, that he carelessly jogg'd the Table himself, and would have been inevitably scalded had not the Ministress sav'd him. It is hard for the Publick to come at the Truth in these Cases.

At six o'Clock this Afternoon News came by the Post, that her Majesty arrived safely at Rochester on Saturday Night. The Bells immediately rang——for Candles, to illuminate the Parlour; the Court went into Cribbidge, and the Evening concluded with every other Demonstration of Joy.

It is reported that all the principal Officers of the State, have received an Invitation from the Dutchess Dowager of Rochester to go down thither on Saturday next. But it is not yet known whether the great Affairs they have on their Hands will permit them to make this Excursion.

We hear that from the Time of her Majesty's leaving Craven Street House to this Day, no Care is taken to file the Newspapers; but they lie about in every Room, in every Window, and on every Chair, just where the Doctor lays them when he has read them. It is impossible Government can long go on in such Hands.

To the Publisher of the Craven Street Gazette.
Sir,
I make no doubt of the Truth of what the Papers tell us, that a certain great *Person* has been half-starved on the bare Blade-bone, *of a Sheep* (I cannot call it *of Mutton* because none was on it) by a Set of the most careless, thoughtless, inconsiderate, corrupt, ignorant, blundering, foolish, crafty, and Knavish Ministers, that ever got into a House and pretended to govern a Family and provide a Dinner. Alas, for the poor Old England[7] of Craven Street! If these nefarious Wretches continue in Power another Week, the Nation will be ruined——Undone!——totally undone, if the Queen does not return; or (which is better) turn them all out and appoint me and my Friends to succeed them. I am a great Admirer of your useful and impartial Paper; and therefore request you will insert this without fail; from Your humble Servant   INDIGNATION.

To the Publisher of the Craven Street Gazette.
Sir,
Your Correspondent *Indignation* has made a fine Story in your Paper against our excellent Cravenstreet Ministry, as if they meant

7. One of BF's *noms de plume*; see above, XV, 14, 19.

to starve his Highness, giving him only a bare Blade Bone for his Dinner, while they riot upon roast Venison, &c. The Wickedness of Writers in this Age is truly amazing! I believe we never had since the Foundation of our State, a more faithful, upright, worthy, careful, considerate, incorrupt, discreet, wise, prudent and beneficent Ministry than the present. But if even the Angel Gabriel would condescend to be our Minister and provide our Dinners, he could scarcely escape Newspaper Defamation from a Gang of hungry ever-restless, discontented and malicious Scribblers. It is, Sir, a piece of Justice you owe our righteous Administration to undeceive the Publick on this [Occasion], by assuring them [of] the Fact, which is, that there was provided, and actually smoaking on the Table under his Royal Nose at the same Instant, as fine a Piece of Ribbs of Beef, roasted, as ever Knife was put into; with Potatoes, Horse radish, pickled Walnuts, &c. which Beef his Highness might have eaten of, if so he had pleased to do; and which he forbore to do, merely from a whimsical Opinion (with Respect be it spoken) that Beef doth not with him perspire well, but makes his Back itch, to his no small Vexation, now that he hath lost the little Chinese Ivory Hand [at] the End of a Stick, commonly called a *Scratchback*, presented to him by her Majesty. This is the Truth; and if your boasted Impartiality is real, you will not hesitate a Moment to insert this Letter in your very next Paper. I am, tho' a little angry with you at present. Yours as you behave   A HATER OF SCANDAL.

JUNIUS and CINNA *came to Hand too late for this Days Paper, but shall have Place in our next.*

Marriages. None since our last; but Puss begins to go a Courting.
Deaths.   In the back Closet, and elsewhere, many poor Mice.
Stocks.   Biscuit very low.
               Buckwheat and Indian meal, both sour.
               Tea, lowering daily in the Canister.

Postscript. Wednesday Sept. 26.

Those in the Secret of Affairs do not scruple to assert soundly, that our present First Ministress is very notable, having this day been at Market, bought excellent Mutton Chops, and Apples 4 a penny, made a very fine Applepye with her own Hands, and mended two pair of Breeches.

From William Franklin
ALS: Historical Society of Pennsylvania

Honoured Father   Burlington Septr. 23d 1770.

Mr. Thos. Hopkinson, Son of your old Friend, calling on me for a Letter of Introduction to you, it is with Pleasure that I comply with his Request as he has the Character of a very sober, ingenious and promising young Gentleman.[8] He intends to take the Gown, tho' I understand much against the Inclination of many of his Friends who have taken Pains to dissuade him from it. His Knowledge of the World is but small, having confined himself ever since he left College to his Studies, your Advice and Countenance will therefore be particularly serviceable to him.

I am to set out Tomorrow for Amboy to meet the Assembly. At Dr. Witherspoon's Request I shall stop at Princeton in my Way in order to be present at a Commencement.[9] I have but just Time to add that I am, Honoured Sir, Your dutiful Son

WM. FRANKLIN

From Jane Mecom
ALS (torn): American Philosophical Society

Boston Sept 25[1] [1770]

I have trobled my Ever Dear Brother [with] several Leters Since I have had the P[leasure of] won from Him but cannot omit Ading won more by my well Respected and much Esteemed Kinsmen whome wee all Part from with Regrett Notwithstanding we hope Ther Future Benifit and saif return will be occasion of Joy to all there Friends.[2]

Josiah says He fears nothing He Shall have to Incounter so much as your Disaprobation of His Sceme. He Expects you will advise

8. See Mary Hopkinson to BF above, Sept. 3, 1770.

9. Witherspoon had been for two years president of the College of New Jersey, now Princeton, and WF as governor was *ex officio* president of the board of trustees. The two men were, Ezra Stiles believed, in league to undercut Presbyterian opposition to BF; see above, XVI, 125.

1. Dated Sept. 22 by Van Doren, *Franklin–Mecom*, p. 115, because he misread her weird but consistent 5 as a 2. Her brother misread it as a 9; see the postscript of his letter to her below, Nov. 9.

2. BF's nephew, John Williams, and two grandnephews, Josiah and Jonathan Williams, Jr.; see Jonathan Williams, Sr., to BF above, Aug. 27.

Him to Return in the first Ship, yet He cant conquer His Inclineation. I tell Him you have seen so much of the Follies of Human Nature and So L[ittle] Els in the comon Run of man kind, that you will know Beter how to Pitty and Advice him.

[There is?] a Rumer Hear that you have mett with some [harsh?] Treetment[3] and I cant Help being conserned about [you tho' you?] forbad me, I Fansey by this time you have [found there?] are more wicked folks in the world than [you thou]ght there was; and that thay are capeble of Doing [you hu]rt. I Pray God to Preserve your Usefull Life among them and that Every Good man may not be Distroyed from of the Face of the Earth.

I am Desiered by a Lady of my Acquaintanc to send you the Pamphlit Discribed by this note[4] and says if I will send for two she will make me a Present of won. She is won I should [be] Glad to oblige and think it may be Agreable to me to have won. [I] beg the favour of you to send a Cople if to be had. Cousen Josiah will be Able to Inform you Every thing that Conserns me that will be Agreable to you to know that I need not make my Leter more Lengthy and only [to] add that I am with much fear about your wellfare Your Ever Affectionat Sister   J[ANE MECOM]

From Joseph Galloway   ALS: American Philosophical Society

Dear Friend   Philada. Septr. 27. 1770
In the Midst of Hurry, I take up my Pen to write you a few Lines. Our Sup. Court and Assembly Sitting and our Election approaching leaves me scarcly a Moments Lieusure.

As to our Election, we are all in Confusion; The White Oaks and Mechanicks or many of them have left the old Ticket and tis feared will go over to the Presbyterians, and yet I believe the Proprietary Party will not Stir. Under these Circumstances what will be the Event as to my Self is uncertain. Thus much indeed I have always found certain——a great deal of Abuse and Calumny instead of grateful Returns for the most faithful Services. So much of them have fallen to my Share, since your Departure, that was it not for

3. For the threat to BF's position in the Post Office see BF to Le Despencer above, July 26, and his reply to this letter below, Dec. 30, 1770.
4. BF's reply, just cited, indicates that the pamphlet was a religious tract.

my Connections in Politics, Nothing woud induce me to serve the Public.[5]

I have it from many, and those on whom I can depend, that General G——ge has sent to the Ministry a Copy of your Letter to Ch. Thomson: This has truely given me much Concern and uneasiness as I fear the Consequences not only on your private Account but on that of the Publicks. Pray be cautious in future what you write to that Man, who is void of Principle or Virtue. I have found him so on more Occasions than one, and I am confident you will also should you continue your free Correspondence.[6]

I will write to you fully by C. Falkner and to Mr. Strahan. My Time now will only admit me to assure you that I shall always remain with great Truth and Sincerity yours most Affectionately

J. GALLOWAY

Addressed: To / Benjamin Franklin Esquire / in Craven Street / London / per Michael McGraw

From Thomas Gilpin[7]　　　　ALS: American Philosophical Society

Esteemed friend　　　　　　　　Philada. Septm 28th 1770
This will Convey to thee an account of this Places Breaking through the non importation agreement which happened on the

5. For the White Oaks, a group of artisans and mechanics who had supported BF and Galloway in 1765, see above, XII, 316 n. The failure of Galloway and the Quaker leadership to stand out for nonimportation in 1770 aligned the White Oaks with those who did, notably Charles Thomson, John Dickinson, and their faction of the "Presbyterians." In the election, which was the beginning of the end of Galloway's party, he lost his Philadelphia seat in the Assembly and had to content himself with representing Bucks County. See James E. Hutson, "An Investigation of the Inarticulate: Philadelphia's White Oaks," 3 *W&MQ*, XXVIII (1971), 18, 22–3; and "The Campaign to Make Pennsylvania a Royal Province, 1764–1770, Part II," *PMHB*, XCV (1971), 48–9.

6. On July 6 Gage wrote Lord Barrington, Secretary at War, about BF's letter to Thomson of March 18; and five days later Alexander Colden, New York postmaster, sent printed copies to Anthony Todd, secretary to the Post Office. Carter, ed., *Gage Correspondence*, II, 546–7; *N.Y. Col. Docs.*, VIII, 218–19. Galloway's view of Thomson was naturally colored by the latter's part in the political upset described in the preceding note.

7. This is the only letter from Gilpin that is extant in MS. The others printed in this volume and its predecessor are, as mentioned in the headnote to that

20th by a Large Majority of the Votes of the Subscribers about 5 to 1.[8] I am Sorry it has So happend but it is only what Might have beene Expected from the first and what I Realy Did Expect and thiarefore Wold not Meddle in it for I always thought it a Verry great Risque wheather the acts wold be Repealed Whilst those Interested on this Side Cold be kept in any Degree of quietude. It is a hard thing for So maney to Sacrifise their Living one year after another at So high a Rate and Maney of those who were averse to a partial Importation at first and Realey prevented it from being Came into near 6 months before the generall non importation Commenced, are now most forward to Relax. Every one is at Libertey now to Import any goods Exept tea or any article as may be Taxed for the use of Raising a Revenue. Those who have held out obstanate against a Disolution are trying now to forme a new plan Similar to that of Maryland[9] but I think it is too Late they have Delayed too Long and have beene too obstinate. On the 5th of june it was Contended for by the other but was oposed by the old Committee and by availing them Selves of Some Letters thine in particular[1] for which I was Sorry, and by Some other Stratigems they prevented an alteration then which was Realey the Right time to have Done it. I have always Compared our Proceedings Like young giddey Q[uick?] furnished troops going against a Strong fortifyed City wheare as Wee aught to have gone with the greatest Caution and well Supleyd. If wee had decliard against all Dutey goods Superfluitys and Such as wee Cold Manufacture at a tolerable Rate, then the Marchant wold have had Some thing to do the artificer Incouradged, wee have Payed no Duteys, and the acts Rendered a Real Advantage to the Couloneys. This Might with

---

of June 1 above, extracts included in a memoir written by a descendant. Comparison of the spelling, punctuation, and even style of this letter and of the extracts indicates how much liberty the memoirist must have taken with the originals.

8. The defection of New York doomed the Philadelphia nonimportation agreement, which was not, however, given up without hot controversy. See Arthur M. Schlesinger, *The Colonial Merchants and the American Revolution, 1763–1776* (New York, 1918), pp. 229–32.

9. For the Maryland agreement, which was less strict than the one that the Philadelphia merchants had adopted and then abandoned, see *ibid.*, pp. 138–9, 199–202, 218.

1. BF's letters above, to Thomson of March 18 and to Galloway of March 21.

Justice [have] beene Contended for and wold have beene Observed. This was Contended for but over Ruled and now I am a fraid little or no order will be observed. Wee began wrong. Wee had the Mode from the Northward but town Meetings are not the thing nor the noyse of a promiscus assembly the way to Digest good politicks by. Although I think the Ministry and parliment is Very Impolitick and wrong in attempting to Tax us without a Representation, yet I think it is highly Proveble that america ought to Contribute but the mode is the thing to fix who Shall be Judges. Aplying to So many provances will always be attended with Intricaceys and great Delay it will be harder for Each to Degist a Measure than all in one. A Representation in parlimint wee are afraid of wee think they will Corrupt our Members and over Rule them. I think a better way wold be to propose a Committee of Each to meete Some whare and a Eaquill number of [in?] Each or for England to Borrow of america and pay Interest to her owne People Instead of forignors and the paying this Interest will be a Real Advantage to hir as it will be Done in the Labour of Manufacturors and tend to keep the nation full of people which is hir Stranth. Thiase are Trantiant thoughts I have had which please to Excuse my troubling thee with and believe me to be thy friend   THOMAS GILPIN

Addressed: To / Doctr / Benjamin Franklin / agent for Pensylvania / in London

From Daniel Roberdeau

AL (letterbook draft): Historical Society of Pennsylvania

Dear Sir   Philada. Septr. 28th. 1770

I am honoured with your favour of the 11th. June which lais me under great obligation; I should not have been so tardy in my reply but that I have for some considerable time past been greatly afflicted in my wife's Illness the latter part of her pregnancy and since her delivery occasioned by repeated Accidents which very much endangered her life which blessed be God is spared and health within these few days restored,[2] which cleared the way for my writing not

2. Mary Bostwick Roberdeu recovered; her son, their third child, was born August 22 and died Sept. 14. Roberdeau Buchanan, *Genealogy of the Roberdeau Family*... (Washington, 1876), pp. 124–5.

only to you at greater length, but also to my worthy friends Dr. Fothergill and Mr. Pearce, but a meeting yesterday at the State House and in consiquence my being employed with others as a Committee to endeavour to counter act the detestible conduct of some of our Merchants the 20th Inst. in violating the non Importation agreement,[3] but alas! I feer it is a forlorn Hope, I say these Circumstances have embarrassed me and must plead in excuse for me to Dr. F and Mr. P——that I cannot by this Opportunity write them as I intended and in Apology to you for my abruptness. I doubt not that each of you have zealously endeavoured for my Interest and that I shall very shortly be favour'd with your answer, in the very important Affair committed to you.[4] I am surprised that you write that Dr. F had no notice of the Affair from me, whereas at the same time that I wrote to you I also wrote to him.

I flatter myself Mr. Boyd has acceded to the terms of purchase proposed to him, if not, as I would provide against the possibility of its being otherwise, I beg you will be pleased to inform me per first Opportunity what Terms he will approve, for I am more and more determined on a Sale. I beg you will be pleased to be particular when you write that I may know how to make an effectual End of this Affair. I am with respectful Regard Dear Sir Your sincere friend and most obedient Servant

Benja. Franklin Esqr.

From Ezra Stiles

ALS: Yale University Library

Dear Sir Newport Sept. 28. 1770

Yesterdy I received your Favor of 16 May ult with *Relandi Analecta Rabbinica* you was so obliging as to send me.[5] For which please to accept my Thanks. One of the Tracts I wanted is contained in Relandi Hist. Hebraea.[6] I am sorry to have given you so much Trouble. I could wish for an Answer from Mr. Dow——as I

3. For a report of the meetings see *Pa. Gaz.*, Sept. 27, Oct. 4, 1770.
4. See Roberdeau's five letters above, Feb. 27, where the people to whom he refers in this letter are identified.
5. See above, XVI, 271.
6. Adriaan Reland, *Antiquitates Sacræ Veterum Hebræorum* (Utrecht, 1708).

have a very great Thirst after Oriental Antiquities.[7] With the greatest Respect, I am Dear Sir Your most obliged Friend and very humble Servant   EZRA STILES

Dr Benja Franklin R.S.S. London

To Jacques Barbeu-Dubourg

Extract: reprinted from William Temple Franklin, ed., *Memoirs of the Life and Writings of Benjamin Franklin, LL.D., F.R.S. &c.* (quarto ed., London, 1817–18), III, 319.

London, October 2, 1770.

I see with pleasure that we think pretty much alike on the subjects of English America. We of the colonies have never insisted that we ought to be exempt from contributing to the common expences necessary to support the prosperity of the empire. We only assert, that having parliaments of our own, and not having representatives in that of Great Britain, our parliaments are the only judges of what we can and what we ought to contribute in this case; and that the English parliament has no right to take our money without our consent. In fact, the British empire is not a single state; it comprehends many; and though the parliament of Great Britain has arrogated to itself the power of taxing the colonies, it has no more right to do so, than it has to tax Hanover. We have the same king, but not the same legislatures.

The dispute between the two countries has already lost England many millions sterling, which it has lost in its commerce, and America has in this respect been a proportionable gainer. This commerce consisted principally of superfluities; objects of luxury and fashion, which we can well do without; and the resolution we have formed of importing no more till our grievances are redressed, has enabled many of our infant manufactures to take root: and it will not be easy

7. Alexander Dow (d. 1779) was an officer in the army of the East India Company, and a dramatist and orientalist by avocation. While on leave in England in 1768 he had published two translations from the Persian, one of tales and the other of a history of Hindustan. *DNB*. Stiles had read a review of the history, and had written Dow in December, 1769, to inquire about early Hindu writings and religion. His questions were numerous and explicit; he clearly had no more hesitation about troubling a stranger than about troubling BF. See Abiel Holmes, *The Life of Ezra Stiles . . .* (Boston, 1798), pp. 134–6.

233

to make our people abandon them in future, even should a connection more cordial than ever succeed the present troubles. I have indeed, no doubt that the parliament of England will finally abandon its present pretensions, and leave us to the peaceable enjoyment of our rights and privileges.

To Pierre Samuel du Pont de Nemours

ALS: Henry Francis DuPont Wintherthur Museum

Dear Sir,   London, Oct. 2. 1770

I received with great Pleasure the Assurances of your kind Remembrance of me, and the Continuance of your Goodwill towards me, in your Letter by M. le Comte Chreptowitz.[8] I should have been happy to have rendred him every Civility and Mark of Respect in my Power (as the Friend of those I so much respect and honour) if he had given me the Opportunity: But he did not let me see him.

Accept my sincere Acknowledgements and Thanks for the valuable Present you made me of your excellent Work on the Commerce of the India Company, which I have perused with much Pleasure and Instruction.[9] It bears throughout the Stamp of your Masterly Hand, in Method, Perspicuity, and Force of Argument. The honourable Mention you have made in it of your Friend is extremely obliging. I was already too much in your Debt for Favours of that kind.

I purpose returning to America in the ensuing Summer, if our Disputes should be adjusted, as I hope they will be in the next Session of Parliament. Would to God I could take with me Messrs. Dupont, Dubourg, and some other French Friends with their good Ladies! I might then, by mixing them with my Friends in Philadelphia, form a little happy Society that would prevent my ever

8. Probably Joachim Chreptowicz (1729–1812), who was vice-chancellor and later chancellor of the Grand Duchy of Lithuania. He was in Paris in 1769 and may well have gone to England before returning home. He is said to have possessed a brilliance that would have appealed to the French intelligentsia. *Polskislownik biograficzny* . . . (15 vols. to date, Krakow, 1935–70), III, 441–3; Constantine R. Jurgela, *History of the Lithuanian Nation* (New York, 1948), p. 333.

9. *Du commerce et de la Compagnie des Indes* . . . (2d ed., Amsterdam and Paris, 1769).

wishing again to visit Europe. With great and sincere Esteem and Respect, I am, Dear Sir, Your most obedient and most humble Servant   B FRANKLIN

M. Dupont

To Jean-Baptiste LeRoy   ALS: Yale University Library

Dear Sir,   London, Octob. 2. 1770

I always think it too much to put you to the Expence of Postage for any Letters of mine; and one so seldom meets with private Hands that one can trouble with a Letter, that our Correspondence must suffer long Interruptions.

Your last Favour was dated July 4. recommending to me, and to Sir John Pringle, your Friend the Baron Darcy; to whom we should have gladly render'd any Civilities in our Power here; if we could have seen him. He very obligingly brought or sent to my House your Letter, with the Book and Pump Machine; but I was abroad, and no Note was left of his Lodging.[1] As Dr. Matty had before at the Coffeehouse mention'd to me his Arrival, I went immediately to the Museum, two Miles from my House, to enquire for him of the Doctor, who could give me no Satisfaction.[2] He had seen him, but knew not where he lodged. After enquiring at some other Places, I went to Sir John Pringle's, who had not seen him or heard of his being in London, but suppos'd we might learn where to find him at the French Ambassador's. Sir John undertook to make that Enquiry, went accordingly, and was told by M. Francois,[3] that Baron Darcy had indeed been there, and had left a Letter, but no Note of his Lodging, and had not call'd since, so that he could not

1. The letter has been lost. Patrick d'Arcy (1725–79) was an Irish-born officer in the French Army, highly skilled in mathematics, who had been a member of the Académie des sciences since 1749. *DNB*; Richard Hayes, *Biographical Dictionary of Irishmen in France* (Dublin, 1949), pp. 52–3. The book was Fernando Galiani, *Dialogues sur le commerce des bleds*; see LeRoy to BF above, April 22. The machine is discussed below.

2. Matthew Maty (1718–76), foreign secretary of the Royal Society, had been closely associated with the British Museum since its founding in 1753. *DNB*.

3. Jacques Batailhe de Francès had been secretary to the Ambassador; see LeRoy to BF above, April 22. In late May, when the Ambassador left, Francès became chargé d'affaires: *Lloyd's Evening Post*, May 28–30.

tell where he might be found. Perhaps my Writing all this may seem too particular; but it is to assure you, that we should have shown all possible Regard to your Recommendation if the Gentleman had put it in our Power.

We are both exceedingly mortify'd at the Disappointment of our Expectations of seeing you here in London. But still hope, that if it is too late this Year, you will not fail to give us that Pleasure early in the next. The Affairs of America keep me still here as you supposed, and I do not now think of going home till May or June 71. Sir John and I have made no long Excursion together this Summer. If we had, I think we should have taken Paris in our way, as you French People above all the rest of Mankind have the Art of making Strangers happy, and we are never more so than when among you.

I am much obliged to you for sending me the Chandelier à Pompe; and also for the Book of Abbé Galliani. Your Brother's excellent Work contains a great deal of curious Information; my Thanks and best Wishes attend him.[4]

The late Comet had something singular in its Appearance.[5] I long to receive your Ideas of those wonderful Bodies, which you promis'd some time since to favour me with. I find many Difficulties in attempting to explain their Phenomena.

Capt. Frey did me the Favour the other Day to take a Packet for you, which had been made up Six Weeks, waiting for an Opportunity to send it. It contains some of our American Observations of the Transit of Venus.[6] I had sent you some others before, which I hope you received, tho' they had not come to hand when you wrote to me in May last.

I am happy to think that the Translation of my Book will have the

4. For Pierre LeRoy's book, see the letter just cited. "Chandelier à Pompe" was obviously the "Pump Machine" that d'Arcy brought, but what it was we cannot guess.

5. See above, XVI, 186.

6. Frey is mentioned again in LeRoy's reply below, Nov. 25. Although neither reference is specific enough for confident identification, this may well be the first appearance in the correspondence of a man who later figured prominently in it. Joseph-Pierre, Baron de Frey (1740–96), was either an Austrian or a Swiss, who had seen service in Poland; in 1777 he was recommended to Washington by BF, joined the American army, and served throughout most of the war. The packet that Frey carried for BF presumably contained some or all of the observations of the transit that are described in BF's correspondence in 1769.

Advantage of your Inspection: For as your Language is now almost universal, and will make me more known than any other, I wish to appear in it under as few Disadvantages as possible; and by what little I perused of the Manuscript, I had reason to fear that my Meaning was not always clearly taken by the Translator.[7] I am ashamed to request that you should be at so much Trouble; but your thorough Examination and Correction of the whole, would oblige me infinitely.

Sir John Pringle has charged me, that whenever I write to you, I should, with mine, join his Respects and best Wishes for your Health and Prosperity. With the sincerest Esteem and Affection, I am, my dear Sir, Your most obedient and most humble Servant

B FRANKLIN

M. Le Roy

Addressed: A Monsieur / Monsieur Le Roy / aux Galeries du Louvre / à Paris.

Daniel Roberdeau to Benjamin Franklin, John Fothergill, and Charles Pearce

AL (letterbook draft): Historical Society of Pennsylvania

Dear Sirs   Philada. Octr. 2d. 1770

You'll please to be refered to what I wrote you some Months past respecting the Sale of my Estate in St. Christophers,[8] since which I have not been favoured with any answer but an obliging kind Letter from Doctor Franklin informing that you had appointed a meeting to converse on that subject, so that I am ignorant of the steps you have taken, but daily expect the Pleasure of hearing fully from you. An undetermined Mind occasioned me to delay this matter so long, that I am now streightned in point of Time, as Mr. Rawlins's Leese expires next January, and I am informed he is determined then to give up the Estate into my hands, when all income from thence will cease without you have succeeded in obtaining the Terms last

7. The Abbé Jean Baptiste l'Écuy. LeRoy's missing letter of July 4 must have said that he had agreed to check the translation of BF's works, which he had known nothing about in April. See above, p. 127 and n. 6.

8. Most of what is discussed in this letter has been explained in the annotation of Roberdeau's earlier letters above, Feb. 27.

limited, for I have put it out of my own power to treat with any Person respecting a Sale, but if I do not hear from you in a fortnight I have thoughts, which yet do not amount to a resolution, to give Orders to let the Estate for one year only, but in such Case I shall aim at a Condition to allow for any improvement in the way of planting if the Estate should be sold to be determined by a reference to impartial Men for all such work, who may be the appointment on my part of the Purchaser, if you Sell the Estate to be given up immediately on such Sale which I should prefer. I have copied and enclosed you an abstract of Mr. Robt. Thomson's Letter to me dated the 31st. March last, who is the surviving Partner of Messrs. Hyndman & Thomson my Attorneys in St. Christophers,[9] to this I shall only add that rather than Risque this Opportunity of sale to Mr. Boyd, to whom my sincere regard also inclines me to give a preference, and now determined to make a full end of this Affair, scarce admitting the possibility of a failure if Mr. Boyd has any the least inclination to purchase you have now my warrant to sell for any sum not less than £4000 Guineas exclusive of all Charges, but I flatter myself that if you have not obtained £5,500 Sterl. my last limitation you will at least obtain some thing considerably above this low limitation, low indeed, for could I settle the Estate myself it would be worth to me double that money, but as I dare not purchase negroes or even leave the Temptation in the way of my Children, from such Considerations necessity compels me. I have Records of the Island of St. Christophers in my hands which with the Papers you have no doubt obtained from Mr. Grossvenor Bedford Mr. Wm. Woodmass or Mr. Jno. Boyd particularly the Instrument docking the Entail which is not on record in St. Christophers, as will enable me to make an indubitable Title, which Mr. Boyd does not dispute. I must beg you to be at the trouble to get copies sent of such Papers in your hands as will be necessary in Case of my Conveying. I do not pretend to limit you as to any time to be allowed me for drawing in case of sale for the money, you know my motive was

9. The will of William Hyndman of Nevis, proved on Sept. 25, 1770, named Robert Thomson, also of Nevis, as one of his executors. Vere L. Oliver, *The History of the Island of Antigua*... (3 vols., London, 1894–99), II, 94. These were undoubtedly Roberdeau's attorneys, for Antigua, Nevis, and St. Kitts were part of the same government. Thomson, or a man of the same name, died in 1776. *Caribbeana*, II, 311.

to avail my self of the rise of Exchange and I entirely leave it to your discretion, but the money must be subject to my draft as soon as I choose to draw except by any allowance of Credit on the best security my Interest could be considerably promoted, but this cannot well happen in case of a sale to Mr. Boyd. I am ashamed and confounded to think what trouble [I] Immerse you in, even in reading my scrawls, pray pardon me I lay at your mercy[1] and am Dear Sirs Your inexpressibly obliged friend and Servant

Doctor Benja. Franklin Doctor John Fothergill and Charles Pearce Esqrs.

To Deborah Franklin　　　ALS: American Philosophical Society

My dear Child,　　　　　　　London, Oct. 3. 1770
　I received your kind Letter of Aug. 16. which gave me a great deal of Satisfaction. I am glad your little Grandson recovered so soon of his Illness, as I see you are quite in Love with him, and your Happiness wrapt up in his; since your whole long Letter is made up of the History of his pretty Actions. It was very prudently done of you not to interfere when his Mother thought fit to correct him; which pleases me the more, as I feared, from your Fondness of him, that he would be too much humoured, and perhaps spoiled. There is a Story of two little Boys in the Street; one was crying bitterly; the other came to him to ask what was the Matter? I have been, says he, for a pennyworth of Vinegar, and I have broke the Glass and spilt the Vinegar, and my Mother will whip me. *No, she won't whip you* says the other. Indeed she will, says he. *What*, says the other, *have you then got ne'er a Grandmother?*
　I am sorry I did not send one of my Books to Mr. Rhodes, since he was desirous of seeing it. My Love to him, and to all enquiring Friends. Mrs. West was here to day, and desired me to mention her Love to you.[2] Mr. Strahan and Family are all well, always enquire how you all do, and send their Love. Mrs Stevenson is at present in

　1. Within a few months he tired of being at their mercy, and decided to take matters into his own hands. He went to England in May, 1771, and sold the plantation to Boyd for £4,500, slightly more than the minimum price he set in this letter. See Roberdeau Buchanan, *Genealogy of the Roberdeau Family* . . . (Washington, 1876), p. 58.
　2. A return of the greeting in DF's letter above, Aug. 16.

the Country. But Polly sends her Love to you and Mrs Bache and the young Gentleman. My Love to all. I am, a[s ever,] Your affectionate Husband   B FRANKLIN

Addressed: To / Mrs Franklin / at / Philadelphia / viâ New York / per Packet / B Free FRANKLIN

From Mary Parker   ALS: American Philosophical Society

N York October 6th 1770

Since writing the foregoing[3] My Daughter is returned from Philadelphia without the Comptrollers Books: Mr. Foxcroft Intends to bring them himself; when he does shall Answer yours as particularly as I can. I received yours with a protested bill of Mr. Vernon. Your Letter and bill I (by the Next post) sent to Mr. Foxcroft; who I suppose (and make no Doubt) will do what is needful therein. When my Daughter left Philadelphia Mrs. Franklin and Mrs. Bache were very well. So is the Governor and his Lady; he is now at Amboy to Meet the Assembly.

As Soon as Mr. Foxcroft returns my Books Shall Draw out and Send you a General Account of the Post Office Affairs, also an Account of the Different Post Masters in as particular a Manner as I am able from the books; with your own Account as it Stands in Mr. Parkers books.

Inclosed is a Small Account Due me, shall take it as a favour youl git Some one to receive for me.[4] After my best wishes and prayers for your health and Happiness, give me leave to Subscribe myself with Gratitude your Most faithful and Obliged Humble Servant

MARY PARKER

Benjamin Franklin Esqr.

Addressed: Benjn. Franklin

3. The wording strongly suggests that this is the postscript of a letter, which to judge by the subject matter alone would seem to have been that above, Aug. 12. But did Mrs Parker wait for almost two months before sending off to BF what she had then written about her husband's last illness? Our guess is that she did not—that she wrote again to explain the delay in settling the accounts, and that all but the postscript of her letter has been lost.

4. The people and financial matters referred to are discussed in BF's correspondence earlier in the year with James Parker, and in his wife's letter above of Aug. 12. The postal account she enclosed, which is not extant, probably had to do with the balance of her husband's salary as comptroller.

Thomas Coombe, Jr., to His Father[5]

Extract of ALS: Historical Society of Pennsylvania

London Ocr: 8th 1770

I dined with Dr. Franklin the Day before yesterday, when he desired to be kindly remembered to you. My Affection for the good old Dr. increases every Time I visit him, which I do very frequently. An Anecdote just occurs which will make you smile. Calling to'ther Day to ask Dr. Franklin "how he did," I found him sitting, with only a *single* Cap on—the Day was cold—and the Dr. usually wore a *double* one. Upon this, I undertook to remonstrate, and received for Answer, that "his Head grew warm". I said that "Dr. F was never accounted hot-headed." "Aye (says he) but Nature seems to think so, for she is taking all the Hair off my Head." An hundred other such Things come from him in an Evening. He told me some time ago, that Christians did not debate about the Essentials, but about *"the Paper and Packthread of Religion."*

From Noble Wimberly Jones

ALS: American Philosophical Society

Dear Sir   9th. October 1770

Your very kind favours I duly received and should have answered them respectively, only that I waited in expectation of transmitting the sum then supposed necessary, trust however to your goodness to excuse the omission being at that time disappointed; your un-parralell'd kindness in so readily complying with the request (through me) of the Assembly demands as it heartily has our most sincere and best thanks. By Mr. Crouch I receiv'd agreable to your last The Mace which is in the Oppinion of all that has seen it ex-treemly neat and Ellegant the Gouns also quite compleat and in very good order[6]. You will herewith Sir, receive in part recom-

5. Young Coombe had come to London in 1768 for ordination in the Church of England, and his acquaintance with BF had begun on arrival. We have often cited information on BF's affairs contained in Coombe's letters to his family, but this is the first extract that merits printing for its own sake.

6. For the ceremonial mace and the gowns see BF to Jones, above, July 6.

pence of these kind offices two setts of Bills of Exchange vizt. one on Mssrs. Greenwood & Higginson £100 and the other on John Campbell Esquire Kings Agent for this Province £20 which doubt not will be respectively honourd.[7] Please to accept my best thanks for the Pamphlets and Speeches &c. you favour'd us with, the subject on which they are Wrote cannot but render them very pleasing and agreable to an American Mind.[8]

Permit me Sir to assure you that the Assembly esteem themselves extra happy in being represented by a gentleman of your known Integrety, whose sentiments coincide with theirs and every true American, and every branch of the Legislature express their highest approbation of your past conduct and greatfully accept the continuance you kindly offer of those faithful endeavours to serve the Province for the future.

That you may long enjoy health and prosperity to receive the warmest acknowledgements of a greatful Assembly of Georgia is the very sincere Wish of Dear Sir Your Most Obliged and Obedient humble Servant   N W JONES

To Benjamin Franklin Esqr.

To Noble Wimberly Jones

ALS: Blumhaven Library and Art Gallery, Philadelphia

Sir,   London, Oct. 10. 1770

The within is a Copy of mine that went with the Gowns and Mace, which I hope got safe to hand.[9] One of the Bills, (that for the Mace) contain'd, by the Silversmith's Mistake, an Article of Buckles that should not have been in it. The true Amount of that Bill, on Account of your Province, is only - - - - - - - - - - £88 8s. 1d.
That for the Gowns was - - - - - - - - - 19 4s. 9d.

107 12s. 10d.

---

7. Greenwood & Higginson were merchants at 97 Queen Street in Cheapside. *Kent's Directory...* (London, 1770), p. 76. For John Campbell see the Assembly's letter above, May 11.

8. The speeches were Pownall's; see BF to Jones, above June 7.

9. See BF to Jones above, July 6.

A War with Spain is just now talk'd of here as inevitable.[1] And a Disposition to accommodate amicably all Differences with the Colonies begins to shew itself more strongly among Persons in Power. The American Agents will not fail, as it is both their Duty and Interest, to cultivate as much as possible that Disposition. With great Respect, I am, Sir, Your most obedient and most humble Servant, B FRANKLIN

Honble. N. W. Jones, Esqr

From Joseph Galloway ᴌs: Historical Society of Pennsylvania

Dear Sir   Philada. Octr. 10. 1770

This will be deliver'd to you by Mr. William White for whose Parents, as well as himself, I have a particular Regard.[2] His Arrant to London is with Design to finish his Studies in Divinity, and to obtain Orders in the Church. If great Goodness and Rectitude of Heart, improved by a virtuous and liberal Education, and free from the Vices and Licentiousness too frequently the Attendants on unguarded Youth, render a young Gentleman fit for the great and important Duties of Religion, I have good Reason to beleive, the Object of this Letter will not prove an inferiour Ornament to the Sacred Profession. Under this Opinion of him, permit me, to recom-

1. This is the first mention in the correspondence of a crisis that had been brewing for months. In the 1760's France and Britain both laid claim to the Falkland Islands, and established small settlements. In 1767 France ceded her claim to Spain, and in June, 1770, a Spanish force from Buenos Aires attacked and captured the British post at Port Egmont. The news reached London in the late summer, when Lord North was out of town; Lord Weymouth, the Secretary of State for the Southern Department, took matters into his own hands, and protested so belligerently to Madrid that war seemed for some months to be inevitable. North gradually succeeded in regaining control, in securing the good offices of France, and in moderating the tone of British diplomacy. In December Weymouth resigned in disgust. In January, 1771, Spain disavowed the expedition and agreed to restore Port Egmont. Alan Valentine, *Lord North* (2 vols., Norman, Okla., [1967]), I, 208–11. In August, September, and October, 1770, the *London Chron.* constantly reported preparations for war; the general opinion in the City, according to its issue of Oct. 6–9, was that expressed by ʙꜰ.

2. Young White was coming well-furnished with letters: see ᴅꜰ's fourth note in the following document.

mend him to your Advice Assistance and Friendship. I will not offer an Apology on this Occasion, as I well know the Pleasure you recieve in lending your Aid to Mankind in general, but to Youth in particular, in their laudable Pursuits, will more than compensate for any Pains you may be at in performing the benevolent Office. I am with much Esteem your most obedient humble Servant

JOS. GALLOWAY

Addressed: To / Benjamin Franklin Esquire / Deputy Post Master General of / North America in / Craven Street / London / per Favor / Mr. White

Endorsed: White

From Deborah Franklin

ALS: (1) Historical Society of Pennsylvania; (2) and (4) American Philosophical Society; (3) Yale University Library

In early October, 1770, four young men left Philadelphia together for London, two to study law and two to seek ordination in the Church of England.[3] All were family friends of the Franklins, and for each Deborah wrote a note of introduction to her husband. The notes were written on the same day, and we have arranged them in the alphabetical order of the bearer's last name. She fully realized what a remarkable group it was ("I donte remember such a wortheyer Cargo never wente from this plase"), and she was confident that Franklin would appreciate its arrival.

My Dear child   Ocktober the 11 1770
    the bairer of this is the Son of Dr. Phinis Bond his only Son and a worthey young man.[4] He is a going to Studey the Law he desired

3. They cleared from Chester on Oct. 15 in the *Britannia*, Nathaniel Falconer's ship, along with a number of other Philadelphians. *Pa. Gaz.*, Oct. 18, 1770. The four between them carried a total of eight letters of introduction to BF; see the following notes.

4. For the father see above, II, 240 n. The son, Phineas Bond, Jr. (1749–1815), graduated from the College of Pennsylvania in 1766 and studied for the bar; he was going to England to complete his studies, and carried a note to BF from Galloway as well: below, Oct. 12. He returned in 1773, subsequently became a Loyalist, and left for England in 1778. In 1786 he returned again, this time as British consul for the Middle Atlantic States, and held this position until the outbreak of war in 1812. Joanne L. Neel, *Phineas Bond, a Study in Anglo-American Relations, 1786–1812* (Philadelphia, [1968]).

a line to you I beleve you have Such a number of worthey young Jentelmen as ever wente to gather. I hope to give you pleshuer to See such a number of fine youthes from your one [own] countrey which will be an Honour to their parentes and Countrey. I am my Dear child your Afeckshonet wife   D FRANKLIN

Addressed: To / Benjamin Franklin Esqr / Craven Street / London / per favor of / Mr Bond

My Dear Child   ocktober the 11 1770
   the bairer of this is Mr. T Hopkinson[5] Son of your old friend and a young man as is as good as lives he asked a line to you from me his mother and he dranke tee on Satter day laste. I supose he has letters to you from his friends to you he will tell you a boute your Grand son as he is a quinted with him. I am your Afeckshonet wife
                                         D FRANKLIN
Mr Hopkison

Endorsed: Hopkinson Recommendations of White, Bond, Hopkinson and Rush

My Dear Child   Ocktober the 11 1770
   the bairer of this is Dr. Rushes Brother[6] a young [man] of a good Carreckter live with Mr. Dickison[7] severel years is Coled a hones young man heard his friends desierd I wold write to you. I have told I Cold not write as I am not Capabel of writin a boute my selef[8] I

5. For young Thomas Hopkinson, a candidate for holy orders, see his mother's letter to BF above, Sept. 6. Hopkinson also carried a noncommittal note of introduction from Richard Bache: below, Oct. 14.

6. Jacob Rush (1748–1820), was the younger brother of Benjamin, from whom he also carried a letter of introduction to BF: below, Oct. 14. In addition he had one from Galloway: below, Oct. 12. Jacob graduated from the College of New Jersey in 1765, and was admitted to the Pennsylvania bar in 1769. After two years at the Middle Temple he returned to America, served in the Continental Congress and later in the Pennsylvania Assembly, and eventually became a circuit judge in Pennsylvania. See Lyman H. Butterfield, ed., *Letters of Benjamin Rush* (2 vols., [Princeton,] 1951), I, 44 n.

7. Possibly John Dickinson, the author of the *Farmer's Letters.*

8. DF's meaning, as so often, is conjectural. None of the other notes indicates that she considered a letter of introduction as "writin a boute my selef"; perhaps what she was declining to do was to send a personal message to her husband by young Rush.

Cold not deney him and his relashons and severel young nabors is a going in Capt. Folkner. I am your afeckshonet wife

D FRANKLIN

Mr Rush

Endorsed: Rush

My Dear Child   ocktober the 11 1770
  the bairer of this is Mr. White the only Son of our Nabor White.[9] I beleve he is as worthey a young Jentelman as ever wente over to Ingland he desired a line to you tell good Mrs. Stephen Son I donte remember such a wortheyer Cargo never wente from this plase I hope thay will be a credit to us I am your Afeckshonet wife

D FRANKLIN

Mr. White

Addressed: To / Benjamin Franklin Esqr / Craven Street / London / per favor of / Mr White

Endorsed: White

From Thomas Fitzmaurice   ALS: American Philosophical Society

Dear Sir,   Isle Wight Octr. 12. 1770
  You must do Doctor Hawkesworth and me the Justice to believe that we were very much mortified at being deprived of the pleasure which we were happy in the thought of enjoying from your Company here. What has added to our mortification has been the being deprived of that satisfaction which God forbid but that we sho'd

9. Young White also had a letter of introduction to BF from Joseph Galloway: above, Oct. 10. He and DF were befriending a young man who came to be one of the best known American clergymen of his day. William (1748–1836), the son of Col. Thomas White (for whom see above, III, 428 n), graduated from the College of Pennsylvania in 1765 and presumably studied for the ministry, because he was ordained a deacon almost immediately after reaching London (Dec. 23, 1770). He was admitted to the priesthood in 1772, returned to Philadelphia to be curate of Christ Church, became its rector during the Revolution, and retained this position until his death. In the 1780s he took a leading part in organizing the Protestant Episcopal Church in the United States, and was chosen to be the first Bishop of Philadelphia. He became Presiding Bishop on the death of Samuel Seabury in 1796, and held that office for the next forty years. *DAB.*

enjoy with the rest of our fellow Creatures, of abusing you as plenti-fully as we were disposed to suppose there might have been room for doing, this pious intention the politeness and sincerity of your excuse obliges us to lay aside. But, for the next Summer the Doctor and I propose to carry a similar engagement with you into execu-tion in a manner that may possibly prove more successfull.

Sir Chas. Knowles, who left us about a fortnight ago, has been obliged, from some un-foreseen inconvenient circumstances to postpone the trial of his Experiment and likewise to adopt a dif-ferent Situation for the purpose from that which he originally in-tended, instead of making it in this neighbourhood he has been induced to prefer other Downs on the opposite side of the Water which being nearer to Portsmouth will prove, it seems, in many res-pects more Convenient. The object of his intended Experiment is to ascertain with precision the force and direction of the Wind. It w'd be difficult for me to describe the nature of a Machine which having never seen I can not say that I understand as well as I c'd wish. When I mentioned your desire to Sir Chas., he seemed not less desirous of describing his Ideas to you himself than he is of carrying those Ideas into execution, so that Dr. Hawkesworth and myself have each of us promised that we w'd bring you together the first Opportunity.[1]

As to the aspersion thrown upon the Doctor's Maggy, the best Characters he sees are not free from reproach, and comforts him-self that the Accident may one day or other bring his Maggy into the first Company.[2] He sets out from hence, much to my concern, on Sunday next, but desires me to present his best respects to you 'till such time as he has an Opportunity of presenting them in person.

The War like preparations in this part of the World[3] seem to grow fainter and fainter daily, so that I am not without hopes but that in profound peace I may have an Opportunity, after Xmas of assuring

1. For Hawkesworth and Knowles and the wind experiment, whatever it was, see Fitzmaurice to BF above, Sept. 10.

2. An impossibly obscure reference. We have a hunch, which scholarly re-search can scarcely prove or disprove, that Maggy was Dr. Hawkesworth's mare, and that she had been accidentally exposed to a stallion of higher status than her own.

3. Related to the Falkland Islands crisis. See BF to Jones above, Oct. 10.

you in person myself of the truth and Esteem with which I have the pleasure of subscribing myself, Dear Sir, Most faithfully and Sincerely Yours &c   THOMS. FITZMAURICE

From Joseph Galloway: Two Letters of Introduction

ALS: (1) Historical Society of Pennsylvania; (2) University of Pennsylvania Library

Dear Sir   Philada. Octr. 12. 1770.
    The Bearer Mr. Phineas Bond, Son of Doctr. Phineas Bond of this City, is desirous of finishing his Education at the Temple; and for that Purpose now visits London.[4] I have a particular Regard for his Parents, and from a considerable Acquaintance with his Conduct during his Apprenticeship, he also claims my Esteem; I therefore wish to render him any acceptable Service: I know, I can offer him none greater than a cordial Recommendial to your Advice and Friendship, during his Stay in England. I am confident, he will prove neither ungrateful, or unworthy of any Favors you shall confer upon him. I am Dear Sir, with much Esteem, your most Obedient humble Servant   JOS. GALLOWAY

Addressed: To / Benjamin Franklin Esquire / Deputy Post Master General / of No. America / in / Craven Street / London / per Favor / Mr. Bond

Endorsed: Bond

Dear Sir   Philada. Octr. 12. 1770
    This will be deliverd to you by Mr. Jacob Rush Brother to Doctr. Rush with whom you are well acquainted.[5] After having obtained Admission, as a Practitioner at Law, in our Several Courts of Justice, he is desirous of completing his Studies at the Temple. The Pleasure you ever take in assisting the Progress of Youth in their laudable Pursuits is a strong Motive with me, to recommend him to your Notice and Friendship. Favors confer'd on him will be esteemed additional Obligations recieved by Dear Sir your most Obedient humble Servant   JOS. GALLOWAY

4. See above, p. 244 n.
5. See above, p. 245 n.

248

Addressed: To / Benjamin Franklin Esquire / Deputy Post Master General of / North America / in Craven Street / London
Endorsed: Rush

From Ebenezer Kinnersley[6]

ALS: the Royal Society[7]

Dear Sir, Philada. Octo. 13. 1770

I received your Favour of March 18. I thank you for speaking to Mr. Nairne;[8] he has now sent a Thermometer that pleases. The English School has indeed been discouraged, and, in Consequence, declining;[9] Particulars would be too tedious to mention now; I have been almost determined to seek my Fortune abroad again.

The Conducting Quality of some Sorts of Charcoal is indeed very remarkable. I have found Oak, Beech and Maple to conduct very well; but try'd several Pieces of Pine Coal without finding one that would conduct at all; perhaps they were made in a Fire not hot enough, or not continued in it long enough. A strong Line drawn on Paper with a black Lead Pencil will conduct an electrick Shock pretty readily; but this perhaps may not be new to you.

On the 12th. of last July, three Houses in this City and a Sloop at one of the Wharfs were, in less than an Hour's Time, all struck with Lightning. The Sloop and two of the Houses were considerably damaged; the other was the Dwelling House of Mr. Joseph Moulder, in Lombard Street,[1] which being provided with a round iron Conductor, Half an Inch thick, its several Lengths screwed to-

6. Clergyman, teacher, and BF's principal scientific associate; see above, IV, 192 n.

7. An extract, containing all but the first and last paragraph and with some phrases italicized, was printed in *Phil. Trans.,* LXIII (1773–74), 38–9.

8. The electrician and instrument-maker, for whom see above, X, 171 n.

9. The English School of the Academy of Philadelphia, of which Kinnersley was the master, had for some time been declining in favor of the Latin School. See above, VIII, 415 n; Thomas H. Montgomery, *A History of the University of Pennsylvania from Its Foundation to A.D. 1770* (Philadelphia, 1900), pp. 244–51.

1. See *Pa. Gaz.*, July 19, 1770. Joseph Moulder (1729–79) had been a sail-maker as a young man, and presumably still was; during the Revolutionary period he was involved in Pennsylvania politics and became an officer in the militia. *Pa. Geneal. Mag.*, XXII (1961), 121; *Decennial Register of the Pennsylvania Society of Sons of the Revolution, 1888–1898* (Philadelphia, 1898), p. 369.

gether so as to make very good Joints, and the lower End five or six Feet under Ground; the Lightning, leaving every Thing else, pursued its Way thro that, melted off six Inches and a Half of the slenderest Part of a brass Wire fixt in the Top, and did no further Damage within Doors, or without. Capt. Falconer, who brings you this, was in the House at the Time of the Stroke, and says it was an astonishing loud one. If you publish this Paragraph, do please to correct it first. I am, Dear Sir, with very sincere Respect, your most obedient humble Servant   EBENR. KINNERSLEY

Dr. Franklin

From Richard Bache   ALS: Pennsylvania Historical Society

Dear Sir   Philada. 14th: October 1770.

I did myself the pleasure of writing you a few Lines the other day per packet. Mr. Thomas Hopkinson has strongly sollicited to be the Bearer of a few Lines, and tho' I am conscious that any Introduction of him from me to you, will have but little Weight, yet I cannot help complying with his Request.[2] I must at the same time trouble you with the inclosed Letter for my Mother,[3] which you will be pleased to forward per first post. I am with due Respect Dear Sir Your Affectionate Son   RICHD BACHE

Addressed: To / Benjamin Franklin Esqr. / London. / per favor Mr. / Thos: Hopkinson.

From Deborah Franklin   ALS: Pennsylvania Historical Society

[My Dea]r Child   Ocktober the 14 1770

I have bin so much taken up of Laite I Cold write only a line or two which I desired Billey to in close in his letter to you, to tell you that when he and mrs. Franklin is in town I am much taken up; the laste I got Mr. Beach to excues me to you for we had Several friends in

2. Hopkinson's mother had already written BF about him, and he was also armed with a note of introduction—more outgoing than this one—from DF. See above, Sept. 6, Oct. 11.

3. For Mrs. Mary Bache see above, XIV, 136 n.

the house and this day I am told Folkner Sailes on Satter day.[4] So I muste write when I Can as to aney thing of publick Affairs I leve to your friends to give you an acounte. This is to tell you Mr. Beach and Salley is gon to Burlinton to See Mrs. Franklin as Shee did not go to Amboy and I thinke Shee will cume down to the Roses.[5] Yisterday came the a Counte of the Death of our verey kind Friend Mr. White Feld it hurte me indeaid you will See all a bought him in the Papers and in the Same paper Came the a Counte of the Deth of John Mecum.[6] Hough is our Sister Mecum but Shee is much Suported and Shee has a dubel Shair of Sperrites I am a fraid Shee is angarey with me but I Cante tell for what Shee thinkes I donte thinke quite as Shee dus but I love her and will as long as I live. I did reseve a letter by two Ladeys by the way of Scotland it was a wrong time I fair as everey bodey has laid all finery is laid on sid I did all in my power but that is but Small.[7] I have Seen our friend Rhodes he is much plesed with your writing to him his wife and Dafter much plesed as did our old friend mrs. Paskel Shee cumes to See as Shee is verey fond of your Grand Son the day he was Crisond he was taken in to her house as did his unkill and ante and Pason Petters and mrs. paskel rememberd that Salley was carreyed to her house the firste time [s]he wente oute.[8]

Our Dear mrs. Grasce is in town Shee and mrs. Suel and her Dafter mrs. Hunte. Shee loves you as well as ever. Shee is a fine woman in dead and has a fine Son[9] her mother and Shee Lay in att

4. Falconer actually left on Monday, Oct. 15 (*Pa. Gaz.*, Oct. 18); DF doubtless started her letter several days before the date on it.

5. Probably BF's friends John Ross (above, XI, 531 n) and his wife, Elizabeth Morgan Ross (1714?–76), for whom see Geneal. Soc. of Pa. *Publications*, XI (1900–03), 305.

6. The *Pa. Gaz.*, Oct. 11, carried the news of George Whitefield's death at Newburyport, Mass., on Sept. 30. John Mecom, Jane's son and BF's nephew, had died in New Brunswick, N.J., on the same day: Van Doren, *Franklin–Mecom*, p. 113.

7. BF had recommended the Misses Farquarson and Smith, identified only as a milliner and a dressmaker, in a note of introduction to DF above, April 20.

8. For Samuel Rhoads and his family see above, II, 406 n; XII, 205 n. Mrs. "Paskel" was Ann Chandler Paschall, Rhoads' sister-in-law and the widow of Thomas Paschall; for the Rev. Richard Peters, rector of Christ Church, see above, III, 187 n.

9. Rebecca Nutt Grace was twice widowed; her second husband, Robert Grace, had died in 1766. Above, I, 209 n; II, 286; XIV, 281 n. Elizabeth Fordham

the Same time I wente to See them all thow I donte visit more. I
Send you a barrel of Cranbarey I Cold not get aney thing eles it is
two airley in the Seson but I Shall have an opertunety Soon I hope.
I hear mr. Bambridg is Cume to his Fathers house near Frankford.[1]
I give you Joy in the marraige of all your friends marraigis be So
kind as to tell our Dear Polley if I Cold Write I wold Say much and
to our good mrs. Stephenson I give her as much Joy as Shee wish or
deseyer and our Kinswoman I wishe her all hapeynes mrs. Franklin
knows the Captin[2] but I Cante Say aney thing more only I hope
them all hapeynes. I Cante Say aney thing more of our [Gran]dson
then he is sound [torn] teeth and has maney readey to a peer he
walkes Strong [torn] not with oute [torn] for he is verey prudent and
will hold by everey bodey. He has charmin fine eyes and a fine littel
mouth in [torn] Lovelay. Laste evening Mr. Bache and Salley re-
tarnd from B[urling]ton. Mrs. Franklin is well thay thoute Shee
wold a Cume down to the rosses but shee did not as shee desires to
Cume down and Stay Sume time as Soon as the Assemby rises att
amboy. I had Miss Parker att our House for 6 weeks her mother is
to Cume and live att Woodbridg Jenkey[3] as you onse told me is
hansumer then my Dafter and as I Sed then Shee was hansumer the
[than] two dafters Such as mine. Shee is a fine Gorle in dead. Senes
I wrote the a bove I Saw Mr. Banbridg he did not Stay as he had
Severel letter to deliver he looks verey well he lefte a letter for
Billey and mr. Suell was in the room[4] I gave it to him to take Cair
of it to Send it to him. Capt. Folkiner ofred to due aney kind ofis but
I told him I did not desier to give him aney trubel. Franklin had bin

---

Shewell (1731–94) was the wife of Stephen Shewell (1747–1809), Benjamin
West's brother-in-law. The Shewells' second daughter, Mary, had married
Isaac Hunt in 1767. Her "fine Son" was probably Isaac, the eldest of three
brothers; the youngest, born in 1784, became the famous Victorian critic and
poet, Leigh Hunt. Theodore F. Rodenbough, *Autumn Leaves from Family
Trees*... (New York, 1892), p. 196.

1. The painter, Henry Benbridge, was returning from a sojourn in Europe;
his stepfather was Thomas Gordon. See above, XVI, 38, and BF to DF, July 19.

2. Anne Johnson had married Capt. Peter Clarke, R.N.; see BF to Folger
above, Aug. 21. The Clarkes, like WF's wife, came originally from the West
Indies.

3. James and Mary Parker's daughter Jane, whose usual nickname was
Jenny.

4. Presumably Stephen Shewell, for whom see Sabine, *Loyalists*, II, 374.

to See him and mrs. Folkener and we talked of a hobbey Horse but it is as you plees. It wantes but a verey few day of 6 years Senes you lefte home and then you thought it wold be but Seven munthes. Be plesd to tell Mr. Whorton I did Send the in closed I Sente to his House[5] I have Seen Mrs. Moungomorey Senes Shee arived her edest Son deyed her Husbands Corpes is brot and bureyed in this plase[6] I told you Shee had Sente me a worke bag from Lisbon Billey did fawl in Love with it and I presented it to his wife I hope it was well. I had Sum thing eles but it is Sliped my mind and I am to write to Sister Macum as I have dun a Small Caske of Poke melos and muste Send them a way today[7] and write to her. I did not write a boute mr. Foxcrofte as I remember Senes he went and as he is to be hear Soon I say aney thing a boute him only that he has a verey a greabel Ladey and he may be verey happey.[8] Salley will write So I donte say aney thing of her or Mr. Beach only that thay air well and our Dear King bird. Mr. Hall has bin un well I wente to See him yisterday he Ses he is better agen. Cusin Molley is in a bad Staite of helth and look verey poorly as yousal. Capt. Sparkes loste his wife laste week[9] our frand Rhodes is gon to N york to be thair a while with her[1] as her mother is not a bell to go so he and his dafter hannah is gon all my old friend air well I cante menshon them by name

5. In the absence of the enclosure DF's meaning is undecipherable, but her message was clearly for Samuel Wharton.

6. For Robert Montgomery's widow see BF to DF above, June 10. Their elder son Thomas (1768–70) had died on Aug. 9: Thomas H. Montgomery *A Genealogical History of the Family of Montgomery* (Philadelphia, 1863), p. 152.

7. Presumably some concoction of pokeweed, which we cannot identify. The berries and roots, although emetic and purgative, are also mildly narcotic; and Jane was still in pain from her fall the winter before.

8. John Foxcroft had married Judith Osgood in London on Aug. 2; see above, p. xxviii. The newlyweds returned to America almost at once, and arrived in Philadelphia in late October: *Pa. Gaz.*, Nov. 1.

9. Mary or Molly (F.2.2.3) was David Hall's wife and DF's second cousin, and lived until 1781. Capt. James Sparks and his second wife, Sarah Ozier, had been married less than five years: J. Granville Leach, "The Record of Some Residents in the Vicinity of Middle Ferry, Philadelphia, during the Latter Half of the Eighteenth Century," Geneal. Soc. of Pa. *Publications*, IX (1924–26), 68.

1. DF omitted the antecedent, but in all likelihood she meant to refer to the Rhoads' elder daughter, Mary Rhoads Franklin, for whom see above, XII, 205 n. She apparently lived in New York: *PMHB*, XIV (1890), 424 n.

[*torn*] Person is a going with this vesill[2] Shee desired a line to you but I fair [*torn*] write Shee has bin in London ones you was thair my beste Compley m[ents to] all our friends as those menshoned [*torn*] I muste [*torn*] this has bin writ in Severel day and now I Can tell your Son has a temted to walke a lone but he is verey Caushou[s] and is verey Cairfull he has be gon to tolke he has a Swet voyse he Ses babey and Coles his maid mamah and his mother he Coles mamah the boy Bob and is quit fond of his father thay whip top and play marbels and Sing and maney other Such things. Salley has desired me to Send to you for a Doz. pair of the beste of fine white threed Stocking and large mens[3] for her to present to a portickler friend of hers. I told her to write her Self but Shee insiste on me to due it for her now I muste due her the Caireckter as to Say Shee has bin one of the best mother I ever Saw Shee wonte Spile her Son Shee ones has whiped his ones and twise he has bin behind the dore and is Sadley afraid and dus what he is bid. I thing you wold be much plesd Billey is verey much plesd with them boath and mrs. Franklin verey hapey with them all So and Ses Sister is the best mother. Thay [are] to Cume and Stay with us a time and then thay muste go and Stay att Burlinton but you will Cume and See hough thay all So hapey with this one Child.

I observe what you Say a boute the 6 tees you tell me of. Mr. Beach is in my mes he drinke Sage and Balms laste evening I reseved a letter from Sister Jeney I was a littel Jeles which proseded from two much love[4] Shee tells me that our Cusin Polley Ingersole was deliverd of a Ded Son after be in Ill for days. Polley marreyed a Weste Indey man his name is Jarvis an elderly man.[5] Sister did not like him but he was thought rich.

I shall write to her next week this is Sonday afternoon and I a lone

2. Perhaps Miss Ann Pearson, who sailed with Capt. Falconer (*Pa. Gaz.*, Oct. 18), and who later became James Sparks's third wife: Leach, *loc. cit.* n. 9.

3. BF did not refer to this commission in any letter that is extant, and if he carried it out he must have been a mind-reader. DF either meant large men's stockings, or intended to ask for stockings and large men's handkerchiefs or something of the sort.

4. DF was presumably "jealous" (*i.e.*, solicitous) because of John Mecom's death.

5. Elizabeth Ingersoll Jarvis (C.12.1.1) was BF's grandniece; almost nothing is known about her or her husband, but before her marriage she had lived with Jane: above, XII, 418 n.

this evening I Send it of [off] my love to good Mrs. Stephenson and as I have Sed be fore everey bodey. I hope your Dear arme is well. As to the hurte I had with Sliping down Dr. Shippins Stairs is worse and dus everey falls and I Sufer pain.[6] My Dear child I hope you will not Stay longer then this fall I muste Conclud your Afeckshonet wife   D FRANKLIN

My beste Compleymente to Sir John Pringal for his regard to my kingbird and my Selef.[7]

From Benjamin Rush   ALS: University of Pennsylvania

Honoured Sir   Philadelphia October 14. 1770
The many Advantages which I derived from your Friendship Whilst in London have emboldened me to take the Liberty of recommending to your friendly Notice the Bearer of this Letter—— my Brother who proposes to spend two Years in the Temple in Order to finish his studies in the Law.[8] The Civilities you confer upon him will add greatly to the very many Obligations already confered upon Sir Your Most Obedient Most Obliged Humble Servant   BENJAMIN RUSH.
Endorsed: Rush

From Israel Pemberton[9]   ALS: Historical Society of Pennsylvania

[Oct. 17, 1770. Is going on a long journey and wants Franklin to pay the balance due from five years' ground rent of property in Pewter Platter Alley.[1] The total rent was £101 5s., of which Franklin had paid £60 in 1769, leaving £41 5s. due.]

6. Dr. William Shippen, Sr., was an old family acquaintance. DF had doubtless mentioned the fall in an earlier and missing letter, but part of the sentence remains gibberish to us.
7. Sir John Pringle had advised a second inoculation of the baby (BF to DF above, June 10), but what his advice to DF had been we do not know.
8. See DF's recommendation of young Rush above, Oct. 11.
9. A wealthy Quaker merchant, for whom see above, v, 424 n.
1. BF had bought the property in 1764 from James Pearson, to whom Pemberton had sold it with the reservation of the ground rent. See above, XI, 319–21.

From the Pennsylvania Assembly Committee of Correspondence

Printed in *Votes and Proceedings of the House of Representatives of the Province of Pennsylvania,* 1770–1771 (Philadelphia, 1771), p. 210.

Sir,   Philadelphia, October 19, 1770.

In Pursuance of the Directions of the House of Assembly to the Committee of Correspondence, we inclose you their Resolves, appointing us that Committee, and you the Agent to solicit and transact the Affairs of this Province in Great-Britain for the ensuing Year.

Upon considering the Instructions given by preceding Assemblies,[2] the present House find them so full, as well on the important Matters which relate to the general Rights and Liberties of America, as those which concern this Province, that they think it unnecessary to repeat them; and, as nothing new has occured, they content themselves at present with recommending them to your serious Attention.

The Experience they have had of your Abilities and Fidelity, leaves them no Room to doubt that you will at all Times exert your utmost Endeavours to obtain Redress of every Aggrievance which in any wise affects the Rights and Liberties of the Colonies, and to promote the Welfare of this Province. We are, with great Regard, Your assured Friends and very humble Servants,[3]

> JOSEPH GALLOWAY, *Speaker.*
> THOMAS LIVEZEY,
> JOSEPH FOX,
> SAMUEL RHOADS,
> JOSEPH WATSON,
> ISAAC PEARSON.

2. For an example of such instructions see above, XIV, 285–8.

3. All have been identified in previous volumes except Joseph Watson (1729–1805). He was a Quaker who lived in Lower Makefield township, Bucks Co., represented Bucks in the Assembly, 1767–71, and was a member of the county Committee of Safety in 1774. See 8 *Pa. Arch.,* VII, 6062, 6582; *PMHB,* XV (1891), 259–60, 264; Jane W. T. Brey, *A Quaker Saga: the Watsons of Strawberryhowe...* (Philadelphia, [1967]), p. 290.

From Harvard College

Reprinted from William C. Lane, "Harvard College and Franklin," Colonial Society of Massachusetts *Publications*, x (1907), 237.

Octor 22, 1770.
That the Thanks of this Board be given to Dr. Franklin for his repeated good Services to this College, and particularly in his Care of a valuable achromatic Telescope lately received thro' his hands:[4] and that Professor Winthrop Transmitt this Vote to Dr. Franklin.

Resolution of the Massachusetts House of Representatives Appointing Benjamin Franklin as Agent

DS: Massachusetts Historical Society

This resolution marks the beginning of Franklin's most troubled agency. The root of trouble was the inability of the two chambers of the General Court, the Council and the House of Representatives, to agree on a single agent. For years, in consequence, each had its own, William Bollan for the Council and Dennys DeBerdt for the House, and the latter's position was questionable: Lord Hillsborough had already expressed doubt of his status, on the ground that the House had appointed him only to oppose the Stamp Act.[5] When he died in the summer of 1770 a single provincial agent, named by an act of the legislature and the governor as Franklin had been named in Georgia, was as remote a prospect as ever. Some members of the House saw no point in having an agent at all, to lobby fruitlessly against the measures of an obdurate Parliament. The majority wished to continue, but was divided over who the agent should be. The faction led by James Otis and Samuel Adams, after rejecting several candidates as too moderate, came up finally with the name of Arthur Lee. He was a Virginia-born and Scottish-trained physician, then studying law in London, who had first achieved prominence by his letters to the press against the Stamp Act, and in the fall of 1769 had begun a series of articles in London papers, signed Junius Americanus, which were effective propaganda against the Townshend Acts. Franklin was also in the running, and the contest narrowed to one

4. For the telescope see above, xvi, 65, and BF to Winthrop, June 6; see also Winthrop to BF below, Oct. 26.

5. See above, xv, 198 n. Hillsborough soon went further, and challenged the right of the House to appoint an agent at all; see BF's memorandum of his conversation with him on Jan. 16, 1771.

between him and Lee, the two chief American propagandists in London. Some attacked Franklin for having too many agencies already, others for being the father of a colonial governor and hence too friendly to officialdom. But his reputation was enhanced by his recent answers to Strahan's queries, which were circulated by Samuel Cooper;[6] and Franklin was eventually chosen by a considerable majority. As a sop to the opposition, however, Lee was named as his alternate to serve in the event of his absence or death.[7] This subordination bitterly antagonized the younger man, who was soon accusing Franklin of being Hillsborough's tool.[8] The action of the House, in short, first yoked together two colleagues who were not designed for that yoke. They bore it for a decade, as agents first for Massachusetts and then for the infant United States, and it sorely galled them both.

In the House of Representatives Octo. 24th: 1770.
Wednesday, 3 o'Clock. P.M.
The House according to Order proceeded in the Choice of an Agent, and upon sorting and counting the Votes it appeared that Dr. Benjamin Franklin was chose by a majority.

It was then moved, and thereupon Resolved, That Dr. Benjamin Franklin be, and hereby is appointed and authorized (on behalf of this House) to appear before his Majesty in Council, in the several Houses of Parliament, and at any other Board whatever in Great Britain, there to plead and defend as the Exigency of the Case, and the Service of the Province may require, for the Space of one Year, agreable to such Directions or Instructions as from Time to Time he may receive from the House, (or from such Committee as may be by them authorized and appointed for that Purpose,) entirely relying on his Vigilance and the Exertion of his utmost Endeavors, to support the constitutional Rights of this House, and of the Province, and to guard against, and (as far as in him lies) to obviate whatever may have a Tendency to prejudice the same.

THOMAS CUSHING Speaker

Endorsed: Dr Franklin's appointment as Agent to the House of Representatives Massachustes. 1770

6. See above, XVI, 243–9, and Cooper to BF below, Nov. 6.
7. Mass. Hist. Soc. *Collections*, 6th ser., IX (1897), 213–14; Thomas Cushing to Stephen Sayre, Nov. 2, 1770, Mass. Hist. Soc.; Cooper to BF below, Nov. 6; Harry A. Cushing, ed., *The Writings of Samuel Adams* (4 vols., New York, 1904–08), II, 58–9; Kammen, *Rope of Sand*, pp. 148–51.
8. Crane, *Letters to the Press*, p. 212.

From Joseph Priestley

ALS (transcript): the Royal Society[9]

Dear Sir   Leeds 26th. Octr. 1770

I think myself happy in an opportunity of giving you a species of pleasure, which I know is peculiarly grateful to you as *the father of modern electricity*, by transmitting to you an account of some very *curious and valuable improvements in your favourite* science. The author of them is *Mr. Henly, in the* Borough, who has favour'd me with the communication of them, and has given me leave to request, that you would present them to the Royal Society.[1]

In my history of Electricity, and elswhere, I have mention'd a good *Electrometer*, as one of the greatest *desiderata* among practical electricians, to measure both the precise degree of the electrification of any body and also the exact quantity of a charge before explosion with respect to the size of the electrified body or the jar or battery with which it is connected; as well as to ascertain the moment of time, in which the electricity of a jar changes, when, without making an explosion, it is discharg'd by giving it a quantity of the contrary electricity. All these purposes are answer'd, in the most complete manner, by an electrometer of this Gentleman's contrivance, a drawing of which I send you along with the following description.[2]

The whole instrument is made of Ivory or wood. (a) is an exceeding light rod, with a pith ball at the extremity, made to turn upon the center of a semicircle (b), and so as always to keep pretty near the limb of it, which is graduated: (c) is the stem that supports it, and may either be fixed to the prime conductor or be let into the brass knob of a Jar or Battery, or set in a stand, to support itself.

9. Read at a meeting of the Society, May 8, 1772, and published in *Phil. Trans.*, LXII (1772), 359–64, from which minor errors in the transcript have been silently corrected.

1. William Henly, or Henley, was a linen draper; he made enough of a name for himself as an electrical experimenter to warrant a brief notice in the *DNB*. BF, who had known him at least since the spring of 1770, suggested some improvements in his electrometer, and in 1773 was instrumental in having him elected an F.R.S. Henly to John Canton, June 7, 1770, Royal Soc., and to BF below, Jan. 29, 1771; above, VIII, 359.

2. The drawing has disappeared. Our illustration is taken from the letter as published in *Phil. Trans.*, where the capital letters correspond to those in low case in the description that follows.

The moment that this little apparatus is electrified, the rod (a) is repelled by the stem (c) and, consequently, begins to move along the graduated edge of the semicircle (b); so as to mark with the

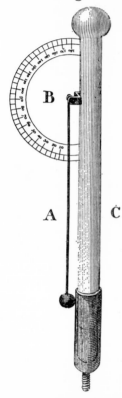

utmost exactness, the degree in which the prime conductor etc. is electrified, or the height to which the charge of any Jar or battery is advanced; and as the materials of which this little instrument is made are very imperfect conductors, it will continue in contact with any electrified body, or charged Jar, without dissipating any of the electricity.

If it should be found, by trial in the dark, that any part of this instrument contributes to the dissipation of the electric matter, (which when the electrification was very strong, I once observ'd mine to do) it should be baked a little which will presently prevent it. If it is baked too much it will not receive electricity readily enough; and then the motion of the index will not correspond with sufficient exactness, to the degree in which the body to which it is connected is electrified; but this inconvenience is easily remedied by moistening the stem and the index; for the semicircle cannot be too dry.

I find by experience, that this electrometer answers all the purposes I have mentioned with the greatest ease and exactness. I am now sure of the force of any explosion before a discharge of a Jar or battery, which I had no better method of guessing at before, than by presenting to them a pair of Mr. Canton's balls, and observing their divergency at a given distance.[3] But the degree of divergency was still to be guessed at by the eye, and the balls can only be applied occasionally; whereas this Instrument, being constantly fixed to the prime conductor or the battery, shews without any trouble, the whole *progress* of the charge; and, remaining in the same situation, the force of different explosions may be ascertained with the utmost exactness before the discharge.

If a Jar be loaded with positive electricity, and I want to know the exact time when by attempting to charge it negatively, it first becomes discharged, I see every step of its approach to this state by

3. For John Canton's device see above, IX, 351 n.

the falling of the Index; and the moment I want to seize, is the time when it has got into a perpendicular situation, which may be observed without the least danger of a mistake. Accordingly I find that, in this case, not the least spark is left in the Jar. If I continue the operation, the Index after having gained its perpendicular position, begins to advance again, and thereby shews me the exact quantity of the opposite electricity that it has acquired.

Considering the admirable *simplicity*, as well as the great *usefulness* of this instrument, it is something surprising that the Construction should not have occurred to some electrician before this time. Nollet's and Mr. Waits's invention of *threads, projecting shadows upon a graduated board*, resembled this apparatus of Mr. Henly's, but was a poor and awkward contrivance in comparison with it; nor was *Richmans gnomon*, tho' a nearer approach to this construction, at all comparable to it;[4] and the ingenious author of it had no knowledge of either of those methods when he hit upon this.

I have made a receptacle for this instrument in my prime conductor, and I have also a pedestal in which I can fix it; and by means of which I can very conveniently place it on the wires of a battery.

In either of those situations it answers almost every purpose of an electrometer, without removing it from its place.

I doubt not that you and all other electricians will join with me in returning our hearty thanks to Mr. Henly for this excellent and useful instrument.

Many of the effects of my battery, in breaking of glass, and tearing the surfaces of bodies, Mr. Henly performs by a *single Jar*, only increasing the weight with which the bodies are pressed, while the explosion is made to pass close under them.

By this means he raises exceeding great[5] weights and shatters strong pieces of glass into Thousands of the smallest fragments. He even reduces thick plate glass by this means to an impalpable powder. But what is most remarkable is that when the pieces of glass are thick, and strong enough to resist the shock, they are mark'd by the explosion with the most lively and beautiful *colours*, generally

4. The Abbé Jean-Antoine Nollet was the leading French electrical authority, Jacob Siegismund Waitz was a German pioneer in the subject, and Georg Wilhilm Richmann was the Swedish experimenter who lost his life in St. Petersburg while testing his "gnomon," or electrometer. See above, IV, 423–8; VIII, 331 n; V, 155 n, 219–21.

5. [*Priestley's note:*] frequently 6 pounds Troy.

covering the space of about an inch in length, and half an inch in breadth.

In some of the pieces which he was so obliging as to send me, these colours lie all intermixed and confused; but in others I observe them to be disposed in prismatic order, in lines parallel to the course of the explosion, and in some (as No. 1) I have counted three or four distinct returns of the same colour.

He has lately inform'd me, that, since he sent me this piece, he has struck these prismatic colours into another mass of glass, in a still more vivid and beautiful manner, the colours shooting into one another. This effect, he says, was produced by making a second explosion, without moving any of the apparatus after the first.

When the glass in which these colours are fixed is examined, it is evident that the surface is shattered into *thin plates*, and that these give the colours, the thickness of them varying regularly, as they recede from the path of the explosion.

In the middle of some of these coloured spots (as in No 2) some of these thin plates, or scales, are struck off, I suppose by the force of the explosion; and with the edge of a knife they are all easily scraped away, when the surface of the glass is left without its polish (as in No. 3).

The piece of glass on which I have marked these Numbers, as well as that on which he has struck the colours in a still more beautiful manner, Mr. Henly will present to the Royal Society, for the inspection of the members.

Besides these improvements, Mr. Henly has likewise, in a very ingenious manner, diversified several of the more entertaining experiments in electricity, particularly in his imitation of the effects of Earthquakes by the lateral force of explosions; and he has also hit upon several curious facts, that, unknown to him, had been observed before by others. The following particular however I believe is new, Exciting a stick of sealing wax, and using a piece of Tin foil for the rubber, he found that it wou'd electrify *positively*, as well as *glass* rubbed with *silk and Amalgama*.

Wishing we had *more* such fellow labourers as Mr. Henly, I am Dear Sir your oblig'd Humble Servant   J PRIESTLEY

To Doctor Franklin

An Account of a new Electrometer contrived by Mr. William

Henly and of several electrical experiments made by him, in a letter from Dr. Priestly F.R.S. to Dr. Franklin F.R.S.

Endorsed: Read May 28. 1772

From John Winthrop

Reprinted from the Massachusetts Historical Society *Proceedings*, xv (1878), 12–13.[6]

Dear Sir, Cambr., Octr 26. 1770.

I received your favors of June 6 and July 9 at the same time. I am very glad to find your admirable invention of Lightning Rods is coming into fashion in England, and cannot but think your circulating particular directions for making them, by the magazines will greatly promote the use of them. I have on all occasions encouraged them in this country, and have the satisfaction to find, that it has not been without effect. A little piece I inserted in our news papers last summer induced the people of Waltham (a town a few miles from hence), to fix rods upon their steeple, which had just before been much shattered and set on fire by lightning.[7] They are now becoming pretty common among us, and numbers of people seem convinced of their efficacy.

I received the Transactions for 1768, but was disappointed in not finding the Print which I had requested, with them. I hope you will soon meet with a good opportunity to send it. The Achromatic Telescope is come safely. It is very elegant and I believe, by the trials I have hitherto made of it, a very good one. I have the honor to transmit to you the thanks of the Corporation for the repeated instances of your kindness to the College. I suppose Mr. Hubard has or will direct the payment out of moneys in the hands of Mr. Mauduit. The Galilean glasses did arrive from Philadelphia the end of May last, accompanied with a very polite Letter from Mr. Galloway dated in August preceding. I am directed to thank Mr. Ellicott for them, which I shall do by this conveyance if possible.

I thank you very kindly for the care of my papers and in for-

6. A transcription of the original draft ALS, also in the Mass. Hist. Soc. and in Winthrop's peculiar and difficult shorthand. We have collated the two versions to establish the accuracy of the transcription.

7. For the incident at Waltham and Winthrop's article see *Mass. Gaz. and Boston Weekly News-Letter*, Aug. 9, 1770.

warding Mr. Maskelyne's obliging Letter and the Nautical Almanac for 1770 to me. I am greatly obliged to that Gentleman for his favorable acceptance of my dissertations and for the valuable present of that Almanac, which I find a most useful performance; and shall be very glad of that for 1771, if he has sent it to you, as you intimate he talked of doing. I will do my self the honor to write Mr. Maskelyne, when I have any observations that seem worth laying before him.[8]

I look on my self as under singular obligation for your friendship in communicating my paper on the aberration to the Rev. Mr. Price, before you ventured it in public. It gives me pleasure to find my self supported by so judicious a person. I have with satisfaction perused his paper on that subject, which you inclosed to me; but that I may not swell your Letter shall throw what I have to say upon it into a separate paper; which if you think worth while, may be sent to Mr. Price.[9]

Upon this occasion Sir give me leave to mention to you, that a year or two ago I was informed by some Gentlemen of our Corporation, that you had intimated a desire to Mr. Nathaniel Rogers when in London, that Mr. Price should have a Doctorate from the College.[1] The Gentlemen appeared ready to fall in with your proposal; but hearing nothing further from you upon it, nothing has been done in the affair. I know, Gentlemen here have the highest

8. Most of the matters discussed in these two paragraphs have been covered above: XVI, 65–7; BF to Winthrop, June 6; and Harvard's vote of thanks, Oct. 22. Thomas Hubbard was the College treasurer, Jasper Mauduit a London merchant, and John Ellicott a clockmaker and scientist; see above, respectively, VII, 69 n; XVI, 65 n; X, 248 n. Maskelyne's gift was *The Nautical Almanac and Astronomical Ephemeris for the Year 1770*... (London, 1769); the 1771 volume was published in the same year.

9. The sequence of the exchange between Winthrop and Price, via BF, can be at least conjecturally reconstructed. Winthrop sent his paper on the aberration of light during the transit of Venus (above, XVI, 195–8) to BF to show to Price before publication. Price seems to have replied in a letter to BF, now lost, that was an early draft of his discussion printed below, Dec. 20; if so, Winthrop is here acknowledging receipt of that draft. His MS has at this point a bracketed insertion, "See Cover [?] of this Letter," which may mean that he enclosed his comments—the separate paper to which he refers—for forwarding to Price. In any case that paper, Winthrop's second on the subject, has been lost.

1. For Nathaniel Rogers see above, XVI, 66. Price never did receive a Harvard degree.

opinion of Mr. Price's merit: I know too, they will be glad upon all opportunities to express the sense they have of their obligations to you. If you should think proper to signify a desire of this kind, I cannot think the affair would meet with any difficulty. At least I would do all in my power to promote it.

I congratulate my Countrymen on the judicious choice our Representatives made yesterday of Dr. Franklin for their agent in this Time of difficulty. I have no doubt every thing will be done that is possible to be done, to avert the cruel blow aimed at our Charter rights by those implacable enemies to this Province and to the general cause of Liberty. I am with the most entire esteem and respect Dear Sir Your most obliged and most humble Servant

JOHN WINTHROP

P.S. I send by the Bearer of this 52s. sterling for the Volume of Transactions for 1769.

From Thomas Cushing   ALS: Massachusetts Historical Society

Sir.   Province of the Massachusetts Bay Oct: 31: 1770

In pursuance of the directions of the House of Representatives of this His Majesty's Province, I have the pleasure to Inform you that they have made choice of you as their Agent in Great Britain for the purposes mentioned in the Vote which I now transmit you. I am directed also to acquaint you that the House will write you more fully by the next Conveyance and will then furnish you with such Instructions or directions as may be necessary, entirely confiding in your Ability Fidelity and Zeal in Execution of the Trust Committed to you.[2] I am with great Esteem Your most humble Servant

THOMAS CUSHING Speaker

Benjamin Franklin Esqr

Endorsed: T. Cushing to Dr. B. Franklin anouncing his appointment to the agency of Massachusetts 1770

2. For BF's appointment see above, Oct. 24, and for the instructions see below, Nov. 6.

An Expostulation   Printed in *The Public Advertiser*, Nov. 3, 1770[3]

For the PUBLIC ADVERTISER
An AMERICAN, *to those* ENGLISHMEN *who virulently write and talk against his* COUNTRYMEN, *sends this Expostulation:*

If it be true, as some of you say it is, that our Non-Importation Agreements are not observed, but that we clandestinely import and consume as much British Goods as ever, why are you so angry with us, and why do you propose compelling us to trade with you by Force?

If, as others of you say, we do indeed generally forbear importing at present, but must soon from Necessity be obliged to break our Agreements, can't you have a little Patience?

Can you Englishmen think your abusing us in all the British Papers as Rebels, Knaves, Fools, Traitors, &c. &c. will put us into a better Humour, make us more inclined to come to your Shop, buy your Superfluities, and follow your Fashions?

Are you absolutely certain that there are no possible Means whereby we may supply ourselves with Conveniences and Necessaries without importing them from Britain?

If through the high Price of Labour, Manufactures are, as you assert, impracticable in America, cannot you be quiet, and let us convince ourselves of our own Folly by Experience, since that will make our future Commercial Connexions with you still stronger, and discourage future Attempts when perhaps become more practicable? Is it mere Good-will to us, and Fear of our hurting ourselves by such Attempts, that you take such Pains to prove they cannot succeed? Or is it to convince Government that we may be used very ill, without the least Danger of Prejudice to your Trade and Manufactures?

If those Colonies, that entered into the Non-Importation Agreement, have done it, as some of you assert, because they are in bad Circumstances, deep in Debt to your Merchants, and on the Verge

3. The essay exists in two other forms. An incomplete copy of BF's draft, in the APS, contains roughly five-sixths of the printed version; a fragmentary copy made by WTF is printed in W. A. S. Hewins, ed., *The Whitefoord Papers* . . . (Oxford, 1898), p. 179. The numerous variations between these, particularly the former, and the printed essay are mostly in stylistic details that do not affect the sense; for the few that do have a slight effect see the notes in Crane, *Letters to the Press*, pp. 213–15.

of Bankruptcy, can their refusing to take more of your Goods, and get deeper into your Debt, be so heinous a Crime as to provoke your calling down upon them National Vengeance?

If the Colonists are indeed generally such bad Paymasters; if your Factors and Agents among them find such infinite Difficulties in getting in your Debts; if the People of America are such a set of Hypocrites, Knaves and Cheats as you represent them to be, why, in the Name of Common-sense, are you so desirous of continuing the Commerce with them? Why in such Rage at their refusing it? Why in such Raptures when you heard that a few in New York had broken through the Agreement?

If the American Trade is of so little Consequence to this Nation, as others of you tell us, that your Merchants and Manufacturers do not miss it, that additional Demands from other Countries more than supply the Loss of it, and that it is not therefore of the smallest Importance whether the Americans are pleased or displeased with any Treatment they may receive from Britain, would you then punish them for doing you no Injury? If the Trade be only advantageous to them, cannot you leave them (like froward Children that quarrel with their Bread and Butter) to punish themselves by going without it?

On the other Hand, if our Commerce and Friendship are of some Advantage to you, while you are exasperating this Country against the Colonies by Misrepresentations and Falsehoods, if you are at the same Time by your Abuses so exasperating that Country against this, as that they will from Resentment exert themselves more earnestly to give Encouragement, and finally should succeed in every Manufacture, as they have already in several, will your Country then think that you have been doing it Service?

Don't you suppose it possible that civil Dissentions may encourage foreign Insults? Can you conceive the least Use in destroying all mutual Regard and Affection between Britain and America? Can you imagine a more diabolical Employment than that of fomenting Mischief, sowing the Seeds of Civil War, provoking a Prince against his Subjects, Fathers against their Children, and promoting deadly Feuds between different Branches of the same Family?

Do you think it impossible that England may ever need Assistance from the Colonies? Do you think it quite out of the Course of human Affairs that Britons should ever have Occasion to seek an Asylum in America? Would it not be more comfortable to you and your Children to find there LIBERTY and Friends, than SLAVERY and Enemies?

The Rise and Present State of Our Misunderstanding

Printed in *The London Chronicle*, November 6–8, 1770[4]

To the PRINTER *of the* LONDON CHRONICLE,
Sir,

Much abuse has lately been thrown out against the Colonies, by the Writers for the American part of our Administration. Our Fellow Subjects there are continually represented as Rebels to their Sovereign, and inimical to the British nation; in order to create a dislike of them here, that the harsh measures which have been taken, and are intended against them, may not be blamed by the People of England. Therefore to prevent our being led into mistakes in so important a business, it is fit that a full and particular account of the rise and present state of our misunderstanding with the Colonies should be laid before the Public. This, from the opportunities I have had, and the pains I have taken to inform myself, I think I am enabled to do, and I hope I shall do it with truth and candor.

The fact then is, that there is not nor has been any rebellion in America. If the rescue of a seizure by Smugglers, or the drubbing an Informer or low Custom-house Officer, were rebellion, England, Scotland, and Ireland, might be said to be in rebellion almost every week in the year; and instances of that kind are much fewer in America than here. The Americans were ever attached to the House of Hanover, and honour their present gracious Sovereign sincerely. This is therefore a groundless calumny. Nor have they any enmity to Britain: they love and honour the name of Englishman; they were fond of English manners, fashions, and manufac-

4. A draft of the latter part of the essay, in BF's hand, is in the APS; and Crane, with his usual care, has collated the draft with the printed version: *Letters to the Press*, pp. 215–20.

tures; they had no desire of breaking the connection between the two countries, but wished a perpetual intercourse of good offices, commerce, and friendship. They are always willing to give aids to the Crown in proportion to their abilities: They think, however, and have always thought, that they themselves have alone the right of granting their own money, by their own Representatives in Assembly met, and that the Parliament of Britain hath no right to raise a revenue from them without their consent.

The Parliament hath, nevertheless, of late made several attempts to raise such a revenue among them.

Heretofore, whenever the Colonies thought themselves aggrieved by British government, they applied for redress by humble petition; and it was usual to receive and consider their petitions, and give them a reasonable answer.

They proceeded in the same manner on the late occasions. They sent over petitions after petitions to the House of Commons, and some to the House of Lords. These were scarce any of them received. Some (offered while the acts were under consideration) were refused on this reason, that it was against an order of the House to receive petitions against money bills; others, because they contained expressions that called the right of Parliament in question; and therefore, it was said, no Member dared to present them. Finding the petitions of separate Colonies were not attended to, they thought to give them more weight by petitioning jointly. To this end a congress of Committees from all the Assemblies was held at New York, when petitions to the King and both Houses of Parliament were agreed to and sent hither. But these could not be received, or were rejected, on the pretence that the congress was an illegal assembly which had no right to petition. Lastly, on occasion of the Duty Act, the Assemblies proposed by a correspondence with each other to obtain attention, by sending at the same time similar petitions. These were intended to the King their Sovereign, requesting his gracious influence with his Parliament to procure them redress. But this they were told by the American Minister was a FLAGITIOUS[5] attempt! All the Governors were by him directed to prevent it, or to dissolve the Assemblies that persisted in it; and several of them were accordingly dissolved. And of those petitions

5. [BF's *note*:] See Lord H[illsborough]'s Letters to the Governors [of April 21, 1768].

that nevertheless came hither and were presented, it is said that no notice was ever taken, or any answer given to them.

By this management the ancient well contrived channel of communication between the head and members of this great Empire, thro' which the notice of grievances could be received that remedies might be applied, hath been cut off. How wisely, the Publick will judge. History of a similar conduct in the Ministry of Spain with regard to the Low Countries, makes one doubt a little the prudence (in any Government how great soever) of discouraging Petitions, and treating Petitioners (how mean soever) with contempt.

Instead of *preventing* complaints by removing the causes, it has been thought best that Soldiers should be sent to *silence* them.

The Soldiers have behaved in such a manner as to occasion more complaints.

They took possession of the publick building in which the Assembly or Parliament of New England usually convenes, obliged the Members to pass through lanes of men in arms to get to their Chamber, disturbing them in their debates by drumming and piping in and round the House, and pointed the cannon against the doors, treating the Province and People with every indignity and insult, proper to provoke their resentment, and produce some rash action that might justify making a massacre among them.[6] And they have fired upon and murdered several of the inhabitants.

The Americans, upon the treatment their Petitions had repeatedly received, determined to petition no more: But said to one another, "We are too remote from Britain to have our complaints regarded by the Parliament there, especially as we have no share in their Election, nor any Representatives among them. They will not hear *us*, but perhaps they will hear *their own people*, their Merchants and Manufacturers, who are maintained and enriched in some degree by the commerce with our country. Let us agree to with-hold that commerce till our grievances are redressed. This will afford those people a foundation for petitioning, and they will be attended to

6. After the troops arrived in Boston in October, 1768, some were quartered for a short time in the Town House or Old State House, where the General Court met. The wording of this paragraph is unlike BF ("Parliament of New England," for example), and a few earlier turns of phrase do not sound like his. The draft proves his authorship of most of the essay, but he may have had a collaborator in this part.

as they were on a former occasion, and meet with success." This reasoning and expectation were the sole foundation of the Non-Importation agreements in America, and *not any enmity to Britain*.

In this expectation it seems they were mistaken. The Merchants trading to North America not well liking the Ministry, unwilling to solicit or be obliged to them for any thing, and hoping soon to see a change for others more to their mind, were backward in petitioning the Parliament. And when they did petition, the City being out of favour at Court, their Petition was very little attended to, and produced no effect. To prevent the Manufacturers from taking any part in the affair, they have been artfully amused with assurances that the Colonies could not long subsist without the trade, that manufactures among themselves were impossible, that they might depend there would be an extraordinary demand for goods as soon as the total want of conveniencies should compel the Americans to resume the commerce; and therefore they would do well to be quiet, mind their business, and get a great stock of goods beforehand to be ready for that demand, when the advanced price would make them ample amends for the delay.

In the mean time the Merchants in America have reaped great advantages. They have sold off most of the old goods that lay upon their hands; they have got in most of their debts from the people, and have in a great measure discharged their debt to England, that bore a heavy interest; this they have done at an advantage of near 20 per cent. in most of the Colonies, by the lowness of exchange, occasioned by the non-importation; and this nation has lost near that proportion (if I am rightly informed) on all the money drawn for these by British Agents, to pay and provide for the troops and ships of war, and to discharge other expences of contingent service. This loss must amount to a very great sum, besides the loss in commerce.

Many of these Merchants in America, however, having nearly compleated these points, and seeing the main end of their agreement, (the total abolition of the duties) not likely to be so soon obtained as they expected, begin to grow uneasy under the delay, and are rather desirous of altering the agreement made against general importation, and reducing it to the exclusion of those commercial articles only, on which the duties are, or shall be imposed. But the generality of the people in America, the artizans in the towns, and

271

the farmers throughout the country, finding the non-importation advantageous to them all; to the artisans, as it occasions fuller employment, and encourages the beginners that introduce new arts; and to the farmers, as it prevents much useless expence in their families, and thereby enables them more expeditiously to improve their plantations to the raising a greater produce, at the same time that it is a spur to domestic industry, in such manufactures as though not fine, are now become fashionable and reputable, and from their superior strength are much more serviceable than the flimsy fineries that used to be made for them in Britain; and all feeling the advantage of having had money returned into the country for its produce, from Spain, Portugal, Italy, (and even from England since the balance of trade has turned against her) instead of those British superfluities for which all that cash was formerly remitted, or ordered into England. I say, the generality of the people in America, pleased with this situation of things, and relishing the sweets of it, have now taken the lead in a great degree, out of the hands of the Merchants, and in town and county meetings are entering into solemn resolutions not to purchase or consume British commodities, if they are imported, till the acts they esteem injurious to their privileges are repealed: and that if any Merchants do import before that time, they will mark them as enemies to their country, and never deal with them when the trade shall be opened. This is now become a restraint upon the Merchants. A party, however, of those at New-York, have broken through the agreement, and ordered goods; and the Merchants here, who had long lain idle, being rejoiced at this opening, have sent them over immense quantities, expecting a quick sale and speedy returns. But the event is yet very uncertain. The trade of New-York was chiefly with East New Jersey and Connecticut, their two neighbouring Colonies, and these have resolved to have no farther dealings with that city. Several counties, too, of the Province of New-York, and the greatest part of the inhabitants of the city itself, have protested against the infraction of the agreement, and determined not to buy or use the goods when they arrive. So that the exporters begin now to apprehend that their sanguine hopes will be disappointed. And as Rhode Island has returned to the agreement, some think it not unlikely that New-York may do the same.

What remedy, if any, the wisdom of Parliament shall think fit to apply to these disorders, a little time will shew. Mean while, I cannot but think that those writers, who busily employ their talents in endeavouring to exasperate this nation against the Colonies, are doing it a very ill office: For their virulent writings being dispersed among the inhabitants of the Plantations (who read all our papers and pamphlets, and imagine them of greater estimation here than they really are) do in some degree irritate the Colonists against a country which treats them, as they imagine, think so injuriously: And on our side, as nothing is likely to be well done that is done in anger; as customers are not naturally brought back to a shop by unkind usage; as the Americans are growing, and soon will be, a great people, and their friendship or enmity become daily of more and more consequence; as their fisheries, their coasting trade, their West-Indian and European Trades, greatly increase the numbers of English seamen, and thereby augment our naval power; as their joint operations with our's in time of war must make the whole national effort more weighty and more effectual; as enmities between countries, fostered and promoted till they have taken root, are scarce ever to be eradicated; and, when those countries are under the same Prince, such enmities are of the most mischievous consequence, encouraging foreign enemies, weakening the whole empire, and tending to its dissolution; therefore I cannot but wish, that no steps may be taken against the Colonists, tending to abridge their privileges, alter their charters, or inflict punishments on them, at the instance of *angry Governors, discarded Agents, or rash indiscreet Officers of the Customs*, who, having quarrelled with them, are their enemies, and are daily irritating Government here against them, by misrepresentations of their actions, and aggravations of their faults, with much malice: I hope the great principle of common justice, that *no man should be condemned unheard*, will not by us be violated in the case of a whole people; and that lenient measures will be adopted as most likely to heal the wound effectually: For harsh treatment may increase the inflammation, make the cure less practicable, and in time bring on the necessity of an amputation; death indeed to the severed limb, weakness and lameness to the mutilated body.   N.N.

From Samuel Cooper

ALS (draft): British Museum

Dear Sir, 6. Novr. 70.

My State of Health, and Excursions upon that Account into the Country must be my Excuse for not taking an earlier Notice of your very obliging Packet of 8th June, for which I return you my particular Thanks. Your Letter and Replies to Mr. Strahan's Questions gave me great Pleasure, tho the closing and prophetic Part coming from one so capable of discerning amidst the Uncertainties of Futurity which may probably take Place, could not but impress me with melancholy Ideas.[7] Some of them have since been realised, but may Heav'n forbid a further Fulfillment. In this Wish I doubt not of your own hearty Concurrence; for I do not take you to be of the Turn of Swift's Physicians of whom he some where says,

> They rather chuse that I should die,
> Than their Predictions prove a Lie;[8]

and yet I am afraid I shall not soon see you thoroly refuted by Events. So many hope to find their own Interest in Misrepresentations, so many seem willing to be deceiv'd, and so much Art is employ'd to make Whatever is tho't convenient appear just and true, that the happy Day for establishing the Prosperity of Britain, by composing the Troubles, and securing to her the united affections of America seems to be at too great a Distance. We ought not however to be discourag'd from employing the most likely Means to promote so desireable an End. Such a Means I esteem the choice which our House of Representatives have made of you to be their Agent——Your Letter came most seasonably for this. I communicated it with great Caution knowing the Delicacy the Times require: I allow'd however some of the leading Members of the House; in Confidence to read your Sentiments. They exprest the highest Satisfaction. And tho it was objected that you were Agent for other Provinces, and we ought to enlarge the Number of our Friends, and that you and your Son the Governor, held Places of Importance under the Crown, and tho the House from various Causes had been much divided respecting an Agent, yet such was their Opinion of your Abilities and Integrity, that a Majority

7. See above, XVI, 248–9.
8. The single physician in Swift has become plural; see Sir Walter Scott, ed., *The Works of Jonathan Swift . . .* (2d ed., 19 vols., Boston, 1883–4), XIV, 321.

readily confided the Affairs of the Province at this critical Season to your Care. I am this Moment told the Vessel is just upon sailing. I must break off. You see the Hurry of this Script——but it is to a Friend. I shall write more fully soon. Your very respectful and obliged Humble Servant   SAML COOPER

Dr Franklin

Copy to Dr Franklin

Endorsed: To Dr Franklin   6. Novr -70.

From the Massachusetts House of Representatives: Instructions to Benjamin Franklin as Agent[9]

DS: Massachusetts Historical Society

These instructions introduced Franklin to the boiling cauldron of resentment in Massachusetts. Anger was directed at more than the troops in Boston—at what the colonists took to be the helplessness of the civil authority before the military, the secret and false reports sent home, the subordination of the legislature to an executive controlled by undisclosed instructions from London, the arbitrary power of the admiralty courts and the threat to the whole legal system of the province. These grievances, whatever their reality, combined to create among the leaders in Boston a mood that already foreshadowed rebellion. Through Samuel Cooper, Franklin had urged them to put their faith in the crown, for he was not yet ready to abandon hope of redress from the throne.[1] They were. Such hope seemed to them mere romanticism; they made no distinction between royal and ministerial policy, which they regarded as a threat to their property and their rights. Although they had chosen as their new agent a moderate who still preached restraint, their own sense of restraint was wearing extremely thin.

Sir,   Province of the Massachusetts Bay Novembr. 6th, 1770
The House of Representatives of this his Majesty's Province, having made Choice of you to appear for them at the Court of

9. Attributed by Thomas Hutchinson to Samuel Adams, and printed in Harry A. Cushing, ed., *The Writings of Samuel Adams* (4 vols., New York, 1904–08), II, 46–56, from which a few mistakes in the copy have been silently corrected.

1. BF to Cooper above, June 8.

Great Britain, as there may be Occasion, it is necessary that you be well informed of the State and Circumstances of the Province, and the Grievances it labours under, the Redress of which will require your utmost Attention and Application.

You are sensible that the British Parliament has of late years thought proper to raise a Revenue in America without our Consent, by divers Laws made expressly for that Purpose: and to dispose of the Monies raised, for the Administration of Justice and the Defence of the Colonies: The Reasons and Grounds of our Complaint against these Acts, are so well known and understood by you, that it is needless for us to mention them at this Time.

The Measures which have been taken by the American Assemblies, to obtain the Repeal of these Acts, though altogether consistent with the Constitution, and clearly within the Bounds of the Subjects Rights, have been nevertheless disgustful to Administration at home; to whom we have been constantly represented, by Servants of the Crown, and others on this Side the Water, in the most disagreable and odious Light.

Whether this Province has been considered as having a Lead among the other Colonies, which they have never asserted; or whether it is because Governor Bernard, the Commissioners of the Customs, and others who have discovered themselves peculiarly inimical to the Colonies, have had their Residence here, Certain it is that the Resentment of Government at home has been particularly pointed against this Province. For it is notorious, that we have been charged with taking inflammatory measures tending to create unwarrantable Combinations, to excite an unjustifiable Opposition to the constitutional Authority of Parliament, and revive unhappy Divisions among the Colonies, and we have frequently been censured as disobedient to Government, for Parts of Conduct taken by us, in no wise dissimular to those which have been taken by other Colonies, without the least Censure or Observation.

While Administration appeared to have conceived undue Prejudices against us, our Enemies here, have not failed to take every Measure to increase those Prejudices: and particularly by representing to the King's Ministers that a Spirit of Faction had so greatly and universally prevailed among us, as that Government could not be supported, and it was unsafe for the Officers of the Crown to live in the Province and execute their Trust, without the

Protection of a military Force.[2] Such a Force they at length obtained; the Consequence of which was a Scene of Confusion and Distress for the Space of seventeen Months, which ended in the Blood and Slaughter of his Majesty's good Subjects.

It was peculiarly mortifying to us, to see the whole System of civil Authority in the Province yeilding to this most dangerous Power: And at the very Time, when the Interposition of the civil Magistrate was of the most pressing necessity, to check the wanton and bloody Career of the Military, the Lieutenant Governor himself declared, as Governor Bernard had before, that "he had no Authority over the King's Troops in the Province;" and his Majesty's Representative in Council became an humble supplicant for their Removal out of the Town of Boston! What would be the Feelings of the Subjects in Great Britain, if contrary to *their* Bill of Rights, and indeed to every Principle of civil Government; Soldiers were posted even in their Capital, without the Consent of their Parliament? And yet the Subjects of the same Prince in America, who are intitled to the same Freedom, are compelled to submit to as great a military Power as Administration shall be pleased to order, to be posted among them in a time of profound Peace, without the Consent of their Assemblies.[3] And this military Power is allowed to trample upon the Law of the Land, the common Security, without Restraint. Such an Instance of absolute, uncontrouled military Tyranny must needs be alarming to those, who have before in some Measure enjoy'd, and are still intitled to the Blessings of a free civil Government, having never forfeited the Character of loyal Subjects.

After the fatal Tragedy of the 5th. of March last, the Regiments under the Command of Lt. Colonel Dalrymple were removed from the Town of Boston, to the Barracks on Castle Island, in Consequence of a Petition of the Town to the Lt. Governor, and his *Prayer* to the Colonel. Since which in Pursuance of Instruction to the Lt. Governor the Garrison there in the Pay of the Province has been withdrawn, and a Garrison of his majesty's Regular Troops

2. The fear of false reports, mentioned here and later in the instructions, was deep and long-lasting. See the letters from the Boston committee above, XVI, 44, and July 13, 1770.

3. This sentence echoes BF's own views of military power; see his letter to Cooper above, June 8.

placed in their Stead: and by the inclosed Affidavits [*in the margin:* Capt. Phillips and Mr. Hall's] it appears, that merely in Obedience to Instructions the Lieutenant Governor has made an absolute Surrender of that Fortress to Colonel Dalrymple: and altho' the Surrender was made by him ostensively as Lieutenant Governor, yet even the Shew that was made of the Authority of the Governor, served only to make the Surrender the more solemn and effectual; the Governor by Charter has the Right of committing the Custody and Government of the Fortress to such Person or Persons as to him shall seem meet; But he has given up this Right to Colonel Dalrymple, by vesting him with the Power of garrisoning the Fortress with such Person or Persons as *to him* shall seem meet; and so far forth he has in an Instance of the greatest Importance, divested himself of the Government of this Province.[4]

We cannot help observing upon this Occasion, that the Instructions which have of late been given to the Governor, some of them at least, have directly militated, as in the present Instance, with the Charter of the Province; and these Instructions are not always adapted to promote his Majesty's Service, or the Good of the People within this Province, but often appear to be solely calculated to further and execute the Measures and enforce the Laws of a different State; by which Means his Majesty's Colonies may be entirely subjected to the absolute Will of his other Subjects in Great Britain, for which there can be no Pretence of Right, but what is founded in meer Force.

By Virtue of such positive Instructions, the General Assembly of the Province has been removed from its ancient, established and only convenient Seat in Boston, and is still obliged to hold its Sessions at Harvard-College in Cambridge, to the great Inconvenience of the Members, and Injury of the People, as well as Detriment of that Seminary of Learning, without any Reason that

4. The point at issue, the governor's constitutional authority not only by the charter but by his commission under the great seal, was one that BF and Thomas Pownall had discussed almost a year before; see above, XVI, 298. Captain John Phillips and Mr. Hall were commander and chaplain, respectively, of the provincial militia at Castle William; their affidavits related to the transfer of the Castle to Dalrymple. For further details see Carter, ed., *Gage Correspondence*, I, 265, 271; II, 116, 564; Thomas Hutchinson, *History of the Province of Massachusetts Bay . . .* (3 vols., London, 1828), III, 307–12; Cushing, *op. cit.*, II, 70–7.

can be assigned but Will and Pleasure. And thus the Prerogative of the King, which is a Trust reposed in him, to be improved only for the Welfare of his Subjects, is perverted to their manifest Injury.

And what is still more grievous is, that the Governor of the Province is absolutely inhibited, as we are told, from laying before the Assembly any Instructions which he receives, even such as carry in them the evident Marks of his Majesty's Displeasure; by which means the House of Representatives cannot have it in their Power to obtain here that precise knowledge of the Ground of our Sovereign's Displeasure, which they are in Reason and Justice entitled to; nor can the ministry be made responsible for any Measures they may advise to in order to introduce and establish an illegal and arbitrary Government over his Majesty's Subjects in the Colonies.

We have an Instance of this Kind now before us; the Lieutenant Governor of the Province having in his Speech at the Opening of this Session given a dark Hint of something intended against the Province: and when the House of Representatives earnestly desired him to explain it, that they might have a clear understanding of what was intended therein, he declared, as he had before done in other like Cases, that he was not at Liberty to make publick or to communicate to them by Speech or Message an Order of his Majesty in Council, which he had received, altho' in Consequence therof the State of the Province was to be laid before Parliament. And yet, extraordinary as it may appear, he at the same Time, by a message declared, that although he was not at Liberty to lay the Order before the House, he was very ready to give all the Information in his Power, to any Committee they might think proper to appoint of the Facts and Grounds upon which it was founded, so far as should be consistent with his Instructions.[5]

5. For the removal of the General Court see *ibid.*, pp. 19–35. Lieut. Gov. Hutchinson's "dark Hint" was about reforming the provincial charter; see the House Committee of Correspondence to BF below, Dec. 17. As early as February, 1769, Hillsborough had suggested to the Cabinet that changes be made in the charter, but had run into opposition from his colleagues and the King. Gipson, *British Empire*, XI, 238, 241. He did not, however, abandon the idea; instead he asked Hutchinson's opinion on what reforms would be advisable in the charter and in colonial administration. The Lieutenant Governor, on the assumption that changes were impending, replied with lengthy recommendations. It was presumably at this time also that William Knox, Hillsborough's under-secretary, drew up specific proposals for submission to Parliament. See Hutchinson's letters in Mass. Archives (State House, Boston), XXV, 441–7;

By such Conduct in the Ministry it appears, that we again may be accused and censured by Parliament, as we have heretofore been, and perhaps suffer the greatest Injury without knowing our Accusers, or the Matters that may be alledged against us.

At the same Time, by an Order of Parliament that the names of Persons giving Intelligence to Ministry which may at any time be laid before Parliament, shall be made secret even to the Members themselves, the greatest Encouragement is given to Persons inimical to the Province, to send home false Relations of Speeches and Proceedings, in publick Assemblies and elsewhere, containing injurious Charges upon Individuals as well as publick Bodies; Some of which have been transmitted home under the Seal of the Province, without the least notice given to those Bodies, or to any but the few in the Secret, to attend and cross examine such Witnesses. And thus even the Parliament itself may be misled into Measures, highly injurious and destructive to the Province, by the Calumny and Detraction of those, who are not and cannot be known, and whose Falsehoods, therefore cannot be detected. So wretched is the State of this Province, not only to be subjected to absolute Instructions given to the Governor to be the Rule of his Administration, whereby some of the most essential Clauses of our Charter vesting in him Powers to be exercised for the Good of the People are totally rescinded, which is in reality a State of Despotism; but also to a Standing Army, which being uncontrouled by any Authority in the Province, must soon tear up the very Foundation of civil Government.

Moreover we have the highest Reason for Complaint that since the late parliamentary Regulations of the Colonies, the Jurisdiction of the Court of Admiralty has been extended to so enormous a Length, as itself to threaten the very Being of the Constitution. By the Statute of 4 Geo. 3: Chap. 15. all Forfeitures and Penalties inflicted by this or any other Act, relating to the Trade and Revenue of the British Colonies and Plantations in America which shall be incurred there, may be prosecuted, sued for and recovered in any Courts of Admiralty in the said Colonies. Thus a single Judge, independent of the People, and in a civil Law Court, is to try these ex-

---

XXVII, 83, 87–8, 98–101; Hist. MSS. Commission, *Fourteenth Report*, App., Pt. X (Dartmouth MSS., vol. II; London, 1895), p. 75. No change was actually made in the charter until the Coercive Acts of 1774.

traordinary Forfeitures and Penalties without a Jury;[6] whereas the same Statute provides, that all Penalties and Forfeitures which shall be incurred in Great Britain, shall be prosecuted, sued for and recovered in any of his majesty's Courts of Record in Westminster or in the Court of Exchequer in Scotland respectively. Here is the most unreasonable and unjust Distinction made between the Subjects in Britain and America, as tho' it were designed to exclude us from the least Share in that Clause of Magna Charta, which has for many Centuries been the noblest Bulwark of the English Liberties, and which cannot be too often repeated. "No Freeman shall be taken, or imprisoned, or deprived of his Freehold or Liberties or free Customs, or be outlaw'd or exiled or any otherwise destroyed nor will we pass upon him nor condemn him but by the Judgment of his Peers or the Law of the Land."

These are some of the insupportable Grievances which this Province has long been labouring under, and which still remain altogether unredressed: For although they have been set forth in the clearest Manner by humble Petitions to the Throne, yet such an Ascendancy over us have the Officers of the Crown here in the Minds of Administration that our Complaints are scarcely heard, our very Petitions are deemed factious, and instead of obtaining any Relief, our Oppressions have been more aggravated, and we have Reason to apprehend will still be increased.

For by the best Intelligence from England we are under strong Apprehensions, that by Virtue of an Act of Parliament of 7. Geo. 3. which empowers his Majesty to appropriate a Part of the Revenue raised in America, for the support of Government and the Administration of Justice in such Colonies where he shall judge it necessary, Administration is determined to bestow large Salaries upon the Attorney General, Judges and Governor of this Province; whereby they will be made not only altogether independent upon the People, but wholly dependent upon the Ministry for their Support. These Appointments will be justly obnoxious to the other Colonies, and tend to beget and keep up a perpetual Discontent among them. For they will deem it unjust as well as unnecessary to be obliged to bear a Part of the Support of Government in this Province, when it is

6. For the complexities of admiralty jurisdiction and procedure in Massachusetts see the many cases in L. Kinvin Wroth and Hiller B. Zobel, eds., *Legal Papers of John Adams* (3 vols., Cambridge, Mass., 1965), II.

now as it always has been amply and honorably supported by the People here. And the making those Officers thus independent will be to introduce into this Province an arbitrary Administration in the State, and even in the Courts of Law: especially if Designs are also meditating to make other very important Alterations in our Charter, by appointing the Council from home, whereby the Executive will be rendered absolute and the Legislative totally ineffectual to any valuable Purpose. The Assembly is in all Reason sufficiently dependent already upon the Crown: One Branch annually for its Being as it is subject to the negative of the Governor and both Branches for every Grant and Appropriation of their money, and also for their whole Defence and Security as he is Captain General and has by Charter the sole military Command within the Province: All civil Officers are either nominated and appointed by him with the Advice and Consent of his Majesty's Council, or if elected they are subject to his negative. And our Laws after being consented to by his Majesty's Governor, are by the first Opportunity from the making thereof to be transmitted to his Majesty for his Approbation or Disallowance. Three years they are subject to the Revision of the Crown Lawyers in Britain, who may always be Strangers to our internal Polity, and sometimes disaffected to us; and at any Time within the three years, his Majesty in his Privy Council may if he thinks proper reject them, and then they become utterly void. Surely the Parliament cannot even wish for greater Checks both upon the Legislative and Executive of a Colony, unless we are to be considered as Bastards and not Sons; a Step further will reduce us to an absolute Subjection.[7] If Administration is resolved to continue such Measures of Severity, the Colonies will in time consider the Mother State as utterly regardless of their Welfare: Repeated Acts of Unkindness on one Side, may by Degrees abate the Warmth of Affection on the other, and a total alienation may succeed to that happy Union, Harmony and Confidence which had before always subsisted, and we sincerely wish may always subsist. If Great Britain instead of treating us as their Fellow Subjects, shall aim at making us their Vassals and Slaves, the Consequence will be, that altho' our Merchants have receded from their non importation

7. The similarity between this discussion of executive authority and Cooper's in his letter to BF below, Nov. 15, suggests that both were in response to BF to Cooper above, June 8.

Agreement, yet the Body of the People will vigorously endeavor to become independent on the Mother Country for their Supplies, and sooner than she may be aware of it, may manufacture for themselves.[8] The Colonies like healthy young Sons, have hitherto been chearfully building up the Parent State, and how far Great Britain will be affected, if they should be rendred even barely useless to her, is an Object which we conceive is at this very Juncture worth the Attention of a British Parliament.

Inclosed are the Proceedings of his Majesty's Council of this Province upon an Affidavit of Mr. Secretary Oliver, which this House apprehend has a Tendency to make a very undue Impression on the Minds of his Majesty's ministers and others respecting the Temper and Disposition of the People, previous to the tragical Transaction of the Town of Boston on the 5th. of March last. You are therefore desired, so to improve them as to prevent such unhappy Consequences from taking Effect.[9]

Your own Acquaintance with this Province, and your well known warm attachment to it, will lead you to exert all your Powers in its Defence: And as the Council have made choice of Mr. Bolland for their Agent, you will no doubt confer with him, and concert such measures as will promote our common Interest. Your Abilities we greatly confide in; but if you shall think it for the Advantage of the Province to consult with and employ Council learned in the Law, the Importance of your Agency, will be a Motive sufficient for us to acquiesce in such Expence on that Account, as your own Judgment shall dictate to you to be necessary. In the name and by order of the House I am with respect your most humble Servant

THOMAS CUSHING Spkr.

8. This point scarcely needed to be made to BF, who had been harping on it for some time in letters to American correspondents.

9. On the two days following the Massacre charges were made and denied, in angry meetings of the Council, that the attack on the troops had been premeditated. Unofficial minutes of the meetings were kept by Andrew Oliver, secretary of the province; he gave a sworn copy to Hutchinson, who sent it to Gov. Bernard in London. When published there, and reprinted in Boston in October, it appeared to be an official report. Oliver was attacked in the Council for misrepresentation and for divulging privileged information. BF seems to have done nothing to "improve" these charges, but Arthur Lee, after Oliver had been promoted to lieutenant governor, vilified Hillsborough in the London press for having appointed such a "perjured traitor." *Sibley's Harvard Graduates*, VII, 403–4.

PS. The House have made Choice of Dr. Lee as their Agent in case of your Death or Absence from Great Britain.[1]

Benjamin Franklin Esqr

Endorsed: No. 1. 1770 Agent To Dr Francklin

To Jane Mecom

ALS: American Philosophical Society

Dear Sister, London, Nov. 7[-9]. 1770

I received your kind Letter of July 6. and was glad to hear (since you chose to return) that you were got so well home. I hope the Hurt you receiv'd will be attended with no bad Consequences.[2] My Arm, that had given me no Uneasiness for several Years, has lately began again to pain me, from a slight Strain, and I am now afraid will continue to do so as long as I live, since it has not mended for some Months past. But as I grow old, being now near 65, it is a Comfort that nothing can pain me long. You had not I hope, any Offence at Philadelphia, that induc'd you to leave it so soon. I must stay here this Winter but hope to be in that dear Place pretty early in the next Summer, being quite uneasy under so long a Banishment from my Country and my Family. I have been for a great part of my Day engag'd abroad in the Bustle of Publick Business: It is time now, that I should return home, spend the Evening with my Friends, and be ready to go chearfully to Bed. My Respects to Dr. Cooper, Love to Cousin Jenny,[3] and believe me ever, Your affectionate Brother B FRANKLIN

I condole with you on the Death of my dear old Friend Mr. Whitefield which I have just heard of.[4]

Nov. 9. –70

Since writing the above I have received yours of Sept. 29. by our Kinsmen, who are safe arrived, and lodge with Mrs. Stevenson.[5]

1. The postscript and previous sentence are in Cushing's hand. For the background of Lee's appointment as alternate agent see above, pp. 257–8.
2. While staying with DF in Philadelphia the previous winter, Jane had fallen down the stone steps to the Franklins' garden; her recovery was slow.
3. The Rev. Samuel Cooper and Jane's daughter, BF's niece.
4. The news traveled fast. The great Methodist, George Whitefield, had died in Newburyport, Mass., on Sept. 30.
5. John Williams and his two nephews; see Jonathan Williams to BF above, Aug. 27.

George Whitefield

We shall endeavour to make their Residence here as agreable to them as possible. Be in no Concern about any Abuses I receive here in the Newspapers. 'Tis the Fashion to roast one another, and I sometimes take a little of that Diversion myself. I inclose you a Newspaper or two which you may show to Dr. Cooper: but if you think you see any thing of mine there, don't let it be publish'd as such; for I am obnoxious enough here already on Account of some Letters I wrote to Philada. I will endeavour to get the Books you desire, but suppose it will be difficult.[6]

From Thomas Foxcroft[7]   ALS: American Philosophical Society

[Philadelphia, Nov. 10, 1770. Encloses a bill of exchange from the Quebec post office for £50 and will send the duplicate by Capt. Osborne.[8]]

From Samuel Cooper   ALS (draft): British Museum

Dear Sir,   Novr. 15. 1770.
    I wrote you the 6. Inst. acknowledging the Receit. of your very obliging Packet of June 8th. and mentioning the Use I have made of your Letter &c among some of the leading Men in our H. of Represent. in whom I could confide. They agreed with me that your Principles were incontestible, your reasoning clear and conclusive, and supported by History and Fact. The King has an undoubted Right to absolve any of his Subjects from their Allegiance to himself; certainly then from their Subjection to Parliament, which was evidently done by our Charters. The Security for every reasonable Advantage we can afford our Fellow Subjects in Britain is, that their Sovereign is our's: That living with them as the superior state he may be suppos'd to have a Predilection for them; that the Consent of a Governor appointed by himself, and removeable at his Pleasure is necessary to constitute a Law; That even these Laws, for I particularly refer to the Massachusetts, the chief Object of Jealousy, and Malice are subject to the Royal Controll by

6. Jane had requested two copies of a pamphlet in her letter above, Sept. 25.
7. John Foxcroft's brother and the Philadelphia postmaster.
8. Peter Osborne, Falconer's successor as the master of the *Pa. Packet*; his sailing was announced in *Pa. Gaz.*, Nov. 29, 1770.

the Advice of a British Council: that the Governor has a Negative upon the Council, not only a Branch of the Legislative, but of that Authority and Influence in other Respects which Negative creates a greater Dependence than the Choice of the Council by the Representatives in Conjunction with themselves: that the Governor has the Appointment of all officers civil and military, (the Advice and consent of the Council having long been reduc'd to a mear Shadow) which creates naturally a great Interest in the lower House, and among the Body of the People in Favor of Prerogative:[9] To all which may be added the natural affection of an infant Colony to the Parent State, unless subdu'd by hard Usage, and the natural Authority deriv'd upon the former by the latter. Whoever takes a View of these Advantages collectively and in all their Extent, as they have in Fact been found to operate, must be convinc'd that had Things been left exactly as they stood before the Stamp Act Britain would have been far from having any just Reason to complain of the Independence of our Constitution. We had indeed scarce any Thing left on the Side of Privilige but the Granting of our own Monies for the Support of Government and the furnishing necessary military Aids to the Crown. This Palladium seems about to leave us; for after all the Complaints made of our Obstinacy and Ungovernableness we are daily paying Taxes not granted by us, but exacted from us for both these Purposes; so that we are in a worse Situation than our fellow Subjects in Ireland——We have an Army quarter'd among us independent of any Supplies to be freely given by us; We have Pensioners not indebted for what they receive to any Grant of our own Parliaments; and this may soon become the Case of our governor, and principal Civil officers: for

9. The procedure to which Cooper is referring was as clumsy as his prose. Members of the lower house were popularly elected each spring. At the opening session of the General Court they and the outgoing members of the Council ("themselves") chose the new Council, subject to the governor's approval. He also had to approve not only bills passed by both houses but also appointments made by the Council. What Cooper is trying to say is that the role of the lower house in choosing the upper is insignificant, that the Council has lost its appointive role ("Influence in other Respects"), and that the governor's resultant control of patronage has subjected the representatives and the people at large to his "prerogative." The central contention in this monstrous sentence, that the governor as agent of the crown already has more than enough power in the colony, echoes one of the points in the instructions to BF from the House of Representatives above, Nov. 6.

already Lord Dunmore has a Warrant upon the American for £2000 sterling per Annum, commencing from the Date of his Commission in January last.[1] I doubt not of your best Endeavors to obtain a Redress of so capital a Grievance, and of all others which we have just reason to complain of. The House I am told have addrest a long Letter to you, in which I suppose they will be enumerated. I send you this by a safe hand, Mr. Isaac Smith, a young Gentleman of good Sense, and literary accomplishments; who goes abroad for the Improvement of his Mind, and the enlarging his Observations.[2] With great Esteem, and the warmest Attachment, I am, dear Sir, Your most obedient and most humble Servant

S. COOPER

Dr Franklin.

Copy to Dr Franklin.

From Thomas Gilpin[3]

Extract: reprinted from "Memoir of Thomas Gilpin," *Pennsylvania Magazine of History and Biography*, XLIX (1925), 314–15.

November 15th [1770]

Politics are now rather at a low ebb: nor do I expect they will revive; it will take some time to restore the public agitation and eradicate the remembrance of what has passed: the cause of injury is yet fresh and like a man that has been prompted to delirium time must be allowed to restore quietude and heal the pain of exertions that have been made. I think the late blunderers here deserve thanks

1. Lord Dunmore, the new governor of New York, had a warrant for his salary on the American Board of Customs Commissioners. In Massachusetts Hutchinson had been receiving a royal salary as chief justice since 1768, and the House of Representatives was beginning to fear that the General Court would lose control over his salary as lieutenant governor; see the House Committee of Correspondence to BF below, Dec. 17.

2. Isaac Smith, Jr. (1749–1829), the son of a member of the Boston merchants' committee to enforce nonimportation, was John Adams' cousin by marriage. The young man graduated from Harvard in 1767, stayed in England until 1784, and later became librarian of Harvard. See above, XVI, 273; Lyman H. Butterfield *et. al.*, eds., *Diary and Autobiography of John Adams* (4 vols., Cambridge, Mass., 1961), IV, 250 n.

3. BF may not have been the recipient: see the headnote to Gilpin's letter of June 1.

from your side the water as nothing could have been more effectual to weaken the measures and destroy the unanimity which prevailed. A scene of intemperate violence has been too much used instead of the cool unyielding firmness which the state of affairs demanded. We have had summonses by ballots, town meetings, hasty resolutions made and then repealed, proclamations and measures carried by clapping, stamping hissing, hallooing &c; in fact too much of that violence which however it denotes the public feeling is inimical to the adoption of those cool measures which the state of the country and the injuries it was exposed to required.[4]

From Jonathan Williams, Sr.

ALS: American Philosophical Society

Boston Novr 16 1770

Since I Clos'd my letter I Received your Verry agreeable favour adviceing of the good fortune of Our Cousin Nancey in her Maraige too Capt. Clark.[5] We Wish them all Happiness We are much Pleased With the Connection. Our Young folks are aquanted With his Late Uncles Famley that Lives at Salem. I Will take Particular Care to have a thrrough Repaire to the Tomb.[6]

I have Given your Account Credit for the Balance of my Lottery Account £38 3s. Sterling.[7] I am your Dutifull Nephew and Humble Servant   JONA WILLIAMS

To Benja Franklin Esqr

Addressed: To / Benjamin Franklin Esqr / at Mrs Stevinson in Cravin Street / London / per Scot

4. Earlier letters from Gilpin and Galloway describe the agitation in Philadelphia over the end of nonimportation and the annual election campaign.

5. Nancy Johnson and Peter Clarke; see above, p. 210 n.

6. The "late uncle," John Clarke, the eldest son of Francis and Deborah Gedney Clarke, had died in 1764; see Henry F. Waters, "The Gedney and Clarke Families of Salem, Mass.," Essex Institute *Hist. Collections*, XVI (1879), 271–2. Neither Williams nor BF, we assume, was interested in Clarke's tomb; the one that Williams was promising to refurbish was probably that of BF's parents, Josiah and Abiah, in the Granary Burying Ground in Boston, for which BF composed the epitaph discussed and printed above, VII, 229–30. Josiah was Grace Williams' grandfather.

7. For the complicated business of Williams' lottery tickets see above, XVI, 178, 211; BF to Smith, Wright & Gray, May 10, and to Williams, June 6, 1770.

From Joseph Priestley

ALS: American Philosophical Society[8]

Dear Sir   Leeds 21 Novr 1770.

I took the liberty to trouble you with a line the last post, and being but just able to finish my letter in time, I recollect a mistake in the catalogue of books wanted, which I beg you would rectify as follows,

Vitelliones Optica best edition 1572
Kepler's Paralipomena in Vitellionem

I also very much want *De la Hire's differens Accidents de la vue*. But I should think it might be got without a public advertisement. I have already collected from that writer as much as will make a considerable section. I cannot well do without *Du Hamel's History of the French Academy*, and tho' it is inserted among books I have got, it is only in the library at Manchester, and I cannot, without great loss of time, and expence, go and study there. Many other books I foolishly inserted in the catalogue of those I had access to, which are only there, particularly the *Petersburg Memoirs* which I must absolutely purchase, tho they will cost me, I believe, above £20. I shall give Johnson orders for them this post. I have not yet got *Boyle's Works*, and I find a tract of his on colours quoted, but I believe it relates to the chymical production of colours. However it is within my subject, but Johnson, tho he has had my order for Shaw's *Boyle* several months, has not yet been able to get it.[9]

8. Parts of the letter, illegible in photocopy, have been silently supplied from the printed version in Robert E. Schofield, ed., *A Scientific Autobiography of Joseph Priestley* (Cambridge, Mass., [1966]), pp. 81–2.

9. Priestley was beginning a comprehensive study of the development of experimental philosophy, for which see his letter to BF above, June 2. The books he wanted from Joseph Johnson, the London bookseller and one of his publishers, were the following: a treatise on optics by the thirteenth-century Polish mathematician Vitello or Witelo, first published in 1535 and reprinted with the translation of a work on the same subject by the Arabian philosopher Alhazen in Friedrich Risner, trans. and ed., *Opticæ thesaurus...* (Basel, 1572); Johann Kepler, *Ad Vitellionem paralipomena* (Frankfurt, 1704); Philippe de la Hire, *Mémoires de mathématique et de physique, contenant...un traité des differens accidens de la vue...* (Paris, 1694); Jean Baptiste du Hamel, *Regiæ scientiarum academiæ historia...* (Paris, 1698); two series of the proceedings of the Russian Academy, *Commentarii Academiæ scientiarum imperialis petropolitanæ* and *Novi commentarii...* (St. Petersburg, 1728–), which eventually came to 34 vols.; and Peter Shaw, ed., *The Philosophical Works of the Honourable Robert Boyle, Esq.; Abridged...* (3 vols., London, 1725).

I have just dispatched the discoveries of Newton and his Contemporaries, and from his time to the present have such a number of *Memoirs, dissertations, tracts,* and *books* on the subject of Light and colours to read, compare, and digest, as, I think, would make any person not practised in the business of arrangement, absolutely despair: Till I had actually taken a list of them, I did not think there had been a tenth or a twentieth part so much upon the subject. And other subjects, I see, will be much times more embarassing than this.

If you be obliged to advertise for the books I think it would be better not to mention my name, but only say *A Person being employed &.* I am, with the greatest respect Dear Sir your friend and Servant

J PRIESTLEY

From John Bartram   ALS: American Philosophical Society

My dear worthy friend   November the 24th 1770
    I have thy Kind letter of August the 26th before me which Comforted me as comming from my dear intimate ould friend. The pamphlet and espetially the picture of my dear Peter was very acceptable, and now I am furnished with four of our worthies Lineus, Franklin Edwards and Collinson (but I want Dr. Fothergill,) to adorn my new stove and lodging room which I have made very Convenient for thair reception alltho I am no picture Enthusiast.[1] Yet I love to looke at the representation of men of inocency integrety ingenuity and Humanity. I can hear nothing this year whether the King continueth his bounty to me or not: William Young Blusters stoutly and publishes it in the news and perticular advertisements all over the countrey that he is Botanist to thair Majesties the King and Queen of Great Britain.[2]
    I have sent according to thy desire a small Box of seeds with a list of them in the Box which I have Consighned to James Freeman

    1. The disappearance of BF's letter of Aug. 26 precludes identifying the pamphlet. The picture of Peter Collinson was doubtless a print of the Gainsborough portrait, which is reproduced as the frontispiece of Norman G. Brett-Jones, *The Life of Peter Collinson...* (London, [1926]). The other Englishman in Bartram's gallery was George Edwards, the ornithologist and F.R.S.
    2. For William Young and his rivalry with Bartram see above, XI, 353 n; Brett-Jones, *op. cit.*, p. 137.

who hath two Boxes to dispose of for me.[3] He lives in the same house where our dear Peter formerly lived. This comes with great love and respect from thy Sincear friend   JOHN BARTRAM

Pray my dear friend squeese out a few lines as often as Convenience will alow to comfort thy ould friend in his new stove room.

Addressed: To / Mr Benjamin Franklin / London / per Mary & Elizabeth / Capt. Sparks

Endorsed: Red Lion Grace Church Street 39

[From Jacques Barbeu-Dubourg]

AL: American Philosophical Society

Monsieur et cher Ami,   A Paris ce 25e. 9bre. 1770

J'ai reçu dabord deux, puis cinq exemplaires de la traduction que vous avez daigné faire faire de mon petit Code,[4] et je ne puis assez vous en remercier. Il est si bien rendu en Anglois qu'on auroit pu facilement en faire passer la version pour un original, et il est imprimé tout au mieux. [La seule] faute bien remarquable mais sans consequence, c'est à la page 7e où il y a [*twelfth*] pour *second*, c'est a dire douzieme pour deuxieme. Je suis tres flaté du suffrage de vos dignes amis, un petit nombre de persones icy l'ont également goûté, mais en general il n'y a pas fait une grande sensation, cela viendra peutetre, et puisqu'on veut m'honorer d'une 2e edition a Londres, je crois que j'en risquerai une aussi à Paris, l'encouragement que vous m'avez donné m'ayant fait faire de nouveaux efforts pour l'ameliorer autant qu'il est en moi. Je l'ai presque tout refondu et étendu de 35 articles jusqu'a 51, comme vous verrez par la copie que j'ai l'honneur de vous envoyer cyjointe, et que je soumets a votre revision.

Si ma respectable Traductrice ne dedaigne pas de s'amuser a faire passer cette addition en votre langue, je vous serai fort obligé de vouloir m'en envoyer quelques exemplaires comme de la 1e edition et si j'osois vous prier d'en faire remettre aussi un a Mademoiselle Pitt soeur du Comte de Chatam, et qui est ou a eté Bour-

3. James Freeman was Dr. Fothergill's nephew; see above, XVI, 250.
4. Polly Stevenson's translation of the writer's *Petit code de la raison humaine.* See BF to Polly above, [before July 10].

siere de la Princesse de Galles. Cette Demoiselle m'a honoré de ses bontés et de sa confiance, surtout lors [de] son dernier sejour en france, et j'en ai encore eu des temoignages signa[lés] depuis [son] retour en Angleterre; mais j'ai eté si confus d'une lettre tres m[auss]ade qu'on me poussa à lui ecrire vers le commencement de la derniere guerre que je n'ai plus osé cultiver une connoissance si precieuse à tant de titres. Je ne sais si vous la connoissez personellement mais je doute fort que son frere puisse avoir plus d'esprit.[5]

A l'egard de mes recherches sur nos Pairs et nos Magistrats, comme on auroit eu de la peine à en faire entrer l'edition de chez vous icy, je l'ai envoyée en endroit où les Difficultes seront moindres, quoique trop grandes encore; et cela apres avoir vainement sollicité la permission de le faire imprimer icy. Je ne vous importunerai donc point à ce sujet, je vous prierai seulement d'en agréer un exemplaire.

Mais je me reserve à mettre votre bienveillance à une autre épreuve; j'ai travaillé à des momens perdus à un digeste de l'humanité, ou commentaire du Code, sous le nom de M. Jone de Philadelphie, il sera ecrit un peu plus longuement et plus negligemment, mais j'espere qu'il pourra encore interesser par l'ordre et le developement des matieres,[6] et j'ai bien a coeur de pouvoir vous l'envoyer avant votre depart dont la seule pensée me fait fremir, et gemir de ne pouvoir vous suivre en un pays, où, graces a vous principalement, on a bientôt secoué tous les prejugés de notre vieil hemisphere, et où nos Neveux pourroient bien voir un jour le siege de l'empire Britannique et le foyer de la raison universelle.

5. The flighty and eccentric Ann Pitt had been maid of honor to Queen Caroline, the wife of George II, and then after the death of the Prince of Wales had been briefly Keeper of the Privy Purse for the Dowager Princess, George III's mother. This position she lost because of her involvement in court intrigue, and she spent a short exile in France, where she presumably met Barbeu-Dubourg; after her return the favor of Lord Bute secured her a pension from George III. She had, according to Horace Walpole, "excellent parts and strong passions." Matthew Hodgart, ed., *Horace Walpole: Memoirs and Portraits* (New York, [1963]), pp. 121–2.

6. Barbeu-Dubourg's work on the peerage continued to occupy him for months to come, but it was so badly mauled by the censor that he never published it in the form he had intended. His "digeste de l'humanité" was a revision and expansion of his *Petit code*. See his letter to BF below, May 27, 1771, and Alfred O. Aldridge, "Jacques Barbeu-Dubourg...," APS *Proc.*, XCV (1951), 342.

Sans vanité, je vous dirai par occasion qu'il y a icy 2 ou 3 sorbonistes qui me traitent souvent de demi-Quaker, quoique je rende le pain beni a mon tour que je tapisse le devant de ma porte a la fete Dieu, et que j'ôte mon chapeau presqu'a tous pretres et moines.

On nous flatte que nous n'aurons point de guerre avec vous, je vous proteste que j'en suis fort aise. Louis 14 reconnut en mourant qu'il avoit trop aimé la guerre, pour moi, si peu qu'on l'aime, je trouve toujours que c'est trop.

Je vous rens graces du bon accueil que vous avez fait a notre ami M. frey,[7] il n'a pas repassé par Paris, mais il m'a donné de ses nouvelles, et il regrette beaucoup de n'avoir pu sejourner plus longtems a Londres; et moi je suis desolé de ne pouvoir pas y faire le moindre voyage, soyez sûr qu'il faut que les entraves qui me retiennent soient bien fortes apres votre gracieuse invitation à me procurer la facilité de loger a portée de vous, et de jouir à toute heure d'un commerce dont je sens tout le prix. Ma femme vous assure qu'il ne seroit pas moins delicieux pour elle, quoiqu'ell'ait bien de la peine a revenir de l'eloignement qu'on lui a inspiré pour tout ce qui est retranché de la s[ainte?] communion Romaine.

A propos de cela, nous avons en france une petite innovation qui peut s'etendre loin; c'est la liberté de conscience dans une villotte naissante; je crois qu'on en est redevable au Duc de Choiseul; il ne sera pas toujours en place, mais si comme je l'espere, on se trouve bien de cet essay, et que la raison continue a faire des progrès, cet arrangement sera difficile à renverser grands et petite reclameroient de toutes leurs forces. Je joins icy un extrait de lettre à ce sujet.

From Thomas Life[8]   AL: American Philosophical Society

30th Novr. 1770.

Mr. Life presents his Complements to Dr. Franklin and acquaints him that the Georgia Acts are referred to Mr. Jackson,[9] that Mr.

7. Presumably the Capt. Frey mentioned in BF to LeRoy above, Oct. 2.

8. The London lawyer and agent for Connecticut; see above, x, 369 n.

9. BF had consulted with Richard Jackson, counsel for the Board of Trade, about the Georgia act for governing slaves; see BF's comment on the Assembly's instructions to him above, May 10. Life was pursuing that matter and others raised in the instructions.

Life has told Mr. Jacksons Clerk that Mr. Life wishes to have an Attendance on Mr. Jackson before he makes his Report, that Mr. Life ever since he received the Papers, has been very busy in some Conveyancy that must be executed by some officers in the Navy, who are going abroad, but hopes to be more at leisure in a Week or Ten Days, and will in the meantime wait on Mr. Jackson and get an Appointment for an Attendance on him and acquaint Dr. Franklin of it.

Addressed: To / Dr. Franklin at Mrs / Stevensons in / Craven Street

To Deborah Franklin   ALS: American Philosophical Society

[November, 1770[1]]
This is just to let you know I am well, but so busy that I cannot now write more than to acknowledge the Receipt of your kind Letter of Oct. 14. with Sally's and Mr. Bache's, which I shall answer per next Opportunity. Thanks for the Cranberrys. I am as ever Your affectionate Husband   B FRANKLIN
Endorsed: D Franklin

From Joseph Smith   ALS: American Philosophical Society

Respected Friend   Burlington December 8. 1770
    Thy several favours of the 19th of March 10th. and 12th. April and 11th of June have been duly received and communicated to the Committee of Correspondence and by them laid before the House of Assembly at a late sessions at Amboy where they gave very general satisfaction.
    In answer to that part of thy Letter of 19th March respecting Sherwoods Accounts I may inform thee it has been determin'd by the House not to allow him the Ballance he mentions to be due to him, it was apprehended there was a considerable Ballance in his

1. The letters that BF is acknowledging were carried by Capt. Falconer, who arrived in late November: *Lloyd's Evening Post*, Nov. 28–30, 1770.

hands before his Accounts appear'd, which it was said were extravagant the services considered.[2]

In thy Letter of 12 April thee mentions having mov'd "for their Lordships favourable Report on the Act for Septennial Assemblys and that for giving Representatives to the Countys of Morris Cumberland and Sussex which they were pleas'd to say should be taken into speedy Consideration." and in thy next that of 11 June after mentioning the Repeal of the Paper Money Bill and the Secaucus Law thee says "but the others have received his Majestys Royal Assent." from which it was imagin'd by some that the two former Acts were allow'd of by the King, but the Governor not recieving any intelligence of it made it doubtful, the Committee of Correspondence would be glad to be inform'd respecting this matter in thy next.[3] No particular Business of the Province that I know of make it at this time necessary for any Directions from the Committee of Correspondence respecting thy Conduct as Agent, the Laws pass'd at the late Session together with the Votes of the House I shall send thee as soon as they are printed when if any Directions should be necessary the Committee of Correspondence will without doubt give them.

I am much Obliged to thee for Gov. Pownal's Speech &ca.[4] thee was so kind as to send and am Very Respectfully Thy Friend

JOS: SMITH

Benjan. Franklin Esqr.

Endorsed: New Jersey Jos. Smith Dec. 8. 1770 Recd Feb. 5. 1771 via Bristol

2. BF's letter of March 19 has disappeared. Joseph Sherwood, a London Quaker and lawyer, had been New Jersey agent, 1760–66: above, XIII, 498; XIV, 217 n.

3. The Board of Trade does not appear to have acted at all until July. Its minutes are almost as uninformative as its procedure was dilatory, but the only act approved, as far as we can discover, was that for representatives from the three counties; consideration of the act for septennial assemblies was postponed. *Board of Trade Jour.*, 1768–75, pp. 203–4. On Dec. 12, 14, and 19 the Board discussed with Jackson and eventually took action on some New Jersey laws (*ibid.*, pp. 219–20), but what laws and what action its minutes do not reveal.

4. See BF to Smith above, April 12.

From Benjamin Gale[5]   ALS: American Philosophical Society

Honored and Dear Sir   Killingworth 10th Decr 1770

Your Favor per Mr. Bayard,[6] dated 10th Aprill Last, Inclosing a Gold Medal granted me by the Society of Arts, for an Improvement on the Drill plow,[7] I duely receivd, the 10th July, the receipt of which, (with my gratefull returns of Thanks for Your Care in transmitting the same) I should before this time have Acknowledged, but have been prevented by frequent Interruptions of Health, which (through divine Goodness) is again in great Measure Confirm'd.

I am likewise duely sensible of my Obligations to return my most gratefull Acknowledgments to the Society, for the Honour they have been pleas'd to Confer upon me, and Sincerely Wish, my Abilities were Equal to my most Ardent desire, to promote the Laudible designs for which they Incorporated, a Neglect of which, is not from an Insensibility of my Obligations, but from my being Unacquainted, to whom they may with propriety be directed.

I Was Apprized of the Death of Dr. Templeman by the Publick Papers, but never could Learn (although I Carefully Attended to know,) who was elected by the Society to Succeed him. Neither has it been in my power to get sight of any of the late Books of Premiums by which I could attain that Knowledge,[8] which is the

5. For Dr. Gale and his many scientific and political interests see above, XI, 183 n, where the wrong date is given for his receiving the medal mentioned below.

6. Col. William Bayard, the prominent New York merchant (above, XV, 125), had returned from trying to establish in England his claim to some land in Secaucus, N.J.: Bayard to WF, Oct. 18, 1768, APS.

7. Before his death in 1763 the Rev. Jared Eliot, Gale's father-in-law, had worked on an improved plow with Benoni Hillyer, or Hilliard, a wheelwright of Killingworth, Conn., who may well have been the "mechanic" mentioned below. For Eliot's contribution see the fifth essay in Harry J. Carman and Rexford G. Tugwell, eds., *Essays upon Field Husbandry...by Jared Eliot* (New York, 1935). Gale's plow may have been Eliot's (whose executor he was) or may have included improvements of his own. In any case Hillyer subsequently disputed his claim to the invention in an unsuccessful damage suit: George E. Groce, Jr., "Benjamin Gale," *New England Quarterly*, X (1937), 708.

8. Peter Templeman, the secretary of the Society (above, IX, 322 n), died in 1769 and was succeeded by Samuel More. The book of premiums was the Society's annual announcement of its awards.

only reason I do not at this time make proper Acknowledgments, for which neglect when known, I hope they will be kind enough to Excuse.

My Last was from Dr. Templeman, Dated 17 July 1766, requesting a Model of our Drill plough, and a specimen of Sarsaparilla, the Growth of this Colony, both which I transmitted, together with a Model of a Hand Drill, for planting Cabbages and Turnips at a Certain Distance in the Same Line, which was presented to the Society by the Mechanic, who was the principal Contriver of the several Movements of our Drill, for throwing Manure Into the Same Channels with the Wheat, for its first Nourishment and Growth, but Remaind wholly Unacquainted, whether they had ever receivd them, or whether any of them had met with the Approbation of the Society, Untill the Receipt of Your Letter Inclosing the Medal.

I likewise at the Same time Sent a Specimen of White Iron Oar, and should have been Glad to have known Mr. Horns Sentiments of its Quality.[9] Conclude it is the Only one known of the Kind In America.

As I well know You take pleasure in the Prosperity of the Colonies, which if properly Encouraged will add a Certain Lusture to the Throne, Afford Commerce to the Merchants, and Employment to the Manufacturers of Great Brittain, I can with Pleasure Acquaint You, That several Gentlemen in this Colony, are Engagd to promote the Culture of Mulberry Trees, in Nurseries from the Seed, in Order for to Set forward the Culture of Silk. But as You are well Acquainted with this Country, and know its Poverty, And that nothing will Stimulate the lower Class of People, but a prospect of Immediate profits, by which their Families may be Cloathed and fed, and that frequently those who have Affluent Fortunes, and Can Afford to Expend Mony, without Immediate returns of profit, are prevented carrying such things into Execution, either from Inattention to the Importance of such an Undertaking, or diverted by their several peculiar Amusements, and that many who have a Turn of mind that way, are discouraged by the Tedious process of raising

9. Gale was again following his father-in-law, who had also been interested in making iron from the local ores: Henry H. Pierce, *Colonial Killingworth*... (Clinton, Conn., 1961), p. 7. The sample of ore was probably the white-iron pyrites found in Haddam, Conn. Henry Horne had had an article on sand iron in *Phil. Trans.*, LIII (1763), 48–61.

the Trees from the seed, who would Gladly purchase them if to be sold, fit to be transplanted into Feilds for Growth and Immediately set about the Culture of Silk, wherefore I have frequently thought, had the Society given a Premium for the Cultivation of Mulberry Trees, In Nursiries from the Seed, fit to be Transplanted——Another Premium for the Trees when Transplanted Into Feilds, Well secured by Fence, it would have had a more Extensive and Effectual Influence, as when the Trees are once Transplanted, and Afford Nourishment for the Culture of Silk, their own Interest to Improve them for that purpose would be a Sufficient Stimulus for that End.[1]

In this Colony the Culture of All kind of trees in Nurseries from the Seed, is very much left to Youth Under Age, Apprentices &c, in order to make a private purse to themselves, and on that Account much Neglected by the Farmer; if there is any thing In this Suggestion I make no doubt of Your Influence to promote it. I may not Add least I take up too much of your Time but that I am with great Truth and Regard Sir Your Most Oblidged and Most Humble Servant   BENJA GALE

To Dr. B Franklin F.R.S.

From Noble Wimberly Jones

ALS: American Philosophical Society

Dear Sir   Savannah 13 Decr 1770

By Capt. Thomas Hall I did myself the pleasure of writing you and then inclosed two Bils of Exchange in part to recompence your kindness and discharge the ammount of the Mace and Gouns for which you have Sir the sincere and greatful thanks of the Assembly.[2] I inclose the second of each of the Bills of same tenor and date which wish safe. I have now the pleasure to acquaint that an Ordinance Reappointing you Agent for another year lies for a Third reading to morrow morning,[3] and that on all occasions the highest

1. For the Society's bounty on silk production, and its impact on Connecticut, see above, X, 321 n. Here too Gale was continuing his father-in-law's work: the sixth essay in Eliot's book, cited above, urged the planting of mulberry trees.

2. See Jones to BF above, Oct. 9.

3. The Commons House, after the earlier lapse of BF's legal appointment, was attempting to be forehanded for the year 1771–72. The attempt failed: the

approbation of your conduct is apparant. We have no news that can recollect worth Notice beg leave therefore to conclude and subscribe myself Sir Your Very Sincere and Obedient Servant

N W JONES

To Benj. Franklin Esqr.

From Noble Wimberly Jones

ALS: American Philosophical Society

Dear Sir   13th. December 1770

Convinced of your good inclinations to every species of mankind, emboldens me to trust you'l excuse my thus troubling you. Mr. Cornelius Winter the gentleman by whom you'l receive this has been employ'd on the Estate of the late worthy Rector of this Parish by the Trustees of the said Estate as Instructor &c to the Negroes thereon agreable to the Will of the deceased, but as the intention thereof cannot be fully carried into execution but by a person in Holy Orders, and this gentlemen having that in veiw sometime and being well esteem'd here, he now comes in hopes of obtaining that end, and he thereby rendered more useful to the community, in case he succeeds he intends returning as quick as posible.[4] If without intruding too much on your valluable time and

---

ordinance had not passed when the legislature was dissolved in February, 1771; it was reintroduced in the next Assembly in April, but on the day that that too was dissolved. Candler, ed., *Ga. Col. Recs.*, XV, 251, 260, 313; XVII, 623–4.

4. The rector was Bartholomew Zouberbuhler, the son of the pastor of the Swiss colony in Purysburg, S.C. The young man was educated in Charleston, received Anglican orders in 1745, and obtained from the Georgia trustees the parish in Savannah. Before his death in 1766 he had built a strong congregation, accumulated a handsome fortune, and owned a plantation of some size. In his will, of which Noble Wimberly Jones was a trustee, he made provision for employing a suitable person to teach his slaves Christianity on Anglican principles.

Cornelius Winter (1742–1808) then entered the story. He was a London orphan, and spent some time in the workhouse before George Whitefield converted him and turned him into an itinerant preacher. In 1769 he went to Georgia with Whitefield, who persuaded him to apply for the position created by Zouberbuhler's will. Winter was accepted and spent a year on the plantation, then decided to return to London for Anglican ordination. This was sub-

goodness you can be of service to Mr. Winter in effecting this desireable purpose it will be greatfully acknowledged among the many other obligations your kindness has laid me under. I remain with the most sincere Respect Sir Your Most Obliged and Very humble Servant   N W JONES.

To Dr Franklin

Addressed: To / Benjamin Franklin Esqr / Agent for the Province of Georgia / in / London / per the Britannia / Captn. Deane / Q:D:C

Endorsed: Letter from N W Jones Esqr Speaker of the Georgia Assembly to B Franklin, dated Decr. 13. 1770 Recommending Mr Winter.

From Thomas Crowley⁵ ALS: American Philosophical Society

Worthy Friend   Gr[ace] Ch[urch] Street: 17 dec 1770
  On Wednesday last when I scribled a few Lines to accompany the Return of one of the Pamphlets which you was kind enough to Lend me I was then about mounting my Horse, then waiting for me, in Company with a Friend, to Ride about twenty Miles to attend the Funeral of an Intimate Friend, who died suddenly a few Days before; I had not then lookd into the other, now Returnd; The Merit of This appears to me very different from that first so Returnd; I find Many of J Otis sentiments exactly simalar to my Own.⁶ I never saw his Performance before, but I like it in general

---

sequently refused him because of his association with Whitefield, and he never returned to Georgia. Edgar L. Pennington, "The Reverend Bartholomew Zouberbuhler," *Ga. Hist. Quarterly,* XVIII (1934), 354–63; William Jay, "Memoirs of the late Rev. Cornelius Winter," *Standard Works of the Rev. William Jay...* (3 vols., Baltimore, 1842), III, pt. 2, pp. [9]–12, 25–6, 31–40; Luke Tyerman, *The Life of the Rev. George Whitefield...* (2 vols., London, 1876–77), II, 346, 508–9, 573.

5. The Quaker merchant and proponent of imperial union, for whom see above, XIII, 121 n; XV, 238–41.

6. Crowley was presumably referring to two of James Otis' three pamphlets, all of which had been reprinted in London: *The Rights of the British Colonies Asserted and Proved...* (Boston, 1764); *A Vindication of the British Colonies* (Boston, 1765); and *Considerations on Behalf of the Colonists...* (Boston, 1765).

so well I think it highly Deserves another Edition; and If any should Ensue I will take off a dozen, or two, of them, to give away: I am not a little affected in the Considerations a Man of so just sentiments should have met with so much oppression; and That the observation made by Solomon, apropos, has been so unhappily Verifyd in him; I do heartily wish the fix'd Recovery of his Health.[7] And have sent one of the Pamphlets on Representation to a Friend at Boston to deliver to him mine own also to accompany.[8] I am very respectfully Your sincere well wishing Friend   THOS CROWLEY

Endorsed: To Dr. Franklin

From the Massachusetts House of Representatives Committee of Correspondence   LS: Maine Historical Society

Sir,   Boston Decembr. 17th. 1770

The House of Representatives of this Province after appointing you their Agent at the Court of Great Britain, directed us to correspond with you in the Recess of the Court upon matters that concern the Interest of the Province. In general there is nothing that will more promote the true Interest of this Province as well as Great Britain herself than a happy Settlement of the Disputes that have too long subsisted between the Mother Country and the Colonies. These are justly tenacious of their constitutional and natural Rights, and will never willingly part with them and it certainly can never be for the Advantage of the Nation to force them away. Great Britain can lose nothing that she ought to retain, by restoring the Colonies to the State they were in, before the passing the obnoxious

7. John Robinson, a customs officer, had injured Otis in a brawl in a coffee house in 1769; the injury accentuated Otis' mental unbalance, and he withdrew from politics. *DAB*. The Biblical reference is probably to Prov. 3: 11–12.

8. The idea of American M.P.s was discussed in so many pamphlets that the present to Otis cannot be identified. Crowley's own plan for imperial union included representatives from Ireland, Canada, the thirteen colonies, and the West Indies; two MS versions, dated Nov. 17 and Dec. 10, 1770, are in the Franklin Papers in the APS, and the latter is endorsed by Crowley, "Be pleased to send to the Assembly of Massachusetts Bay...." He does not appear to have published this plan until it was included in his *Letters and Dissertations on Various Subjects...* (London, [1776]), pp. 137–44; he presumably sent Otis a MS copy, and furnished BF with another.

Stamp-Act, and we are persuaded that if that is done they will no further contend. This we think it necessary early to inform you of as *our own* Opinion, because we have Reason to think that there are Persons on both Sides the Atlantic whose Interest it may be to keep alive a Spirit of Discord, who are continually insinuating to Men in Power that such a Concession on the Part of Great Britain would only serve to increase our Claims, and there would be no End of them, which we believe and may even venture to assure you is without the least Colour of Foundation in Truth.

The House had during two Sessions contended with the Lieutenant Governor concerning the Exercise of a Right to call and continue the Assembly out of the Town House in Boston. The Proceedings of the two Houses and the messages that passed between the Lieut[enant] G[overnor] and them are partly contained in the enclosed Pamphlet: the Remainder is now in the Press, which we shall send to you as soon as it is printed. The House was prevailed upon at the third Session to proceed to the publick Business principally from the necessity of attending to the Affairs of the Province on the other Side the Water; his Honor having informed them in his Speech at the opening of the Session that the State of this Government would be laid before Parliament at the Winter Session, and some of the Members having received good Intelligence that Administration was meditating some fatal Alteration in our Charter.[9] In the Course of Business a Grant was made to the Lieutenant Governor for his Support equal to what had ever been before made, and at the Rate of Five Hundred Pounds Sterling per annum nearly, and a Bill was passed for the Purpose which went thro' both Houses, but his Honor did not think fit to give his Assent to it. The House had thought it proper to revive the ancient Stile in the enacting Clause of their Bills, that is, by averring therein that they were enacted by the three Branches *in General Court assembled*, which Words, "*in* General Court assembled," had been omitted for near thirty years. The messages on this Subject you have in the inclosed

9. For the removal of the General Court from Boston, and the threat that Parliament might alter the provincial charter, see the House's Instructions to BF above, Nov. 6. The pamphlet sent BF was *The Proceedings of the Council, and of the House of Representatives . . . Relative to the Convening, Holding and Keeping the General Assembly at Harvard-College in Cambridge . . .* (Boston, 1770). The "remainder," with nearly the same title but prefaced by *A Continuation of*, contained the protests by the House.

Papers.[1] We cannot but observe upon this and other like Occasions, that there seems to be a Determination to have this Province, and perhaps all the Colonies governed by the mere Force of Instructions, which we conceive in no other Light than as setting up an absolute despotic Power, an Attempt to which can never tend to conciliate the Affection of the Colonies. The Bill for his Honor's Support was delayed in the House for some Days by the difference of Sentiments between the Governor and the House on the Importance of the Words in Dispute. Whether his Honour's refusing to sign the Bill was owing to its not being the first Bill laid before him, which we can hardly believe, or to his expecting from another Quarter a more ample Subsistance than this Province has ever provided for their Governors, or to whatever other Course, perhaps may be better ascertained by you than by us.

There is a Circumstance lately arisen here, which had it not been noticed by the Lt. Governor in Council, we should not have thought worth our while to have mentioned. After a State of perfect Peace in this Town during the late Trials of Preston and the Soldiers, some imprudent Person [*line missing*] the minds of People against the Judges of the Courts. It was early taken down, perhaps by the first Person who saw it. A Proclamation *immediately* within a few Hours was issued, and a Reward of One Hundred Pounds offered for a Discovery. Our Enemies who have an excellent Talent at Representation may probably set forth what in all Likelyhood was the Act of a single indiscreet Person, as a Combination of seditious Persons, and an Extract from Otway's Venice preserved (which the Paper is said to contain) may be construed Treason.[2]

1. The restored phrase, which touched off the quarrel, was designed to assert that the determination of public salaries rested with the Governor, Council, and House jointly. The messages on the subject were doubtless those reprinted in [Alden Bradford, ed.,] *Speeches of the Governors of Massachusetts, from 1765 to 1775; and the Answers of the House of Representatives* . . . (Boston, 1818), pp. 278–86, 290–3.

2. On the night of Dec. 12, two days after the last trial of those accused in the Massacre, a handbill threatening the judges was displayed on the Town House. The threat, against leaders who attempt to enslave the people, consisted of mangled quotations from the first scene of Thomas Otway's *Venice Preserv'd; or, a Plot Discover'd: a Tragedy* (London, 1682). The text of the handbill is in Catharine B. Mayo, "Additions to Thomas Hutchinson's 'History of Massachusetts Bay,'" American Antiquarian Soc. Procs., LXIX (1950), 33.

We shall constantly advise you of every thing material which occurs here, and shall be happy in your communicating to us what you may think worth Notice, relating to the Affairs of this Province on your Side the Water. We are with strict Truth Sir your most humble Servants, THOMAS CUSHING
SAML ADAMS
JOHN HANCOCK
JOHN ADAMS

Benjamin Franklin Esqr

From Richard Price: On the Effect of the Aberration of Light on the Time of a Transit of Venus over the Sun

Printed in the Royal Society, *Philosophical Transactions*, LX (for 1770; London, 1771), 536–9.

Dear Sir, [Before December 20, 1770.[3]]

I Cannot doubt but that the observation made by your ingenious friend in the paper you sent me is right.[4] The aberration of Venus must, I think, affect the phases of a transit, by retarding them, and not by accelerating them. This retardation is $55\frac{1}{2}''$; for that is the time nearly which Venus, during a transit, takes to move over $3''.7$. This, however, is by no means the whole retardation of a transit occasioned by aberration. There is a retardation arising from the aberration of the Sun, as well as from that of Venus. The aberration of the Sun, it is well known, lessens its longitude about $20''$. and the aberration of Venus, agreeably to your friend's demonstration, increases its longitude at the time of a transit $3''.7$. Venus, therefore, and the Sun, at the instant of the true beginning of a transit, must be separated from one another by aberration $23''.7$; and, since Venus then moves nearly at the rate of $4'$ in a hour, it will move over $23''.7$ in $5':55''$. And consequently, from the instant of the *real* beginning of a transit, $5':55''$ must elapse before it can begin *apparently*.

It may, I know, be objected here, that the aberration of the Sun ought not to be taken into consideration, because the calculations from the solar tables give the apparent places of the Sun, or its

---

3. When the letter was read before the Royal Society.
4. The friend was John Winthrop; see above, XVI, 195–8, and Winthrop to BF, Oct. 26, 1770.

longitude with the effect of abberation included, and therefore always about 20″ too little. But from this observation a conclusion will follow very different from that which the objection supposes. The retardation I have mentioned is properly the time that the calculated phases of a transit of Venus will precede the apparent phases, supposing the tables from which the calculation is made to give the true places of the Sun.

If they give the apparent places of the Sun, this retardation, instead of being lessened, will be considerably increased. In order to prove this, I must desire it may be remembered, that in deducing by trigonometrical operations the geocentric places of a planet from the heliocentric, the Earth is supposed to be in that point of the ecliptic which is exactly opposite to, or 180° from the place of the sun, and that this supposition is just only when the sun's true place is taken. In reality, the Earth is always about 20″ more forward in its orbit than the point opposite to the Sun's apparent place; and in consequence of this it will happen, that in calculating a transit of Venus from tables which give the Sun's apparent places, a greater difference will arise between the calculated and the observed times than if the tables had given the Sun's true places.

For, let S be the Sun, T the Earth, V Venus. Were there no aberration of light, the Sun would be always seen in its true place, or in the direction TS. But, in reality, in consequence of aberration, it will be seen 20″ less advanced in the ecliptic, or in the direction Ts, supposing STs to be an angle of 20″. Now a calculation from tables giving the true places of the Sun, would fix the moment of a conjunction, to the time that Venus gets to TS; but this, though the time of the true conjunction, would not be the time of the observed conjunction; for the Sun being then really seen in the direction Ts, Venus, after getting to TS, must move 20″, or from a to c, before the apparent conjunction can take place.

But if the calculations are made from the apparent places of the Sun, the conjunction will be fixt to the time Venus gets to t S, or a line drawn through S parallel to s T, for in this case t will be the point of the ecliptic opposite to the apparent place of the Sun, and the longitude of the sun seen from t will be 20″ less than its true longitude, and therefore the same with its apparent longitude. But the Earth being then really at T, Venus will, at the calculated time of a conjunction, be observed at a distance from the Sun equal to the angle L T *s*. This angle, supposing V T 277, and V S 723, may be easily found to be 72″.2. Add to this 3″.7, the proper aberration of Venus at the time of a transit, removing it more towards E, and the whole visible distance of Venus from the Sun's center at the calculated moment of a conjunction, will be 75″.9, over which it will move in 19 minutes of time. And this, consequently, will be the retardation of the phases of a transit of Venus occasioned by aberration, on the supposition, that in calculating, the Sun's apparent, and not his true place is taken.

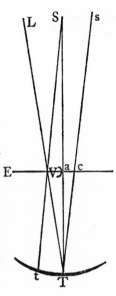

I believe these observations have not been attended to by astronomers; and therefore I am the more desirous of communicating them to you. I am, Dear Sir, with much respect, your obliged humble servant,

RICHARD PRICE.

P.S. In a former letter which I sent you, I gave, by mistake, the error occasioned by aberration less than I have now given it.[5] The discovery of this mistake I owe to the kind assistance and correction with which Mr. Maskelyne, the astronomer royal, has been pleased to favor me.

I have, for the sake of more distinctness and clearness, supposed Venus to move in the plane of the ecliptic. Some differences will arise from the inclination of the path of Venus to the ecliptic, and also from taking the aberration of the Sun, and the proportion of Venus's distance from the Earth to her distance from the Sun, exactly as they really are at the time of a transit. Thus, at the time of the last transit of Venus, supposing light to come from the Sun to the Earth in 8′.2, the aberration of the Sun was 19″.8. The distance of Venus from the Earth was to its distance from the Sun as 290 to 726, and therefore the retardation 18′:16″.

Mr. Canton has observed, that in the *Con. des Temp*, Mr. De la Lande makes the effect of aberration at the inferior conjunction of

5. Probably an earlier draft, now lost; see above, p. 264 n.

Venus and Mercury to be an augmentation of their longitudes. Indeed, Mr. Bliss himself observes this; and yet, through an oversight, makes the effect as to time to be an acceleration. Vid. Phil. Trans. Vol. LII. p. 249.[6]

To Thomas Cushing[7]

Reprinted from Jared Sparks, ed., *The Works of Benjamin Franklin...* (10 vols., Boston, 1836–40) VII, 492–4.

In his letter to Samuel Cooper six months before, Franklin had put more emphasis on loyalty to the King than was perhaps welcome to leaders of the Massachusetts House. During the debate over the agency he had been criticized for being, as a postal official and the father of a colonial governor, too much the servant of the King to represent a province that had suffered by the acts of the King's soldiers, customs officers, and governors. Although the House chose Franklin as agent, both it and Cooper pointed out to him that the crown and ministry already exercised too much control of provincial government.[8] He turned in the letter below from speaking of loyalty to the throne to another point, the contractual relationship between the monarch and the colonies. The attempt to alter that relationship by amending the Massachusetts charter in Parliament he considered unconstitutional, but he was certainly justified in his modest denial that he had played much of a part in quashing the move. For his argument against it was one that Parliament, as he himself had said, "would deem little less than Treason."[9]

Sir,   London, 24 December, 1770.

Your favor of October 31st came to hand a few days since, with the vote of the House of Representatives appointing me their agent here, which, as it was unsolicited on my part, I esteem the greater

6. John Canton was citing the French astronomer, Joseph Jérome le Français de Lalande (1732–1809), who was editor of the almanac *Connaissance des temps.* Nathaniel Bliss's letter on the first transit of Venus appeared in 1762.

7. Here and later BF was replying to a committee's public communications by what was in form a private letter. This practice tended to blur the distinction between statements that he intended to be confidential and those that he intended to be publicized.

8. See the House to BF above, Nov. 6, and Cooper to BF, Nov. 15.

9. To Cooper above, June 8.

honor; and shall be very happy, if I can, in that capacity, render my country any acceptable service.

I have also just received your letter, of November 6th, containing an account of the state and circumstances of the province, and the grievances it labors under, with sundry depositions and other papers. Another of November 17th, with a pamphlet, entitled, the "Proceedings of Council," &c.; another of November 23d, containing an order on Mr. DeBerdt for papers.[1] I can at present only say, that I shall immediately endeavour to make myself master of the business committed to my care, that so, when the Parliament and public boards, which are now adjourned for a month, shall meet again, I may be ready to proceed, in such manner, as, on conferring with Mr. Bolan,[2] shall appear advisable for obtaining redress of the grievances so justly complained of.

I have the pleasure to acquaint you, from good authority, that the project formed by the enemies of the province, for bringing into Parliament a bill to abridge our charter rights, though at first it received some countenance, and great pains were taken to recommend it, is now laid aside. I do not presume to suppose, that the opposition I gave to it, (by showing the imprudence of the measure, and declaring openly my opinion on all occasions, that, the charter being a compact between the King and the people of the colony who were *out of the realm* of Great Britain, there existed nowhere on earth a power to alter it, while its terms were complied with, without the consent *of* BOTH *the contracting parties*,) had any weight on the occasion. I rather think, that a disposition prevails of late to be on good terms with the colonies, especially as we seem to be on the eve of a war with Spain;[3] and that, in consequence of that disposition, which I hope we shall cultivate, more attention has been paid to the sober advice of our friends, and less to the virulent instigations of our enemies.

I beg you will present my dutiful respects to the House of Repre-

1. See above for Cushing's letter of Oct. 31 and the instructions of the House, Nov. 6. The other communications are missing. The pamphlet sent on Nov. 17 dealt with the Council's interrogation of Oliver, for which see *ibid.* The fourth letter doubtless empowered BF to take custody of the provincial documents that had been in the hands of the former agent, Dennys DeBerdt, at his death.

2. William Bollan, the agent for the Massachusetts Council.

3. The Falkland Island crisis was almost over; see above, p. 243 n.

sentatives, and assure them of my most faithful endeavours in their service. With great esteem and regard, I have the honor to be, &c.

B. FRANKLIN.

From Anthony Tissington[4]

ALS: American Philosophical Society

Dear Sir   Alfreton 29th. Decr 1770.

By this Letter my Wife sends best Compliments to you and Mrs. Stevenson, and by this days Carrier (Clarks Wagon which will be at the Ax in Aldermanbury[5] next Saturday) a Turkey which she hopes will come to hand Sweet and good.

In July I left you in London; in August went into Scotland; in September into South Wales to Swansey; have been upon the move most of the time since; so that I am but Just set down, to my Books and papers; so soon as I shall have put them in some order, I hope to return to my more pleasing Studies, and not give you peace by so long a Silence again—provided I am permitted to live at home this winter, which is not quite certain.

I am glad to see by the papers, that your affairs in America do well; and that you settle with the Ministry, and not with the Parliament, who, I think have nothing to do with you; therefore shou'd repeal all the Acts they have made.

This rambling, has set me as well in health as ever in my life but my Wife has had a bad summer; has had much of the Gravell, and has pass'd three large Stones, by which she is now pretty well and intends to take Chittick's Medicine as directed by Blackrie.[6]

We shall be glad of a line, to tell us how you and Mrs. Stevenson are in health, and also your friends in North america when you heard; hope this will find you very well, and Join in best wishes

4. A regular if intermittent correspondent; see above, IX, 42 n, and subsequent volumes.

5. An inn in Aldermanbury St., Cripplegate: Henry A. Herben, *A Dictionary of London*... (London, 1918), p. 38.

6. Mrs. Tissington seems to have enjoyed permanent bad health; see above, XIII, 403. Alexander Blackrie (d. 1772) was an apothecary whose writings popularized the medicine of a Dr. Chittick which supposedly dissolved stones. See *Gent. Mag.*, XXXIII (1763), 471–5; *DNB* under Blackrie.

and the Compliments of the Season to you and I am Dear Sir Yours most affectionately ANTH TISSINGTON

I have gather'd some Materials in my rambles, for a philosophical paper to you when I get time to put them together.

Addressed: To / Benjamin Franklin Esqr / Craven Street Strand / London

Endorsed: Mr Tissington Dec. 29.70

To Samuel Cooper

ALS: British Museum

The letter below belongs with those above to Cooper of June 8 and to Cushing of December 24, for in each Franklin discusses a different aspect of the constitution as he sees it. In the earliest he stresses the colonists' recourse of petitioning their sovereign for protection against an arbitrary and corrupt Parliament. In the second he argues that Parliament has no right to alter the sovereign's relationship with a colony by amending its charter. In this letter he insists that the King's surrogate, the governor, should be dependent on the colonial assembly and not on the dictates of Whitehall, and that the only way to re-establish that dependence is to persist in nonimportation. Thus each of the letters develops, in Franklin's pragmatic way, a constitutional point; and the points are interrelated parts of his concept of the empire as a group of autonomous states with a common sovereign.

Dear Sir,   London, Decem 30. 1770.
    I duly received your several Favours of July 12, Nov. 6. and 15. and am glad that my little Communications afforded you any Pleasure.[7] I join with you most cordially in Wishes of a perfect happy Union between Great Britain and the Colonies: This is only to be expected from Principles of Justice and Equity on both sides, which we must endeavour to cultivate. I think there is now a Disposition here to treat us more equitably, and I hope it will increase and prevail.
    I esteem the Appointment to the Agency of your Province, unexpected and unsolicited by me, as one of the greatest Honours, for which I must think myself indebted to your Friendship: I wish I

7. Only Cooper's November letters have survived; see above. BF's "communications" were presumably in his letter to Cooper above, June 8.

may be able to do my Country effectual Service; nothing could make me more happy: I shall however use my most faithful Endeavours. I had, before I heard of this Appointment, openly oppos'd the Project of abridging our Charter Privileges, which some of our Adversaries were extreamly busy in; designing to do it by an Act of Parliament; a Bill for the purpose being, as I have heard, actually drawn ready to be brought in. I boldly and openly asserted that Parliament had no such Power; and that an Attempt of that kind, would, by alarming all America, raise a new Flame there, and tend more to loosen the Connections now subsisting, than any Step that had yet been taken. I do not know that the Freedom I used in declaring and publishing these Sentiments had much Effect; I rather think the Apprehension of an approaching War, inclin'd Government to milder Measures, and to hearken less to the mad Projects of our Adversaries. So it is, however, that the Scheme has been laid aside, and will, I think, hardly be resum'd, tho' the Expectation of War is much lessened.[8]

It makes me happy to learn that my Ideas on a certain Subject, appeared just to you and your Friends. I have now in hand a Piece (intended for the Publick at a convenient Time) which I hope will satisfy many others even on this side the Water, that every Lady of Genoa is not a Queen of Corsica.[1] Just at this Juncture here, perhaps 'tis more prudent to be quiet, to stir no new Questions, to let Heats abate; and when Minds are cooler Reason may be better heard. I think I shall send my Manuscript to America for the Perusal and Correction of my Friends, and for their Advice on the Expediency of its being published, before I venture it into the World. You I hope will give me leave to trouble you with it, as it seems to me a Question of great Importance to us all.[2]

8. This paragraph covers the same ground as BF to Cushing above, Dec. 24.

1. BF must have recently encountered a remark, which we have been unable to trace, that every Genoese lady considered herself Queen of Corsica—that every citizen of the Republic, in other words, claimed sovereignty over the island because Genoa did. For BF's varied uses of this remark see above, p. 214, and below, p. 340.

2. BF did not send the MS, for in Cooper's reply below, July 10, 1771, he expressed the hope of seeing it. What it was cannot be established. It was certainly neither of BF's two known literary productions in 1771, his "Plan for Benefitting Distant Unprovided Countries" or the first instalment of his *Autobiography*. Crane suggests that BF was writing a treatise on his concept of

You have given, in a little Compass, so full and comprehensive a View of the Circumstances on which is founded the Security Britain has for all reasonable Advantages from us, tho' things were put into the same State in which they were before the Stamp Act that I cannot refrain communicating an Extract of your Letter, where I think it may be of Use; and I think I shall publish it.

There is no doubt of an Intention here to make all our Governors independent of the People for their Support, as fast as the American Duties will bear the Expence. In this Point I think all Parties are against us: And nothing appears to them more unreasonable than that we should wish to have our Governors under such Influence, when the King himself, as they say is always made independent of the Parliament here in that respect, by a fixed Civil List Revenue. I have endeavoured to show the Injustice of Taxing the Colonies (who have always supported their own Government) for the Support of other Governments in which they have no Interest; and the great Difference between a Prince, whose Welfare and that of his Family is intimately connected with the Prosperity of the Nation, and a Governor who comes from another Country to make Money, and intends to return to the Place from whence he came, where he will not hear the Complaints and Curses of those he has oppress'd and plunder'd, nor his Children be less respected or fare the worse for the Malfeasance of their Father. But it is so sweet a thing to have the Giving of Places of great and sure Profit to Friends and Favourites; and the Prospect of doing it out of other Revenues than those of this Nation, at which Parliament is therefore less likely to take Umbrage, is so tempting, that I think scarce any thing said or to be said here will avail much towards discouraging the Project. There is indeed one Thing (if that is in our Power) the Refraining absolutely from the Use of all Commodities subject to the Duty. The Deficiency of the Revenue to pay the Salaries, and those to be

---

empire growing out of his marginalia, that he had alluded to this treatise as early as his letter of Nov. 28, 1768 (above, XV, 273), and that this was what he intended to send to Cooper and never did. Verner W. Crane, "Franklin's Marginalia, and the Lost 'Treatise' on Empire," *Papers* of the Mich. Academy of Science, Arts, and Letters, XLII (1957), 163–4, 172, 175. This suggestion is plausible, and would help to explain the time and effort that BF spent on his marginalia in 1769–70. But, unless the lost treatise turns up, we can only conjecture that it was what BF was talking about.

made good by the Treasury here, might possibly put some Check to the Career. And if the Assemblies should at the same time decline giving any more annual Supports, and leave all Governors to their Appointments out of the Revenue, giving bountifully to a good Governor at the End of his Administration, and leaving bad ones to be rewarded by their Masters; perhaps by this means some of that Influence with Governors might be retained, which induces them to treat the People with Equity and Moderation. But if our People will, by consuming such Commodities, purchase and pay for their Fetters, who that sees them so shackled will think they deserve either Redress or Pity? Methinks that in Drinking Tea, a true American, reflecting that by every Cup he contributed to the Salaries, Pensions and Rewards of the Enemies and Persecutors of his Country, would be half choak'd at the Thought, and find no Quantity of Sugar sufficient to make the nauseous Draught go down.

I hope your Health is restored, and that your valuable Life will be long continued, for the Benefit of your Friends, Family and Country. With sincere and great Esteem, I am, Dear Sir, Your affectionate and most obedient Servant   B FRANKLIN

Revd Dr Cooper,

To Jane Mecom   Transcript:[3] American Philosophical Society

Dear Sister   London Dec. 30. 1770
This Ship staying longer than was expected, gives me an Opportunity of writing to you which I thought I must have miss'd when I desir'd Cousin William[s] to excuse me to you. I received your kind Letter of Sept. 25 by the young Gentlemen, who, by their discreet Behaviour have recommended themselves very much to me and many of my Acquaintance. Josiah has attained his Heart's Desire of being under the Tuition of Mr. Stanley, who, tho, he had long left off Teaching, kindly undertook at my Request to instruct him, and is much pleased with his Quickness of Apprehension and the

3. Made in 1833, according to an endorsement, by Rebecca Burroughs. An extract consisting of the long second paragraph, in Jane Mecom's hand, is in the British Museum; she perhaps copied it for Samuel Cooper, whose papers the British seized in 1775.

Progress he makes; and Jonathan appears a very valuable young Man, sober, regular, and inclin'd to Industry and Frugality, which are promising Signs of Success in Business: I am very happy in their Company.[4]

As to the Rumour you mention (which was, as Josiah tells me, that I had been depriv'd of my Place in the Post Office on Account of a letter I wrote to Philadelphia) it might have this Foundation, that some of the Ministry had been displeas'd at my Writing such Letters, and there were really some Thoughts among them of shewing that Displeasure in that manner.[5] But I had some Friends too, who unrequested by me advis'd the contrary. And my Enemies were forc'd to content themselves with abusing me plentifully in the Newspapers, and endeavouring to provoke me to resign. In this they are not likely to succeed, I being deficient in that Christian Virtue of Resignation. If they would have my Office, they must take it——I have heard of some great Man, whose Rule it was with regard to Offices, *Never to ask for them*, and *never to refuse them*: To which I have always added in my own Practice, *Never to resign them*. As I told my Friends, I rose to that office thro' a long Course of Service in the inferior Degrees of it: Before my time, thro' bad Management, it never produced the Salary annex'd to it; and when I receivd it, no Salary was to be allow'd if the office did not produce it. During the first four Years it was so far from defraying itself, that it became £950 Sterling in debt to me and my Collegue. I had been chiefly instrumental in bringing it to its present flourishing State, and therefore thought I had some kind of Right to it. I had hitherto executed the Duties of it faithfully, and to the perfect Satisfaction of my Superiors, which I thought was all that should be expected of me on that Account. As to the Letters complain'd of, it was true I did write them, and they were written in Compliance with another Duty, that to my Country. A Duty quite Distinct from that of Postmaster. My Conduct in this respect was exactly similar with that I held on a similar Occasion but a few Years ago, when the then Ministry were ready to hug me for the Assistance I afforded

4. For the Williamses' journey see their father to BF above, Aug. 27. While Josiah started studying music with Stanley, Jonathan began what was to be a long career as BF's financial clerk.

5. See above, BF to Charles Thomson, March 18, and to Lord Le Despencer, July 26.

them in repealing a former Revenue Act. My Sentiments were still the same, that no such Acts should be made here for America; or, if made should as soon as possible be repealed; and I thought it should not be expected of me, to change my Political Opinions every time his Majesty thought fit to change his Ministers. This was my Language on the Occasion; and I have lately heard, that tho I was thought much to blame, it being understood that every Man who holds an Office should act with the Ministry whether agreable or not to his own Judgment, yet in consideration of the goodness of my private Character (as they are pleas'd to compliment me) the office was not to be taken from me. Possibly they may still change their Minds, and remove me; but no Apprehension of that sort, will, I trust, make the least Alteration in my Political Conduct. My rule in which I have always found Satisfaction, is, Never to turn asside in Publick Affairs thro' Views of private Interest; but to go strait forward in doing what appears to me right at the time, leaving the Consequences with Providence. What in my younger Days enabled me more easily to walk upright, was, that I had a Trade; and that I could live upon a little; and thence (never having had views of making a Fortune) I was free from Avarice, and contented with the plentiful Supplies my business afforded me. And now it is still more easy for me to preserve my Freedom and Integrity, when I consider, that I am almost at the End of my Journey, and therefore need less to complete the Expence of it; and that what I now possess thro' the Blessing of God may with tolerable Oeconomy, be sufficient for me (great Misfortunes excepted) tho' I should add nothing more to it by any Office or Employment whatsoever.

I send you by this Opportunity the 2 Books you wrote for. They cost 3s. a piece. When I was first in London, about 45 Years since, I knew a person who had an Opinion something like your Author's ——Her Name was *Ilive*, a Printer's Widow. She dy'd soon after I left England, and by her Will oblig'd her son to deliver publickly in Salter's Hall a Solemn Discourse, the purport of which was to prove, that this World is the true Hell or Place of Punishment for the Spirits who had transgress'd in a better State, and were sent here to suffer for their sins in Animals of all Sorts. It is long since I saw the Discourse, which was printed.[6] I think a good deal of

6. The pamphlet of which Jane wanted two copies cannot be identified, but was clearly a religious tract because of what follows. Elizabeth Ilive (1669–

Scripture was cited in it, and that the Supposition was, that tho' we now remember'd nothing of such pre-existent State; yet after Death we might recollect it, and remember the Punishments we had suffer'd, so as to be the better for them; and others who had not yet offended, might now behold and be warn'd by our Sufferings. In fact we see here that every lower Animal has its Enemy with proper Inclinations, Faculties and Weapons, to terrify, wound and destroy it; and that Men, who are uppermost, are Devils to one another; So that on the establish'd Doctrine of the Goodness and Justice of the great Creator, this apparent State of general and systematical Mischief, seem'd to demand some such Supposition as Mrs. Ilives, to account for it consistent with the Honour of the Diety. But our reasoning Powers when employ'd about what may have been before our Existence here, or shall be after it, cannot go far for want of History and Facts: Revelation only can give us the necessary Information, and that (in the first of these Points especially) has been very sparingly afforded us.

I hope you continue to correspond with your Friends at Philadelphia, or else I shall think there has been some Miff between you; which indeed, to confess the Truth, I was a little afraid, from some Instances of others, might possibly happen, and that prevented my ever urging you to make such a visit especially as I think there is rather an overquantity of Touchwood in your Constitution.[7] My Love to your Children, and believe me ever, Your affectionate Brother   B FRANKLIN
Let none of my Letters go out of your Hands.

1733) required the oration of her son Jacob (1705–63) a printer, type-founder, and author; he not only delivered but published it, in two editions, and went on to give similarly heterodox talks at nearly all the City Companies' halls. He thereby gained a reputation for insanity and a three-year jail sentence for blasphemy. *DNB*; Talbot B. Reed, *A History of the Old English Letter Foundries*... (A. F. Johnson, ed.; London, [1952]), pp. 338–40.

7. Touchwood is tinder. After Jane's visit to Philadelphia DF had written that her guest was angry with her, "but I Cante tell for what" (to BF above, Oct. 14). That remark was doubtless behind BF's comment.

Note on Marginalia in *Another Letter,* an Anonymous Pamphlet, [1770?]

MS notations appear on pp. 139–40 of a copy in the Historical Society of Pennsylvania of *Another Letter to Mr. Almon, in Matter of Libel* (London, 1770). The author is discussing the American claim that Parliament has no jurisdiction over the colonial assemblies because they are constitutionally coequal with it. Franklin's comments were largely obliterated when the copy was cropped in rebinding, and most of them cannot be even conjecturally reconstructed. The few that can be suggest that he was adding little to what he said in other marginalia.

Marginalia in *An Inquiry,* an Anonymous Pamphlet

MS notations in the margins of a copy in the New York Public Library of *An Inquiry into the Nature and Causes of the Present Disputes between the British Colonies in America and Their Mother-Country; and Their Reciprocal Claims and Just Rights Impartially Examined, and Fairly Stated* (London, 1769).

This anonymous and, today, very rare pamphlet was once tentatively ascribed to Franklin.[8] Even if he had not annotated a copy, the ascription would be absurd. The writer, whoever he may have been, was patently an Englishman, and one with more goodwill than logical acumen. He was deeply imbued with the concept of natural rights, but quite incapable of reconciling that concept with the hard realities of the British Empire at the time he wrote. At moments he seemed to understand the position of the colonists, and to recognize the inequity as well as uselessness of attempting to coerce them; at other moments his outrage at their rowdy protests made him almost a Grenvillean, and he breathed dire threats about where their defiance would lead them. His shift from one attitude to the other bewilders the modern reader, and makes the pamphlet a study in inconsistency. That is its value. It illuminates the dilemma of thoughtful, well-intentioned, and not overly intelligent Englishmen, of the sort who were numerous in the House of Commons and the offices of Whitehall, and who made British policy in the decade of wobble that converted a quarrel into a revolution.

8. Joseph Sabin, Wilberforce Eames, and R. W. G. Vail, *Bibliotheca Americana: a Dictionary of Books Relating to America from Its Discovery to the Present Time* (29 vols., New York, 1868–1936), IX, 111.

Franklin waded into the author's arguments and in the process developed his own. His marginalia have almost the immediacy of a dialogue, in which he responds occasionally with approval, more often with criticism, and at moments with angry defiance. Sometimes he reiterates a point that he has often made before, such as that the British and Americans are fellow subjects of the King, and harps on it repetitively; but he also elaborates it by arguing that there is no union between the parts of the empire except royal sovereignty. He gives careful consideration to the idea of an imperial parliament, with representatives from the colonies, and insists that the practical difficulties are less than the author believes; yet he makes clear his preference for leaving the constitution as it is. His championship of colonial rights leads him to the startling position that Americans, because of their risks and expenses in settling the wilderness, are entitled to more than the King's other subjects. He dismisses contemptuously the threat to keep the colonies in line by returning Canada to France, and gives a new twist to the common assertion that the ousting of the French has encouraged American intransigence: it has encouraged the British, he says, to treat America as they have, and as they would never have dared to do if the French were still on the frontiers. His marginalia, in short, are a disorganized but illuminating compendium of his views on the large questions that the pamphlet raises.

The date of his comments is particularly important for the development of those ideas. By a rare stroke of luck he dated one remark 1770, and it may reasonably be assumed that the others were made at the same time. They contain a single reference to what is clearly the year 1768–69, but none to anything later. Hence we are assigning them all, with more confidence than usual, to 1770. The method of reproduction is the same as that with similar marginalia in Volume XVI. The printed original is paraphrased and drastically condensed in the right-hand column, with direct quotation only of words or passages that Franklin specifically noted. All emphases in this column are his: what he underlined once is italicized, what he underlined twice is capitalized. Gaps to accommodate the marginalia do not indicate any break in the paraphrase. Franklin's comments are printed verbatim in the left-hand column, where the emphases are again his and are similarly reproduced.

[1770]
The dispute with the colonies has gone beyond the point where charters and statutes are the relevant issues; the question now is what policy ought to underlie legislation. Although we live

in a scientific age, "*where our interest is concerned, we meet with such a narrowness both of thinking and acting upon every occasion, as is far from distinguishing us from the most barbarous period of antiquity....*" Otherwise Britain would behave quite differently, and her colonies would be "*more obliging and dutiful.*"

This essay will pursue three lines of inquiry: Should the colonies have the same political advantages and privileges as the mother country? Does the British constitution make this possible? If it does not, should it be changed?

We are inclined to view colonies as existing for our wealth and aggrandisement, but this view is mistaken. The existence of an empire increases the power of the whole, not of one part at the expense of the others. If the parts are governed, "from *no reasonable,* or...from the *most unjust* motives, with a *partiality,...divisions* and *murmurings,* if not actual rebellions, are evidently unavoidable." The larger such an empire is, the weaker it is.

Hence all parts demand equal attention, or, if anything, the most distant demand the most. Abuses creep into all government, and flourish best in the remote provinces, which are always first to revolt against ill usage.

It is "*wholly* the effect of the *illiberal notions,* and *partial views* of government,...that the *trade and manufactures* of different provinces are *laid under the restraints we often see them.* And, in short, from the same unhappy source, spring most of the *inequitable laws and inhibitions,* to which colonies and the more remote parts of an empire are frequently subjected." Sound policy dictates the minimum of regulation; trade and commerce should be permitted to thrive wherever they can most advantageously. Britain rejects this argument, and commits "*the folly* and

319

Marginal notes (left column):

I hope the Author will be on his Guard upon this point, and not suffer his Interest to run away with his Judgment.

Already the Colonies seem to be condemn'd by this impartial Writer!

Right and Just.

Certainly.

Just Reasoning. The King should look to this.

Very true.

Injustice is always

Folly.

injustice of not treating all the parts and provinces of an empire, with the exactest impartiality."

Does the British constitution permit impartiality? Among classical empires Rome was the most liberal, but the inhabitants of its provinces did not and could not enjoy all the privileges of Roman citizenship; if they had the state would have been reduced to anarchy. "Supreme power must not, cannot reside equally every where throughout an empire." This is true despite the fact that authority in a free state derives from and resides in the people.

The laws by which they are governed derive from them through their representatives, and are as binding upon the executive as upon them. A free government extends throughout the whole empire, but out of its many parts

Writers on this Subject often confuse themselves with the Idea that all the King's Dominions make one State, which they do not nor ever did since the Conquest. Our Kings have ever had Dominions not subject to the English Parliament; as first the Province of France, of which Jersey and Guernsey remain, always governed by their own Laws; appealing to the King in Council only, and not to our Courts or

to the House of Lords. Scotland was in the same Situation before the Union: It had the same King, but a separate Parliament; and the Parliament of England had no Jurisdiction over it. Ireland the same in truth, tho' the

British Parliament has *usurp'd* a Dominion over it. The Colonies were originally settled on the Idea of such extrinsic Dominions of the King, and of the King only. Hanover is now such a Dominion.

But different States may have different Assemblies of Representatives. As is the Case.

"*one only* supreme assembly of representatives, for making laws, *can regularly be formed.*" If there are many assemblies, one is supreme and the powers of the rest abridged; otherwise there

This is the only clear Idea of their real present Condi-

would be "many different governments *perfectly independent of one another.*" These truths are self-evident.

tion. Their only
Bond of Union is
King.

Within Great Brit-   Because Britain has *"exactly the kind of govern-*
ain, if you please,   *ment* I have been here speaking of," the Ameri-
but no farther.   can assemblies cannot have an authority equal

It would not be   to that of Parliament *"without actually dismem-*
dismembring of it,   *bering the British empire"*; for government
if it never was   implies subordination as well as union. All its
united, as in truth it constituent parts, however, have a right to par-
never yet has been.
Breaking the present ticipate in regulating the affairs of the whole.
Union between
England and Scot-
land would be dis-
membring the
Empire; But no such
Union has yet been
formed between
Britain and the
Colonies.

True, But why do   Hence, although the British Parliament may
you use the Expres- legislate for Britain, *"it cannot with the same*
sion, OUR DOM-   *propriety exercise the like power with respect to*
INIONS? Are the   *America, while those parts of our dominions are not*
King's Subjects in *fairly represented* in it." Neither can the colonies
England Sovereign legislate independently without "declaring
over his Subjects in
America? No. The
King is the Sover-
eign of all.

They are such.   themselves *independent states"*; their legislation
must be subject to amendment or reversal by
The Parliament of *"the parliament of Great Britain."* While their
Britain has no Right power is thus limited by an authority in which
to repeal an Ameri-
can Law that the
King has assented
to.

They would not indeed [be], if that were the Case.

they have no part, however, they are not a free people. They are subject to regulation outside their control, *"which is the very definition of slavery"*; their rights and liberties therefore remain precarious.

Here appears the Excellency of the Invention of Colony Government, by separate independent Legislatures. By this means the remotest Parts of a great Empire, may be as well governed as the Center; Misrule, Oppresions of Proconsuls, and Discontents and Rebellions thence arising prevented. By this Means the Power of a King

The freer a constitution is in its nature, the less widely it applies. "Where divers remote and distant countries are united under one government, an equal and fair representation becomes almost impracticable, or, at best, extremely inconvenient."

may be extended without Inconvenience over Territories of any Dimensions how great soever. America was thus happily governed in all its different and remote Settlements, by the

Crown and their own Assemblies till the new Politicks took place, of governing it by our Parliament, which have not succeeded and never will.

Water, so far from being an Obstruction, is a Means of facilitating such Assemblies from distant Countries. A Voyage of 3000 Miles by Sea, is more safely performed than a Journey of 1000 by Land.

The difficulty is compounded when the parts of a state are divided by the ocean. Convening a parliament from provinces widely separated by land would be much more feasible than convening one from Britain and America. Yet such an Anglo-American parliament is the only way to make government equal for all: our system requires general and impartial representation, and America has none. This fact reveals "the stubbornness and inflexibility...of the genius of our constitution,"

It is in my Opinion, by no means impracticable, to bring Representatives

which in itself is the best in the world.

conveniently from
America to Britain:
But I think the
present Mode of
letting them govern
themselves by their
own Assemblies
much preferable.
They will always be
better governed;
and the Parliament
has Business enough
here with its own
internal Concerns.

They have it already.
All the Difficulties
have arisen from the
British Parliament's
Attempting to de-
prive them of it.

Right.

Certainly

Very just. Only that
the arbitrary Gov-
ernment of a single
Person is more
eligible than the
arbitrary Govern-
ment of a Body of
Men. A single Man
may be afraid or
asham'd of doing
Injustice. A Body is
never either one or
the other, if it is

The next question is whether, if the nature of
the constitution precludes giving the Americans
their full privileges as Englishmen, "they should
not *be allowed such a form of government*, as will
best secure them their just rights and natural
liberties?"

This question may strike many as absurd.
"Yet I cannot help thinking it much more absurd, to hold that the British parliament, as it
now stands, hath an undeniable right to make
laws for North-America." Few of us openly assert that it is just "for *one half of a kingdom*, to
hold the other half in chains," and those who do
would change their tune if the situation were
reversed; "justice requires that we should do by
others, as we would…be done by ourselves."
Is it not folly to condemn the Stuarts for governing without Parliament, when most of us would
govern America on equally unjustifiable principles?

strong enough. It cannot apprehend Assassination; and by dividing the Shame among them, it is so little apiece, that no one minds it.

The question should be how high we can raise the colonies without making them independent and thereby abrogating "*our rights of sovereignty over them.*" This is at once the liberal and the politic approach, "for the most *lasting*

I am surpriz'd that a Writer, who in other respects appears often very reasonable and consistent, can talk of *our Sovereignty* over the Colonies! As if every Individual in England, was Part of a Sovereign over America! See the preceding Page.

Surely

empires are always founded in principles the most agreeable to justice." A thoughtful man would never wish, even if it were possible, "to *make*

See Page 25 [p. 323 above] where the Author defines Slavery.

slaves of the Americans"; for they would then be

And if you ever succeed in making Slaves of us, depend upon it, we shall always be ready to return the Compliment.

dangerous to Britain. "A people...in whom the love of liberty as well as all sense of the just value of it, was extinguished, would certainly be the most proper instruments to reduce others to the like condition." Although in some things we are wildly apprehensive of our liberty, in the altercation with the colonies our apprehension is dormant, and that is the measure of our folly.

The true basis of the Americans' grievance is wider than their complaints indicate. The right of taxation touches on two of "the *three principal objects* of government," which are securing the citizen's person, property, and religion: disposing of his property without his consent threatens his person with starvation. "Hence then it appears what alarming consequences a right of imposing taxes involves in it. Can it therefore surprise any one that the colonies should be jealous of this right? or rather would it not be much more surprising, were they not jealous of it?

"However, a right of legislation in general over them, they certainly may with equal jus-

The Americans think, that while they can retain the Right of disposing of their own Money, they shall thereby secure all their other Rights. They have therefore not yet disputed your other Pretensions.

tice and propriety dispute, so long as they continue unrepresented in our parliament, or some other way are not admitted to a due share of power, in making those laws to which they are subject." At present they complain only of taxation, and to this point I shall confine myself. If it can be settled, other arguments about legislation will doubtless prove negotiable.

Just.

"*That England has an undeniable right to consider America as part of her dominions, is a fact, I presume, which can never be questioned.*" Few empires can produce as good a claim to their provinces as England to hers.

You do indeed *presume* too much. America *is not* part of the Dominions *of England*, but of *the King's* Dominion. England is a Dominion itself, and has no Dominions.

"It was England, *in some sense*, which at first gave them being...and ever since has defended them with her arms, and governed them with her laws. It is therefore but just and equitable that they should, in return,

In some Sense. In what Sense? They were not planted at her Expence. As to Defence. All Parts of the King's Dominions have mutually always contributed to the

325

Defence one of the other. The man in America who contributes Sixpence towards an Armament against the common Enemy, contributes as much to the common Protection as if he liv'd in England.

They have always been ready to contribute but by voluntary Grants according to their Rights. Nor has any Englishman yet had the Effrontery to deny this Truth.

contribute a reasonable proportion for the support of that government, by which they are protected. *This they have not as yet had the effrontery openly to deny.*"

1.

2.

3.

4.

The Author here is greatly mistaken. Such a Requisition as [he] describes, where a Sum certain was fixed for the Colonies to raise and *the Manner* only left to them, was never acquiesced in by the Colonies,

The question at issue is how they should contribute. Four ways are possible. One is by requisition from the King in council "of a certain sum by *them fixed,* to be raised in each province, *in such manner* as their own assemblies shall think fit." The second is a similar requisition from Parliament and raised in the same way. The third is taxation by Parliament as it is now constituted. The fourth is taxation by a Parliament in which the Americans are represented.

The first of these ways, "*however acquiesced in on the part of the colonies,*" is the most exceptionable, because it enables the ministry to set the amount. If such a requisition "*is to be indispensibly complied with,*" the Americans

326

indeed it was never propos'd to them. The Requisitions have only been (after stating the Occasion) that they should grant such Sums as were suitable to their Abilities and Loyalty, the Quantum being intirely left to their Judgment. And this is the only kind of Requisition that will ever be approv'd there.

will be subject to ministerial government and therefore to ministerial tyranny. Yet it is obvious that the requisition, if made, "*should without reserve be complied with*," for otherwise the Americans will have discretionary power and

Certainly. And therefore they never had an Idea of being oblig'd to comply indispensably with such Requisitions.

He still confounds himself and Readers with this *Sovereignty of England*.

"the *sovereignty of England*" will be nominal: if they are free to decide how much to raise as well as how to raise it, "*It is scarcely to be*

Why is it to be doubted that they will not grant what they ought to grant? No Complaint was ever yet made of their Refusal or Deficiency.

doubted but their allowance will be found *extremely short*."

He says, if they are not without reserve oblig'd to comply with the Requisitions of the Ministry,

"*They may, upon this footing, absolutely refuse to pay any taxes at all.*" If so, England would be better advised to break connection with them than to continue *her protection* of them at her own expense.

327

they may absolutely refuse to pay any Taxes at all. Let him apply this to the British Parliament, and the Reasoning will equally prove, that the Commons ought likewise to comply absolutely with the Requisitions of the Ministry. Yet I have seen lately the Ministry demand 4s. in the Pound, and the Parliament grant but 3.[9] But Parliaments and Provincial Assemblies may always be safely trusted with this Power of Refusing or granting in part. Ministers will often demand too much. But Assemblies, being acquainted properly with the Occasion will always grant what is necessary. Protection is (as I said before) mutual, and equal in Proportion to every Man's Property. The Colonies have been drawn into all British Wars, and have annoy'd the Enemies of Britain as much in Proportion as any other Subjects of the King equal in Numbers and Property. Therefore this Account has always ballanc'd itself.

The second method, a requisition by Parliament, is preferable because "in so large a body of men, both justice and the true interest of the empire are more likely to be duly regarded"; Americans may therefore "reasonably expect the burden will be more equitably laid upon them." Proceedings in Parliament are less rapid than in the Privy Council, so that if need be the Americans "will have more time *to petition or*

An American will hardly ever be of this Opinion. When the *Taxers* may lighten their own Burthen by so much the greater Weight they lay on the *Taxed*, Equity is scarce to be expected.

make remonstrances.

Late Experience has fully shewn that American Petitions and Remonstrances are little regarded in Britain.

9. The episode in February, 1767, when Charles Townshend asked for the usual rate of four shillings in the pound and the opposition, led by Grenville, succeeded in having the rate reduced to three. See William R. Ward, *The English Land Tax in the Eighteenth Century* (London, 1953), p. 76. The resultant shrinkage in revenue was a factor in Townshend's subsequently formulating his program for taxing the colonies.

The Privilege of Petitioning has been attempted to be wrested from them. The Assemblies uniting to petition has been called a *flagitious Attempt* in the Minister's Letters,[1] and such Assemblies as would persist in it, have therefore been dissolved!

For *this privilege, the least which a subject can enjoy, is not to be denied them,* however an ultimate compliance may be insisted on as indispensable." The Americans' financial position, furthermore, will probably be better understood in Parliament than in the ministry and "their

'Tis a Joke to talk thus to us, when we know that Parliament so far from solemnly canvassing our Petitions, have refus'd to receive or read them.

petitions and remonstrances more solemnly canvassed."

The impropriety of the third method, taxation by Parliament as presently constituted, has been demonstrated by the repeal of the Stamp Act. The Americans argued that the act was an unlawful exercise of authority; the justice of this argument the legislature, by repealing the act, "notwithstanding all their declarations and resolutions to the contrary, seem tacitly to have acknowledged."

Very true.

The question with me touches the rights of mankind, one of which is to the greatest degree of liberty that government can secure. No people is free when it is without a voice in making its laws, and to say that the Americans have any such voice in Parliament is irrational. Those who insist on *"our right of legislation over them"* have a point; the right is essential. "But...this

True.

1. Hillsborough's circular letters to the colonial governors, for which see 1 *N.J. Arch.*, x, 14–5.

The Author here grows reasonable again.

perhaps may be otherwise effected, than at the expence of the just birth-right of our fellow-creatures; yet were it only to be accomplished by such a violation, I am perfectly at a loss how to demonstrate the equity of such a procedure, unless it can be fully proved that the safety of the state can be secured by no other means. For nothing less can justify it." But we are not yet

Our Sovereignty!

at the extreme of securing *"our sovereignty* over them" at the expense of their natural rights.

Then be very sure of the Right before you attempt to exercise it.

"To claim and exercise an authority we have naturally no right to, is an action in itself as wrong as any, I think, that we can put in supposition.... Our right of legislation* over the Americans, un-represented as they are, is the point in question. This right is asserted by most, doubted of by

I am one of those few, but am per-suaded the time is not far distant, when the few will become the many; For *magna est Veritas, et prevalebit.*

some, and *wholly disclaimed by a few.* But to put the matter in a stronger light, the question, I think, should be,

A very proper State of the Question.

Whether we have a general right of making slaves, or not."

Imperfect governments administer justice and preserve order, or there would be little of

How can we Americans believe this? When we see almost half the Nation paying but 1*s.* 6*d.* in the Pound while others pay full 4*s.*, and that there is not Virtue and Honesty enough in the Par-liament to rectify this Iniquity?[2] How can we suppose they

either in the world. Parliament may be as equable and tender toward the colonies as their own assemblies are; this is *"possible,* although perhaps not *very probable,"* if only because our distance from them makes us poor judges of their grievances and what they can afford in taxes.

An empire will not necessarily dissolve when "some *parts thereof are possessed of a power, by no means consistent with that unity of government* I have been speaking of. Nay it is possible that

Note 2 appears on page 331.

330

will be just to us at
such a Distance,
when they are not
just to one another?
It is not, indeed, as
the Author says,
very probable. The
unequal Representa-

tion, too, that pre-
vails in this King-
dom, they are so far
from having Virtue
enough to attempt
to remedy, that they
make use of it as an
Argument why we

should have no
Representation at
all. Be quiet, says
the Wag in the
Story, I only p[iss]
o[n] y[ou]: I sh[it]
o[n] t[he] o[the]r.³

This Power in the American Assemblies has never been found inconvenient.

such a power may never be found productive of any great inconvenience." The Irish parliament, for instance, may throw out money bills: here *"is a*

Very true. Then let us [not] trouble ourselves and others with a useless Theory.

great defect in point of theory; and yet the inconveniences arising therefrom, in practice, have been hitherto by no means considerable.... The truth of the matter is, it is not so much the best form of government, as the most exact and regular administration of justice, that most effectually fastens together the different parts of an empire, whereon the stability and duration of it must ever necessarily depend." The people abuse such power as they have only after they receive

Take care.

"very heavy provocations to enrage them, from the excesses of their governors." We should not think ill of the Americans for considering our mode of taxation provocative.

A Representation in the British Parl[iamen]t.

I wish that the *"fourth and last"* method of taxation were as feasible as it is just. "To the

Provided they had an equitable Number of Representatives allow'd them.

equity of this measure the Americans themselves, I presume, *could have nothing fairly to object."* Apportioning members among them

---

2. The iniquity as BF describes it is incomprehensible. The land tax was raised again to 4s., it is true, in December, 1770; but what was the half of the nation that paid 1s. 6d.? British taxation was such a welter of special levies on commodities, windows, professions, etc.—not to mention the local rates— that BF's generalization makes no sense.

3. We have been unable to locate the story, which by its nature was more likely to have circulated orally than in print.

Let the old Members continue till superseded by new Ones from America.

would be a transient difficulty; a more lasting one would be the distance involved, particularly when a new Parliament is to be elected. If Parliaments were annual, as they should be, the difficulty would be heightened, and could

By the above it might.

scarcely be overcome when only a few weeks elapse between the dissolution and the election.

Let the Members be chosen by the American Assemblies, and disputed Elections settled there, if any, but there would be none.

Another problem would be contested elections, which would have to be decided on a different basis in America and in England. But removing these difficulties is not my purpose, because "*it*

I think so too. Where neither Side approve a Match it is not likely to be made.

is not...probable, that an American representation will ever be convened in England." Other and greater difficulties stand in the way: If the Americans wanted Parliament to intervene in a particular colonial affair, distance would preclude action; if they wanted the benefit of private Parliamentary acts, the expense of time and money would preclude it, yet

They may make them at home. The expence of private Acts in England is shamefully great.

Scarce ever

they might often have to apply for such acts. There would be many other matters, such as the cost of highways, rivers, and canals, where Parliament would have to be consulted but the

All this may be done by their own Laws at home.

colonists would bear the charges. How could witnesses be brought across the ocean? The Americans have a right to representation if they want it; but it is a last resort, and cannot be realized "*without immense trouble.*"

Evidences may be taken in Writing when necessary.

Very little.

All four methods of raising money are full of difficulties; what then should be done? This is as

Then leave it as it

is. It was very well till you attempted Alterations and Novelties.

important a question as the British government has ever faced. "If they should be *divided in their sentiments* upon it, and *uncertain what measures to adopt and follow*, it cannot be matter of just wonder or censure."

Very just.

The best guide to policy is the disposition of those we deal with, but "the truest policy...is ever founded in the soundest morality." The Americans, if unrepresented in Parliament, have a right to any other form of government that is consistent with "*the sovereignty of England over them.*" England has only the right to have them "*continue in subjection to her, and form a part of her*

England is not a Sovereign. The King is.
   They are in Subjection only to him. England is itself a Dominion, but has no Dominions.

But you are mistaken.

dominions.... The one I think, she has a right to command; and the other they have a right to claim." Any concessions she makes are by favor; if the Americans gained the same taxing power as the Irish, for instance, "it should be deemed only as *matter of grace*, to be resumed at pleasure. And custom, of however long a standing, can never convert it into matter of undeniable *claim*." If, on the other hand, the Americans agreed to be taxed by the present British Parliament, they could not equitably be held to that agreement; for they would not thereby lose their right to be represented in the House of Commons.

Your humble Servant. We thank you for nothing. Keep up your Claim and make the most of it.

Strange! that the Parl[iamen]t should have *a Right* to do what they cannot do *equitably*. And the Colonies a Right that is contrary to the Right of Parl[iamen]t.

These are the limits of right and equity on both sides. "To be placed upon a level with the rest of the subjects of the British crown, *is the utmost the colonies can challenge.*"

No. They may

333

challenge all that was promis'd them by Charters to encourage them to settle there. They have perform'd their

Part of the Contract, and therefore have a Right to expect a Performance of the other Part. They have by the Risques

and Expences they incurr'd additional Merit and therefore to be considered as *above the Level* of other Subjects.

and more,

I am quite sick of this *our Sovereignty.*

To refuse them this, on any ground except an immediate danger to England, would be dishonesty. We may not abridge the liberty of a country "merely because we cannot otherwise maintain *our sovereignty* over it, unless

Your Safety is only endangered by quarreling with the Colonies; not by leaving them to the free Enjoyment of their Liberties.

our safety were actually at stake, and absolutely required it."

The Colonies were not planted at your Expence.

The case may be altered when the country in question has been founded "*at our own expence.*"

They well knew the contrary. They would never have gone if that had been the case. They fled from your Government which oppress'd them. If they carried your Government with them and of course your Laws they had better have staid and endur'd the Oppression at home, and

The first settlers presumably "*well knew...they were still to continue the subjects of the same government.*"

not have added to it all the Hardships of making a new Settlement. They carried not your Laws but [*line missing*] they had carried your Government and Laws, they would now

have been subject to Spiritual Courts, Tythes, Church Acts of Parl[ia-men]t, Game Acts, &c &c which they are not and never were since their being OUT OF THE REALM.

334

Although their charters were less explicit than they should have been, the Americans "knew they were not to be independant." Any powers the charters seemed to give them that were inconsistent with British sovereignty might be removed; "no government can be supposed to alienate prerogatives necessary to its safe existence." By the same token we in turn should remove any unnecessary limitations on colonial liberties.

They were to depend on the King only.

Every Government is suppos'd to be *compos mentis* when it grants Charters, and shall not be allow'd to plead Insanity. If you break the Charters or violate them, you dissolve all Tie between us.

But *"a right of sovereignty in this case, we may undeniably claim and vindicate:*

You may claim it, but you have not, never had, nor, I trust, ever will have it.

and though we may safely grant them absolute independency, yet whatever generosity might suggest, justice does not seem to require it....

You, i.e. the People of England, cannot grant the Americans Independency of the King. It can never be, but with his Consent *and theirs.*

"Now, our title and pretensions to all our American provinces are of that sort that seem fairly to justify our asserting and preserving our sovereignty over them, although at the expence of some portion of their natural prerogatives."

Our Sovereignty! Our Sov[ereign]ty for ever.

The colonies partly consist of our own planta-

Of *their* not *our* Plantations.

tions, and partly of the conquests we have made from France. In both cases we have the right to

The Conquests may be yours, partly; but

335

they are partly Conquests belonging to the Colonies, who join'd their Forces with yours in equal Proportion.

keep them on a footing that will support our government. If we declared them independent they would fall to France, help to give her mastery of the seas, and endanger the liberties of

Take care then how you use them.

Europe; our existence as a free people, therefore, depends on retaining the colonies. So does

The direct contrary is true. They are not redressed, they are refused to be heard. Fresh Oppressions and Insults are continually added. (1770)

their existence as a free people. "They are now treated as children; *their complaints are heard, and grievances redressed*; but then they would be treated rather as slaves, having the swords of

English Swords are now held at our Throats. Every Step is taking to convince us that there is no Difference in Government.

their masters perpetually held at their throats, if they should presume to offer half the indignities to the officers of the French crown, which they have often, with impunity, done to those of the British."

It is well they have.

At present they enjoy the full benefit of English citizenship, and have their own assemblies to redress their grievances. The power of these assemblies is little inferior to that of Parliament, and threatens to equal it. In that case "what marks of *sovereignty* will they allow *us* to enjoy? What sort of claim will they indulge us with? Only, I suppose, a mere titular one." Then why should we continue to defend them, or do they

What would you have? Would you the People of England be Subjects and Kings at the same time?

expect to defend themselves? "This *they certainly at present are not able to do*, if they were not sheltered by the wings of Great Britain."

Don't be under any Apprehensions for them. They will find Allies and Friends somewhere;

We only ask them to contribute within reason to their own defense. They may say they are willing to do so, if it is on their own initiative;

and it will be worth no one's while to make them Enemies or to attack so poor a People so numerous and so well armed.

and this is the alternative to their receiving Parliamentary representation. If they do receive it, the number of their members should be

A *proper limitation* can only be this, that they shall from time to time have such a Number of additional Members as are proportion'd to their increasing Share of the Taxes and Numbers of People.

"*properly limited*," as Scottish members were in the Act of Union.

Americans and Englishmen must contribute their due proportions to the support of government. But it is almost impossible to estimate,

The Protection is mutual.

for the colonies, "what expense their *protection stands in to Great Britain*. Besides, we can *cer-*

They are always in time of War at as much Expence as would be necessary to protect themselves; first, by the Troops and armed Ships they raise and equip. 2. By the higher Price they pay for all Commodities, when drawn into War by English European Quarrels. 3. By Obstructions to the Vent of their Produce by general Embargos.

tainly afford to protect them at less expence than they could afford to protect themselves, were they either so many independent states, or only one general community." For the forces we must keep in being for our own protection will largely guard them as well. Such addition as we must make for them they ought to pay for. If they remonstrate that this additional strength, and the cost of maintaining it, can be safely reduced,

this is little to the purpose. Although their remonstrances "should be *candidly heard*, and

337

This never was the Case.	*duly regarded,*" England must remain the judge;
England is no Governor; it is governed. The King governs.	if they dictate to her, "it is no longer *England*, but her colonies, that govern." The Americans are also chargeable with part of the civil list,
I will tell you how it is managed. The Colonies maintain their Governors, who are the King's Representatives. And the King receives a Quitrent from the lands in most of the Colonies.	but how this is managed is
But not 100th part so great. Lessen these Expences, they are exorbitant. There is no Occasion to oblige them to do what they do voluntarily. Many profitable Offices too are held by Patentees from the Crown residing in England.	not my business to inquire. "The pomp of government" always requires such expenses, and they are considerable. It is only fair that the colonies should bear their share, and I see no reason why they should complain at being obliged to do so. An Englishman pays heavier taxes than an American can. But if one contributes a day's pay a week, the other might afford a day's pay a
Most of these Writers seem to forget, or not to know, that American Governments have heavy Taxes of their own to pay.	fortnight. Americans have great expenses of converting a wilderness into habitable land; but the cost varies in different parts of the colo-
As these Differences cannot be known in Parliament here, how can you pro-	nies, and some parts are as well off as the mother country. We should not be over-rigorous, nevertheless, in taxing the colonies, for we thereby depress them and discourage improvement. In

338

portion and vary your Taxes of America so as to make them equal and fair? It would be undertaking what you are not qualified for, as well as doing what you have no right to do.[4]

a northern province of Denmark, it is said, the lands were so heavily taxed that the peasants petitioned the King to take their farms into his

If it were once established that the Parliament had a Right to tax America *ad libitum*, we might as well give up our Lands, for we could call nothing our own that might be taken from us at the Pleasure of a Body wherein we had no Representatives.

own hands; this he did not want to do, knowing that they would be useless to him unless cultivated. Excessive taxation may have the same effect in any country.

Whether the Stamp Act would have been that kind of taxation I cannot say. The English may be considered incompetent judges, but the Americans are equally so because the matter so closely concerns their own interests. "*Yet it must be granted, that they know best the state of*

And yet you would be meddling.

their finances, and what taxes they can afford to pay." The difference in the value of their money suggests that the troops there might be paid less, but this would be imprudent even if it were limited to the provincials.

The Provincials are paid nearly double. Men are not to be had there on English pay.

Whatever lenience the colonies may deserve from England, "it is very certain that *England is entitled to a great deal of gratitude from her colonies.*" They must realize that without British help they would have been swallowed up by the French. "That the late war was chiefly kindled, and

The English are eternally harping on this String; the great Obligations the Colonies are

4. BF is here elaborating a point that he made earlier in commenting upon Governor Pownall's *State of the Constitution of the Colonies*, for which see above, XVI, 298–304.

339

under for Protection from the French. I have shown already that the Defence was mutual. Every Man in England, and every Man's Estate, has been defended from the French: But is it Sense to tell any particular Man, The Nation has incurr'd a Debt of 148 Millions to protect you and your Estate; and therefore you owe a great deal of Gratitude to the Nation, &c.? He will say, and justly, I paid my Proportion, and I

am under no Obligation. The Colonies, as I have shown in preceding Notes, have always paid more in various Ways. And besides, [*line missing*] extending your Trade sometimes (from which you exclude the Colonies) and for Whims about the Ballance of Power, and for the Sake of continental Connections in which they were separately unconcerned. On the other hand, they have from their first

Settlement had Wars in America in which they never engag'd you. The French have never been their Enemies but upon your Account. The French were at peace with them when you came into America with your Troops and began a War which you now say was on their Account, tho' it was really for Lands which the King claimed, not the Colonies, and to protect your Indian Trade.

It is denied.

carried on upon their account, can scarcely be denied," and Britain's loss of money and lives was heavy. She admittedly furthered her own interests thereby, but the Americans endorsed those interests by joining with her; why do they now jeopardize them by trying, it seems, to shake off sovereignty? If they succeed, our peace and safety will become more precarious then ever, and they

Our Sovereignty again. This Writer, like the Genoese Queens of Corsica, deems himself a Sprig of Royalty![5]

We are assured of the contrary. Weak States that are poor, are as safe as great Ones that are rich. They are not Objects of Envy; the

will immediately become dependent upon France.

Even if they could be actually independent, we do not know whose friends they would become or what factors, if any, might dispose them

5. For an explanation of this cryptic remark see above, p. 311 n.

340

Trade that may be carried on with them, makes them Objects of Friendship. The smallest States may have great Allies. And the mutual Jealousies of Great Nations contribute to their Security.

Then be careful not to use them ill.

toward us rather than toward the French. This uncertainty alone is a good reason for us to

It is a better Reason for using them kindly. That alone can retain their Friendship. Your Sovereignty will be of no Use if the People hate you. Keeping them in Obedience will cost you more, than your Profits from them can amount to.

guard our "*sovereignty*."

How little this Writer knows of the Colonies!

They never wanted or desired Protection from Indians.

Do you Englishmen then pretend to censure the Colonies for Riots? Look at home!!! I have seen within a Year, Riots

Whatever benefit Britain derived from the late war, the colonies were the principal gainers. "*Now they enjoy a peace and tranquility, which they scarcely ever knew before.*" Their chief remaining danger is from the Indians, whom they themselves have provoked; and the diligence with which our government has defended them from this and every other danger deserves some gratitude. But if their claims are just, wherein are they blameworthy? Not for claiming their rights and liberties, but for their riotous and seditious way of asserting them. England has much to justify her conduct. "She is conscious she has a right of sovereignty over

in the Country about Corn, Riots about Elections, Riots about Work-houses, Riots of Colliers, Riots of Weavers, Riots of Coalheavers, Riots of Sawyers, Riots of Sailors, Riots of Wilkites, Riots of Government Chairmen, Riots of

Smugglers in which Customhouse Officers and Excisemen have been murdered, the King's armed Vessels and Troops fired at; &c &c &c.[6] In America if one Mob rises and breaks a few Windows, or tars and feathers a single

rascally Informer, it is called REBELLION: Troops and Fleets must be sent, and military Execution talk'd of as the decentest Thing in the World. Here indeed one would think Riots part of the Mode of Government.

No, nor before.

In the last War America kept up 25000 Men at her own Cost for 5 Years, and spent many Millions. Her Troops were in all Battles, all Service: Thousands of her Youth fell a Sacrifice. The Crown gain'd an immense Extent of Territory and a great Number of new Subjects. Britain gain'd a new

them, which perhaps may not be quite so easy to maintain, when the point in dispute is given up. And *this sovereignty* she knows to be a matter of the last consequence for her to support." For the Americans it is of equal consequence: in the recent peace treaty Britain sacrificed every other object to "*procuring them a safe establishment.*" In return she might expect a dutiful instead of an outrageous demeanor; firmness would have been more becoming for an American, and would have gained him more from Parliament.

6. Enough of these riots can be identified to establish that BF was referring to the year 1768, when the *Lond. Chron.* mentioned disturbances over elections in its issues of March 19–21, April 7–9, Dec. 8–10, disturbances by weavers in its issues of Jan. 5–7 and April 23–6, by coal-heavers in those of April 21–3, 26–8, May 7–10, 17–19, June 11–14, and July 9–12, by sailors in those of May 7–10, 10–12, and Aug. 27–30, by sawyers and others in that of May 10–12. The battle with the smugglers, which occurred at Milford Haven, is recounted in the issue of Oct. 13–15, 1768. For the Wilksite riots of the same year see, for example, above, xv, 98.

Market for her
Manufactures and
recover'd and
secur'd the old one
among the Indians
which the French
had interrupted and
annihilated. But
what did America
gain, except that *safe*
Establishment,
which they are now

so taunted with?
Lands were divided
among none of
them. The very
Fishery which they
fought to obtain,
they are now re-
strain'd in, (Labra-
dor). The Plunder
of the Havanah
was not for them.[7]
And this very *safe*

Establishment they
might as well have
had by Treaty with
the French their
Neighbours, who
would probably
have been easily
made and continu'd
their Friends, if it
had not been for
their Connection
with Britain.

Then don't be in-
solent with your
Power.

"It seldom happens that one fares the better for his insolence."

If the Americans choose to defy us, to gain some points that England might prefer to surrender than contest, it is an imprudent course. For their insolence may increase with our concessions until nothing will content them but independence, and we may be forced into other measures which they will be the first to repent. In an extreme crisis with the colonies "England may yet produce both a ministry and a parliament that would rather *share them once more with the French*, than totally relinquish her present pretensions, from a very just conviction that such a step would be *much more politic* than to suffer them to *throw themselves wholly* into the arms of that nation; and such a measure... would be abundantly defensible, however awkward it may be found at the first mention." Though I hope they will never compel us to take that step, if they do they will find them-

We have been often
threaten'd with this
wise Measure of
returning Canada to
France. Do it when
you please. Had the
French Power,
which you were 5
Years subduing with
25000 Regulars, and
25000 of us to help
you, continu'd at

7. By the Peace of Paris of 1763 the French retained a share in the fisheries off Labrador and Newfoundland, but their activities scarcely constituted a restraint on the colonists. A few years earlier BF had been well satisfied with the American role in the fisheries (above, XIII, 363–4) and with reason, for it was a predominant one; see Gipson, *British Empire*, X, 17–18. The British captured Havana in 1762, and to obtain its return in the peace settlement Spain ceded Florida.

selves involved in the same bloodshed out of which they have recently emerged. This prospect may dispose them to some moderation, which otherwise we cannot expect.

It may be asked what is the limit of their demands, because hitherto they do not seem to have known where to stop. But I return to my underlying premises. The first is that the Americans have as much right as the English to be represented in the legislature that taxes them and passes the laws by which they are governed.

The second is that imperial authority must center in one supreme assembly. The third, which follows from the first two, is that the Americans should be represented in Parliament if they so desire. The fourth is that, if the third is not practicable, they should be allowed "such an establishment,

---

Marginal notes:

our Backs, ready to support and assist us whenever we might think proper to resist your Oppressions, you would never have thought of a Stamp Act for us; you would not have dared to use us as you have done. If it be so politic a Measure to have Enemies at hand to keep (as the Notion is) *your Subjects* in Obedience; then give Part of Ireland to the French to plant [*line missing*] another French Colony in the Highlands to keep rebellious Scotland in order. Plant another on Tower hill to restrain your own Mobs. There never was a Notion more ridiculous. Don't you see the Advantage you now have if you preserve our Connection? The 50000 Men, and the Fleet employ'd in America during the last War, is now so much Strength at Liberty to be employ'd elsewhere.

They only desire you would leave them where you found them. Repeal all your taxing Laws, and return to Requisitions when you would have Aids from them.

Distinguish here what *may be convenient* from what *is fact*. Before the Union, it was thought *convenient* and long wish'd for, that the two Kingdoms should join in one Parliament. But till that Union was form'd, the *fact* was that their Parliaments were distinct, and the British Parliament could not make Laws for Scotland. The same *Fact* now subsists in America. The Parliaments and States are distinct. But the British has taken advantage of our Minority, and *usurp'd* Powers not belonging to it.

O Lord!

in *subordination to the sovereignty of England,* as should appear most favourable to their rights and liberties."

The discussion would be greatly furthered if some fixed principles were accepted on all

[*Part of a line missing*] a new Argument, and the Writers on both sides, have found themselves, on a more thorough Examination of Arguments and Facts, obliged to change some of their first Positions. The Subject is now better understood.

sides. For in the heat of argument "what is *granted at one time, is totally disavowed or denied at another.*" This seems to be the case,

And of Old Englanders too. Witness, the *Virtual Representation.*

in particular, of the New Englanders.

Whatever opinion I have of their rights is more favorable than my opinion of their con-

They think the same of yours.

duct, which is "*neither consistent nor prudent.* If they are *willing*

No, none at all. Leave the King, who alone is the Sovereign, to exercise his Acts of Sovereignty, in appointing their Governors, approving or disapproving their Laws, &c.

WE should exercise *any acts of sovereignty among them at all,* the imposition they have so riotously resisted, might...have been allowed better quarter; for it could have occasioned no further hardship than was voluntary,

But do you leave it to their Choice to trade elsewhere for those Commodities, to go to another Shop? No; you say

they having it always wholly left to their own choice to buy the commodities so charged, or not."
If they had submitted to this demand, they might never have been sorry. In any case I am

345

they shall buy of
you, or of nobody.

This mighty Resist-
ance is only doing
what the Author
says above they
might do, refusing
to buy the taxed
Commodities.

convinced that *"the resistance* they have made
to it was absolutely inconsistent with the demeanor usually expected from *subjects towards*

O God!

You have no Reason
for this Hope. It
was your Govern-
ment's refusing to
receive and consider
their Remonstrances,
that drove them
into the Measures
you condemn.

their governors. Less tumultuous proceedings
would...have been deemed much more becoming: and our government, I should humbly
hope, would have paid full as favourable an attention to their just remonstrances."

The reciprocal rights and claims of both sides
must be defined and adjusted before grievances
can be redressed and harmony return. Once the
adjustment is made, we may hope that the colonies will no longer complain of encroachment

The English have no
such Cause of
Complaint.

The Charters are
sacred. Violate
them, and then the
present Bond of
Union (the Kingly
Power over us) will
be broken.

on their liberties, or the mother country *"complain of the unequal payment of taxes on the part of
the colonies*; both being obliged equally to do
justice by each other....Nor should any mere
custom, *nor any charter or law in being, be allowed
any great weight in the decision on this point....*
The Americans may insist

Surely the Ameri-
cans deserve a little
more. They never
put you to the
Trouble and Ex-
pence of conquering
them, as Ireland has

upon *the same rights, privileges, and exemptions
as are allowed the Irish,* because of the similarity,
if not identity, of their connections with us."
But the situations of the two are in some respects
different, and, if any distinction is to be made
between them,

done three times over.[8] They never were in Rebellion. I speak now of the Native Irish. The English Families settled there certainly lost no Rights by their Merit in conquering that Country.

I wonder much at this *most certainly*.

"*most certainly...the Americans are least entitled to any lenity* on that score; and yet...they have been hitherto, by far, the most favoured."

The terms England may think safe to grant the Irish she may consider "dangerous and *imprudent* to grant the Americans: for...they may have it much more in their power to create disturbances with impunity; because, *long before we could send among them any considerable number of forces, they might do a great deal of mischief,*

It is very imprudent to deprive America of any of her Privileges. If her Friendship and Commerce are of any Importance to you, they are to be had on no other Terms, than leaving her in the full Enjoyment of her Rights.

They will take Care to preserve Order and Government for their own sakes.

if not actually overturn all order and government." Hence it would not

Where you can not so conveniently use Force, there you should endeavour to secure Affection.

be convenient to use the same coercive measures against America as against Ireland.

If the Americans "*would...contribute their quota of taxes,*" I should rather leave their pre-

8. The reconquest of Ireland by the forces of Queen Elizabeth after Tyrone's rebellion in 1598, by Cromwell in 1649–50, and by William III after the Battle of the Boyne, 1690–91.

347

Why then don't you try them? When did they refuse?	sent constitution undisturbed, however imperfect it may be, than try innovations that threaten an open rupture. For when we insist that they support the expense of government, they may justly insist upon enjoying the full benefit of it. [*The last two pages of the pamphlet are missing.*]

Marginalia in a pamphlet by Josiah Tucker

MS notations in the margins of a copy in the Historical Society of Pennsylvania of [Josiah Tucker], *A Letter from a Merchant in London to His Nephew in North America* (London, 1766).

The Rev. Josiah Tucker, Dean of Gloucester, was one of the more prolific pamphleteers of his time, and one of the few whose work still commands attention.[9] He was an economist as well as a theologian, and his economic ideas led him gradually to the conclusion that the colonies were an encumbrance that the mother country could best do without. The conclusion was based solely on British self-interest as he saw it; with the colonists' arguments about their rights he had no patience. The sovereignty of Parliament was for him unlimited: the Americans were virtually represented in it and hence might be taxed by it.[1] He was singularly contemptuous of them, even by the standards of the day. His contempt showed in the form in which he cast this pamphlet, which was ostensibly the letter of a wise old man to his young and callow relative, an imaginary background that gave the "uncle" free rein to write with a condescension that seems almost designed to infuriate.

Franklin was infuriated. He tore into the Dean's arguments with his usual vigor and at unusual length; he commented more fully than on any other pamphlet that has survived. The bulk of his notes permits extensive quotation, rather than paraphrase, of Tucker's accompanying text, from which its tone as well as style becomes all too clear.[2] Franklin's responses

9. For a brief biographical note on Tucker see above, IX, 123 n. The standard modern edition of his works is Robert L. Schuyler, ed., *Josiah Tucker: a Selection from His Economic and Political Writings* . . . (New York, 1931), in which this pamphlet appears on pp. 305–29.

1. *Ibid.*, pp. 30–9.

2. The complete text, together with BF's comments, is printed in *PMHB*, XXV (1901), 307–22, 516–26; XXVI (1902), 81–90, 255–64.

are interesting for their range (and occasionally their rage) rather than their originality: except for his views on property qualifications for voting, most of these marginalia repeat, at times almost verbatim, those in other pamphlets. Like them, these cannot be dated with confidence, although they were clearly written after news of the Boston Massacre reached London—more than four years, in other words, after the pamphlet was written. Franklin bought it and kept it on his shelves intending to read it, we conjecture; when he finally did so he exploded into rebuttal.

This is quoted upon the Supposition that the Point disputed is indisputable, viz. The Power of Parliament to make Laws binding in America, and to repeal Laws of the Colonies after they have had the Royal Assent. This Clause is void in itself, being contrary to the original Compact contained in the Colony Charters.

The letter deals with the colonists' position, discusses the supposed violation of their charters and other grievances, and explains the consequences if they attempt to gain independence. There follows a quotation from 7-8 Wm. III, c. 22, asserting the supremacy of parliamentary statutes over all colonial usages or legislation.

This is wickedly intended by the Author (Dean Tucker) to represent the E[nglish] North Americans as the Cause of the

"Your Letters gave me formerly no small Pleasure, because they seem to have proceeded from a good Heart, guided by an Understanding more enlightened than is usually found among young Men." The indignation you express against the frauds, robberies, and insults that lost us the affections of the Indians is particularly commendable, for those acts involved us in the bloodiest and most expensive war ever known and, if repeated, will drive the savages

349

War, Whereas it was in fact begun by the French, who seized the Goods and Persons of the English Traders on the Ohio: encroached on the King's Lands in Nova Scotia and took a Fort from the Ohio Company by force of Arms; which induc'd England to make Reprisals at Sea, and to send Braddock to recover the Fort on the Ohio, whence came on the War.

to seek revenge. You were therefore right in expressing your detestation of such practices.

But recently your tone has changed. Your mind seems agitated, and your reasoning incoherent and contradictory. Perhaps you want changes in your government, or perhaps you have the mistaken notion that we are making changes. Why do you keep harping on the

There is no doubt but Taxes laid in Parliament where the Parliament hath Jurisdiction, are legal Taxes; but doth it follow that Taxes laid by the Parliament of England on Scotland before the Union, on Guernsey, Jersey, Ireland, Hanover, or any other Dominions of the Crown not *within the Realm*, are therefore legal. These Writers against the Colonies all bewilder themselves by supposing the Colonies *within the Realm*, which is not the Case, nor ever was.

spirit of the constitution? It does not help your cause. "Magna Charta, for Example, is...the Basis of the English Constitution. But, by the Spirit of Magna Charta, *all Taxes laid on by Parliament are constitutional legal Taxes*; and Taxes raised by the Prerogative of the Crown, without the Consent of Parliament are illegal. Now remember, young Man, That the late Tax or Duties upon Stamps was laid on by Parliament; and therefore, according to your own Way of reasoning, must have been a regular, constitutional, legal Tax. Nay more, the princi-

350

This then is the *Spirit* of the Constitution, that Taxes shall not be laid with[out] the Consent of those to be taxed. The Colonies were not then in being and therefore nothing relating to them could be *literally* express'd. As the Americans are now *without* the Realm, and out of the Jurisdiction of Parliament, the *Spirit* of the British Constitution dictates, that they should be taxed only by *their own* Representatives as the English are by theirs.

pal End and Intention of Magna Charta, as far as Taxation is concerned, was to assert the Authority and Jurisdiction of the three Estates of the Kingdom, in Opposition to the sole Prerogative of the King: so that if you will now plead the Spirit of Magna Charta against the Jurisdiction of Parliament, you will plead Magna Charta against itself."

These subjects, like changeable silks, have different colors when seen in different lights. Let us move from the spirit of the constitution

This Position supposes, that Englishmen can never be out of the Jurisdiction of Parliament. It may as well be said, that wherever an Englishman resides, that Country is *England*. While an Englishman resides in England he is undoubtedly subject to its Laws. If he goes in to a foreign Country he is subject to the Laws and Government he finds there.

to the constitution itself, which is a factual matter. "The first Emigrants, who settled in America, were certainly *English Subjects;*—subject to the Laws and Jurisdiction of Parliament, and consequently to parliamentary Taxes, before their Emigration; and therefore subject afterwards, unless some legal constitutional Exemption can be produced.

"Now this is the Question, and the sole Question between you and me, reduced to a plain, single Matter of Fact. Is there therefore any such Exemption, as here pretended? And if you have it, why do you not produce it?—'The King, you say, hath granted Charters of Exemption to the American Colonies.' This is now coming to the Point: and this will bring the

351

If he finds no Government or Laws there, he is subject there to none, till he and his Companions if he has any make Laws for themselves. And this was the Case of the first Settlers in America. Otherwise and if they carried the English Laws and Power of Parliament with them, what Advantage could the Puritans propose to themselves by going, since they would have been as subject

Dispute to a short Issue. Let us therefore first enquire, Whether he could legally and constitutionally grant you such a Charter? And secondly, Whether he did ever so much as attempt to do it? And whether any such Charters are upon Record?

"Now, upon the first settling of an English Colony, and before ever you, Americans, could have chosen any Representatives,...to whose

to Bishops, Spiritual Courts, Tythes, and Statutes relating to the Church in America as in England? Can the Dean on his Principles tell us how it happens that those	Laws, the Game Acts, the Statutes for Labourers, and an infinity of others made before and since the Emigration, are not in force in America, nor ever were?

The Author here appears quite ignorant of the Fact. The Colonies carried no Law with them, They carried only a Power of making Law, or adopting such Parts of the English Law, or of any other Law, as they should think suitable to their Circumstances. The first Settlers of Connecticut, for Instance, at their first Meeting in that Country, finding themselves out of all Jurisdiction of other Governments, resolved and enacted, That till a

Laws, and to what legislative Power were you then subject? To the English most undoubtedly; for you could have been subject to no other. You were Englishmen yourselves; and you carried the English Government, and an English Charter over along with you. This being the Case, were you not then in the same Condition, as to Constitutional Rights and Liberties, with the rest of your Fellow-subjects, who remained in England?

Code of Laws should be prepared and agreed to, they would be governed by the *Law of Moses,* as contained in the Old Testament.[3]

You are too positive, Mr. Dean.

Certainly you were.... You ought not to have been placed in a worse: and surely you had no Right to expect a better. Suppose therefore, that the Crown had been so ill advised, as to have granted a Charter to any City

If the first Settlers had no Right to expect a better Constitution, what Fools were they for going over, to encounter all the Hardships and Perils of new Settlements in a Wilderness! for these were so many

Additions to what they suffer'd at home from tyrannical and oppressive Institutions in Church and State if they carried those Institutions with them, with a Subtraction of all

their old Enjoyments of the Conveniencies and Comforts of an old Settled Country, Friends, Neighbours, Relations, Homes, &c &c.

The American Settlers *needed no Exemption* from the Power of Parliament; they were necessarily exempted as soon as they landed out of its Jurisdiction. Therefore all this Rhetorical Paragraph is founded on a Mis-

or County here in England, *pretending to exempt them from the Power and Jurisdiction of an English Parliament;*—what would the Judges? what would the Lawyers? nay, what would you Americans have said to it?... Is it possible for you to believe, that the King has a Power vested in him by the Constitution of *dividing his Kingdom into several independent States, and petty Kingdoms, like the Heptarchy in the Times of the Saxons?*... Is it possible, I say, for you to be-

3. BF is referring to the reception in the colony of New Haven of John Cotton's "Moses his Judicials," which despite its title was based more on the law of Massachusetts Bay colony than on the Mosaic code. See Charles M. Andrews, *The Colonial Period of American History* (3 vols., New Haven, [1934–38]), II, 156–9.

take of the Author; he talks of is of his own Making.

lieve an *Absurdity so gross and glaring?*" The alternative is to believe that the King can do in America what he can not do in England, which

What Stuff! Why may not an American plead for the just Prerogatives of the Crown? And is it not a just Prerogative of the Crown to give the Subjects Leave to settle in a foreign Country if they think it necessary to ask such Leave? Was the Parliament at all considered or consulted in making these first Settlements? [No]r did any Lawyer then think it necessary.

means exalting his power. "An American pleading for the Extension of the Prerogative of the Crown? Yes, if it could make for his Cause;—and for extending it too beyond all the Bounds of Law, of Reason, and of Common Sense!"

It was not a Renunciation of [a] Right of Parliament; There was no Need of such a Renunciation, for Parliament had not then pretended to such a

Although I have supposed for argument's sake that the crown was so ill advised as to grant illegal and unconstitutional charters, the fact was very different. [*Footnote:* Kings formerly claimed the right to tax without the consent of Parliament; but this right was not insisted on in any of the charters, and was explicitly surrendered in that of Maryland.[4] Now this renunciation of an obsolete prerogative is made into the renunciation by Parliament of the right to raise taxes. The King was promising only for himself, not for Parliament.] No such unconstitutional charters were ever

4. In the Maryland charter of 1632 Lord Baltimore acquired remarkable palatine rights, among them that to all duties levied upon the commerce of the province.

Right. But since the Royal Faith was pledg'd by the King for himself and his Successors, how can any succeeding King, without violating that Faith, even give his Assent to an Act of Parliament for such Taxation?

A Fib, Mr. Dean: In *one* Charter *only*, and that a later one, is the Parliament mentioned: And the right reserved is only that of laying Duties on Commodities imported from the Colony or exported to it.[5]

granted. "Nay, *many of* your Colony Charters assert quite the contrary, by containing express Reservations of Parliamentary Rights, particularly that great one of levying Taxes. And those Charters which do not make such Provisoes in express Terms, *must be supposed* virtually to

Suppositions and *Implications* will not weigh in these important Cases.

imply them; because the Law and Constitution will not allow, that the King can do more either at home or abroad, by the Prerogative Royal,

No Law or Constitution forbad the King's doing what he did in granting those Charters.

than the *Law and Constitution* authorize him to do."

This Instance would be something, if London was not *within* the Realm. Whereas the

If you want a striking proof of this argument I will give you one, "and *such an one too, as shall convince you*, if anything can, of the Folly and Absurdity of your Positions." The City of London has long enjoyed great liberties under its

5. The charter of Pennsylvania granted by Charles II; for the provision to which BF refers see William Macdonald, *Select Charters* ... (N.Y. and London, 1899), pp. 188–9.

Colonies are *without*; and therefore 'tis nothing to the purpose, convinces no American of any thing but the pert positiveness and Ignorance of the Author.

charter, but no Londoner would think of pleading them as ground for being exempted from Parliamentary authority or taxation. If any one did he would be sent, not to prison, but "to

The difference between a Fool and a Madman is said to be, that the Fool reasons wrong from right Premises, the Madman right but from wrong Premises. This seems the Case of our Author, and therefore *that Place* perhaps more suitable for him.

another Place of Confinement, much fitter for a Person in his unhappy Situation.

"And now, my good Friend, what can you say to these things?—The only thing which you ought to say, is,—that you did not see the Affair in its true Light before: and that you are sincerely sorry for having been so positive in a

This is Hollowing before you are out of the Wood.

wrong Cause. *Confuted most undoubtedly you are beyond the Possibility of a Reply....*" But your letters indicate that you have other arguments than the charters. What are they? The cruelty of taxing a free people without permitting them to have representatives? "Strange, that though

False! Never before the Restoration.

the British Parliament has been, *from the Beginning*, thus unreasonable,...you should not

The Parliament, it is acknowledged, have made many oppressive Laws relating to America, which have passed without Opposition, partly thro' the Weakness of the Colonies, partly thro' their

have been able to have discovered, that you were without Representatives in the British Parliament, of your own electing, till this enlightening Tax upon Paper opened your Eyes! And what a pity is it, that you have been Slaves for so many Generations, and yet did not know, that you were Slaves until now."

But let that pass. If you mean anything by the cruelty of the mother country, you must mean

356

Inattention to the full Extent of their Rights while employ'd in Labour to procure the Necessaries of Life. But that is a wicked Guardian, and a Shameless one, who first takes Advantage of the Weakness incident to Minority, cheats and Imposes on his Pupil; and when that Pupil comes of Age urges those very Impositions as Precedents to justify continuing them and adding others!

This is all Banter and Insult, when you know the Impossibility of a Million of Freeholders coming over Sea to vote here. If their Freeholds in America were *within the Realm*, why have they not, in virtue of those Freeholds, a Right to vote in your Elections as well as an English Freeholder? Sometimes we are told, that our Estates are by our Charters all in the Manor of East Greenwich and therefore all in England, and yet have we any Rights to vote among the

that she deals worse with you than with her own inhabitants, by denying you rights and privileges that they enjoy. But what are these rights? Name them if you can. The right of voting for members of Parliament? "But surely you will not dare to say, that we refuse your Votes, when you come hither to offer them, and

choose to poll: you cannot have the Face to assert, that on an Election Day any Difference is put between the Vote of a Man born in America, and of one born here in England. Yet this you must assert, and prove too, before you can do any thing to the present purpose. Suppose therefore, that an American...is become a Freeman, or a Freeholder here in England;—on that State of the Case, prove if you can, that his Vote was ever refused, because he was born in America: —Prove this, I say, and then I will allow, that your Complaints are very just; and that you are indeed the much injured, the cruelly-treated People, you would make the World believe.

357

Voters of East Greenwich?[6] Can we trade to the same Ports? In this very Paragraph you

This is all beside the Mark. The Americans are by their Constitutions provided with a Representation, and therefore need nor desire any in the British Parliament. They have never ask'd any such Thing. They only say, since we have a Right to grant our own Money to the King; since we have Assemblies where we are represented for such Purposes, why will you meddle out of your Sphere, take the Money that is ours and give it as yours without our Consent?

An absolute Falshood: We never demanded in any Manner, much less in the Manner you mention, that the Mother Country should change her Constitution.

suppose that we cannot vote in England if we come thither, till we have by Purchase ac-

quired a Right, therefore neither we nor our Estates are represented in England.

"But, my good Friend, is this supposed refusal the real Cause of your Complaint?...Oh! no, you have no Complaint of this sort to make: but the Cause of your Complaint is this; that you live at too great a Distance from the Mother Country to be present at our English Elections....It may be so; but pray consider, if you yourselves do choose to make it inconvenient for you to come and vote, by retiring into distant Countries,—what is that to us?" You live in the colonies because you prefer to do so; why should we be compelled to remodel our ancient

constitution at your behest? "*You demand it* too with a loud Voice, full of Anger, of Defiance, and Denunciation."

But let us be reasonable. Grant that the colonies are unrepresented; what does this mean?

6. See above, XIII, 18–22.

At least six million inhabitants of the British Isles are also unrepresented, not from the necessity

Why then do you not give them a Representation?

of distance as in your case, but because of accidents of property-holding. *"Copyholds and Leaseholds of various Kinds"* have no representatives; I myself am possessed of *"property in London, and of* several Copyholds and beneficial Leaseholds in the Country, and yet... I never had a Vote. Moreover, in some Towns neither Freedom, nor Birth-right, nor the serving of an Apprenticeship, shall entitle a man to give a Vote.... In other Towns the most numerous, the most populous, and flourishing of any, there are no Freedoms or Votes of any Sort; but all is open; and none are represented. And besides all this,... the *great*

Copyholds and Leaseholds are suppos'd to be re-presented in the original Landlord of Whom they are held. Thus all the Land in England is in fact represented notwithstanding what he here says.

As to those who have no Landed Property in a Country, the allow-ing them to vote for Legislators is an Impropriety. They are transient In-habitants, and not so connected with the Welfare of the State which they may quit when they please, as to qualify them properly for such Privilege.

By this Argument it may be prov'd that no Man in England has a Vote. The Clergy have none as Clergymen; the Lawyers none as Lawyers, the Physi-cians none as Physicians, and so on. But if they have Votes as Free-

East India Company, which have such vast Settlements, and which dispose of the Fate of Kings and Kingdoms abroad, have not so much as a single Member, or even a single Vote, *quatenus a Company*, to watch over their In-terests at home. What likewise shall we say in regard to the prodigious number of Stock-holders in our public Funds?

holders that is
sufficient: And that
no Freeholder in
America has for a Re-
presentative in the
British Parliament.

The Stockholders
are many of them
Foreigners, and all
may be so when
they please, as
nothing is more easy
than the transferring
of Stock, and con-
veying Property
beyond Sea by Bills
of Exchange. Such
uncertain Subjects
are therefore not
properly vested
with Rights relating
to Government.

And may not their Property, perhaps little short
of One hundred Millions Sterling, as much deserve to be represented in Parliament, as the
scattered Townships, or straggling Houses of
some of your Provinces in America? yet we
raise no Commotions; we neither ring the
Alarm-Bell, nor sound the Trumpet; but submit
to be taxed without being represented;—and

This is wickedly
false. While the
Colonies were weak
and poor, not a
Penny or a single
Soldier was ever
spared by Britain
for their Defence:
But as soon as the
Trade with them
became an Object,
and a Fear arose
that the French
would seize that
Trade and deprive
her of it, she sent
Troops to America
unask'd. And now
brings this Account
of the Expence
against us, which
should be rather
carried to her own

taxed too, let me tell you, *for your Sakes.* Witness the additional Duties on our Lands, Windows, Houses;—also on our Malt, Beer, Ale,
Cyder, Perry, Wines, Brandy, Rum, Coffee,
Chocolate, &c. &c. &c. for defraying the Expences of the late War,—not forgetting the
grievous Stamp-Duty itself. All this, I say, we
submitted to, when you were, or at least, when
you pretended to be, in great Distress: so that
neither Men, almost to the last Drop of Blood
we could spill,—nor Money, to the last Piece of
Coin, were spared; but all was granted away,
all was made

Merchants and Manufacturers. We join'd our Troops and Treasure with hers, to help her in this War. Of this no Notice is taken. To refuse to pay a just Debt is Knavish. Not to return an Obligation is In-

gratitude: But to demand Payment of a Debt where none has been contracted, to forge a Bond or an Obligation in order to demand what was never due is infamous Villainy. Every Year both King and Parliament

(during the War) acknowledged that we had done more than our Part, and made us some Return, which is equivalent to a Receipt in full and entirely sets aside this monstrous Claim.

Never.

a Sacrifice, when you *cried out for Help*." In the war we acquired a debt unparalleled in history, just as "the *Returns which you have made us for these Succours*" are also unparalleled.

But let us come to the subject that you are trying to make the basis of your case: the fact that you, like so many of us, are unrepresented. Which lack of representation *"deserves first to be redressed?"* Suppose that we ought to increase the size of the House of Commons in order to accommodate representatives of those British subjects who now have none, we must first settle the proportions. If the two million now represented elect 558 members as at present, six million will need 1,674, and the two million colonists will require an additional 558, making

By all means redress your own Grievances. If you are not just to your own People, how can we trust you? We ask no Representation among you: But if you have any thing wrong among yourselves, rectify it, and do not make one Injustice a Precedent and Plea for doing another. That would be increasing Evil in the World instead of diminishing it.

You need not be concern'd about the Number to be added from America. We do not desire to

a total assembly of 2,790 members. "A goodly Number truly! and very proper for the Dispatch of Business! Oh, the Decency and Order of such an Assembly! The Wisdom and Gravity

come among you. But you may make some Room for your own additional Members by removing those that are sent by the rotten Burroughs.

of Two thousand Seven hundred and Ninety Legislators all met together in one Room! What a Pity is it, that so hopeful a Project

This Banter very useless and silly.

should not be carried into immediate Execution!

In the same Manner Mr. Dean, are the Pope and Cardinals Representatives of the whole Christian Church. Why don't you obey them?

"But... I must now tell you, that *every Member of Parliament represents you and me, and our Interests in all essential Points, just as much as if we had voted for him.*" For as soon as he is elected

What occasion is there then, my dear Sir, of being at the Trouble of Elections? The Peers alone would do as well for our Guardians tho' chosen by the King or born such. If their present Number is too small, his Majesty may be good enough to add 558, or make the present House of Commons and their Heirs male Peers for ever. If having a Vote in Elections would be of no Use to us, how is it of any to you? Elections are the Causes of much Tumult, Riot, Contention

he becomes responsible for the interests of all, a guardian of the general welfare rather than of the particular interests of his constituency. Boston and New York are as truly represented as Manchester and Leeds by the 558 members, who are numerous enough to secure the rights and liberties of all.

But you may say that each member must look out for his own interests in order to secure re-election. Perhaps, but who can guard against all dangers? What system is perfect? Your objection, furthermore, proves too much—that no man ought to pay any tax until his own particular representative has consented to it, and therefore that whoever does not have a repre-

362

and Mischief; get rid of them at once and for ever.

You seem to take your Nephew for a Simpleton, Mr. Dean. Every one who votes for a Representative knows and intends that the Majority is to govern; and that the Consent of the Majority is to be understood as the Consent of the whole, that being ever the Case in all deliberative Assemblies.

sentative in Parliament is not obliged to obey its laws or pay its taxes.

Where will you turn to extricate yourself from your logical difficulties? You cannot say that representatives whom such a man never chose have a right to tax him "because he makes a Part of the Body Politic implied in, and concluded by the rest;—you cannot say this, be-

How far, my dear Sir, would you yourself carry the Doctrine of Implication? If important Positions are to be imply'd when not express'd, I suppose you can have no Objection to their being imply'd where some Expression countenances the Implication. If you should say to a Friend, I am your humble Servant, Sir, ought he to imply from thence that you will clean his Shoes?

cause the *Doctrine of Implication* is the very Thing to which you object, and against which you have raised so many Batteries of popular Noise and Clamour. Nay, as the Objection is entirely of your own making, it must go still further: for if your Argument is good for any thing, it is as good for North America as it is for Great Britain: and consequently you must

No Freeholder in North America is without a Vote. Many who have no Freeholds have nevertheless a Vote, which indeed I do not think was necessary to be allowed.

maintain, that *all those in your several Provinces who have no Votes* (and many Thousands of such there are)" and also all those whose representatives did not consent to a provincial tax should not be compelled to pay it. *"These now are the*

Not of our Principles but of what you are pleas'd to imagine such.

happy Consequences of your own Principles, fairly, clearly, and evidently deduced: Will you abide by them?"

What would you say if you discovered that the House of Commons has been more partial to you than to the British? This can be proved from the statute book. You have the choice, for example, "whether you will accept of my Price for your Tobacco,—or *after bringing it here,*

A great Kindness this, to oblige me first to bring it here that the Expence of another Voyage and Freight may deter me from carrying it away, and oblige me to take the Price you are pleas'd to offer.

whether you will carry it away, and try your Fortune at another Market: but I have no alternative allowed, being obliged to buy yours at your own Price; or else to *pay such a Duty* for

You lay a Duty on the Tobacco of other Countries, because you must pay Money for that, but get ours in Exchange for your Manufactures.

the Tobacco of other Countries, as must amount to a Prohibition. Nay, in order to favour your Plantations, I am

Tobacco is not permitted to be planted in England, lest it should inter-

not *permitted to plant this Herb on my own Estate, though the Soil should be ever so proper for it.* Again, the *same Choice,* and the same Alterna-

fere with the Corn
necessary for your
Subsistence.

Rice you cannot
raise. It requires 11
Months, your Sum-
mer is too short.
Nature not the Laws
denies you this
Product.

tive are allowed to you, and *denied to me*, in regard to Rice; with this additional Advantage,
that in many Respects you need not bring it into
England at all, unless you are so minded. And
what will you say in Relation to Hemp? The

Did ever any North
American bring his
Hemp to England
for this Bounty? We
have yet not enough
for our own Con-
sumption. We begin
to make our own
Cordage. You want
to suppress that
Manufacture and
would do it by
getting the raw
Material from us:
You want to be
supply'd with Hemp
for your Manu-
factures, and Russia
demands Money.
These were the
Motives for giving
what you are
pleased to call a
Bounty to us. We
thank you for your
Bounties. We love
you and therefore
must be oblig'd to
you for being good
to yourselves. You
do not encourage
raising Hemp in
England, because
you know it im-

Parliament *now gives you a Bounty of £8 per Ton
for exporting your Hemp from North America*; but
will allow me nothing for growing it here in
England; nay, will tax me very severely for
fetching it from any other country; though it be
an Article most essentially necessary for all the
Purposes of Shipping and Navigation. Moreover in respect to the Culture of Raw Silk, you
have an immense Parliamentary Premium for
that Purpose; and you receive farther Encour-
agements from our Society for Arts and
Sciences, which is continually adding fresh
Rewards:—but I can receive no Encouragement either from the one, or from the other, to
bear my Expences at first setting out;—though
most undeniably the white Mulberry-Trees
can thrive as well on my Grounds, as they can
in Switzerland, Brandenburgh, Denmark, or
Sweden, where vast Quantities are now raising.
Take another instance: Why shall I not be
permitted to buy Pitch, Tar, and Turpentine,—
without which I cannot put my Ships to sea,—
and Indigo, so useful in many Manufactures;—
why shall not I be permitted to purchase these
Articles wherever I can, the best in their kind,
and on the best Terms?—No, I shall not; for
though they are all raw Materials, which therefore ought to have been imported Duty free,

poverishes the richest Grounds; your Land Owners are all against it. What you call Bounties given by Parliament and the Society are nothing more than Inducements offered us, to induce us to leave Employments that are more profitable and engage in such as would be less so without your Bounty; to quit a Business profitable to ourselves and engage in one that shall be profitable to you; this is the true Spirit of all your Bounties. Your Duties on foreign Articles are from the same Motives. Pitch, Tar and Turpentine used to cost you £5 a Barrel when you had them from Foreigners, who us'd you ill

yet I am restrained by an heavy Duty, almost equal to a Prohibition, from purchasing them anywhere, but from you:—Whereas you on the contrary, are paid a Bounty for selling these very Articles, at the only Market, in which you could sell them to advantage, viz. the English.

into the Bargain, thinking you could not do without them. You gave a bounty of 5s. a Barrel to the Colonies, and they have brought you such Plenty as to reduce the Price to 10s. a Barrel. Take back your Bounties when you please, since you upbraid us with them. Buy your Indigo, Pitch, Silk, and Tobacco where you please, and let us buy our Manufactures where we please. I fancy we shall be Gainers. I am sick of these *forged Obligations*. As to the great

Kindness of these 558 Parliamentary Guardians of American Privileges, who can forbear smiling that has seen the Navigation Act, the Hatters Act, the Steel, Hammer and Slit Iron Acts, and numberless others restraining our Trade, obstructing our Manufactures, and forbidding us the Use of the Gifts of God and Nature? Hopeful Guardians truly! Can it be imagined that if we had a reasonable Share in selecting them from time to time they would thus have us'd us?

See the Statutes too for the Navigation Act.

[*Footnote:* Those who have not the Statutes at large, *may see the Things* here referred to, and many others of the like Sort, in Crouche's or Saxby's Book of Rates.]"

It is your Confutations that are imaginary.

Of all people on earth you have least reason to complain, but complain you will. No sooner is "one Recital of *imaginary Grievances silenced and confuted*" than another appears. Your last one is that this tax is inexpedient, ill timed, ill

All these Objections were only to show, how unequal the Parliament was to the Business of Taxing the Colonies if the Right had been with them, from their Ignorance of Circumstances and Abilities &c.

digested, and unrelated to the colonists' ability to pay. This objection would be unnecessary if you had succeeded in showing, as you have not, that the tax was illegal. But, as you were probably dissatisfied yourself

We see in you abundance of Self Conceit, but no convincing Argument.

with the legal argument, "and must have seen abundant Reason before this Time to have altered your former hasty, and rash Opinion," I will debate the question of expediency. You cannot claim that you are too poor to pay after

This should be a Caution to Americans how they indulge for the future in British Luxuries. See here British Generosity! The People who have made you poor by their worthless I mean useless Commodities, would now make you poorer by Taxing you: And from the very Inability you have brought on yourselves by a Partiality for their Fashions and Modes of Living, of which they have had the whole Profit, would now urge your Ability to pay the Taxes they are

having given us "such *displays of your growing Riches and increasing Magnificence,* as perhaps never any People did in the same Space of Time." Remember how I expostulated with your father on the tremendous increase of American luxury. He attributed it to the growing wealth of the country, and told me to suit my wares to my customers' tastes. He and then you ordered richer and richer goods of all sorts. Have you now put them aside? Have you given up concerts and plays and gambling and horse races? "And is the *Luxury of your Tables, and the Variety and Profusion of your Wines and Liquors* quite banished from among you?" You must answer these questions before pleading that the tax is excessive. Even if you were poor, which you are not by comparison with thirty years ago, it may be that we are relatively poorer. In that case which people can better bear the tax burden?

pleas'd to impose. Reject then their Commerce as well as their pretended Power of Taxing. Be frugal and industrious, and you will be free. The Luxury of your Tables, which could be known to the English only by your hospitably entertaining, is by these grateful Guests now made a Charge against you, and given as a Reason for taxing you.

I have heard, Mr. Dean, that you have studied Political Arithmetick more than Divinity, but by this Sample of it I fear to very little purpose. If personal Service were the Matter in Question, out of so many Millions of Souls so many Men might be expected, whether here or in America. But when raising Money is the Question, It is not the Number of Souls but the Wealth in Possession, that shows the Ability. If we were twice as numerous as the People of England it would not follow that we are half as able. There are Numbers of single Estates in England each worth a hundred of the best [of] ours in N A. The City of London alone is worth all the Provinces of N. America.

Assume "that you are two Millions of Souls: ...that the Public Debt of the several Provinces amounts to about 800,000 Sterling: and...that were this general Debt equally divided among the two Millions, each Individual would owe about the Value of Eight Shillings. Thus stands the Account on one side. Now we in Britain are reckoned to be about Eight Millions of Souls; and we owe almost One hundred and forty-four Millions of Money: which Debt, were it equally divided among us, would throw a Burthen upon each Person of about £18 Sterling. This then being the State of the Case...would it be High-Treason in us to demand of you, who owe so little, to *contribute equally with ourselves*, who owe so much, towards the public Expences;—and such Expences too as *you were the Cause of creating?*...Surely no:—And yet, my gentle Friend, we do not so much as ask you to

This Lie is forever repeated by these Writers.

contribute equally with ourselves, we only demand, that you would contribute something." In other words £100,000, the most that the stamp duty can amount to, which comes to a

The Colonies have ever been willing and ready to contribute in Proportion to their Ability, and have done it in various Ways.

shilling a person. "Blush! blush for shame at your perverse and scandalous Behaviour!"

Perhaps you will say—and it is all that is left for you to say—that you have other taxes of your own to pay. Undoubtedly you have, but so have we, many others "besides those which ...are to be accounted for at the Exchequer....

Blush for Shame at your own Ignorance Mr. Dean, who do not know that the Colonies have Taxes and heavy ones of their own to pay, to support their own Civil and military Establishments! and that the Shilling should not be reckon'd upon Heads, but upon Pounds. There never was a sillier Argument.

Witness our County Taxes, Militia Taxes, Poor Taxes, Vagrant Taxes, High Road and Turnpike Taxes, Watch Taxes, Lamps and Scavenger Taxes, &c. &c. &c.—all of them as numerous and as burthensome as any that you can mention. And yet with all this Burthen, yea, with an additional Weight of a National Debt of £18 Sterling per Head,—we require of each of you to

And have we not all these Taxes too, as well as you, and our Provincial or Public Taxes besides? And over and above, have we not new Roads to make, new Bridges to build, Churches and Colleges to found, and a Number of other Things to do that your Fathers have done for you and

which you inherit
from them, but
which we are oblig'd
to pay for out of
our present Labour?

How fond he is of
this One Shilling
and twenty!

contribute only *One Shilling to every Twenty*
from each of us!—yes; and *this Shilling too to be
spent in your own Country, for the Support of your*

Who has desired
this of you, and
who can trust you
to lay it out? If you
are thus to provide
for our Civil and
military Establish-
ments, what use will
there afterwards be
for our Assemblies?

own Civil and Military Establishments;—together with many Shillings drawn from us for
the same Purpose.—Alas! had you been in our

No. We will pay
nothing on Com-
pulsion.

Situation, and we in yours, would you have
been content with our paying so small, so inconsiderable a Share of the Public Expences?"

The Americans
never brought
Riots as Argu-
ments. It is unjust to
charge two or three
Riots in particular
Places upon all
America. Look for
Arguments in the
Petitions and Re-
monstrances of the
Assemblies, who
detest Riots, of
which there are ten
in England for one
in America.

You are the world's most unfortunate people
in your handling of this controversy: the way
you prove your inability to pay is "by breaking
forth into Riots and Insurrections, and by committing every kind of Violence, that can cause
Trade to stagnate, and Industry to cease. And
is this the Method ... to make the World believe,
that you are a poor People? Is this the Proof you
bring, that the Stamp Duty is a burthen too
heavy for you to bear? Surely, if you had really

How impudent it is to insinuate that the Americans chose no other Medium.

When? Where?

intended our Conviction you would have *chosen some other* Medium." If you are in fact poor, you are taking the best way to make yourselves poorer. For if "you can still afford to idle away your Time, and to waste Days, *and Weeks*, in Outrages and Uproars," you are demonstrating your prodigality and extravagance.

The stamp duty, despite what you say, is neither unfair, unduly burthensome, nor badly timed. In the recent past you were draining us dry to pay for our fleets and armies "acting in Defence of America," and at the same time our blood was being sucked by the extortionate demands of "*your Jobbers* and *Contractors*." Mean-

Defence of your Trade in America.

Your Jobbers and Contractors if you please. We had none of those dainty Morsels.

while you were growing rich by "continually acting the double Part either of Trade, *or War*, of Smuggling, or *Privateering*, according to the Prospect of greater Gain." While we were

Is the War we made on your Enemies then among our Offences?

An infamous Lie! They always have warlike Stores cheaper than ours: Our Supplying them with Provisions was a Cry only to found an Embargo on for the Benefit of English Contractors, that they might buy our Provisions cheaper. All this Page is Falshood and Misrepresentation. Money was actually much scarcer in the Colonies after the War than before. This is a

striving to end the war you were prolonging it, "and were supplying *our enemies with all Manner of Provisions, and all Sorts of warlike Stores for that Purpose*. Nay; because forsooth a Part of these ill-gotten Riches were laid out in English Manufactures...your Advocates and Authors trumpeted about the prodigious Profits of this North American Trade;—not considering, or rather not willing that we should consider, that while a few Individuals were getting Thousands, the Public was spending Millions."

Fact known to all
that know any
thing of them.

If you believe that the tax was ill timed because Britain was "able to bear the additional Load, *which you had brought upon us,*" you are completely mistaken: we are not able, even if we were willing, to bear further taxation. "*The Expenses of America must be borne by the Americans* in some Form...."

Infamous Lie!

Undoubtedly. We
don't desire you to
bear our Expences.

But perhaps you mean that the act was ill timed because it was made "when neither the *French, nor Indians were in your Rear to frighten,* nor the English Fleets and Armies on your Front to *force you to a Compliance.* Perhaps this was your real Meaning: and if it was, it must be confessed, that in that Sense, the late Act was not well-timed; and that a much properer Season might have been chosen. For had the Law been made five or six years

It seems a prevailing
Opinion in England,
that Fear of their
French Neighbours
would have kept the
Colonies in Obedi-
ence to the Par-
liament; and that if
the French Power
had not been sub-
du'd, no Opposi-
tion would have
been made to the
Stamp Act. A very
groundless Notion.
On the contrary,
Had the French
Power continued, to
which the Ameri-
cans might have had
Recourse in Case of

Oppression from Parliament, Parliament would not have dared to oppress them. It was the Employment of 50,000 Men at Land, and a Fleet at the Coast, five Years to subdue the French

only. Half the Land Army were Provincials. Suppose the British 25000 had acted by themselves with all the Colonies against them: what time would it have taken to subdue the whole?

It is wonderful
whence the English
drew this Notion!
The Americans
know nothing of it.

before, *when you were moving Heaven and Earth with your Cries and Lamentations;* not a Tongue would then have uttered a Word against it...." Even the Americans would then have obeyed

The Protection was
mutual.

Britain "in Return for her *kind* and *generous Protection.*"

Not from the
Beginnings. Look
below at your List
of Acts. The first of
them is in the 12 of
Cha. II. Threescore
Years after the
Beginning of Settle-
ments in America.

Your real grievance is not the Stamp Act but
Britain's revival of trade restrictions. "The same
*Restrictions have been the standing Rules of gov-
ernment from the Beginning*; though not en-
forced at all Times with equal Strictness."

False.

[*Footnote:* All European colonial powers have
attempted by legislation to confine colonial
trade to the mother country "ever since the
Discovery of America." A list follows of British
statutes for that purpose.] "During the late
War, you Americans *could not import the Manufactures* of other Nations (*which it is your constant

An absolute Lie!

Aim to do, and the aim of the Mother Country

More conveniently
if we had lik'd
them. But the Truth
is, that Foreign
Manufactures are
not to the Taste of
the Americans.

always to prevent), *so conveniently as* you can in
Times of Peace: and therefore, there was no
Need of watching you so narrowly, as far as

Not a single Manu-
facture of France,
except Brandy if
that be one, ever
used in America.

that Branch of Trade was concerned. *But immediately upon the Peace, the various Manufactures of Europe, particularly those of France, which
could not find Vent before, were spread, as it were,*

A vile Lie.

over all your Colonies, to the prodigious Detriment of your Mother Country." This caused
the revival of trade restrictions. If their administration is faulty, it will be improved; but
the American wants more. "He will ever complain and smuggle, and smuggle and complain,
till all Restraints are removed, and till he can
both buy and sell…wheresoever he pleases."

Infinitely more
Smuggling in Eng-
land! Not a Member
of Parliament that
has not smuggled

373

Goods on his
Wrists.

They are Laws *in*
the Kingdom.

To the King only.

Ignorance!

By suffering us to
enjoin our Rights,
you may expect our
Assistance, and not
otherwise.

These restraints, nevertheless, will remain.
"They are the *standing Laws of the Kingdom....*
In short, while you are a Colony, you must be
subordinate to the *Mother Country.* These are *the
Terms and Conditions, on which you were per-
mitted to make your first Settlements*: they are the
Terms and *Conditions,* on *which alone* you can be
entitled to the Assistance and Protection of Great

Not at all to pro-
mote our Interests,
but your own. See
p. 23, 24, 25 [above,
pp. 363–6].

Britain...." You ought to have restrictions on
your trade in order to promote our interest, because we have restrictions on our trade in order
to promote yours. Do not expect, therefore,
that the present administration will long con-
nive at your disobedience; they will have to
enforce the law.

Another infamous
Lie!

"Many among you are sorely concerned,
That they cannot pay their British Debts with
an American sponge. This is an intolerable

Who proposed this,
you lying Villain!

Grievance: and...you have spoken out, and
proposed an open Association against paying your

Had the French or
Spaniards rais'd
such a Lie on you,
what Name would
you have given
them?

just Debts." Had our debtors, French or Spanish, proposed this, "what Name would you
have given to such Proceedings?"

You resent the sovereignty of Great Britain.
"For you want to be independent: You *wish to
be an Empire by itself, and to be no* longer the
Province of another. This Spirit...is visible in
all your Speeches, and all your Writings, even

We were always
distinct separate
States under the
Same Sovereign.

when you take some Pains to disguise it. 'What!
an Island! A Spot such as this to command the
great and mighty Continent of North America!
Preposterous!'" Let us no longer be subjected
to the paltry Kingdom of Great Britain, you say,
but let the seat of empire be transferred to
Great America.

A silly Speech Mr.
Dean has made for
us.[7]

These extravagant conceits are founded on
calculations which "*I think*...both false and
absurd." But the question is what we are going
to do with you before you become as formid-
able as your dreams. "*You endeavour, with all
your Might, to drive us to Extremities.* For no
Kind of Outrage, or Insult is omitted...and you
do not seem at all disposed to leave Room for an
Accommodation." Only if we recant will you
acknowledge the power of Parliament, which

Your Thought, Mr.
Dean, avails little
against Fact.
On the Contrary, It
is you English that
endeavour by every
kind of Outrage and
Insult to drive us to
Extremities. Wit-
ness your Troops
quarter'd upon us,
Your Dissolution of
our Assemblies, &c
&c &c

means acknowledging "that *we have a Right
and a Power to give you Bounties, and to pay your
Expences*;—but no other."

We desire neither.

7. The idea of this imaginary speech did not seem silly a few years later.
"There is something very absurd, in supposing a Continent to be perpetually
governed by an island." Thomas Paine, *Common Sense*... (Philadelphia,
1776), p. 45.

We have three choices: to coerce you, to procrastinate, or to give you up entirely. The first would not be difficult; an American mob would be no match for British officers and soldiers, "*who passed several Campaigns with your Provincials in America,*" and took their measure. We have faith in our troops, despite some of your friends here and "*their Insinuations*" of the Feasibility of corrupting his Majesty's Forces...by Means of *large Bribes, or double Pay.*" You say you are poor and cannot pay your debts, in other words, while "you *boast of the scandalous Use which you intend to make of your Riches.*"

And who did little or nothing without 'em:

A ridiculous Imagination of the Author's own Head!

A Silly Lie! No such Boast was ever made.

I am, however, opposed to military operations, for how would conquering you benefit us? We might keep ships on your coast, and an army of customs officers to hunt down smugglers; but all this would only "sharpen your Wits, which are pretty sharp already, to elude our Searches, and to bribe and corrupt our Officers." We might in the end force you to buy twenty or thirty thousand pounds' worth of our goods at a cost for enforcement of two or three hundred thousand.

Here appears some Sense.

Procrastinating is no solution, for it would only strengthen your opposition, as would any appearance of yielding to your demands. If the Stamp Act were suspended for the benefit of British merchants, who are in the pitiable position of having entrusted you with hundreds of thousands of pounds' worth of goods, they would find that such indulgence had merely confirmed you in refusing to pay your debts to them. For you demand repeal, not suspension,

Infamous Scandal, without the least Foundation. The Merchants never receiv'd better Payment of the Debts, than during the Suspension of the Trade.

376

Never any Such
Justification was
offered by any
American whatever,
that I can hear of.

Never!

The Impudence of
this Language to
Colonies who have
ever maintained
themselves is
astonishing! Except
the *late attempted*
Colonies of Nova
Scotia and Georgia,
No Colony ever
received Main-
tenance in any
Shape from Britain:
And the Grants to
those Colonies were
mere Jobbs for the
Benefit of ministerial
Favourites: *English*
or *Scotchmen.*[8]

Throughout all
America, English
Debts are more
easily recovered
than in England, the
Process being
shorter and less ex-
pensive, and Lands
subject to Execu-
tion for the Pay-
ment of Debts.
Evidence taken *ex
parte* in England to
prove a Debt is
allowed in their

of the act. "*Consequently if you think you could
justify the Non-payment of your Debts, till a Repeal took place; you certainly can justify the Suspension of the Payment during the Suspension of
the Act.*" Shall we, then, repeal the act "and
maintain you as we have hitherto done?" Or shall
we let you go unless you are willing to be governed by the same laws we are, and to "*pay
something towards maintaining yourselves?*

"The first, it is certain we can not do; and
therefore the next Point to be considered is
(which is also the third Proposal) Whether we
are to give you entirely up?—and after having

obliged you to pay your just Debts, whether we
are to have no farther Connection with you, as
a dependent State, or Colony."

In order to judge this matter properly, we
must consider the prospects before us and before the colonies. "Behold therefore a Political
Portrait of the Mother Country;—a mighty Nation under one Government of a King and Parliament,—firmly resolved not to repeal the Act,
but to give it

8. See above, XIV, 68.

Courts; and during the whole Dispute there was not *one single Instance* of any English Merchants' meeting with the least Obstruction in any Process or Suit commenced there for that purpose. I defy this lying Priest to mention one.

It did indeed execute itself. It was *Felo de se*, before the Parliament repeal'd it.

time *to execute itself*,...determined to protect and cherish those Colonies, which will return

---

This was the Dean's wise Proposal. He at least, thought it wise. The Parliament thought otherwise.

to their Allegiance within a limited Time (suppose Twelve or Eighteen Months)—and as determined to compel the obstinate Revolters to pay their Debts,—and then to cast them off...."

In America there would then be a variety of small colonies, jealous of each other and unable to agree. "By being severed from the British Empire, you will be excluded from cutting Logwood in the Bays of Campeachy and Honduras, —from fishing on the Banks of Newfoundland, on the Coasts of Labrador, or in the Bay of St. Laurence,—from trading (except by Stealth) with the Sugar Islands, or with the British Colonies in any Part of the Globe. You will also lose all the Bounties upon the Importation of your Goods into Great Britain....You will lose the Remittance of £300,000 a Year to pay your Troops;

We have no Use for Logwood but to remit it for your Fineries. We join'd in conquering the Bay of St. L. and its Dependencies, won't you allow us some Share? The Sugar Islands, if you wont allow us to trade with them, perhaps you will allow them to trade with us; or

378

do you intend to starve them? Pray keep your Bounties, and let us hear no more of them. And your Troops, who never protected us against the Savages, nor are they fit for such Service. And the £300,000 which you seem to think so much clear Profit to us, when in fact, they never spend a Penny among us but they have for it from us a Penny's worth. The Manufactures they buy are brought from you, the Provisions we could, as we always did, sell elsewhere for as much Money.

and you will lose the Benefit of these Troops to *protect you against the Incursions of the much injured and exasperated Savages....*" If you have trouble with foreign powers, no one will assist

You know your clear'd Road would do that.[9]

you; "Holland, France, and Spain, will look upon you with an evil Eye,...lest such an Example should infect their own Colonies....

Holland, France, and Spain, would all be glad of our Custom. And pleas'd to see the Separation.

We in Britain shall still retain *the greatest Part of your European Trade; because we shall give a better Price for many of your Commodities than you can have any where else: and we shall sell to you several of our Manufactures, especially in the Woollen, Stuff, and Metal Way, on cheaper Terms."*

Oho! Then you will still trade with us! but can that be without our Trading with you? And how can you buy our Oil if we catch no Whales?

Your internal state will be lamentable, with disputes between colonies and between factions within each. "The Leaders of your Parties will then be setting all their Engines to work, to make Fools become the Dupes of Knaves...." Your people will be borne down by taxes and loss of trade, "and instead of having *Troops to*

Just as they do in England.

To oppress, insult and murder them, as at Boston!

*defend them,...*they must defend themselves, and pay themselves." Soldiers will be needed

These Evils are all imaginations of the

9. BF explains this mysterious reference in his final note.

379

Author. The same were predicted to the Netherlands, but have never yet happened. But suppose all of them together, and many more, it would be better to bear them than submit to Parliamentary Taxation: We might still have something we could call our own: But under the Power claim'd by Parliament we have not a single Sixpence.

for defense against Indians and against neighbors, and fleets as well. All these burdens will soon disillusion the people and open their eyes until, surfeited with republicanism, they will petition for reunion with the mother country.

"And you, my Boy, after you have played the Hero, and spoke all your fine Speeches,...perhaps even you may awake out of your present political Trance, and become a reasonable Man at last."

The Author of this Pamphlet Dean Tucker, has always been haunted with the Fear of the Seat of Government being soon to be removed to America. He has in his Tracts on Commerce some just Notions in Matters of Trade and Police, mix'd with many wild chimerical Fancies, totally impracticable. He once proposed as a Defence of the Colonies to clear the Woods for the Width of a Mile all along behind them, that the Indians might not be able to cross the cleared Part without being seen; forgetting that there is a Night in every 24 Hours.[1]

Marginalia in a Pamphlet by Matthew Wheelock

MS notations in a copy in the Library of Congress of [Matthew Wheelock], *Reflections Moral and Political on Great Britain and Her Colonies* (London, 1770).

This is the true

The writer lives in the country, and has not kept up with the pamphlet controversy on the American question; he may therefore be repeating inadvertently some ideas of others. "*The good of the whole British empire* is what he

1. This crackpot suggestion was apparently sent to America in 1754 or earlier, and either then or subsequently BF attributed it to Tucker. See above, v, 411 n. In searching unsuccessfully for it through the Dean's writings we have come on a few "wild chimerical Fancies," but nothing so grossly stupid.

political Idea, that every Writer on these Subjects should have in View. Most of them think only of the good of *a Part*, Britain.

aims at: the colonies of course must come into consideration; which has obliged him to hasten his work, that it may be printed before the parliament decides what shall be done in regard to them."[2]

Members of the House of Commons represent the public at large, not their particular constituencies. "We may conceive them to be (*in a*

In what Degree?

certain degree) the *representatives* and guardians

Who are British Commoners? Are the American Colonists such?

of all *British commoners*, wheresoever dispersed. It is indeed to be hoped that...

Why don't you set about it?

a better mode of election may be established to *make the representation more equal*," but until then the authority of the Commons must be upheld.

In the present disputes about liberty, it is important to understand the meaning of the word. The benefits we derive from society are apparent only when we lose them, but reflection will

The Difference is not so great as may be imagined. Happiness is more generally and equally diffus'd among Savages than in our civiliz'd Societies. No European who has once tasted Savage Life, can afterwards bear to live in our Societies. The Care

show us "the happiness we enjoy *beyond what is attainable by solitary savages.*" The savage is exposed to continual physical dangers to himself and his family. Society protects a man from these, and he in return owes it obedience. He is not free to pursue his own quarrels, but must submit them to the power that society has appointed for arbitrating differences. That power is in part legal but in greater part moral, for the citizens' sense of morality is what makes the legal system operate. Liberty itself can operate only within the limits that morality prescribes.

2. This suggests that the pamphlet was written in late 1769 or the beginning of 1770, if the author succeeded in having it printed before the crucial debate in early March on repealing the Townshend Acts. The date of BF's comments is, as usual, impossible to determine; but his references to non-importation (pp. 383, 393) suggest that he was writing before the autumn of 1770, by which time he would have known that the movement had collapsed.

and Labour of pro-
viding for artificial
and fashionable
Wants, the Sight of
so many Rich wal-
lowing in super-
fluous Plenty,
whereby so many
are kept poor dis-
tress'd by Want:
The Insolence of
Office, the Snares
and Plagues of Law,
the Restraints of
Custom, all contri-
bute to disgust them
with what we call
civil Society.

A vague Word.

Why should you
oblige those that
never were un-
willing? Only return
to the ancient
Method of Requisi-
tion, and you would
have their Contri-
butions as usual.

This Author
decides before he
examines.

What ancient Laws?
Probably Magna
Charta, the Bill of
Rights, Petition of
Right, &c.

"This parliament and ministry have been
vilified by all means possible, because they have
supported the *pre-eminency* of Great Britain over
her colonies, and *would oblige them* to contribute
to the public expence, which lies at present on
Great Britain. The colonists do not approve of
this, and threaten us with the loss of trade, if
their *extravagant and unjust demands* of exemption from parliamentary taxations, are not complied with." British traders are alarmed, and the
colonists fan their fears "by applying the words
of *ancient laws* to their own case," to which
those laws are irrelevant.

Because the present Parliament has resolved
to assert its authority over all British subjects,

This Author supposes the Colonists want a new Parliament in order to have the Duties taken off. He is mistaken. They did petition; they were *not heard*, and they will petition no more. They have taken their Measures. Keep up your Duties, if you please; they will not pay them, because they will not use the Commodities. And because they think you use them ill in laying such Duties, they will manufacture for themselves. They now find they gain and save infinitely more by your Continuing the Duties, than they should by your repealing them.

"they (*the colonists* and traders) cannot expect to *carry their point* whilst this parliament subsists; they, therefore, desire a new one; in which they hope to get several of their friends elected, in order to allow the colonists to do as they please...."

Merchants and manufacturers have petitioned for the dissolution of Parliament, and to obtain the support of the landed interest have pretended that the ground of their petitions was the expulsion of Wilkes. In fact they are trying to secure the election of a new Parliament that will repeal the duties so obnoxious to the Americans. The latter rest their case on what they call the spirit of the constitution. They acknowledge the King personally, but not "as

He is the executive Power *of* Great Britain *in* Great Britain. In the Colonies he is the Executive Power of the Colonies; i.e. in each respectively.

the *executive power* of Great Britain. They allow, that Great Britain has been so *generous* as *to spend an infinite quantity*

This is a most iniquitous Account trump'd up against the Colonies. It might with more Propriety be

of blood and treasure, to procure them secure settlements in America, and to supply them with great numbers of its useful and industrious families [*interlined by Franklin:* and all your Rogues]; in return for which, the colonists have taken such manufactures from Great Britain, as they wanted...." Now they will take no more unless Britain allows them independence of Parliament in one essential point, taxation.

But the colonists, like the King's subjects in Great Britain, hold their lands from the crown.

> Man for Man with you to fight these Battles? They bring no Account against you for the Blood and Treasure they have spent in your Wars: Then be silent on this Head if you are wise; for whenever the Account comes to be settled you will be found in Debt, the Ballance will be against you.

"Whatever *British subject* holds lands of the King, then holds them for the benefit of the *British public* in the first place; in the second place, he holds them according to the political situation of the country in which the said lands lie. *The Irish are British subjects*;" they have settled revenues on the crown, and no more is required except in emergencies. "But the British legislature extends itself to Ireland, when it sees cause." The Irish have the same liberties as the British, but their land and trade depend "on the *superior power*.

"The chief view of *Great Britain* in establishing colonies in North America was, to promote trade with the Indians; and to furnish us with several articles of commerce which America

Marginal notes:

> brought against the Clothiers of Yorkshire and the West, or the Smiths and Cutlers of Sheffield, or the Buttonmakers of Birmingham. Was it not to secure and extend their Trade and the Vent for their Manufactures, that you fought in America; and did not the Colonies raise and maintain

> Who is a British Subject? Is every Subject of the King such? Then Hanoverians are British Subjects.

> This may be the Case *in Britain.* It is not in Ireland. The Irish are Irish Subjects.

> That is, it *usurps* wherever it can.

> The Superior Power in Ireland is the King and *their* Parliament.

> Great Britain as a Nation had no such Views. The Parliament was not at any

384

Expence gave no
Directions were not
so much as con-
sulted about the
Settlement of
Colonies before
Geo. II's time.

produces. The extension of dominion...was not the *national scheme....*"

The colonists claim that dependence is slavery, but if that is true there can scarcely be any liberty; for all are dependent on authority.

British Empire, a vague Expression. All these Writers (almost all) confound themselves and Readers with the Idea that the British Empire is but ONE State; not considering or knowing that it consists of many States under one Sovereign. As of Great Britain (formerly two, E[nglan]d and Scotland, Ireland, Guernsey and Jersey) every Colony, Hanover, Zell, &c.

"In the *British empire* some power must lead, and the rest of the nation

This is the case in every single State.

follow. If the law of nations allows men to treat

The British Nation had no original Property in the Country of America. It was purchas'd by the first Colonists of the Natives, the only Owners.

The Colonies not *created* by Britain, but by the Colonists themselves.

a conquered country as they please,...*the right of original property, the creation of a colony, and the supplying it with people,* must give a much better title to jurisdiction and superiority. The independency affected by the Americans, is what our old laws would give a very bad name to; the parliament will tell us what to call it now."

American arguments rest on the false premise that their assemblies alone have the right to

The People that went cost the Nation nothing to send them there; they went at their own Expence Nova S[cotia] and Georgia excepted[3] and to these were sent wrong People who dy'd or went away. Why then have you accepted their General Grants heretofore?

grant or refuse supplies for the service of the state. To grant money for the public service of the colony, "*seems* the extent of the assemblies authority." Parliament has the right to grant money for the empire at large. It is implausible

They have agreed heretofore, why not again? How many Wars have they join'd in with Britain? Did ever any of them refuse?

that widely separated assemblies "should *ever agree* in one measure of government, and if they were not unanimous, what must be done with those who dissented?—such a society could

Suppose there were Truth in this, which there is not, Would you argue a Right to enslave us, from an Inconvenience to yourselves if you had not such Right? The same Argument was just as good for the Parliament of England taxing and making Laws for Scotland before the Union.

hardly subsist a twelve-month."

If reason then requires that one power should preside and the rest obey, it follows that the Americans, like the Irish, should not be repre-

3. For fuller remarks by BF on these two "Parliamentary" colonies see above, XIII, 361; XIV, 68.

Dependencies. By this Word you assume what is not granted; and all that follows is therefore unfounded.

sented in Parliament. "All *dependencies* have some peculiar interests of their own," which Parliament should reconcile for the good of the whole. The interest of one dependency often

How came you then to admit Wales, the Principality of Chester, Bishoprick of Durham, Scotland, &c.?

conflicts with that of another; "if they had *each* votes in Parliament, they would be both *parties and judges*; which is against reason and order." The colonists fear oppression by Parliament.

A very poor Security indeed. What would these Apprehensions signify? Many here have long had them already: but is our Case thereby mended? If we should complain of *unequal* Taxation, we should be told that People in England are unequally taxed, Scotland does not pay its Share, &c., just as when we complain of not being represented we are told that many People in England are not represented. Thus you argue from a Wrong to an Injury. But how can we trust you, we who live at such a Distance from you; when you are not just to one another?

But they cannot have "*better security* in the nature of things, than that a parliament, which should unjustly attack your liberty, would give immediate apprehensions to your fellow subjects at home. Besides, the amount of the taxes may be fixed in proportion to what is paid at home, and the manner of raising it be left to the colonists under certain restrictions; but it is not the mode of taxation that the colonists complain of, it is the right itself they contest.

"According to their notions, Great Britain may provide and protect establishments of her subjects in foreign parts, for the advantage of the said subjects personally, but cannot make

She may if she thinks fit. But she is not to apply to her own Advantage unjustly foreign Settlements made by others.

any foreign settlement for her own advantage, nor extend her jurisdiction beyond the island of Great Britain.

"Our old original laws, indeed, were calcu-

Adopted by them. No Power to make Laws for Wales till it was represented.

lated for England...; as our dominions encreased, our law was extended in like manner into Ireland and Wales. When we had establishments in more southern latitudes, the *same*

A great Mistake; no British Law in force in the Colonies but what they voluntarily adopt. Witness the Law of Tythes, Game Laws, Marriage Acts, &c.

law continued, and still continues in force, with such additions and variations, as...required, for the publick good. These alterations...were intended for the benefit of the colonists, on the

The People of Great Britain are themselves Subjects to the King. The Subjects of one Part of the King's Dominions are not Sovereigns over the King's Subjects in another Part of his Dominions. G. B[ritai]n has no Subjects.

supposition, that they were true and loyal *subjects of Great Britain*.

"They are now on as secure a footing, as the subjects who dwell in England: what injustice is there then in subjecting them now to propor-

You forget the Separate Taxes they pay at home.

tionate taxes, with the rest of their fellow subjects? The injustice, indeed, would be to all the British subjects at home, if the Americans were

This was never the Case.

suffered to remain untaxed," because those at home would have to make up the difference.

The Ignorance of the Parliament in these and many other Points shows how improperly they would undertake to tax us.

Proportionate taxes would take into account the differences in the produce of the various colonies, the expense of production, and the price of the necessities of life. In general the products of the northern colonies are less precarious and costly than those of the southern. The way of life also varies. In the north, where large families are common, *"few* can afford to *give their children a liberal education*; after a short schooling, they put them either into a mercantile way, or upon a piece of land (mostly uncultivated). As they have little distinction among

How ignorant this Writer is! There are no less than eight Universities in the Northern Colonies viz. Cambridge in New England, Rhodeisland Do. Newhaven Do. New York, New Jersey, Philadelphia, Williamsburg in Virginia, and Georgia.[4]

As learned and polite, and more so, than any part of Britain, for their Numbers.

them, except what arises from wealth, *learning and politeness of manners* must not be expected: they are very quick in discerning what regards their own particular interest,...and generally

Never without Cause.

suspect that *their governors*, and people in power,

Another Instance of his Ignorance. To stand Candidate for being an Assembly-man is not the Practice in New-England.

enrich themselves clandestinely out of the publick money: in their elections of assembly-men, it is not the sensible and honest man, who *succeeds* by telling them candidly the truth,...it is the violent, noisy *candidate*, who flatters their prejudices, and abuses the governor, that carries

4. Seven of these "universities" are clear enough: Harvard; the College of Rhode Island, subsequently Brown; Yale; King's College in New York City, subsequently Columbia; the College of New Jersey, subsequently Princeton; the College of Philadelphia, subsequently the University of Pennsylvania; and William and Mary. The eighth, in Georgia, existed only in BF's imagination: he was taking for reality the hope that George Whitefield had cherished for his Bethesda Orphanage, for which see above, xv, 28 n.

389

No Gentleman that knew the Country would say this.

the day.... The *character of a gentleman is rare to be met with in these provinces....* A real gentleman

A British Citizen in his Idea is a Colonist that thinks the Parliament has a Right to tax him. There is no such Man.

(in which title that of a good *British citizen* is included) must either hold his tongue, or speak his sentiments at the risk of being insulted."

In Maryland and Virginia the planters give their children a better education, and the gentry have more influence. But their power over slaves makes them haughty, and they some-

No Meaning. Or none to his Purpose.

times forget that they are *British subjects.* Their sense of security, no doubt, makes the Vir-

Query. When and where? The Common Expression is the Mother Country.

ginians talk of Britain as a *sister* state.

The Carolinas and Georgia, threatened by their slaves, the Indians, and the Spanish, are

When did Gr. Britain ever afford any Assistance to Carolina? Never were any English Troops there before the last War.

less secure and depend more on "the *assistance* of Great Britain and the neighbouring colonies."

The colonists in the Sugar Islands are wealthier and better-mannered. Their control of their slaves, and of "the *revenues arising from the*

Would you tax these People beyond those Duties?

duty on sugar," make them self-important. Yet they realize their dependence on Great Britain for protection against their own slaves, who

The poor Creatures know no more of the Existence of such Strength than of a Strength in the Moon.

are kept in subservience only by "the *terror of the European* strength, which *keeps the slaves* from rising; we see them now and then attempt it, even though *they know* there is such assistance in reserve; what would they not do, if the colonists...had no other defense than their own persons?"

The colonists are divided in their attitudes toward Britain. Some live only to make their fortunes and retire to the British Isles, which they regard as home; this is true in general in the West Indies, *Georgia*, and the *Carolinas*. The colonists from Virginia northward, on the other hand, live more affluently than they could in Britain, do not now fear the French or the Indians, "and consider their plantations as their

home, and the people of Great Britain as a check upon them, who limit their trade in favour of the good of the whole, of which the *common people* have little conception."

All the colonists, because they depend on their exports, are associated with merchants in Britain, who fear to be put out of business if the tumults in America ruin trade. "But should the parliament give way to the pretensions of the Americans,...*the strength and dignity of Great Britain, her trade and colonies, would all go to ruin*; for, First, the national credit would be immediately affected, as then *Great Britain alone*

Quite ignorant of these Countries.

Never were apprehensive of the Indians, nor much of the French. Are as much expos'd to Danger from the Indians now as ever.

Neither the Common People nor any others can have much conception that *those* Limitations are for the good of the whole, which they see evidently calculated for the Benefit of Great Britain *only*, and to the Damage of the Colonies.

Take care then how you use us; if your Strength depends on your Union with us.

Is it not already so? *would become responsible for the national debt.*
Would it be respon- Our estimation among all the European powers
sible for more? Does would sink of course; the colonists (who have
it desire to be res- all the necessaries for shipping) would presently
ponsible for the
Irish and Colony

Debts also?
They are dependent interfere with our trade; for *if they are independ-*
only on the King. *ant in one point, why not in another?* The revenue

They will lessen if of the *customs* at home *would lessen,* which de-
you use the Colonies ficiency must be made up by taxes; *this would*
unjustly.

Ignorant of the *raise the price of our manufactures too high* for the
Effect of Taxes. markets; the *manufacturers being unemployed*
They will not make would run to America, and the revenue of ex-
Manufactures too cise diminish of course....
high for foreign
Markets.

You need not be "The *colonists themselves* would not *long enjoy*
concern'd for them. *their independence."* They could not form a single
You are too good.

Very easily. Tis but state on the British model, because representa-
a Weeks Voyage tives from such a large territory could scarcely
from the Extremities attend a central legislature. Could they have a
to the central federal union like the Dutch or Swiss? Scarcely,
Colonies. because the constituent parts differ so much in

Strange, that dif- their *"productions* and interests." Those parts
fering in *Produc-* would soon be at loggerheads, and the weaker
tions, should be a ones, lacking the effrontery to apply for help
Reason of their not to Great Britain, "would *naturally call in the*
being capable of
Agreeing in Govern-
ment.

Silly enough! *French or Spaniards to their assistance."*
Most Americans are doubtless not thinking
of independence, but events are moving in that
direction. A colonial assembly, without the
What has his Con- consent of the governor, communicates its
sent to do with their resolutions to other assemblies, which looks

like confederacy. If Parliament passes legislation that the Americans disapprove of, "the im-

> Resolutions? They know he dare not assent to them whatever his Judgment may be.

portation of British manufactures *is prohibited*: I will not suppose by connivance of the assembly, but have the assemblies

> This which he calls a Prohibition, is no more than a Resolution of any Colonist to buy no more British Superfluities till his Grievances are redress'd, and he is allow'd the Enjoyment of his Liberties. He then persuades others to take the same Resolution. That's all.

discountenanced these proceedings?

> No!

Have they done any thing to suppress them? What do the Americans contend for? Only the enjoyment of all advantages of British subjects, for which they will contribute to the public treasury what they please, and Great Britain to pay the rest. Suppose this is not granted, what will the assemblies do next?

> Why should they?
>
> Do not British Subjects in Britain contribute what they please? If the Americans have, as they ought to have, all Advantages of British Subjects, why not this among the rest?

"The only reasonable hope the North Americans can have of preserving the British constitu-

tion with peace and safety, is their *dependance on Great Britain*, which is the natural umpire when any differences arise between the colonies: take away that resort, and *every colony must decide its*

> There is no such *Dependance*. There is only a *Connection*, of which the King is the common Link.

disputes by the sword. Their division into provinces at present makes

> Why not by Mediation, by Arbitration,

393

or by considerate and prudent Agreement? Suppose England and Scotland differ, are they in a better Case?

every colony a little state of itself," which the governor and assembly can care for better than any central executive and legislature could.

There you hit it.

And they will always (probably) continue so.

The only danger that threatens the colonies is from Europe, and "whilst they *depend on Great Britain"* they are sure to be alerted to such danger and protected against it by men-of-war. "A time in all likelihood will come, when the

While connected with Britain they are sure of being engag'd in all her Quarrels and Wars.

colonies in North America shall exceed Great Britain in strength, and consequently have the

Then don't make Enemies of them if you are wise.

less occasion for her: it is also likely that *in time America will make her own manufactures,* and consequently our intercourse will lessen, and perhaps a separation take place by consent,

You are hastning that time by your Folly.

when the national debt is discharged, and when the European and American Britons can be no longer of service to each other, but as friends and allies."

This Writer seems to imagine the Colonies concern'd in the National Debt. A Notion quite new!

Agriculture is at present more advantageous for the Americans than manufactures. "But when America is fully peopled, the price of land will encrease: the *farther the colonists extend themselves from the sea and great rivers,* the dearer our manufactures must come to them, on account of *land-carriage:* they will then run into manufactures." There is indeed some manufacturing in Philadelphia, but as soon as the

The farther they extend themselves the less likely to be too populous so as to engage in Manufactures. But no Distance they can go from the Sea will add much by Carriage to the Price of British Goods. The Country is full of Rivers and Lakes: which this Writer seems not to know.

And then may not other poor People do as they have done?

poor workers accumulate enough money to buy land "they will probably do as others have done before them."

The Meaning of all this is, The Americans are unable to resist, therefore you may treat them as you please.

The Americans' boasts of unanimity and strength to resist are mere bugbears to frighten us. In slave-holding colonies the whites dare not leave their localities, in the others the mob would be no match for British troops, and everywhere the seacoast is open to attack. The colonists' only hope is to foment discord here, by specious constitutional arguments.

A British subject going to America has all the rights that he had at home, and the mother country renders his possessions in America

How does this appear?

"doubly valuable in point of security." This in-

Britain is not his Sovereign, but the King, who remains the same in America.

creased security does not free him "from the *obedience which he owed to Britain* originally, and

No such Cause and Condition.

which was *the cause and condition of his possessing any lands at all in America.* To bring the spirit of the constitution against the general established law, is oversetting all order and government." That spirit prescribes that all subjects shall be free, whereas the law deprives specific people of their freedom at specific times for the sake of the public good. "To expect perfection in

Does this justify

human institutions is absurd: the highest point

395

any and every Im-
perfection that can
be invented and
added to our Con-
stitution? Why did
you yourselves not
leave our Constitu-
tions as you found
them? Why did you
aim at making them
according to your
Ideas, more perfect,
by taking away our
Rights in order to
subject us to Parlia-
mentary Taxation?

The Salus Populi of
America as impor-
tant to the People
there as that of
Britain here.

that we know in legislation is *salus populi* sup-
prema lex esto." The colonial charters were acts
of the crown, fixing its claims to the soil, "but

The Inhabitants of
that Soil owed no
Obedience to the
British Legislature.
Its Jurisdiction did
not extend out of
the Realm.

could not *exempt the colonists from the obedience
they owed to the British legislature*: if they have
retained and claimed the right of British subjects from their first settlement to this time, it
is plain they did not look upon themselves as

The Crown stipu-
lated that they should
not be Aliens.

aliens.

False in Fact.

In *all distresses they have applied to Great Britain*
as citizens, and *have been protected* as such...."

They would never
have gone if it had
been understood
that they were still
to remain under the
power of the oppres-
sive Laws from
which they fled.

Would they have settled in America if their citizenship had not been their protection? Would a

Very easily. They were too poor to make it worth any Nations Trouble to invade them.

This *very few* was the whole Colony.

Their Allegiance is still untainted. They owe it to the King, not to the Parliament.

Of the King in England if you please.

All this time, when England being out of Debt could so well have afforded it, Did She ever send any Troops to defend them, or give a Shilling for that Purpose? *NOT ONE.*

They are diminished ONE HALF, by the increas'd Plenty of Land at Market, thro' the Conquests.

Did not America pay half of this, and more? They kept up an equal Number of Troops. They suffer'd immensely by the Embargoes.

settlement, once made, have endured for any length of time on any basis except that it belonged to England? The colonists' purpose

in emigrating was to mend their fortunes, "except perhaps *a very few Enthusiasts about Boston.*" England's purpose was to encourage the colonies for the good of the whole; no one at that time doubted their allegiance. They were empowered to provide for their own judiciary, defense, and legislation, "subject

however to the controul *of England.*" They were exposed to the French and Indians, and

their economy was precarious; it would have been unfair for England, with little or no public debt, to have taxed them at that time. But the last war freed the northern colonies from the danger of the French.

"Their estates are *doubled and tripled* in value and security:

the reasons of exempting them from taxes, no longer exist: *the expence of the wars which pro-*

duced these happy events to the Americans, is charged to the publick. There can be no doubt then in equity, that they should now bear a proportionate part in the payment of the debt, since they have more than a proportionate part of the benefit."

Some colonists carry their case further, not only claiming independence of Parliament, but *"paying little regard to the crown"* when its orders are not to their liking. "If this behaviour arises in consequence of their charters, it seems high time to *annul or amend them.*"

A false Charge.

Meddle with them at your Peril. No Alteration can be made in them but by Consent of both Parties, the King and the Colonists. By violating them you break the Link that holds those two parts together.

"There cannot be two *equal legislatures in any state.*" One must be supreme, the others subordinate. The charters of British cities give the corporations autonomy within their areas, but no right to contest the authority of Parliament.

But there may be in *different* States.

The Corporations of Britain are within the Realm, therefore within the Jurisdiction of Parliament. The Colonies are without the Realm. Therefore not.

"It is the essential quality of a province to *depend on* THAT STATE which formed and supported it." The colonists like to fancy that they have the same relationship to the mother country that the Flemish provinces had to

The British State had no Share in forming and supporting the Colonies, except Georgia and Nova Scotia. And New England had a great share in the latter.[5]

Spain, whereas in fact those provinces "depended no more on Spain, than *Hanover* does on Britain"; the inhabitants were not Spanish

The Colonies depend no more on Britain than Hanover does.

5. The New Englanders fought the French in Nova Scotia for years before the Treaty of Utrecht, and after 1755 immigrants from New England filled the lands of which the Acadians had been dispossessed.

subjects. For a province composed of subjects of the state to pretend to equality is "a sort of civil mutiny," and suggests that the colonists may intend "to *withdraw their allegiance.*"

It is great Impudence or Folly in a Man to suppose, that because he is an Englishman every American Owes him Allegiance. If every Englishman is not a Sovereign over every American, neither can he communicate such Sovereignty to another, by chusing him Parliament Man.

"It seems in the present situation of affairs, that either the *rights* and dignity of Great Britain...must be submitted to the apparent (but not real) interest of the colonies; or the colonies *must acknowledge* the *legislative supremacy* of

Never.

Great Britain, and *contribute their proportion* to the good of the whole; or a rupture must ensue."

Their Proportion they always have contributed and more—In the Price of Goods. In the Restraints. In making War for Britain.

Exempting Americans from taxation would create an inextricable dilemma. The prospect of "an exemption from *parliamentary taxes*" would lead the young to emigrate from Britain, and what would Parliament do then? "To let

This Wiseacre seems not to know that there are any other Taxes in the World than those impos'd by the King Lords and Commons of G.B.

399

It is very true. To keep People in England by Compulsion, is to make England a Prison, and every Englishman. The Right of Migration is common to all Men, a natural Right. The Colonists us'd that Right, and seated themselves out of

our people go, depopulates the country; to keep them here by compulsion, would diminish the liberty of the subject.

the Jurisdiction of Parliament, to avoid being subject to Bishops Courts, Tythes, Church Laws, and other Parts and Statutes

of British Law that oppress'd them. Would you now, contrary to the Faith of Charters, bring all those Laws over them again?

No.

"Supposing the Americans acknowledge *their dependance,*

They never refus'd to contribute their Proportion voluntarily.

and pay their proportion, yet...they encrease fast, and we have certainly no subjects to spare." England has fewer inhabitants than it had thirty-five years ago; it is of first

Make your own People as easy as you please, but don't make ours uneasy.

importance to make the populace contented enough to stay in this country.

[The remainder of the pamphlet, which deals with ways and means of improving the lot of the British at home, has no marginal comments.]

Index

Compiled by Mary L. Hart

Caroline, Queen of England, mentioned, 292 n

Carthage, corn trade with Sardinia, 34

Case of Ireland Being Bound by Acts of Parliament (Molyneux), for S. Cooper, 124

Case of Mr. John Harrison, mentioned, 126 n

Cassini, Jean Dominique, *Voyage fait par ordre du roi en 1768...*, mentioned, 126 n

Castle William: British troops withdrawn to, 160 n, 187, 192, 277; Customs Commissioners at, 187, 189, 192–3

"Causes of American Discontents before 1768," mentioned, 33 n

Chalkley (ship), leaves Phila., 180 n

Chamberlain, Mason, BF's portrait by, 94 n

Chapman, Mr., and BF–Hall accounts, 100

Charcoal, and Kinnersley's electrical experiments, 249

Charles I: and ship money, 17; mentioned, 119

Charles II, Pa. charter from, 355 n

Charles, Robert: and N.Y. Currency Act, 121, 170–1, 174; death, 171, 174

Charlotte, Queen of England, coronation anniversary, 220 n

Charming Polly (ship), voyage to Phila., 215 n

Charter, Md.: taxation in, 354; palatine rights under, 354 n

Charter, Mass.: change of, rumored, xxvii, 282, 302, 307, 308, 310, 311; and royal instructions to Hutchinson, 278; as compact, 308

Charter, Pa., taxation in, 355

Charters, colonial: and Parliamentary taxation, 21, 351, 353, 355; and Stuart kings, 22; as compacts, 161, 334, 398; and constitutional role of colonies, 162, 285, 396, 398; possible change of, 335, 346, 397–8; and exemption from British laws, 349, 396, 400; colonial powers under, 397; mentioned, 7

Chatelet-Lamont, Duc de, mentioned, 126 n

Chatham, Lord: ministry of, xxv; on Parliamentary taxation, representation, 14, 15, 68; in Stamp Act debate, 14, 58; speech in Lords, 25; on nonimportation, 25 n; leadership in French war, 46; and efforts to repeal Townshend Acts, 112; Beckford's influence on, 181; mentioned, 29

Chesapeake (frigate), Lawrence commands, 217 n

Chester, Eng., and Parliamentary taxation, representation, 15, 387

Chesterfield, Lord, mentioned, 28 n

China, windmills in, 107

Chittick, Dr., mentioned, 309 n

Choiseul, Duc de, mentioned, 293

Chreptowicz, Joachim, mentioned, 234

Christians, BF on, 241

Chronometer: of Harrison, 126 n; by P. LeRoy, 126 n

Church of England, jurisdiction of, not extended to colonies, 334, 352, 400

Clarendon Press, mentioned, 70

Clarke, Francis and Deborah Gedney, mentioned, 288 n

Clarke, Gedney, mentioned, 210

Clarke, John (of Salem, Mass.), mentioned, 288

Clarke, Peter, marriage to A. Johnson, 210, 252 n, 288

Clifton, Anna Maria, mentioned, 207

Club of Honest Whigs, mentioned, 5

Coal: Perkins on sea, pit, 94–5; BF's theory on, 94 n; from Irish bogs, 95

Coal mines: laws on, in Scotland, 43; BF's visit to, 94 n

Coercive Acts (1774), mentioned, 280 n

Coke, Sir Edward, and Waterford merchants' case, 14 n

Colden, Alexander: bills of exchange from, 13, 55, 132, 141; and BF–Thomson letter, 229 n

Colden, Cadwalader, and N.Y. Currency Act, 121

Colds: tract on, sent to BF, 94; BF's interest in, 94 n

Collinson, Michael: and J. Bartram's journal, 23; letter to, 65–6

Collinson, Peter: BF's memoir on, 65–6; aid to Lib. Co., 65–6; and BF's interest in electricity, 66; portrait of, 290

Colonies, North American: dispute with Britain, xxvi, 5, 6, 28, 60, 115, 123, 143–4, 151, 157, 161, 219, 268, 301, 309, 317, 318, 334, 336, 345–6, 349, 380, 395; BF as spokesman for, xxvii; British policy on western settlement, xxviii; British attitude, policies toward, 5, 25, 33, 36, 58, 59, 64, 92, 110, 112, 115, 116, 150–1, 156–7, 163–4, 170, 174, 177, 187–8, 188–9, 214, 243, 266–8, 273, 276, 282–3, 308, 310, 318, 324, 341, 344, 345, 346, 347, 348, 375, 376, 391, 395; population, 7, 28, 29; dominions of King, not Parliament, 7, 161, 307, 310, 320, 321, 325, 333, 334, 345, 346, 374, 375, 383; views on Parliament, 17, 21, 383, 387; ignorance of, in Parliament, 18, 20, 366–7,